ARTIFICIAL INTELLIGENCE:

principles and applications

ARTIFICIAL INTELLIGENCE:

principles and applications

EDITED BY

Masoud Yazdani
Department of Computer Science
University of Exeter

LONDON   NEW YORK

Chapman and Hall

First published in 1986 by
Chapman and Hall Ltd
11 New Fetter Lane, London EC4P 4EE
Published in the USA by
. Chapman and Hall
29 West 35th Street, New York NY 10001

Printed in Great Britain at the University Press, Cambridge

ISBN 0 412 27240 7 (Pb)
0 412 27230 X (Hb)

British Library Cataloguing in Publication Data

Artificial Intelligence: principles and applications.
1. Aritificial Intelligence
I. Yazdani, Masoud
001.53'5   Q335

ISBN 0–412–27230–X
ISBN 0–412–27240–7 Pbk

Library of Congress Cataloging in Publication Data

Main entry under title:

Artificial Intelligence.
Bibliography: p.
Includes index.
1. Artificial Intelligence.
I. Yazdani, Masoud, 1955
Q335.A7878   1986   006.3   85–22375
ISBN 0–412–27230–X
ISBN 0–412–27240–7 (Pbk)

Contents

Preface   page x

Contributors   xi

Section I
INTRODUCTION   1

1   Principles of Artificial Intelligence
    John Campbell   13
    1.1   Difficulties of classification of Artificial Intelligence   13
    1.2   Heuristics or algorithms?   15
    1.3   Programming methods in Artificial Intelligence   17
    1.4   The level of heuristics   21
    1.5   The level of models   25
          References   28

Section II
TOOLS AND TECHNIQUES   31

2   Artificial Intelligence programming environments and the
    POPLOG system
    John Gibson   35
    2.1   Features of Artificial Intelligence programming
          environments   35
    2.2   The POPLOG environment   40
    2.3   Summary   46
          Annotated references   47

3   LISP, Lists and pattern-matching
    Tony Hasemer   48
    3.1   Introduction   48

3.2   Symbolic computation   50
3.3   List manipulation in LISP   52
3.4   COND and recursion   56
3.5   But that is not the only way to do it   60
3.6   LISP and LISP environments   61
      Bibliography   62
      References   63

Section III
APPLICATIONS   65

4   Computer processing of natural language   69
    Alan Ramsay
    4.1   Why study language?   69
    4.2   Two views of language   70
    4.3   Language processing is a multi-level activity   72
    4.4   Lexical analysis   74
    4.5   Syntactic processing   79
    4.6   Transition networks   83
    4.7   Augmented transition networks   89
    4.8   Semantics   93
    4.9   The function of the utterance   98
    4.10 Putting it altogether   104
          Annotated bibliography   105

5   Levels of representation in computer speech synthesis and
    recognition
    Stephen Isard   111
    5.1   Introduction   111
    5.2   Levels of description of speech   113
    5.3   Processes   116
    5.4   Directions for future work   119
          Acknowledgements   120
          Annotated bibliography   120
          References   121

6   Computer vision   122
    David Hogg
    6.1   Introduction   122
    6.2   The visual image   123
    6.3   Current techniques   126
    6.4   Regions and edges   127
    6.5   Determining visible surface shape   129
    6.6   Object identification   130

	6.7	Limitations	134
		Annotated bibliography	134
		Annotated references	135
7	Artificial Intelligence and robotics		
	Michael Brady		137
	7.1	Robotics and Artificial Intelligence	137
	7.2	The need for intelligent robots	138
	7.3	Robotics as a part of Artificial Intelligence	139
	7.4	Action	141
	7.5	Reasoning about objects and space	153
	7.6	Perception	164
	7.7	Reasoning that connects perception to action	169
	7.8	Conclusions	175
		Acknowledgements	175
		References	176
8	The anatomy of expert systems		
	Richard Forsyth		186
	8.1	Introduction	186
	8.2	Features of expert systems	187
	8.3	The architecture of expert systems	187
	8.4	The knowledge base	188
	8.5	The inference engine	191
	8.6	The acquisition module	193
	8.7	The explanatory interface	194
	8.8	Developing expert systems	195
	8.9	Summary	197
		Annotated bibliography	198

Section IV
FRONTIERS   201

9	Machine learning		
	Richard Forsyth		205
	9.1	Introduction	205
	9.2	A paradigm for learning	206
	9.3	The description language	207
	9.4	Learning by searching	209
	9.5	Perception-type systems	212
	9.6	ID3	215
	9.7	Genetic algorithms	218
	9.8	BEAGLE	220
	9.9	Conclusions	223
		Annotated bibliography	223

10   Memory models of man and machine
     Ajit Narayanan   226
     10.1   The traditional use of the information-processing
            paradigm   226
     10.2   Lower levels of the paradigm   229
     10.3   Some concrete examples of memory models   229
     10.4   Concrete examples of the paradigm at a lower level   236
     10.5   Semantic networks   238
     10.6   Associative memory and content-addressable memory   238
     10.7   Implementing content-addressable memory   240
     10.8   Searching CAM   241
     10.9   CAM responses   242
     10.10 Actors and demons   242
     10.11 The metaphorical revolution   245
     10.12 Justifying neurophysiology, distribution and parallelism   248
     10.13 Spreading activation   249
     10.14 IAM's assumptions   253
     10.15 Inheriting properties   254
     10.16 Intelligence or trickery?   256
     10.17 Conclusions   257
            Annotated bibliography   257
            References   258

Section V
IMPLICATIONS   261

11   Why Artificial Intelligence needs an empirical foundation
     Noel. E. Sharkey and *Gordon D. A. Brown*   267
     11.1   Artificial and human intelligence   267
     11.2   Different methods, different models   275
     11.3   The interaction between psychology and Artificial
            Intelligence   282
     11.4   Conclusions   289
            Acknowledgements   289
            Annotated bibliography   289
            References   292

12   Breaking out of the Chinese room
     Steve Torrance   294
     12.1   Inside the Chinese Room   294
     12.2   Turing's Imitation Game   296
     12.3   Productive and subjective mental states   298
     12.4   Is the mind a unity?   300

12.5   Carbon chauvinism and causal powers of the brain   301
12.6   Flavours to Artificial Intelligence   302
12.7   Language-modelling and neuro-modelling programs   303
12.8   Pure Aritificial Intelligence versus exotic architectures 304
12.9   The limited scope of Searle's argument   306
12.10 Sloman's 'weak strong Artificial Intelligence'   307
12.11 What are the relevant kinds of computational processes?   307
12.12 Mental processes need real subjects   309
12.13 Conclusions   311
       Acknowledgements   312
       Annotated references   312

13 Social implications of Artificial Intelligence   315
Derek Partridge
    13.1   Introduction   315
    13.2   Increased leisure or higher unemployment?   316
    13.3   The computer's image and the human's viewpoint   318
    13.4   The impacts of intelligent computers   322
    13.5   The threats of Artificial Intelligence   324
    13.6   Paradise regained?   328
    13.7   The customization of mass production   329
    13.8   Man's reflection in the computational metaphor   330
           References   333
           Annotated bibliography

    Index   337

Preface

It is a pleasing challenge to introduce a new subject to people who express an interest in knowing more about it. Both the pleasure and the challenge increase with the presenter's involvement and love of the subject matter. The challenge is to present not only the body of knowledge which makes up that subject but also to express the motivation and the enthusiasm for it.

I have taken up the challenge of introducing Artificial Intelligence (AI) to a growing body of interested people on many occasions now, both at a university level, as a lecturer to computer science undergraduates and at a business level as the Chairman of Intellect, a company concerned with the educational aspect of Artificial Intelligence.

This book represents my best achievement so far. The fact that it is an edited compilation of papers gives an indication of my solution to the problem of how best to put across a vast and varying body of knowledge without losing any of the enthusiasm of the workers in each of the subtopics. Texts by a single author, and there are now a few of them, achieve a level of coherence but run the risk of presenting topics which are of no immediate relevance or interest to the author, in a dry and sometimes superficial manner. On the other hand, most compilations of papers, while covering the subtopics well, fail to achieve that level of coherence which allows the book to be read from cover to cover. In putting this book together, my challenge has been to achieve coherence between chapters which have been written by specialists writing in their own area of specialization. I have been fortunate in knowing and having worked with all the contributors during the past few years. In fact the contents of the book read like the programme of some of the commercial tutorial meetings which I have organized in the past, and shall no doubt be organizing in the future to spread the 'gospel'.

No introductory book can hope to fully satisfy the thirst of the enthusiastic reader. The contributors to this book have provided detailed references and/or annotated bibliographies citing other sources where more information can be found.

Masoud Yazdani

Contributors

MICHAEL BRADY is Professor of Information Engineering at Oxford University. Prior to this he was Associate Director of the MIT Artificial Intelligence Laboratory. His degrees of BSc from Manchester University (1967) and PhD from the Australian National University, Canberra (1970) were in mathematics. He taught computer science at Essex University, England until 1980, when he joined MIT. He has authored and edited several books including: *Robot Motion* (1982), *Computer Vision* (1982), *Computational Models of Discourse* (1982), and *The Theory of Computer Science: A Programming Approach* (1977). Professor Brady is a founding editor (with Richard Paul) of the *International Journal of Robotics Research.* His edited collections in print include *The First International Symposium of Robotics Research* (with Richard Paul), and *Artificial Intelligence and Robotics* (with L. Gerhardt). Professor Brady has served on the editorial board of *Artificial Intelligence Journal* and is series editor (with Patrick H. Winston) of the MIT Press series on *Artificial Intelligence.*

GORDON BROWN studied psychology and philosophy at The Queen's College, Oxford, graduating in 1980. He gained a DPhil from the University of Sussex after doing psychological research between 1980 and 1983. Since 1983 he has been working in the Department of Language and Linguistics at the University of Essex on a research project concerned with spoken discourse. He has publications in cognitive psychology and psycholinguistics.

JOHN CAMPBELL is Professor of Computer Science at University College London. Before taking up that appointment he founded the Department of Computer Science at Exeter and worked in various universities and research institutes in several European countries, North America and Australia, in applied mathematics and theoretical physics, as well as computer science. He is the *Artificial Intelligence* series editor for Ellis Horwood Ltd and is editor of *Implementations of Prolog* and co-editor of *Progress in Artificial Intelligence* for that company.

RICHARD FORSYTH has a BA in psychology from Sheffield University (1970) and an MSc in computer science from the City University (1980). From 1979–1984 he was a lecturer, latterly senior lecturer, in computing at the Polytechnic of North London. In 1984 he left the polytechnic to set up his own business, Warm Boot Ltd, which is a software house specializing in machine intelligence applications, and to write books. He is editor of *Expert Systems: Principles and Case Studies* and co-author of *A Hitch-Hiker's Guide to AI* both published by Chapman and Hall.

JOHN GIBSON studied mathematics at Sussex University (BSc 1977) after several years spent in commercial computing. He then stayed on at Sussex to do DPhil research on natural language programming systems. Since 1980 he has been one of the principal architects of the POPLOG system and the POP–11 language.

TONY HASEMER took a BA in philosophy and literature at Sussex University, followed by an MA in philosophy at the same establishment. During the latter he discovered, or was discovered by, Artificial Intelligence. He gained a PhD in that subject at the Open University and is now a lecturer in the Psychology Department there. His main interests are: intelligent user interfaces and the problems faced by novices when learning to program. He is the author of *A Beginner's Guide to LISP* published by Addison-Wesley.

DAVID HOGG has a BSc in applied mathematics (1975) from the University of Warwick, an MSc in computer science (1976) from the University of Western Ontario and a DPhil in Artificial Intelligence (Computer Vision) from the University of Sussex (1984). He has worked at Plessey and been a Charles Hunnisett research fellow at Sussex University on medical image analysis. He is currently a lecturer in Artificial Intelligence at the University of Sussex.

STEPHEN ISARD studied mathematics at Harvard College (BA 1962) and at the University of California at Berkeley (MSc 1964). Since 1967 he has worked in the UK at the Universities of Sussex and Edinburgh, lecturing on mathematical logic, linguistics, psychology and Artificial Intelligence. He has been a lecturer in experimental psychology at Sussex University since 1974.

AJIT NARAYANAN has a BSc in communication science and linguistics from Aston University (1973) and was awarded a PhD in philosophy from Exeter (1975). Worked at Aston University as a lecturer in philosophy and then as a Data Analysis Officer at Aston University. Since

1980 he has been a lecturer in computer science at the University of Exeter. He is co-editor of *Artificial Intelligence: Human Effects* and co-author of *An introduction to LISP*, both published by Ellis Horwood Ltd.

DEREK PARTRIDGE is an Associate Professor in Computer Science at New Mexico State University where he has been since 1975. He has taught computer science at the University of Nairobi, Kenya, the University of Queensland, Australia, and was Visiting Fellow at the University of Essex. He holds a PhD in computer science from Imperial College, London (1972). His research interests are in artificial intelligence and software engineering, two fields that are compared and contrasted in his forthcoming book, *AI: Applications in the Future of Software Engineering* (Ellis Horwood Ltd). He is the author of over 30 papers and publications.

ALLAN RAMSAY studied mathematics and logic at Sussex University (BSc 1974) and logic at London University (MSc 1974). He returned to Sussex to do a PhD in Understanding English Descriptions of Computer Programs (1980). He has worked on a project for the design of distributed programming for Artificial Intelligence (Sussex, 1980–82), lectured in computer science (Essex 1982–83) and is currently a lecturer in Artificial Intelligence in the Cognitive Studies Programme at Sussex University. He is the co-author of *POP–11: A Practical Language for AI* (Ellis Horwood Ltd, 1985).

NOEL SHARKEY was awarded a BA (1979) and a PhD (1982) in psychology, both from Exeter University. He spent a year at Yale University as a research fellow in the Artificial Intelligence laboratory and a year as a senior research fellow in the Department of Psychology at Stanford University. He is currently a lecturer in psycholinguistics and Artificial Intelligence at the University of Essex. He is the co-author of *An introduction to LISP* and the editor of *Advances in Cognitive Science* both published by Ellis Horwood Ltd.

STEVE TORRANCE studied philosophy as an undergraduate at Sussex (BA, 1968) and as a graduate at Oxford where he was awarded a BPhil (1970) and a DPhil (1977). He has lectured in philosphy at Birmingham University and at Middlesex Polytechnic, and is currently a visiting lecturer in Artificial Intelligence in the Cognitive Studies Programme at Sussex University. He has organized several conferences on philosophy, science and AI. He is the editor of the *The Mind and the Machine* (Ellis Horwood Ltd, 1984).

MASOUD YAZDANI was born in Iran, but has lived in England since 1975. He obtained a BSc (1978) at Essex University in computer science before moving on to do research in Artificial Intelligence at the University of Sussex. Since 1981 he has been a lecturer in computer science at the University of Exeter. He is co-editor of *Artificial Intelligence: Human Effects*, and editor of *New Horizons in Educational Computing*, both published by Ellis Horwood Ltd. He is the Chairman of Intellect, a company specializing in Artificial Intelligence applications and the committee secretary of the Society for the Study of Artificial Intelligence and Simulation of Behaviour (AISB). He is also the *Cognitive Science* series editor for Ellis Horwood Ltd.

INTRODUCTION

The fact that it is necessary to start a book on Artificial Intelligence (AI, for short) with an attempt to define the subject is not in itself surprising. What is surprising is that, unlike subjects such as physics and chemistry, any such attempt is bound to be only partially successful. A clear definition of AI is, in itself, a current research topic.

It is true that during the last 25 years the new discipline of AI has been growing on the map of science, somewhere between psychology and computer science. What is not clear is whether AI is yet a science, in its own right, with all that this implies.

The most widely accepted definition of AI is that of Minsky (1968): 'artificial intelligence is the science of making machines do things that would require intelligence if done by men.' Close examination of this definition would, however, find major shortcomings as AI would not, in any way qualify as a science under strict philosophical examination. Furthermore, the community of researchers in AI differ in their motivation and methodologies so dramatically, that it would hardly be possible to claim that the single goal of 'making machines do things that would require intelligence if done by men' binds them together.

We can recognize some of the different trends in AI and the reason behind them by asking: 'To what end are we making machines do these things?'

The answer would differ between people working in different areas of AI and sometimes even between people working on the same topic but in different institutions. One group would justify their actions on the grounds that the result would be better, more useful, machines. At the other end of the spectrum another group would argue that they are not interested in the machine but are using it as a tool to understand human beings better.

We can, however, identify three distinct camps, each of which, when asked this question, would present different answers resulting from their different motivation or background. Consider a class of objects which we would regard as intelligent, i.e. cats, dogs, people and Martians. Outside this class, we have such unintelligent things as tables, chairs and, currently, digital computers (see p. 4).

Group 1 would answer the question by saying that 'AI is about moving computers into the space above (advanced computer technology)'. Group 2 would say 'AI is simulating human behaviour and cognitive processes on a computer (computational theories in psychology)'. Group 3's answer would concern the study of the nature of the whole space of intelligent minds. The volumes in the Annotated Bibliography, present arguments in favour of one or other, or a mixture, of the above three answers from a fair sample of AI researchers.

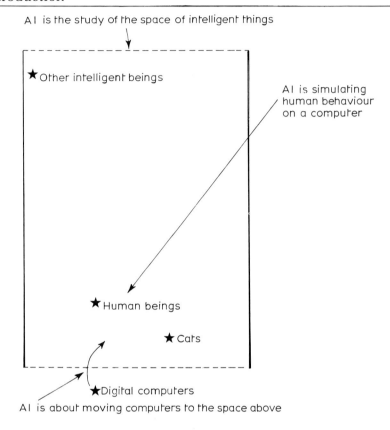

AI is the study of the space of intelligent things

★ Other intelligent beings

AI is simulating human behaviour on a computer

★ Human beings

★ Cats

★ Digital computers

AI is about moving computers to the space above

AN ANALOGY

In order to offer my personal definition, I would ask you to consider an analogy between thinking objects and flying objects. For centuries birds were the ultimate flying objects, just as humans were the ultimate thinking objects. The notion that a machine made out of beer cans could fly was as unintelligible to many as the notion of a thinking machine made out of beer cans is to many people today.

We believe that to claim that it is the biochemical properties of brains which alone can create beliefs and thoughts, is analogous to the claim that it is the biochemical properties of birds which provide the ability for self-sustained flight. What we know now is that it is rather the aerodynamic properties of birds which gives rise to their ability for self-sustaining flight. The aerodynamics analogy also suggests that we have come to know much about natural flight through the creation of artificial flight, though not in a simple direct way. What has emerged is a body of scientific laws governing aspects of the flight of both birds and aircraft.

Artificial flight has progressed, not in direct imitation of natural flight, nor instead of natural flight. It seems reasonable to assume that AI will eventually come to have a similar sort of relationship to natural intelligence. That is to say, AI should expect neither to imitate nor displace human intelligence, but simply to operate within the area defined by a common set of principles – an 'aerodynamics of intelligence' if you like.

That there is such a common set of principles follows logically from the axiom that human intelligent activity is non-mysterious. If human intelligent activity were to be considered impenetrable to scientific advance, then not only AI, but also psychology and certain types of philosophical speculation would be rendered impossible. If there is the possibility of extracting a common set of principles governing the operation of both natural and artificial intelligence, then the creation of AI is, at least in principle, possible.

ARTIFICIAL INTELLIGENCE: A TECHNOLOGY IN SEARCH OF A SCIENCE

Whatever the philosophical foundations of AI, what is clear is that there are numerous applications for it both in military and business spheres. As in aviation, the potential applications of AI are an overriding factor in the development of the field, and a source of influence on the field.

One source of influence on AI has been the attitude of the sponsoring organizations. In the USA the exploratory phase of AI research has been generously sponsored, and now it is results that are expected, rather than exploration. In the UK where, thanks to the Lighthill Report sponsorship of AI research has been rather strict, a turning point has been reached. The Alvey Report recommended rather generous support for areas of AI work where medium-term results are considered possible. This second source of influence has directed AI towards a change of emphasis in favour of building useful computing systems.

The initial phase of AI research has led to a general realization that world knowledge is behind people's ability, which is generally known as intelligent behaviour. AI, in its attempt to produce intelligent behaviour on a computer, is limited by the amount of knowledge about people's general knowledge. Other disciplines, such as psychology, have not been able to provide AI with an explicit exposition of the general knowledge that people show in their behaviour. Due to this problem, some attention is focused on the form of behaviour which most appropriately should be called intellectual behaviour. This is the kind of knowledge which a professional expert has. Such domains are already well defined and well documented in professional journals. Law, citizens advice, geological and mechanical expertise are easily separable from the whole wealth of general human knowledge.

The attempt to deal with only a small bandwidth of human knowledge reduces the complexity of the task faced by an AI researcher, and enables him to offer some working system to users on a reasonable time scale, while major problems of intelligence remain long-term research objectives.

We can view AI's apparent failure in the eyes of people such as Lighthill as an attempt to wage a war against the whole of the domain of human intelligence. As a result, AI achievements have been spread over a large domain, but remain thin on the ground.

We can also view the apparent success of expert systems; they do not attempt to wage a war but are fighting small easy-to-win battles. The effort involved is rewarded by reaching significant depth albeit in a very narrow domain.

Many AI researchers hope that the result of these small successes will also help in the long-term battle to discover the mysteries of human thought processes in general.

ANNOTATED BIBLIOGRAPHY

Alvey, P. (1982), *A programme for advanced information technology* HMSO, London.
    This report was commissioned in the UK by the Department of Trade and Industry in response to the perceived challenge of the Japanese Fifth Generation Initiative. It is a very positive report, favouring short- to medium-term research and development. It identifies Software Engineering, Very Large Scale Integration, Computer-Aided Design, Man-Machine Interaction, Intelligent Knowledge-Based Systems (its term for AI), and infrastructure as areas worthy of investment to a total of £350 million in a five-year programme. This report was accepted and is being acted upon in Britain.

Barr, A. and Feigenbaum, E. (1981–1982), *Handbook of Artificial Intelligence*, Vols 1–3, Pitman Press, London; William Kauffman, Los Angeles.
    This is the book which attempts to make AI look like a respectable scientific discipline. It covers most areas of research in AI like a 'bible'. It succeeds in what it sets out to do, but fails in providing the 'theology' which needs to go with any bible, that is, it cannot offer general principles or theories underlying the vast amount of unrelated research reported in its 1480 pages. Most people would say that the editors would not have found any general principle in AI had they looked for it anyway!

Boden, M. (1977), *Artificial Intelligence and Natural Man*, Harvester Press, Brighton; Basic Books, New York.

This delightful introduction to AI, although now rather dated, still serves as the most coherent introduction for people coming into AI with a humanities background. The beauty of the book is that it attempts to bring together ideas from various areas of AI in order to make some general points about both human and machine intelligence. It still offers one of the best bibliographical sections for a newcomer to the field.

Charnaik, E. and McDermott, D. (1985), *Introduction to Artificial Intelligence*, Addison-Wesley, Reading, MA.

This is the most comprehensive text on AI to date. In its 701 pages it covers almost all aspects of the subject, including general principles which underly different subdomains. Such issues as the role of internal representation, search, memory organization, deduction and planning are covered. Three application areas – vision, language processing and expert systems – are introduced with reference to the general principles described in the book. It is a very thorough book but one which loses out on the communication of enthusiasm and motivation behind the practice.

Dreyfus, H. (1972/1979), *What Computers Can't Do*, 2nd edn, Harper and Row, New York.

This book is similar to Weizenbaum's in its negative view of the potential of AI but, unlike that book, shows a lack of understanding of what AI is all about. On the other hand, it presents its arguments in a more convincing way for a reader with a background in philosophy.

Feigenbaum, E. and Feldman, J. (eds) (1963), *Computers and Thought*, McGraw-Hill, New York.

This is probably the oldest book on AI. It is worth reading for the historical content, as well as being a source of classic papers such as Alan Turing's 1950 paper 'Computing Machinery and Intelligence'.

Feigenbaum, E. and McCorduck, P. (1983), *The Fifth Generation*, Addison-Wesley, Reading, MA; Pan Books, London.

The subtitle of this book 'AI and Japan's Computer Challenge to the World' explains the book well. The book is really about how to use the Japanese challenge to drum up support in the western world. AI is presented as the best thing since sliced bread. It gives a positive view of how AI affects the community in general, and business and the economy in the US and Europe in particular. A good read for people who want to avoid technical issues.

Forsyth, R. and Naylor, C. (1985), *The Hitch-Hiker's Guide to Artificial Intelligence*, Chapman and Hall, London and New York.

This book attempts to bridge the gap between the enthusiasm of mass

microcomputer users and the challenge of AI. It presents programs demonstrating applications of AI in BASIC with a clear exposition of topics such as
expert systems, natural language processing, computer vision and machine
learning.

ICOT (1982), *Outline of Research and Development Plans for Fifth Generation Computer Systems*, Institute for New Generation Computer Technology, Tokyo.
   This is the original report of the Japanese committee set up to give their
country the chance to lead the world in the computer race in the 1990s. It is
now more of historical rather than technical value.

Johnson-Laird, P. N. and Wason, P. C. (eds) (1977), *Thinking: Readings in
Cognitive Science*, Cambridge University Press, Cambridge.
   This is an excellent collection of papers on AI and Cognitive Science. It is
the best value-for-money collection of papers to date. It includes most
papers in a shortened form, which a newcomer to the field would require,
including some by Newell, Winograd, Winston, Minsky, Schank and
Berliner. It also includes papers by cognitive psychologists which emhasize
the inter-disciplinary aspect of AI.

Lighthill, J. (1972), *Artificial Intelligence, Report to the Science Research Council*,
SERC, London.
   This is the report produced by Professor Sir James Lighthill, Fellow of the
Royal Society on AI for the British Science Research Council. It is this
report's negative assessment of the potential of AI which historically is
blamed for the lack of support of basic research in this area in the UK in the
past. The report, in fact, includes replies by Professors Stewart Sutherland,
Roger Needham, Christopher Lonquet-Higgins and Donald Michie which
attempt to defend AI against Lighthill's criticisms.

Michie, D. and Johnston, R. (1984), *The Creative Computer*, Viking, New York;
Penguin, London.
   This book is similar to Feigenbaum and McCorduck's book in its over-
enthusiastic view of the potential of AI but different in its attempt to present
some technical evidence for its claims.

Michie, D. *et al.*, (1982), *Machine Intelligence*, Vols 1–10, Ellis Horwood,
Chichester.
   These volumes contain papers on various aspects of AI in a similar
fashion to a journal, but in a more readable form and of longer length than
technical journal papers.

Minsky, M. (ed.) (1968), *Semantics Information Processing*, MIT Press, Cambridge
MA.
   This is a collection of papers based on a number of early doctoral theses

produced at MIT. The analogy program by Evans contained in this book is still worth reading, whilst most other sections have now been presented in a more up-to-date manner in other publications. There are two short chapters on 'Programs with Common Sense' (John McCarthy), and 'Matter, Mind and Models' (Marvin Minsky), which are classic papers in their own right.

O'Shea, T. and Eisenstadt, M. (eds) (1984), *Artificial Intelligence: Tools, Techniques and Applications* Harper and Row, New York.
A good collection of papers for the advanced undergraduate or post-graduate student studying AI. It is best suited to being read along with a course of lectures as support material. The introductory material on PRO-LOG and LISP, as well as those on computer vision and natural language processing are outstanding.

Rich, E. (1983), *Artificial Intelligence*, McGraw-Hill Singapore.
This is one of the most coherent and thorough textbooks written on AI. It is formal in its presentation and needs the motivation of the student to get through it. As is the case with most single-authored books, the quality of the coverage of topics is uneven. However, it is more balanced in its presentation than Winston's book and more coherent than Charniak and McDermott's.

Weizenbaum, J. (1980/1984), *Computer Power and Human Reason: From Judgement to Calculation*, Freeman, San Francisco; Penguin, London.
This is a strong, well-thought-out critique of AI and its social dangers, by the man who wrote the ELIZA program. It is well worth reading by newcomers to the field who want to grasp some of the basic concepts and basic points of disagreement.

Winston, P. (1984), *Artificial Intelligence*, 2nd edn, Addison-Wesley, Reading, MA.
This is one of the major textbooks on AI. It is written to be read in parallel with *LISP* by Winston and Horn, and gives a clear view of how the subject is considered at MIT. It ignores areas of AI (such as Intelligent Tutoring systems) which are not fashionable at MIT and covers issues such as expert systems (which did not originate at MIT) very superficially. Nevertheless what it does cover is done in a coherent and rigorous manner.

Winston, P. and Prendergast, K. (1984), *The AI Business: Commercial Uses of Artificial Intelligence*, MIT Press, Cambridge MA.
This book is based on a colloquium at MIT which was organized in order to explore the commercial potential of AI. It explains how AI has moved out of university research laboratories into the real world, with a little bit of help from venture capitalists. The book looks at expert systems, robotics, natural language processing and work-stations for advanced programming. It is basically the transcript of the talks and the subsequent discussions at the

colloquium. Therefore its vision is slightly influenced by MIT's version of the truth, and its narrative closer to conversation than to academic prose.

Yazdani, M. and Narayanan, A. (eds) (1984), *Artificial Intelligence: Human Effects*, Ellis Horwood, Chichester; Wiley, New York.
　　This is a collection of papers which looks at the interaction between AI and other human endeavours. It covers medicine, law and education, as well as social and philosophical implications.

PERIODICAL PUBLICATIONS

Artificial Intelligence
This is the oldest (published since 1970) and the most authoritative and technical journal on AI. During the past two years the journal has attempted to shake off its staid technical image in order to attract some of the newcomers to the field of AI. It has changed format to nine issues per year, well over 1000 pages a year, for an annual subscription of $230. For more information contact
　　Elsevier Science Publishers,
　　PO Box 211 1000 AE,
　　Amsterdam,
　　The Netherlands.

Cognitive Science
As a result of the influence of AI on the more established disciplines of psychology, philosophy and linguistics, a new interdisciplinary journal was established in 1976. This journal, although technical, is livelier and more controversial than the *Artificial Intelligence* journal. It costs $36. More information can be obtained from
　　Ablex Publishing Corporation,
　　355 Chestnut Street,
　　Norwood,
　　NJ 07648, USA.

The AI Magazine
This is a quarterly publication of the American Association for Artificial Intelligence (AAAI). It costs $25 per year and includes membership of the association. This is the liveliest and most colourful publication in the field. It concentrates on the American scene and includes technical but well-written papers, alongside conference announcements and the like. For further information contact
　　Claudia Mazzetti,
　　AAAI,
　　445 Burgess Drive,
　　Menlo Park,
　　CA 94025, USA.

AISB Quarterly
This is a quarterly publication of the Society for the Study of Artificial Intelligence and Simulation of Behaviour (AISB). It costs £10 per year and includes membership of the society which, although European in principle, represents most of the British AI community. The *AISB Quarterly* does not, in fact always appear four times a year. When it does it is an enjoyable read, especially as distinguishing between the spoof of Father Hacker and the real article is not that easy! For more information contact

Mike Sharples,
Cognitive Studies Programme,
University of Sussex,
Arts Building,
Brighton BN1 9QN,
England.

The SIGART Newsletter
This is the American counterpart of the *AISB Quarterly*. Both cover news and reports of the activities of their respective research communities. SIGART stands for the Special Interest Groups on Artificial Intelligence, a section of the Association of Computing Machinery. For more information contact

ACM,
11 West 42nd Street,
New York,
NY 10036, USA.

CONFERENCE PROCEEDINGS

The most up-to-date source of research reports is attendance at, and published proceedings of, major AI conferences:

IJCAI   *The Proceedings of the International Joint Conference on Artificial Intelligence*, biennial (odd years) from 1969.

ECAI   *The Proceedings of the European Conference on Artificial Intelligence*, biennial (even years) from 1982 (formerly, *AISB* from 1974).

AAAI   *The Proceedings of the Annual Meeting of the American Association for Artificial Intelligence*, from 1980.

1

Principles of Artificial Intelligence

JOHN A. CAMPBELL

Many of the uncertainties about the exact nature of Artificial Intelligence (AI) are consequences of the fact that it is a science which does not quite fit in with other categories of sciences. For example, although it involves computer programming with a certain amount of formal structure about it, and though formality in computing is usually supported by a mathematical foundation, most areas of AI do not develop in the way that a mathematical area traditionally develops. Nor does AI fit the general model of a physical science: among other differences, we are almost never in the business of finding theories or descriptions for existing physical phenomena which are identified by experiment, or of using experiments to look in nature for phenomena which those theories or descriptions predict. Of the softer sciences, cognitive or behavioural psychology is the one that is most closely identified with AI – occasionally even confused with it – but this has led to some clear identifications (e.g. Hayes, 1984) of the differences. There is a case for considering AI as a proto-science in search of a general framework of description which will allow subsequent abstractions or general theories, rather like botany before Linnaeus, but even this view has obvious weaknesses as well as some strengths. The strengths include the observation that two of the abstractions which should be present in any future description are *heuristics* and *models*.

1.1 DIFFICULTIES OF CLASSIFICATION OF ARTIFICIAL INTELLIGENCE

One feature which distinguishes AI from most other sciences is that it refers to objects (programs or conceptual structures capable of being realized in programs) which are created by humans rather than objects having a prior natural existence. AI can also be viewed as a technology. Technologies deal with created objects, but most of them differ from AI in having to be based on controls imposed by the sciences of the materials out of which the objects are created.

Among the sciences, mathematics is most at home with conceptual structures that are not necessarily inspired by attempts to explain the characteristics of natural objects. In pure mathematics, the inventor of a system of axioms which generates a collection of theorems and other consequences whose size is large, well out of proportion with the size of the initial system, receives considerable esteem from his fellow-mathematicians. This is both a tempting parallel with AI and a useful starting point for discussion of the basics of AI.

The first detail in which the parallel is not exact is the basic building-block used in the two cases. In pure mathematics it is an axiom or a set of axioms. In AI there is no similar clarity. Many workers in AI say implicitly, by their descriptions of what they are doing, that they are investigating computational *models* whose behaviour can be tested by the running of real or imaginary programs. The models have it in common with the mathematician's axioms that they are rated on the basis of the richness, variety or quality of results which they generate.

Models of what? Answers to the question depend in their details on the topic inside AI which is being considered, but the phrase 'intelligent behaviour' is likely to turn up in all of them. If the topic has any overlap with psychology, it is quite common for the model to be intended to represent some aspect of the way in which human intelligent behaviour is achieved. If psychology is not involved, the model is at present more likely to be concerned with achieving results which humans either achieve (by other means) or want to achieve.

The psychological or cognitive-modelling side of the subject is a popular area for debate among AI workers, but the debate generates more heat than light. Seen from the viewpoint of most other sciences, the experimental testability of the computational models' predictions or behaviour against human behaviour is extremely doubtful except in a limited area (e.g. parts of the study of vision) where at least as much neurophysiology as psychology seems to be involved. This is a controversial opinion! Miller (1978) makes some suggestions about the technical difficulties which inhibit communication between workers in AI and psychology. Fortunately, this issue does not need further discussion in a general article on the principles of AI. Practitioners of the cognitive-modelling approach are always welcome in AI if they temper their practice with due care and attention, not to mention due modesty. McDermott (1981) gives some good pointers to both.

It is a standard procedure in AI for models to be realized in computer programs. Because the programs can be quite complex, it is reasonable to look for recurring elements within them which are more helpful than the models themselves as building-blocks for AI. Such elements have been more visible in work that has been driven by applications and even details of programming technology than in specifically cognitive research in AI, although successful technical ideas from any one area of AI migrate quite readily to others. There is a case for regarding them as better than models, as examples of the basic objects which do for AI what sets of axioms do for pure mathematicians, but their character is still not very axiomatic. Therefore, even the mathematical parallel does not settle the question of the kind of science that AI is.

1.2   HEURISTICS OR ALGORITHMS?

The crude definition of AI which says that the subject is about computational ways of providing results or behaviour that are otherwise only the province of human intelligence has many defects. Among them is the fault that it is too general; as far as we know, for example, only human animals understand and use the determination of the greatest common divisor of two positive integers, but nobody has ever argued that a program to compute this number by using the Euclidean method taught in schools is an example of AI.

Many workers in AI would say that this comment is trivial, and that they could explain clearly what distinguishes 'real' AI from the determination of greatest common divisors, given a few seconds' thought. The majority explanation would almost certainly point out that an algorithm is involved, and that no unconditional use of a single algorithm can be AI. But there is a program, part of the larger system MACSYMA (Moses, 1971a, 1971b), which is just as algorithmic while being claimed as an example of AI by people who have not looked at it closely: the MACSYMA component which performs indefinite integrations. The topics in mathematics that underlie its algorithmic performance are described best in a book by Davenport (1981) which has no overtones of AI at all.

One possible argument in favour of regarding the indefinite-integration program as an example of AI is the complexity of the problem which it solves. However, the basic algorithm is not unduly complicated to describe, and there are more algorithmically complex programs, e.g. in plasma physics and probably even in airline-ticket reservations (Gifford and Spector, 1984), which are never mentioned as achievements of AI. A better argument is an historical one: the program's grandfather, Slagle's SAINT symbolic integration program (1963) and its father, the program SIN (Moses, 1967) which was the basis of Joel Moses' PhD thesis, both had heuristic elements whose form (if not the actual representation in the programs) would not be unfamiliar to a builder of modern expert systems.

Heuristics are just rule-of-thumb methods which are not guaranteed to help in the solution of a problem P but which have reasonable records of helpfulness on previous problems which may seem to have something in common with *P*. A good presentation of the heuristic way of looking at problems is a book by Pólya (1945).

Some commentators in AI (Barr and Feigenbaum, 1981) seem to believe that the last word on indefinite integration is still heuristic and therefore still AI, but this is simply a mistake. It is more reasonable, although unconventional, to say that the effort of changing indefinite integration from a mainly heuristic to an algorithmic topic, e.g. by using a mixture of computer-based experimentation and refinement of the accompanying theory or model, was at least partly an effort in AI. This view makes good sense if one uses a definition which says that AI is concerned with the improvement of understanding of processes that require some heuristic elements when they are carried out by human intelligence. There is no evidence that people who have classified MACSYMA as an example of AI have made their choice because of this view, but being right for the wrong reasons is not an unusual human phenomenon.

If the 'algorithmic' state of a topic remains fixed for long enough, while humans continue to tackle the topic heuristically because they cannot make use of the algorithmic insights as part of their own behaviour, then the topic is likely to pay the price of ceasing to be regarded as relevant to AI. This is exactly the situation for the kind of automated chess-playing that is now represented by the chess machines currently on sale in games shops. But the price is not an unfair one: like other sciences, AI can be expected to change its boundaries as it evolves, and to leave behind any topics (even if those were once examples of AI interest) which do not evolve with it.

The most common descriptions of AI involve some mentions of intelligent behaviour. The application of heuristics rather than algorithms or fixed formulae to problems is a good indicator of this behaviour. More technical descriptions of AI tend to take something like this position for granted, and to give examples of computational (programmable) methods whose use is evidence that one is working in AI (Charniak and McDermott, 1985; Winston, 1984). Some of the methods, like the reduction of problems to sets of subproblems which are simpler to solve, are heuristics in themselves. Others, such as backtracking, are components or necessary services which make it possible for various heuristics to be applied computationally. Learning, which is a third consideration in definitions of AI and which is elevated to first place by some authors, is achieved in present practice by the application of heuristics. As such, and as one instance of what one does with intelligence, it falls into the general pattern described above rather than defining an independent dimension in the study of AI.

The picture of AI that has emerged has three levels of detail. At the lowest level, there are computational methods which are common to several fields of application. One level above this, there is the level of heuristics. It includes examples which have also been found useful in different fields of membership. Enough remains to be discovered about heuristics and general methods of assessing their usefulness that novel or untried examples are still worth inspection. For example, even the classic source (Pólya, 1945) has not been fully mined yet, and new sources from outside AI (e.g. Melzak, 1983) appear from time to time. At the highest level, AI deals with processes that use elements from the lower levels to achieve results that are characteristic of the actions of human intelligence, either as products of the actions or as ends that are specified through conscious use of that intelligence. The construction of computational models is a natural way of treating this level of AI.

The answer to the 'Heuristics or Algorithms?' question in the heading for this section is obviously weighted heavily towards heuristics, but it can admit any algorithmic issues that fit the three-level description above. Particularly in robotics, vision and the processing of speech, algorithmic methods figure quite prominently, and legitimately, as contributions to AI.

1.3 PROGRAMMING METHODS IN ARTIFICIAL INTELLIGENCE

The longest-lived example of a standard programming method or set of methods in AI can be summarized in one word – *logic*. In modern practice, computational logic includes such things as inference of consequences from given facts and rules, automated theorem-proving, logic programming (Hogger, 1984) and the language PROLOG (Kluzniak and Szpakowicz, 1985). The founders of formal logic had the aim of establishing a calculus in which consequences of situations could be demonstrated unambiguously, avoiding the imprecision and scope for misunderstanding that were found in ordinary languages. Relative success in this aim would not have been enough for computational logic to have become a basic tool in the AI workshop if the resulting systems, built into programs, had been prohibitively inefficient to use. Robinson's resolution principle (1965, 1983) has made it possible to implement relatively efficient logical computations in 'standard' logics, notably the Horn-clause subset of the first-order predicate calculus, which are adequate to express what most of us mean when we talk informally of 'logic'. This subject is covered too well in existing textbooks (Hogger, 1984; Kowalski, 1979; Nilsson, 1980; Robinson, 1979) to need more detailed treatment here.

A much more recently-recognized programming idea is basic to modern AI and has been abstracted from the understanding of why there are many subjects in which greater experience leads to more effective processing of new requests or solving of new problems in those subjects. There are varieties of the idea: 'frames' and 'scripts' are two words which have been used to name them. Whether at a high or a low level, AI must be concerned with the placing of information into contexts which automatically supply much more information for little or no more computational cost. Generating many productive associations between items of information with little effort or delay is what distinguishes intelligence best from unintelligence. A *frame* is a data structure containing slots for items of information which in principle belong together in some context. The slots can be filled or empty. Any insertion of a piece of information into an empty slot associates with it, in that context, all the pieces of information already filling other slots. Some of the meaning in each case is supplied by the nature or names of the slots holding the information which has been inserted. Among other things, a slot S may be filled with an algorithm which, when applied to the information I in some other slot, will determine the 'S' value of I, e.g. whether I should be regarded as normal or dangerous. S may equally well hold a representation of an heuristic which can determine the same thing at more computational expense. If it is necessary to act quickly on any implications of danger in I, say if I is a measurement of exhaust-gas temperature in a turbine, then reducing the heuristic in S to an algorithm is a very positive achievement, and a legitimate goal of research in the subject.

The concept of frames in its current meaning was first put forward by Minsky (1975) and is also described in the latest textbooks (e.g. Winston, 1984). The concept of a *script* (Schank and Abelson, 1977) is well known informally, but deserves to be defined (or redefined) as that of a frame or set of frames in which some measure of time, 'before' and 'after', or cause and effect, is explicit. In practice, their implementation is just an application of basic knowledge in data structures, but for a purpose, described above, which is currently particular to AI.

The computational use of logic is old and popular in AI, while the use of frames and frame-like means of setting up contexts is relatively new and popular. These examples should not be taken to mean that a method in AI is permanently in fashion once it is adopted. One method which has been around for a long time, but which is currently somewhat in eclipse, is *means-ends analysis*. In such an analysis, the goal which represents a solved problem is described as a state in some space, as is the initial situation or any subsequent situation brought about by attempts to solve the problem. The means available to change the states are regarded as state-changing operators. A metric is imposed on the space: some specification of the distance between any pair of states is thus available. How to use this information is generally a question for the 'heuristics' level of AI, where one looks for good techniques to generate the best path in the space from the initial state to the solved-problem goal state. In the most traditional version of means-ends analysis, the heuristic is simple enough to be lumped in with the basic state-space description of means and ends: choose a next step which reduces (ideally by as much as possible) the distance between the current state and the goal state. There is no obvious present general bias against means-ends analysis as a tool of AI: it is just that other methods on various levels of AI have produced more interesting or efficiently-obtained results lately and have occupied more of the foreground in conferences and books.

Other basic methods of AI use concepts which can be paraphrased in the language of states and changes of state. They do not gain in effectiveness through such a paraphrase – usually quite the opposite – but regarding the paraphrase as possible makes it easy to appreciate that a uniform description which can be applied to several of the basic methods is one of *search* for an appropriate point (a point which specifies a solved problem) in some state-space. Searching is a basic activity in AI. Moreover, only lucky, locally-oriented or deliberately random searches can avoid *backtracking*. Computationally it is more difficult (or requires more care) to set up a system in which backtracking is efficient than to make one where an arbitrary 'next move' in a search is efficient. This is part of the reason why attempts at providing useful implementations of logic programming before PROLOG attracted little following, and why PROLOG itself is still criticized for giving inefficient service in large computations.

In current American AI language, the main source of inefficiency for standard PROLOG implementations and other frameworks for search is that the basic backtracking method is chronological; i.e. when an impasse is met, the first move to be withdrawn on backtracking is the last one that has been made previously. If the essence of that move has nothing to do with the reason for the impasse, then the computing overheads associated with the withdrawal are largely wasted. The alternative is to use dependency-directed backtracking, where the path of backward moves in the search space proceeds only in steps that have something to do with the reasons for the impasse. This essence of efficient backtracking, as an idea, belongs at the 'methods' level of AI. By itself it is of value, but the value is greatly increased by heuristics which can determine possible reasons for an impasse and identify steps in the search space which have some significant association with these reasons. So far, the most powerful techniques of this kind have tended to be problem-specific. However, some of them are general and close enough to the semantics of the programming system in which they work to belong more to the 'methods' level, e.g. the suggestions of Bruynooghe and Pereira (1984) and Cox (1984) for improvements in the efficiency of backtracking in PROLOG and logic programming. An excellent general book on questions of search that arise in AI has been published recently by Pearl (1984).

Pattern-matching is another basic method of AI. In essence, it means that actions are initiated or particular sections of a computation are called up if the data under examination match patterns which are attached as preconditions to those actions or sections. One step of a computation of this kind can change the data or generate new data which can be examined in turn for pattern-matches that initiate the next step. 'Pattern-driven invocation' is the American name for that kind of computation. The method appears in slightly different disguises in many current and historical computing activities in AI: for example, in the formation and use of analogies (Chouraqui, 1985), in Carl Hewitt's landmark MIT AI language or system Micro-planner (Dowson, 1984), and in most current expert systems. Also, it obviously overlaps with and increases the flexibility of the concept of a frame.

Although the repertoire of methods described above is not exhaustive, it covers many of the methods mentioned in standard textbooks (e.g. Charniak and McDermott, 1985; Rich, 1983; Winston, 1984). They are not mentioned here because they can be derived from this repertoire by simple extensions or by re-interpretation. The idea of re-interpretation is of greater value at the 'methods' level, however, for a somewhat different (but equally basic) lesson which it can teach about AI methodology. This lesson is contained many times over in the history of advances in science in general, though workers in AI need to be prepared to confront it once in every new research project, in principle, rather than once in a scientific lifetime or only in reading or courses about the history of science. It is the importance of *finding a good representation for a problem*. In most traditional sciences, there is an overall theoretical framework which can act as a safety-net for difficulties in choice of representation, even though it may not give a direct clue to the best choice. In that sense, for example, quantum mechanics is a safety-net for many specific exercises in solid-state physics and technology. There is no such safety-net for AI.

The best practice in finding good representations for problems is practice in solving problems. It is not necessary to choose a good representation in order to solve a problem, in general, but one can usually learn something about the quality of a representation by examining it again once the solution is to hand. In AI, the difference between a good and a bad representation may not be the difference between possibility and impossibility of finding a solution to a problem, but it will probably be the difference between specifying a means of solution that is computationally feasible and which is capable of useful illumination of future problems, and specifying a means of solution which fails either or both of these tests.

1.4　THE LEVEL OF HEURISTICS

Although some heuristics may be based on specific scientific ideas, most are not. They usually rely on analogy, e.g. 'For one or more previous problems which have contained feature F which is shared by the current problem, doing H has either led to the answer or would have led fairly quickly to the answer. Therefore try applying H to the current problem.' The most useful heuristics in AI are those that are applicable when F is defined very widely, but there is a place in the heuristic game for any scheme that has a record of helping to solve problems with features F that recur in AI.

The study of heuristics has an ambiguous status in most sciences. Mathematics is a good example. In practice, most results in mathematical research are reached first with the help of heuristics, but manuscripts which report these results accordingly, in the form of case studies, are unlikely to be approved for publication by referees and editors of journals. The convention for research papers and the majority of advanced books is that results become acceptable only after they have been tidied up and presented in a polished form, with all the heuristic scaffolding removed. Sets of theorems, in particular, may have an orderly published presentation in which any result may be seen to arise from earlier results in the presentation, but which has no close connection with the sequence that the author actually followed in deriving them, and therefore no reliable indication of mathematicians' intuitions or experience of how to make progress in their subject. The same thing happens routinely in theoretical work in other sciences. It is also not unknown for the orderly pattern that unfolds in an experimental scientific paper to have nothing much to do with the way in which the experiments were first conceived or the panics and sudden changes of plan which may have occurred during the work.

Heuristics are of interest in AI, and respectable, because we know that the 'intelligent behaviour' criterion selects problems for which heuristic or rule-of-thumb behaviour is usually the best way of beginning to tackle them. This situation is a constant of AI. Therefore a proper valuation of heuristics is a legitimate basic element of AI. At the least, this includes an understanding of the types of heuristics.

Because of the recurrence of the idea of 'search' in many AI problems, several of the most general classes of popular heuristics are involved with the simplification of searches for solutions to those problems. For example, in connection with means–ends analysis and the finding of a 'best' path through a search space, there may be too many plausible paths for an exhaustive examination of all of them to be a sensible way to proceed. A better approach, even though it may exclude what is genuinely (on the basis of superior knowledge not available to us) the best available path, prunes the alternatives so that only a subset is explored at each step. A general pruning method must be heuristic: it tries to select such a subset with the help of local information without any guarantee that the selection will always contain part of the best path. The local information usually consists of measures of the goodness of points in the search space (e.g. static evaluations of the quality of board positions in chess) or of distances or costs of moving from a specific point to adjacent points. Where the so-called minimax strategy is used in exploration of the paths that can be followed in a two-person game, alpha–beta pruning is an heuristic with a very precise meaning (Nilsson, 1980) which reduces the size of the search space. Many problems can be cast in the form of two-person games and therefore come within the range of this heuristic.

It is still possible to reduce the size of the space that is searched if no quantitative measures of goodness or distances are available. In fact, some heuristics for reduction can have more power than those that rely on such measures because they can use properties of the space that are easier to relate to the natural statement of a problem. In any problem with a mathematical character it pays to look for symmetries, i.e. transformations of the co-ordinates in the space that leave the essential properties of the problem unchanged. Then, if C and C' are any two sets of such co-ordinates, the computations on the instance of the problem at C need not be repeated for C'. Similar reasoning may be applied to problems that are not specifically mathematical. Another mathematically-based means of pruning paths in a search space is an heuristic which says that equations or similar expressions that may be turned up in the next step by non-mathematical (e.g. pattern-matching or analogical) means are unacceptable unless they are dimensionally consistent. This may be a simple observation in mathematics, but it has non-trivial consequences in problems where algorithms are lacking and where search is the only reasonable way to find the answers (Campbell, 1979).

There is a widely-applicable method or heuristic which is implied by that last comment. If there is no purely algorithmic method of reaching a solution to a problem, a common alternative is to say that anything which passes a given set of tests is a solution. Or, as a US Supreme Court judge is reported to have said about pornography, 'I can't define it, but I know it when I see it.' Hence a possible method, which works in many fields, is to generate candidate solutions and subject them to the relevant tests, retaining only the one or ones which pass those tests. 'Generate and test' is the usual name for the method. The art of applying it to AI problems is to arrange for the amount of computing effort or resources needed for the whole process to be kept within reasonable bounds. This is an heuristic art in some problem-areas because it may be a matter of trial and error, or careful analysis, to choose the best point at which to change from generating to testing of a candidate solution.

Whether or not search is involved, 'divide and conquer' is a valuable organizing principle in the reduction of computational effort. The principle is built into many recursive algorithms that are quoted as examples in undergraduate courses in computer science. In its non-recursive form, it is often the same thing as structured programming. It involves the reduction of the solution of a problem to the solution of a set of smaller subproblems. The power of the idea can be illustrated by a simplified but still realistic analysis, on the assumption that each problem involving n objects can be broken down into two similar problems, each involving $n/2$ objects. If the breaking-down involves inspection of all n objects, which is quite common, then the time for administering the overheads is proportional to n: say cn, where c is a constant. Thus, if $T(x)$ is the time taken to compute a solution for x objects by a divide-and-conquer method, it follows that

$$T(n) = 2T\left(\frac{n}{2}\right) + cn.$$

Suppose that a pedestrian method of finding a solution takes time $t(x)$. We may then choose to use it for very small x as a terminating condition for the recurrence relation above, which becomes

$$T(n) = 2^r T\left(\frac{n}{2^r}\right) + rcn$$

after r divide-and-conquer steps. If $t(x) = kx^p$ for constant k and some fixed power p greater than 1 (common in non-AI textbook problems), and the terminating condition is applied after r steps, then

$$T(n) = \frac{kn^p}{2^{(p-1)r}} + rcn.$$

Alternatively, if the pedestrian method had been applied initially, then the time would have been

$$T(n) = t(n) = kn^p,$$

i.e. approximately $2^{(p-1)r}$ times slower than an r-step divide-and-conquer method (since the n^p term usually dominates the term rcn for all but small n).

In AI problems and others involving search, it is often true that $t(x)$ is exponential in x, and can be reduced to the polynomial form above only if pedestrian methods are supplemented by methods of pruning. Hence the speed-up obtainable by use of the divide-and-conquer method may be even greater than the non-AI factor $2^{(p-1)r}$. It is therefore worth spending significant amounts of time and effort in trying to fit or impose reduction methods or heuristics which have a divide-and-conquer character on AI problems.

A further heuristic of value in AI is one that has been exploited more by researchers with pens and paper than by programs so far. It is worth mentioning here as an interpretation of several of the significant advances in research that have been made in different areas of AI, e.g. in the improvements in efficiency and power of indefinite integration in the MACSYMA family since 1967. Its automation is also a challenge to workers in AI. Search is almost always a less efficient way of finding a solution for a problem than solving the same problem algorithmically (e.g. contrast the treatments of integration by Slagle (1963) and Davenport (1981)). Therefore, the heuristic, 'Try to replace searches by the use of algorithms wherever possible' is a standing instruction in AI (acted upon successfully in other areas besides integration, e.g. computer vision), even though one usually notices it in AI publications only by reading between the lines.

There are still further classes of heuristics whose study has been responsible for advances in AI. For example, in the same spirit as the case above, 'Try to express knowledge in the form of facts and rules that can be used to draw inferences' is a pen-and-paper heuristic which has been responsible for the recent successes in expert systems, among other things. At the purely computational level, each technical variety of the resolution method for automated theorem-proving or inference (e.g. in the selection quoted by Nilsson (1980)) can itself be viewed as a special-instance heuristic for biasing the search for the most appropriate inference in a particular direction.

The subject has even advanced far enough for some researchers to justify spending time on the development of heuristics about heuristics (Davis and Lenat, 1982).

This is not to say that the 'lower' levels are yet satisfactorily explored: there is unlikely to be any useful characterization of a space of basic heuristics, for example, and even quantitative analyses of the expected advantages of using heuristics, such as the treatment of the divide-and-conquer method above, are rare. Nevertheless, the study of heuristics and the attempt to be as systematic as possible about them (rather than brushing them under the carpet) is an essential feature of AI, and a feature which helps to distinguish it from other sciences.

1.5   THE LEVEL OF MODELS

Mathematical modelling is a popular activity in several physical and biological sciences. A provocative definition of a model, from a researcher in one of those sciences, is 'Any set of equations which can't be solved exactly.' This definition is equally fair or unfair to the processes that occur when one writes and runs a program in a simulation language, such as SIMULA (Birtwistle *et al.*, 1973). It is also relevant to high-level programming in AI, especially now that workers in object-oriented programming in AI are discovering that techniques and facilities of use to them, e.g. for inheritance of properties, have already been invented by designers of simulation languages.

A computing analogue of 'a set of equations which can be solved exactly' is a traditional program embodying one algorithm. A computing analogue of mathematical modelling is SIMULA-style simulation. While large programming projects in AI or descriptions of potential AI programming projects have some components of the 'simulation' that one finds in mathematical modelling, they possess a richer structure with no analogue in such modelling. There are at least two sources for this richer structure. First, AI models make essential use of the heuristic level of their subject, while there are almost no examples of features of mathematical modelling that match what workers in AI understand by heuristics. Second, because of the AI interest in intelligent behaviour, there is usually some explicit concentration on cause and effect in AI applications, while standard mathematical models are passive in this respect. (For example, the Newtonian equation of motion $F = ma$ can be read equally well to say that the force causes the acceleration, or that the acceleration causes the force, or that both are caused by something else outside the equation.)

Theories in AI are (or generate) models of how some process related to intelligent behaviour may take place. As in any other science, theories are of very limited value unless they can be tested. Testing in AI can simply involve the running of a program which embodies a model. In physical sciences a program is usually a means of mechanizing the calculation of particular consequences of a theory. Hence the relationship of the program to the physical theory is the same as the relationship of a walking-stick to the man who uses it. There are very respectable programs in AI too with this character, e.g. (to judge by their descriptions) the BACON programs (Langley, Bradshaw and Simon, 1983) for the inference of connections between physical quantities. However, the special importance of many programs embodying theories in AI is that the pen-and-paper theories are only frameworks or walking-sticks while the program itself 'is' most of the theory (of behaviour), and the outputs of the program are the phenomena by which the theory/program entity is judged. In those cases, the theory and the program cannot be separated: both together may be referred to as an AI model.

If this model produces results which parallel those of human behaviour, say in recognition of speech or of visual patterns, then it is logically possible that the elements of the model and its internal functioning *may* correspond to elements of real human behaviour for the same job. Research at the cognitive-science end of the AI spectrum often has this correspondence as the explicit goal of its model-making – after which it has the much harder task of devising actual tests in psychology or neurophysiology which are plausible indicators of success or failure. It is also logically possible that a model which carries out an 'intelligent' job at a good human level of skilled performance does so by using methods that demonstrably share nothing with human methods. Artificial Intelligence research of this kind is equally legitimate AI (with separate problems of its own where automated explanation of actions in human-intelligible terms is concerned), as well as being a useful corrective to the too-common view that humans must use method m to carry out task T if an AI program uses m to reach human standards of performance on T. What this view asserts in logic, if a ranges over a set of agents, m ranges over a set of (sets of) methods that contains the particular element μ, $H(a)$ is true only if a is human, and $T(a, m)$ is true only if a uses m to do T, is

$$\forall T[(\exists m \forall a[H(a) \Rightarrow T(a, m)] \wedge \exists a[\sim H(a) \wedge T(a, \mu)]) \Rightarrow \forall a[H(a) \Rightarrow T(a, \mu)].$$

The complication of this expression may hide the untruth, but the early logicians were public-spirited enough to hope that their notation could be used quite easily to reduce complicated fallacies to simple and self-evident fallacies, and good enough mathematicians to fulfil the hope. Simplifying the expression is an ideal first exercise for people with a background in logic who wish to move into AI (or vice versa)!

The lower-level building-blocks of models need not be combined with each other in a strict hierarchical fashion – another source of complexity in the structures of AI models. Algorithmic methods may interact with algorithmic methods or with heuristics, and heuristics may interact with each other.

There is some bias in the choice of interesting models in AI towards heterarchy rather than hierarchy in as many respects as possible, including the mechanisms used for control and for evaluation of possible courses of action. The work by Hewitt's group at MIT (e.g. Hewitt and de Jong, 1983; Kornfeld and Hewitt, 1981) is a good source for the case for this bias. Where hierarchy is preferred in particular problem-areas in 1985, it is because hierarchical solutions which work can be shown (by construction) to exist, or because hierarchical decomposition of problems has been a powerful aid to human understanding and to scientific progress in the past. Theories or explanations of phenomena in most fields of science and technology are hierarchical, while AI has to admit that heterarchy is also an important principle. It is reasonable to assume that AI will become more explicitly concerned with the scope and properties of heterarchical models in the future – especially if future AI research bypasses some of the shortcomings of the traditional von Neumann computer architecture by using machines which offer significant amounts of parallel or distributed processing power.

Modelling in AI includes the treatment of such apparently unscientific concepts as beliefs and purposes. This is of practical importance to the subject on at least two different levels. It is relevant first in the design and better understanding of heterarchical systems: if choices of actions in an AI model expressed as a program are made by some kind of negotiation or consensus among agents or 'actor' elements, each agent will give any globally-significant choice offered to it a rating which measures how well the choice fits that agent's own local purpose. Specifying clearly what is meant by 'purpose' in general will help to ensure that models get their internal consensual negotiations right. The second level of relevance, where belief and purposes are concerned, is user-modelling – an essential part of the handling of what can be described as issues of the man–machine interface.

Some of the successful user-modelling in past work in AI has been involuntary. An improved understanding of these successes is a further reasonable goal of AI. For example, why have AI programming environments developed in the way that they have, and why is the LISP language (first constructed from a formal mathematical viewpoint (McCarthy, 1963)) so well suited to the 'beliefs and purposes' of people working in AI? Subsequent chapters of the present book should throw some light on those questions.

To sum up: AI is a science where the idea of the testable model embodied in a program is paramount, where it is accepted that not every phenomenon can be reduced to hierarchical form or explained hierarchically, where heuristics and their systematic study are welcome, and where the use of heuristics is intended to guide or reduce the process of automated search for solutions to problems that have something to do with the 'intelligent behaviour' criterion. These are the principles that are most relevant for the achievement of the first central goal of AI that is mentioned in the standard text on AI by Winston (1984): to make computers more useful.

REFERENCES

Barr, A. and Feigenbaum, E.A. (eds) (1981), *Handbook of Artificial Intelligence*, Vol. 1, Pitman, London, pp. 123–7.

Birtwistle, G.M., Dahl, O-J., Myhrhaug, B. and Nygaard, K. (1973), *SIMULA BEGIN*, Studentlitteratur, Lund.

Bruynooghe, M. and Pereira, L.M. (1984), Deduction revision by intelligent backtracking, in *Implementations of Prolog* (ed. J. A. Campbell), Ellis Horwood, Chichester.

Campbell, J.A. (1979), *J. Phys.* A, **12**, 1149–54.

Charniak, E. and McDermott, D. (1985), *Introduction to Artificial Intelligence*, Addison-Wesley, Reading, MA.

Chouraqui, E. (1985), Construction of a model for reasoning by analogy, in *Progress in Artificial Intelligence* (eds L. Steels and J. A. Campbell), Ellis Horwood, Chichester.

Cox, P.T. (1984), Finding backtrack points for intelligent backtracking, in *Implementations of Prolog* (ed. J. A. Campbell), Ellis Horwood, Chichester.

Davenport, J.H. (1981), *On the Integration of Algebraic Functions*, Springer-Verlag, Berlin.

Davis, R. and Lenat, D.B. (1982), *Knowledge-Based Systems in Artificial Intelligence*, McGraw-Hill, New York.

Dowson, M. (1984), A note on Micro-planner, in *Implementations of Prolog* (ed. J. A. Campbell), Ellis Horwood, Chichester.

Gifford, D. and Spector, A. (1984), *Commun. ACM*, **27**, 650–5.

Hayes, P. J. (1984), On the difference between psychology and AI, in *Artificial Intelligence: Human Effects* (eds M. Yazdani and A. Narayanan), Ellis Horwood, Chichester.

Hewitt, C. and de Jong, P. (1983), Analyzing the roles of descriptions and actions in open systems, *Proceedings of the 1983 Annual Meeting of the American Association for Artificial Intelligence*, Los Altos, pp. 162–7.

Hogger, C.J. (1984), *Introduction to Logic Programming*, Academic Press, London.

Kluzniak, F. and Szpakowicz, S. (1985), *PROLOG for Programmers*, Academic Press, London.

Kornfeld, W.A. and Hewitt, C. (1981), The Scientific Community Metaphor, *IEEE Trans. Syst. Man Cybern.*, **11** (1), 24–33.

Kowalski, R. (1979), *Logic for Problem-Solving*, American Elsevier/North-Holland, New York.

Langley, P., Bradshaw, G.L. and Simon, H.A. (1983), Rediscovering chemistry with the BACON system, in *Machine Learning – An Artificial Intelligence Approach* (eds R. S. Michalski, J. G. Carbonell and T. M. Mitchell), Springer-Verlag, Berlin.

McCarthy, J. (1963), A basis for a mathematical science of computation, in *Computer Programming and Formal Systems* (eds P. Braffort and D. Hirschberg), North-Holland, Amsterdam.

McDermott, D. (1981), Artificial intelligence meets natural stupidity, in *Mind Design* (ed. J. Haugeland), Bradford, Vermont.

Melzak, Z.A. (1983), *Bypasses: A Simple Approach to Complexity*, Wiley, New York.

Miller, L. (1978), *Cognitive Science*, **2**, 111–27.

Minsky, M.L. (1975), A framework for representing knowledge, in *The Psychology of Computer Vision* (ed. P. H. Winston), McGraw-Hill, New York.

Moses, J. (1967), Symbolic Integration, Report MAC-TR-47, Project MAC, Massachusetts Institute of Technology, Cambridge, MA.

Moses, J. (1971a), Algebraic simplification: a guide for the perplexed, *Commun. ACM*, **14**, 527–37.

Moses, J. (1971b), *Commun. ACM*, **14**, 548–60.

Nilsson, N.J. (1980), *Principles of Artificial Intelligence*, Tioga, Palo Alto, CA.

Pearl, J. (1984), *Heuristics: Intelligent Search Strategies for Computer Problem Solving*, Addison-Wesley, Reading, MA.

Pólya, G. (1945), *How to Solve It*, Princeton University Press, Princeton, NJ.

Rich, E. (1983), *Artificial Intelligence*, McGraw-Hill, New York.

Robinson, J.A. (1965), A machine-oriented logic based on the resolution principle, *J. ACM*, **12**, 23–41.

Robinson, J.A. (1979), *Logic: Form and Function*, Edinburgh University Press, Edinburgh.

Robinson, J.A. (1983), Logical reasoning in machines, in *Intelligent Systems: The Unprecedented Opportunity* (eds J. E. Hayes and D. Michie), Ellis Horwood, Chichester.

Schank, R.C. and Abelson, R.P. (1977), *Scripts, Plans, Goals and Understanding*, Lawrence Erlbaum, Hillsdale, NJ.

Slagle, J.R. (1963), A heuristic program that solves symbolic integration problems in freshman calculus, in *Computers and Thought* (eds E. A. Feigenbaum and J. Feldman), McGraw-Hill, New York.

Winston, P.H. (1984), *Artificial Intelligence*, 2nd edn, Addison-Wesley, Reading, MA.

TOOLS AND TECHNIQUES

Artificial Intelligence (AI) is concerned with constructing computer programs which exhibit abilities associated with human beings, such as understanding natural language, solving problems, playing games, as well as learning for itself. These applications of the general-purpose computer of today are different from those used in the majority of other cases for such things as payrolls, stock control or calculation of the trajectory of ballistic missiles. Therefore AI requires computing tools which incorporate some of its generally recognized useful techniques.

The two chapters in this section present the two major universal understandings within the AI community: first, that algorithmic number-crunching languages such as FORTRAN are not suited to AI applications and instead we need functional symbolic manipulating languages, and second, that the separation of the language from other components of a programming environment such as an editor, debugging aids, etc. is counterproductive for the experimental nature of rapid program construction in AI. As most AI programs represent an attempt to explore an idea, rather than implement an effective algorithm, the productivity and freedom of the programmer is more important than the efficiency of the computing system. In this section we present one example of each of the two topics.

John Gibson presents an overview of the POPLOG programming environment developed at Sussex University as a cheap but effective solution to the needs of the AI community where the special needs of AI have to be achieved on the same computers which are being used for traditional applications at the same time. There are obviously many points where this system falls short if compared with environments for dedicated AI work-stations. However, for our purpose of expounding on various aspects of an AI programming environment, it serves as a good test case.

Tony Hasemer presents the basic qualities which set an AI programming language apart from the rest. He uses LISP, the oldest and the most established of AI languages, but the primitives and the operations which he describes are the basics of most other popular AI languages such as PROLOG and POP–11.

PROLOG deserves to be mentioned on a number of accounts. It is the language chosen by the Japanese Fifth Generation report as being the most suitable for their project. It is one which it is argued offers new concepts (such as declarative programming) missing from the older AI languages. In my view, PROLOG's strength and weaknesses stem from the same quality of the language, at least within its application to AI. It incorporates some powerful tools and techniques embedded in the language which need to be constructed by the programmer using other tools. LISP offers a database, a pattern matcher and a search mechanism (depth first with backtracking). As these are the primitives of the language, the programmer starts building on top of them and therefore reaches a higher level than he would have done using LISP and with a certain degree of elegance. On the other hand, if the programmer needed to achieve his or her aims with techniques not suited to PROLOG's higher level primitives, most of the programmer's time would be spent undoing what the language had done for him.

Finally, POP–11 deserves a short note too. It is a rather old AI language which has evolved from being LISP with a PASCAL-like syntax, into a language which also offers most of the higher level primitives, such as a database of PROLOG. It seems to be a good compromise between LISP and PROLOG but, as in all compromises, is unpopular with the majority.

Erratum p.34
The word LISP in the first
line on this page should
read PROLOG

2

Artificial Intelligence programming environments and the POPLOG system

JOHN GIBSON

The emergence of Artificial Intelligence (AI) concepts and techniques in recent years has necessitated the concurrent evolution of programming environments designed specifically to complement and support research, development and teaching activities in this area. Although such systems vary widely in their individual capabilities, they generally possess certain characteristic features which most workers in the field have deemed important to the central task of supporting AI program development.

2.1 FEATURES OF ARTIFICIAL INTELLIGENCE PROGRAMMING ENVIRONMENTS

Artificial Intelligence Programming Environments (AIPEs) have evolved to support a style of program development which differs radically from that used in conventional data processing systems. Programs that exhibit some degree of 'intelligence' are generally complex entities, and their construction may well necessitate an evolutionary approach to systems design. That is, the nature of the problem can make it inherently impossible to specify a fully-completed design at the outset, experimentation with possible alternatives being the only way to proceed.

AIPEs have thus developed as test-beds for trying out ideas. Rather than just emphasizing efficient execution of completed programs, they concentrate as much on program development, providing tools to

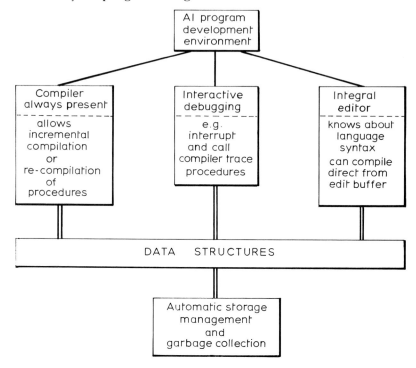

Fig. 2.1 Outline for an AI programming environment.

reduce the cycle-time of this process. A second important factor is the nature of the programs they are intended to run: whereas conventional programming in the past has been largely concerned with the processing of numerical data, AI is characterized much more by *symbolic* computation, i.e. the processing of non-numerical data in such tasks as language comprehension and generation, reasoning and inference, model-based interpretation, etc.

The features of AIPEs that have developed in response to the foregoing are summarized in Fig. 2.1.

2.1.1 Underlying support for symbolic computation

To meet the needs of symbolic computation, AI languages must provide the means for programs to construct and manipulate complex data structures with relative ease. A user program must have available to it a set of primitives which will produce new structures on demand, without having to worry about such low-level details as how memory is allocated, where data is placed in memory, and so on. This implies that the

system must handle storage management automatically, and, in particular, must deal with the problem of reclaiming the space occupied by data
structures that are no longer in use (i.e. garbage collection). Generally
speaking, not only user programs but many parts of the system itself
will rely on this functionality.

An automatic storage management system of this kind can, however,
operate only in the context of a fixed scheme for representing data.
There must be a well-defined set of primitive data structures, where the
type of any object is determinable at run-time. Whereas in conventional
languages data is only typed at compile-time (any run-time typing being
up to the user to implement for himself), in AI languages all data must
carry typing information as part of itself.

A consequence of this is that compile-time type-checking to ensure
program correctness becomes less important (since any operation that
requires to check the types of its operands can do so at run-time). For
this reason, AI languages often have little or no typing restrictions on
variables and expressions, etc., which in itself can ease the task of
program development (quite apart from making possible some operations that would be difficult or impossible in a typed language). On the
other hand, it must be said that type-checking at run-time usually
involves an efficiency overhead, unless this can be done directly by
special-purpose hardware or microcode.

Another important benefit of self-identifying data is that it makes
debugging easier. Being able to recognize any object, and know all about
its structure, the system can automatically display or print it in a
meaningful way. This greatly facilitates the inspection of internal variables and data structures during interactive debugging.

2.1.2 Incremental compiler or interpreter

An essential requirement for an 'experimental' style of program
development is interactive programming. This means eliminating the
conventional cycle of

$$\text{edit} \rightarrow \text{compile} \rightarrow \text{link} \rightarrow \text{run} \rightarrow \text{debug}$$

as separate operations, by the provision of an interpreter or incremental
compiler. The compiler/interpreter is then always present in the running
system, and can be invoked to add to or change existing programs at any
time. In particular, it can be called in contexts such as debugging, where
the ability to use new programs to interrogate the state of the system is a
powerful tool. In general, programs can utilize the compiler/interpreter
to perform a variety of jobs, e.g. evaluating symbolic expressions, or
even to construct new programs in a self-modifying way.

Notice that, being very much concerned with symbolic manipulation and requiring to process complex data structures, the compiler/interpreter itself is a typical example of a part of the system depending heavily on the infrastructure described above. New languages and compilers are often easy to implement on top of an AIPE, precisely because most of the necessary tools (e.g. symbol representation, hash tables and dictionary mechanisms) are already provided.

2.1.3   Interactive debugging tools

As we have said, the presence of a compiler or interpreter at run-time gives the ability to create new code to interrogate the state of a running program (a statement to display the value of a variable would be the simplest example). The system will normally provide a procedure to invoke the compiler to compile input from the current input stream (e.g. the terminal), which procedure can be called at any time.

This may be used in various ways: one option is for the user to call it explicitly from his program at any desired point. Often, the user will want it called after an error has occurred, and the system will provide for this by arranging that the standard error function passes control to a variable procedure whose value can be set to be the compiler-invoker. Interrupts (e.g. from the terminal) will usually be handled by a similar control mechanism, enabling the user to break-in to his program and inspect it at any time.

Other classes of debugging aid often found in AIPEs are tracers and steppers. *Tracers* allow the dynamic sequence of procedure entries and exits in a running program to be followed, minimally with a display of the procedure name and argument values on each entry, and the name and result values on each exit. More sophisticated versions will allow breaking-in and performing some specified action either on entry to, or exit from, any specified procedure. Tracing facilities can also be extended to provide display or trap mechanisms that operate when a specified variable is accessed or updated. *Steppers*, on the other hand, generalize the single-stepping concept of machine-code debuggers to high-level code, by allowing individual program statements to be executed one at a time. These ideas find their ultimate expression in systems that employ high resolution graphic facilities to provide a real-time display of the internal state of a running program, including variable values, procedure calling sequence, etc.

2.1.4   Integral editor

It is somewhat clumsy to have a powerful integrated compilation and debugging system when preparation and editing of programs to be input to the system requires the invocation of a separate text-editing process. Most AIPEs therefore possess an integral editor, having a high-bandwidth communication with other parts of the system. This has many advantages: the editor can know about the structure and syntax of programs, and can perform routine tasks such as syntax-checking and tidying up of program text. It can also provide a variety of operations for helping the user find his way around parts of a program (e.g. find a given procedure definition in a file, move the procedure currently being edited to somewhere else, etc.).

In addition (where an incremental compiler is concerned), the editor can be used to input text directly to the compilation process. So we can request it, for example, to compile the procedure currently being edited, or to compile all program text within a given range in a file; this is far more convenient than being restricted to compilation of whole files. The only real advantage of an interpreter over an incremental compiler is that the former does not require the compilation step; merely altering the source code is sufficient. When this step can be initiated by a single keystroke inside the editor, and (e.g. for a single procedure) reduced to a fraction of a second, the advantage is largely eroded.

The natural extension of this technique is to make the edit 'buffers' become input/output devices for the system as a whole, so that programs can take input directly from one buffer, produce output in another, and so on; all of this text is available for immediate inspection and manipulation with the full power of the editor. The concept becomes more attractive still in the environment of a multi-window display, where each edit buffer can be shown in its own window.

An integral editor can be the basis of many other facilities, such as access to documentation, help systems, etc. Generally, it provides user programs with a built-in library of routines on which to build display-based text processing systems.

2.1.5 Language features: tailorability/extensibility

A common characteristic of AIPEs is their 'softness'. The provision of a built-in compiler or interpreter, and the need for all parts of user programs to be re-compilable, gives rise to a general philosophy of constructing systems with loosely-coupled components, and as a consequence, much of the underlying system is itself constructed in this way. Thus, it is possible for the user to alter and extend many aspects of the system to suit his own tastes and needs. As examples of this we could cite:

• redefining standard system procedures;

- redefining editor commands and functions, or creating new ones;
- changing existing language syntax, and defining new syntactic constructs.

2.2　THE POPLOG ENVIRONMENT

The POPLOG programming environment (Hardy, 1984; Sloman, Hardy and Gibson, 1983) is an ongoing development of the Cognitive Studies Programme at the University of Sussex, founded in the 1970s as a framework for teaching and research in AI. One of the principal aims of the programme is the teaching of computational and AI concepts to humanities undergraduates, and the use of these ideas to elucidate problems in psychology, philosophy and linguistics. The evolution of POPLOG was largely motivated by the need for an environment which would support both beginning programmers (often students with little or no mathematical or scientific background), as well as experienced researchers. Thus, in addition to developing many of the AIPE features already described, POPLOG has also developed in ways designed to make the system friendly and accessible to the naive user.

The result is a system which, although broadly comparable to the kind of LISP–based environments developed in the USA (e.g. INTERLISP (Teitelman *et al.*, 1978)), is in some respects simpler and more approachable than the latter. The choice of POP-11 rather than LISP as the base language was an integral part of this, inasmuch as its syntax and semantics were felt to be more easily comprehensible by the non-scientific user.

2.2.1　Overview of POPLOG architecture

The POPLOG environment incorporates a display editor, programming languages, debugging tools, libraries and documentation in a single integrated system. Figure 2.2 illustrates the interconnections between the basic components; we shall briefly summarize the overall structure before going on to consider some of the components in more detail.

The user interfaces with the system mainly through the display editor VED (although other modes of interaction are possible). VED provides many built-in commands and has links to most parts of the system. It can be used to edit text and program files, and to inspect files that form part of the system. The latter includes accessing the on-line documentation, which comprises a large number of files classified under various headings (described below), as well as the extensive program libraries which augment and extend the basic system facilities. Aside from its use as a straightforward editor, VED has the capability to pass program text

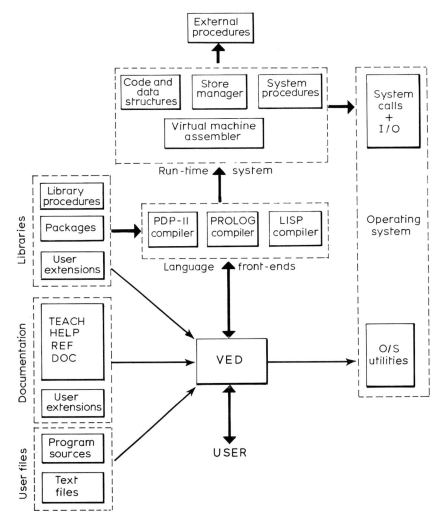

Fig. 2.2 POPLOG architecture.

direct to the language compilers, and to pass data to and from user programs.

POPLOG is a mixed-language environment, currently supporting incremental compilers for the three AI languages POP-11, PROLOG and LISP. A relatively unique feature of POPLOG is the way in which the languages all compile into code for an underlying virtual machine. Code emitted by the compilers is assembled into procedures, which can then be executed in the environment of the run-time system. The run-time system itself comprises a large number of built-in procedures to perform many different functions, including data structure creation and storage management, standard operations on all pre-defined data types, input/ output, etc. It also includes a facility for loading object modules compiled from languages external to POPLOG (e.g. FORTRAN, PASCAL, C, etc.), permitting the user to call routines written in these languages from a POPLOG program.

Although future versions of the system could be self-contained (for example, on single-user work-stations), all existing implementations are hosted on a machine/operating system environment (principally UNIX systems, but also VMS on DEC VAX machines). System procedures are therefore provided in POPLOG to interface with operating system-dependent facilities, but wherever possible, in such a way that the interface is general enough to be independent of any particular host.

2.2.2 POPLOG languages

As already mentioned, POPLOG provides three languages: POP-11, PROLOG and LISP:

- POP-11 is a procedural language with a PASCAL-like syntax (Barrett, Ramsey and Sloman, 1985; Gibson, 1984). It is a development (by the Cognitive Studies Programme) of the language POP-2, originally conceived at Edinburgh University for use in AI research (Burstall, Collins and Popplestone, 1971). Roughly speaking, it provides comparable power to LISP, although in some ways has a cleaner internal structure and semantics than the latter. It is the 'core' language of POPLOG, in the sense that most of the system itself is implemented in POP-11.
- PROLOG probably needs little introduction: a logic-based declarative language, much developed by Edinburgh University from the original conception by Alain Colmerauer at Marseilles. The current PROLOG implementation in POPLOG is largely compatible with the DEC-10 standard PROLOG (Clocksin and Mellish, 1984).
- LISP is also likely to be familiar to the reader, being the principal language used in AI research throughout the world. At the time of writing, the POPLOG version of LISP is being upgraded from a 'toy' system, used mainly for teaching purposes, to a full implementation of Common LISP (Steele, 1984).

Within POPLOG, each language has its own subsystem, including compiler, libraries, documentation, etc. At a given time, a user works 'within' a particular language subsystem, where by this we mean that certain attributes of the overall system operation will be set appropriately for that language, e.g. which compiler is invoked on system reset, which procedures are called on errors or interrupts, which language syntax VED commands will assume, and so on. Each language also possesses built-in commands for switching to the other subsystems; a program file can, for example, start off in PROLOG, switch to POP-11 to define a few procedures, and then switch back to PROLOG.

The subsystem mechanism does not, however, place any restrictions on the ability of a program written in one language to call programs or procedures written in another. Because the language compilers are essentially just 'front ends' to the underlying virtual machine (albeit complicated ones), all languages share a common basis of data representation and procedural control. This makes relatively easy the provision of constructs for inter-language communication, although the exact details depend upon the particular case. Calling LISP from POP-11 or vice versa is straightforward because they are similar kinds of languages, and calling either from PROLOG is also relatively easy since a procedure call can be made to look like an evaluable predicate. On the other hand, invoking a PROLOG clause from LISP or POP-11 is slightly trickier because of non-determinism: the latter languages have no inherent concept of backtracking, and so the problem arises as to whether the PROLOG clause should return just the first solution found, or all possible solutions.

The idea of mixed-language programming is central to the philosophy of POPLOG. While PROLOG, for example, is ideal for implementing certain classes of application (notably rule-based systems, etc), others are far more suited to the algorithmic, procedural style of POP-11 or LISP. One should be free to choose the most suitable language for any particular task, and to mix different languages in a single application where appropriate. The external loading facility in POPLOG extends this idea to non-POPLOG languages too, and (for example) makes quite possible a program written in a combination of PROLOG, LISP, FORTRAN and C.

2.2.3 The virtual machine

In its widest sense, the term 'POPLOG virtual machine' describes most of the run-time system, including all primitives that carry out data structure creation and processing, storage management and interfacing to the host operating system; in fact, everything that is outside the scope of user programs to do. In a more limited sense, it refers to that part of the system which defines an instruction set for use by language compilers, and in terms of which they can turn source code into *procedure records*. These are the objects that actually get executed at run-time. (In general, the content of these records is implementation dependent, but it will normally be host machine-code.)

The virtual machine instruction set is actually rather simple, consisting of no more than about twenty instructions. In addition to the basic data-representation scheme in POPLOG, it assumes a *stack* for pushing and popping objects, a test for a true/false value on top of the stack, the notion of a symbol declared as a *variable*, and the operation of calling a *procedure*. Overall packaging of the code is controlled by instructions which declare the start and end of a procedure, and these may be nested to allow one procedure to be contained within another. Variables may be declared as either *dynamically* or *lexically* scoped, where 'lexical' scoping is defined by the way in which procedures are nested.

In addition to general instructions used by all the compilers, there are instructions intended specifically to support the individual languages. This is particularly true of PROLOG, for which two instructions are provided as a means of interfacing with special run-time support facilities needed by that language.

2.2.4 Program libraries

The content of the program libraries in POPLOG ranges from whole packages down to single procedures (all in source code form). Most of these have been developed over the years for teaching or other purposes. Examples include a relational database package, a 'turtle' graphics program, natural language parsers, simple expert system shells, as well as many other programs designed to illustrate concepts and techniques in AI. We have found at Sussex University that students benefit greatly from being encouraged to examine and understand programs written by other people, and the libraries provide ideal source material for this (quite apart from their practical usefulness).

Although library programs can be loaded explicitly by giving an appropriate command (the exact details of which will depend upon the language being used), an important feature of POPLOG is the *autoloading* mechanism: when a program attempts to use a name (of a procedure or variable, etc.) which is otherwise undefined and for which there is an associated library file, the file will be loaded automatically. Autoloading makes it possible to have procedures and other facilities that appear to the user to be built-in to the system, but which are in fact being loaded on demand.

2.2.5 The VED editor

VED is a multi-purpose display editor. It can be used to edit or view any number of files simultaneously, although the current version for use on ordinary VDUs permits only one or two files to be displayed on the screen concurrently (future versions for systems with window-managed displays will overcome this limitation).

VED has all the normal text-editing functions one would expect from a modern display editor, controlled either by key sequences or named commands. All key sequences are redefinable (an arbitrary procedure can be attached to any sequence), and new commands can be added at any time. Procedures written for both methods can make full use of built-in editor routines. Naturally, VED has many facilities associated with the preparation of ordinary non-program text, and can be used simply as a word-processor if so desired. Its more interesting features are, however, those concerned with the programming system.

Through knowledge of the syntax of POPLOG languages, VED provides a variety of operations for manipulating program text, either at the level of individual syntactic constructs or within a whole file, including automatic formatting and indentation, substitution, cut-and-paste, etc. For ease of program development, one clearly wishes to extend this flexibility to the compilation process itself, and VED makes this possible: an individual construct such as a procedure, a range of lines in a file, or indeed a whole file, can be passed directly from an edit buffer to whichever compiler is currently in use. A procedure being edited can be compiled or recompiled with a single keystroke.

Moreover, compiler error messages and output produced by a running program can be redirected so as to appear in the original file, or in another scratch file. Further development along these lines has led to the point where, in 'interactive' mode, an edit buffer can function like an interactive terminal, in the sense that lines typed into the buffer are compiled and executed immediately, with any output, and a prompt for the next input line, being inserted afterwards. The whole file is thus a complete record of an interactive session; lines previously input can be edited and re-used.

2.2.6 The documentation system

POPLOG incorporates a large amount of on-line documentation, all of it directly accessible from within VED via appropriate commands. The documentation files (and corresponding VED commands) are divided into the four categories, HELP, TEACH, REF and DOC, each designed to meet a different need:

• HELP files are short (average 200–300 word) descriptions of individual system components; for example, each built-in procedure provided in the system will have a corresponding HELP file, describing its function and any associated arguments or results. There are a large number of these (currently around 800). HELP files are aimed at all users generally.

- TEACH files are longer tutorials covering broad aspects of system use, or in some cases, general AI techniques. A user wishing to write a natural language parser, could, for example, consult TEACH PARSING for a general overview of the ideas involved, and later TEACH LISTS to learn how to implement the list-processing required for the task. The TEACH files were developed as an integral component of the course work followed by students learning AI programming at Sussex.

- REF files are reference-level documentation, and contain complete specifications of individual areas within the system, e.g. one for each standard data type and its associated procedures. These files are targeted more at the experienced user, rather than at the beginner.

- DOC files are long files intended more for printing-out in hard-copy format than for on-line use. A typical example is DOC VED-MANUAL, a complete manual for the VED editor.

Needless to say, all the documentation files cross-reference each other heavily: a HELP file will usually refer to several other HELP files, and often a REF file as well. The TEACH files, being designed as a learning vehicle, will encourage the reader to follow up other relevant TEACH or HELP files.

The individual language subsystems also maintain their own language-specific documentation, within the same broad categories. Thus when in PROLOG, for example, the HELP command in VED will look first for an appropriate file in the PROLOG help directory, but failing that, in the main one.

2.3 SUMMARY

Artificial Intelligence programming environments in general, and POPLOG in particular, provide the tools necessary to support a fast turn-around, exploratory style of program development, and encompass languages that are specifically geared to the needs of symbolic computation. POPLOG also lays stress on the philosophy of mixed-language working, by providing both procedural and declarative languages closely integrated within the same system.

In addition to supporting research in AI, AIPEs can also play an important role in education. The exploratory programming paradigm lends itself readily to the needs of beginners, both by allowing them quick feedback on the progress of their efforts, and by supplying powerful debugging tools with which to discover and understand their mistakes. As in POPLOG, the process is further aided and reinforced by the presence of integrated documentation and help facilities.

ANNOTATED REFERENCES

Barrett, R., Ramsey, A. and Sloman, A. (1985), *POP-11: A Practical Language for AI*, Ellis Horwood, Chichester; Wiley, New York.

  This is the first textbook on POP-11, produced by members of the Cognitive Studies Programme. An introduction to the language, covering most of its facilities, with many worked examples and exercises. Assumes some prior knowledge of programming.

Burstall, R.M., Collins, J.S. and Popplestone, R.J. (1971), *Programming in POP-2*, Edinburgh University Press, Edinburgh.

  The principal book on POP-2, including a primer and a reference manual. Very terse in style, and in this respect not ideal for the beginner.

Clocksin, W.F. and Mellish, C.S. (1984), *Programming in PROLOG*, Springer-Verlag, New York.

  More or less the standard introduction to PROLOG. Not always found easy by novices, but this may have more to do with PROLOG itself than any shortcomings of the book.

Gibson, J. (1984), POP-11: An AI programming language, in *New Horizons in Educational Computing* (ed. M. Yazdani), Ellis Horwood, Chichester; Wiley, New York.

  A short overview of POP-11, with examples of its use in some simple AI-type programming. Requires only a general familiarity with programming concepts.

Hardy, S. (1984), A new software environment for list processing and logic programming, in *Artificial Intelligence – Tools, Techniques and Applications* (eds T. O'Shea and M. Eisenstadt), Harper and Row, New York.

  A technical introduction to POPLOG, with particular emphasis on the internal mechanics of the virtual machine and on the way in which the logic programming PROLOG component is integrated into the system.

Sloman, A., Hardy, S. and Gibson, J. (1983), POPLOG: A multi-language program development environment, in *Information Technology: Research and Development*, Butterworths, London.

  This paper presents a general overview of POPLOG and its philosophy. It describes the structure of the system, and presents examples of using it interactively.

Guy, L., Steele, Jr. (1984), *Common LISP – The Language*, Digital Press, Massachusetts.

  You will need some familiarity with LISP for this. A complete specification of the Common dialect of LISP, which may (or may not) become a widely-used standard.

Teitelman, W. *et al.*, (1978), *INTERLISP Reference Manual*, Xerox PARC, Palo Alto, CA.

  A detailed description of the INTERLISP environment, also requiring a knowledge of LISP.

3

LISP, Lists and Pattern-Matching

TONY HASEMER

Very many human cognitive activities can be represented as lists: knitting patterns, recipes, do it yourself car repairs, to mention but three. Each of these lists consists of a set of simple instructions arranged in a certain order, so that if you follow them in that order you eventually achieve some overall purpose – the scarf, the pot-au-feu, the mended engine. A computer program may be thought of in much the same way: it too consists of a set of simple instructions to be carried out (by the machine, of course) in their given order, and the final result achieves some overall objective. LISP is a programming language designed specifically to operate upon lists.

3.1 INTRODUCTION

Every LISP program is a list, conforming very closely to the picture given above. But there are greater similarities. For example, the first instruction in a recipe might say, 'take three ounces of flour'. If you were a TV cook you could do just that: there would be a handy three ounces of flour all ready in front of you. But under normal circumstances to 'take three ounces of flour' itself involves another list of subinstructions, which are implicit rather than explicit in the recipe. In this case, the subinstructions might be:

(1) Get out the measuring scales.
(2) Remove all except the two-ounce and one-ounce weights from the weight pan.
(3) Pour flour into the other pan until the two balance.

Of course, if you have forgotten to buy any flour in the first place there is no point in getting out the scales until you have first completed another set of subinstructions whose overall purpose is 'obtain some flour'.

A LISP program operates like that: any particular instruction within it may well involve a set of subinstructions, and each of these may involve more sub-subinstructions and so on. Eventually, of course, as with the recipe, one reaches sub-sub-(etc.)-instructions which are so simple that they cannot be subdivided any further. One could, in principle, subdivide the instructions in a recipe until they covered every single muscle movement required in cooking a pot-au-feu. Similarly, a LISP program can be subdivided into instructions each of which instruct the underlying computer to perform some very simple action. These very simple actions, the simplest of which LISP is capable, are known as the language primitives.

In languages such as BASIC, and excepting a few very modern dialects of it, a program consists of nothing more than a huge long list of primitive instructions. The language allows you to include certain primitives whose effect is to make the computer skip over some of the lines of the program during execution, or to go back and repeat some earlier section. This helps to shorten the program as a whole, but leads rapidly to the infamous 'Spaghetti Junction' style of programming. Debugging (getting the errors out of) such a program is far more difficult than untangling a ball of wool after the cat has been at it.

LISP handles things a bit more intelligently. Sets of primitive instructions which may be useful again later (later in the program or later in your life) can be bundled up together and given a name. From then on, when LISP sees in any of your programs that name as an instruction, it knows that it should carry out the corresponding bundle of primitive instructions. The proper term for this process is 'defining a function'. Similarly, once you have defined several functions which consist only of primitive instructions, you can then define a new function in terms of the ones you have already written.

However, working like that from the very simplest instructions up to a possibly very complex program (it is known as 'bottom-up' programming) is quite hard to do, and most LISP programmers prefer to work in a 'top-down' fashion. The way they do that is as follows. Suppose that I want to write a program to achieve some complex piece of computation. I start with my single 'top-level' function – the one that eventually I shall type into LISP to tell it to run my whole program. The instructions within that top-level function will be quite broad, like the steps in the recipe. In fact, they will be instructions to the computer to run a series of subfunctions, each of which will achieve one step in the 'recipe'.

Of course, the program will not run yet, because LISP does not yet know how to achieve any of the steps in the recipe. So now I have to consider each step in turn, and write the missing subfunctions. Each of these in turn may consist of no more than a series of calls to (instructions to run) sub-subfunctions, and so on. But eventually I will find that I get down to the level of LISP's primitives, which of course it does know how to do.

To put that another way, a LISP program consists of a master function which calls all necessary subfunctions, and each subfunction may itself be a master function for another set of sub-subfunctions, to any necessary level of complexity.

Another aspect in which a computer program is like a recipe is that both of them are designed to produce *behaviour*: the program causes the computer to behave in a certain way, just as the recipe or whatever causes you or me to behave in a certain way. It is also reasonable to draw a parallel between the fact that when I follow a recipe some kind of knowledge is in the process transferred from the author of the recipe to me – and suddenly I can cook a pot-au-feu where I could not before. If I write a computer program which enables my computer to perform certain tricks, the knowledge of how to perform them has been transferred from me via the program to the machine. If you instinctively disagree with that statement, reflect that in our schools we try to do much the same thing, and we judge our success or failure by testing our pupils' *behaviour*. If they can do what we want them to be able to do, we quite happily say that they have 'learned' – that there has been a knowledge transfer from adult to child.

Later chapters in this book will discuss in greater depth why we should (or should not) say that a running computer program is behaving 'intelligently'. My reason for introducing the argument is merely to point out that, for those who do want to investigate 'Artificial Intelligence' (AI), list processing is a highly convenient technique to use. We ourselves are so accustomed to processing lists in the course of our normal everyday lives that the operations of the computer, incomprehensible though they might be if analysed down to the last free electron, are intuitively perfectly sensible when thought of as operations on lists. All advanced computer languages are attempts to make the internal workings of the machine comprehensible at a higher level than that of moving electric charges, and LISP's particular way of doing that is to let you imagine that inside the computer there actually are various lists of things, which you can instruct the machine to break up, move about, join together, alter the contents of – or simply execute as they stand.

3.2 SYMBOLIC COMPUTATION

So, what kinds of things would these lists consist of? Almost exclusively, LISP lists consist of only three types of thing: constants, function names and variable names. Look at this:

$$x = \frac{-b \pm \sqrt{b^2 - 4ac}}{2a}.$$

Do not worry about the meaning of this formula (or even about whether or not it is right). I seem to remember that it had something to do with quadratic equations. All I want you to notice is that it, too, consists only of three kinds of things: constants (the numbers 2 and 4), various mathematical operators such as **plus** and **square root** and the names of the variables *a*, *b*, *c* and *x*.

Once again, there are similarities with a LISP program which I would like you to notice. Out of nothing more than constants, the available mathematical operators and a handful of variable names it is possible to create a very great many formulae. Each formula is used only in order to produce a specific result – to work out the value of *x* in the example above. If you consider the LISP primitive functions as analogous to the mathematical operators, it is clear that you could similarly write a large number of LISP functions each of which would achieve one goal and one only. And, just as it is possible to write formulae which do nothing useful at all, so it is all too possible to write LISP functions which either do nothing or do something other than they were intended to do!

There is another point here which is very important. Both formulae and functions make use of *variables*. In algebra, the variables *a*, *b* and *c* are assumed to have *values* which, when correctly inserted into the formula, enable you to derive the value of *x*. Similarly, a LISP function will contain variable names; when the function is executed, values are provided for these variables and the function operates upon them in very much the same way as the formula operates on *a*, *b* and *c*.

However, the values given to mathematical variables are for the most part simple numerical values. In symbolic computation a single variable can have an arbitrarily complex value. For example, I now want to talk about my mother.

Notice that as soon as you read the words 'my mother' you already knew quite a bit about her: that she is a woman, that she is older than I, that she gave birth to me, and so on. What you had in your head at that moment might be described as a sort of minimal template for the meaning of 'mother'. All (well, almost all – there are always exceptions) mothers will have the attributes that you now know about my mother.

Now, what about your mother? Of course, it is true that amongst the things you know about your mother are all the things that you know about my mother, plus a great deal more. It is a fact, almost too obvious to mention but nonetheless astonishing when you think about it, that out of all the billions of mothers in the world you could recognize your own without the slightest hesitation. That suggests that your knowledge of your own mother is vastly detailed and rich. What I am saying is that the *meaning* of the word 'mother' varies enormously depending upon *which* mother you are talking about.

In symbolic computation, we could ascribe to the *variable* 'mother' a *value* which represented any stage we liked, between the minimal template such as you visualized when I mentioned my mother, and the (presumably) full version of the mother concept which you see where your own mother is concerned. In fact, we could start with the very simple version, and our program could itself change the concept as it went along, in accordance with the various inputs we gave it. At one level, 'all' such a program would be doing would be progressively modifying the value of a variable, mother. At another level, more interesting to AI research, the program might be a working model of how human beings learn concepts. In symbolic computation the program manipulates its variables much as the mathematical formula does, but the values which the symbols (the variable names) stand for can be vastly more complex, and hence vastly more interesting, than simple numerals. The result of any symbolic computation may well be similarly complex. What it 'means' can only be known by asking the programmer: the machine itself cannot be expected to understand 'mother', for example, the way that you or I do. But it seems only reasonable that the more rich and detailed the ideas (values) your program is manipulating, the more rich and detailed will be the results it achieves.

3.3   LIST MANIPULATION IN LISP

The commonest LISP list consists of one or more elements, the first of which is always a function name, and often the function will be one of LISP's primitive functions. If there are any elements after the first, they will be the 'arguments' to the function, i.e. they will be values (or variables which represent values) supplied for the function to work on. A LISP list is always bounded by one opening and one closing bracket. Here is such a list:

(equal a b)

When LISP seems such a list (you could have typed it in directly to the LISP prompt) it immediately tries to *evaluate* it. This is partly an obvious thing to do: the two arguments a and b are variables, but it is their *values* that we want to test the equality of; so a and b need to be evaluated before equal can be applied to work on them. However, the LISP evaluator is bright enough to know the rule that the first element of any list should be a function name, so before evaluating a or b it goes away and retrieves from memory the 'functional value' of equal. In the case of the LISP primitives, of which equal is one, you the programmer, do not really need to know what that functional value looks like – it is normally only used by the evaluator. But if the first element of the list had been some function which you had defined for yourself, the functional value would contain all the primitives out of which your function had been created.

The net result is that having 'looked up' the functional value of equal, LISP now 'knows how to' perform an equality test. Looking up the values of a and b gives it some data for the test to be performed on, and so your instruction (equal a b)' can be carried out.

There are two things to worry about here: how did a and b get their values in the first place, and what happens to the result of the equality test?

So far, we have imagined a and b as having values much as they did in school algebra – values which we assigned to them when we wanted to use the formula. You might think that in LISP there ought to be some way of telling the machine about such assignations. And you would be right. But before getting involved with that let us assume for a moment that you just wanted to play around with LISP at a very basic level, by getting it to tell you whether or not the two letters a and b – their lexical shapes – were the same which, of course, they are not.

The simple way to do this is to quote the two letters, the two arguments to equal. LISP uses only a single quote mark, but the effect is the same as when in ordinary English you use the double quotes (inverted commas). The LISP expression

(equal 'a 'b)

means 'take the symbols a and b literally, and tell me if they are the same'. The result, or answer, would of course be some LISP equivalent of 'No'. Similarly, we could expect the LISP expression

(equal 'a 'b)

to produce the LISP equivalent of 'Yes'.

Now then, if (somehow) the *value* of a is the lexical shape 'tony' and the *value* of b is the number 5, then the expression

(equal a b)

will produce a LISP 'No', because what we are really asking is 'are tony and 5 the same?' Notice that LISP performed the equality test on tony and 5 rather than on the lexical shapes a and b because in that last example neither a and b was quoted.

When programming in LISP, you are quite free to play around with this simple evaluation rule. For example, if you had given the variable a the value 'b, then

(equal a 'b)

would produce a 'Yes' because the *value of* a is the same as the (quoted) lexical shape 'b'.

The usual way of assigning values to variables is via another LISP primitive, setq. Again, the instruction is a list whose first element is the function name:

(setq a 'tony)

will cause a to have as its value the lexical shape 'tony'. Similarly, with

(setq b 5)

except that in LISP you never need to quote numerals. The purpose of the quote is to prevent evaluation, but if you think about it there would not be much sense in giving '5' any value other than 5. To avoid such possible confusions, every number in LISP behaves as though its value were permanently itself: the value of '5' is 5, the value of '3.142' is 3.142, and so on.

Now, what about the results of the above equality tests, that is, the LISP 'Yes' and 'No'? If you had typed the tests into LISP, then after each had been evaluated there would have appeared on your terminal, just before the LISP prompt reappeared, either a t or a nil. In LISP, t means 'Yes' or 'True'; nil means 'No' or 'False'. The correct description of what happens is that the function equal (after working on its evaluated arguments) *returns* a *value*, which is either t or nil.

In LISP, *every* function, whether it is a LISP primitive or a function written by you, returns a value. equal, being a test, only ever returns either t or nil. But setq, for example, returns the value which it assigned. The two setq expressions above would return, respectively, tony and 5.

Users of LISP very soon get to know what values the various LISP primitives may be expected to return. In the case of a user-defined function, the rule is that the returned value is the value returned by the last instruction within that function. For example, here is a very simple and quite pointless function written by me. As I said earlier, a function of my own can consist of a 'bundle' of LISP primitives, and I can give the bundle a name. I shall call it demo, and here is how I would type into LISP so that LISP 'remembered' it:

```
(defun demo (x)
   (setq a 'tony)
   (setq b x)
   (equal a b))
```

When I came to use my function I might type into LISP:

(demo 'tony)

and the returned value would as above be the result of the (equal a b) expression which is the last expression in my function.

However, there is a lot more to explain first. defun is an inbuilt LISP function – not strictly a primitive, but for the moment you can imagine that it is a primitive. defun is shorthand for 'define-a-function', and it takes arguments just as equal does. But you can give defun any number of arguments – I have given it five. defun's first argument is always the name of the function being defined – in this case demo. You might at once wonder why I did not have to quote it. This is simply because it would be a pain in the neck if every time I used defun I had to quote its first argument. That first argument is *always* a name, a lexical shape. So LISP in its ever-helpful way assumes the existence of the quote, and I can leave it out.

The second argument to defun is always a *list* of variable names. I have only needed one variable name, but still it has to be a list. That is a LISP syntactic rule, so I must not violate it if I expect demo ever to work.

The remaining arguments are simply the 'bundle' of primitive instructions which I want demo to carry out. LISP will faithfully carry them out in the order I have specified.

Suppose that I have defined demo, by typing the above definition into LISP, and that now I want to use it. What happens as the LISP evaluator tackles

(demo 'tony)?

Very much the same thing as happened with equal, in fact. First of all the evaluator retrieves from memory my definition of demo. It can tell from that that demo expects a single argument, symbolized by x in the definition. And I have given demo a single argument: 'tony'. Since the latter is quoted, LISP has no need to check whether or not 'tony' has a value.

What happens next is that LISP evaluates each of the instructions comprising the definition of demo in turn, but with 'tony' as the value of x. Here is the definition again.

```
(defun demo (x)
   (setq a 'tony)
   (setq b x)
   (setq a b))
```

As you can see, the first instruction is to give the variable *a* the value 'tony'. So now x and a have the same value. The next instruction gives the value of x to the variable b. But since x is not quoted, it is xs own value, and not the lexical shape 'x', which becomes the value of b.

Finally comes the all-important equal instruction, the one whose returned value will become the returned value of demo. a and b get evaluated as usual, because they are not quoted. The value of a is 'tony', and the value of b is 'tony'. So equal returns t, and so does demo. If I now typed

```
(demo 'fred)
```

demo would return nil.

Notice that the definition of demo as shown above is still a list, like this:

```
(defun demo . . . )
```

Within that list are other lists:

```
(defun demo (x) . . .)
(defun demo (x) (setq a 'tony) . . . )
```

and so on. In a properly-formed LISP expression, no matter how complex the nesting of lists may become, each one has its own pair of surrounding brackets. You may often hear people who should know better complaining that the abundance of brackets makes LISP hard to read. But, in fact, brackets make LISP unambiguously clear, both to the programmer and to the machine itself.

3.4   COND AND RECURSION

Here is an interesting function definition:

```
(defun match (patt sample)
   (cond ((and (null patt) (null sample)) t)
         ((equal (car patt) (car sample))
          (match (cdr patt) (cdr sample)))))
```

Just look at the shape of the cond expression first:

```
(cond ((and . . . ) t)
       ((equal . . . )
        (match . . . )))
```

cond is another inbuilt LISP function, one which allows *cond*itional choices to be made as a function is evaluated. Schematically, a cond expression looks like this:

```
(cond ( ⟨test1⟩   ⟨action1⟩ )
       ( ⟨test2⟩   ⟨action2⟩ )
         . . . )
```

The angle bracketed tests and actions can each consist of arbitrarily complex LISP expressions. You can have as many tests and actions as you need in a single cond expression. During evaluation, ⟨test1⟩ is evaluated first. If it evaluates to nil, ⟨test2⟩ is evaluated. If that also evaluates to nil, ⟨test3⟩ is evaluated, and so on. If all of the tests evaluate to nil then the whole cond expression returns nil and that is the end of it. If, however, any test evaluates to anything other than nil, then its corresponding ⟨action⟩ is evaluated, and the cond returns whatever that action returns.

Let us watch that in action, as it were. Suppose that I have defined match as above and now want to use it:

(match '(a b c) x)

In other words, I want match to tell me whether or not the expression '(a b c)' is *equal* to the value of x. Imagine that match is being used somewhere inside some complicated series of computations, so that x may have different values at different times; I want to know when xs value is '(a b c)'. So let us consider the case when xs value is '(a b c)'. Here is the definition again:

```
(defun match (patt sample)
   (cond ((and (null patt) (null sample)) t)
         ((equal (car patt) (car sample))
          (match (cdr patt) (cdr sample)))))
```

The two variables patt and sample acquire, respectively, the values '(a b c)' and the *value* of x, which we are imagining also to be '(a b c)'.
The cond's ⟨test1⟩ is:

(and (null patt) (null sample))

null is a LISP primitive which returns t if its argument is an empty list or nil. So the test says, 'If both patt and sample have nil as their values, return t.' But since neither patt nor sample has the value nil, this test will fail.
The cond's second ⟨test⟩ is:

(equal (car patt) (car sample))

car is a LISP primitive which returns the first member of its argument (and, of course, this argument must be a list if no error is to occur). So this test says, 'Are the first element of patt and the first element of sample the same?' And of course they are, because we are imagining patt and sample to be the same list. So this test succeeds (returns t), and now the corresponding ⟨action⟩ must be evaluated:

(match (cdr patt) (cdr sample))

cdr returns its argument (which must also be a list) *without* its first element. Thus

(cdr '(a b c)) returns '(b c)

So what this ⟨action⟩ does is to start match off all over again, but working on lists which are both one element shorter than they were:

(match '(b c) '(b c))

Ultimately, the same ⟨test⟩–⟨action⟩ pair – the same *clause* of the cond will be evaluated again, so calling match a third time. But what is the cdr of a single-element list such as '(c)'? As before, it is what remains after the single element has been remove. That is '( )', which is the same thing as an empty list or nil. So the fourth evaluation of match has nil as both of its arguments. This time the first ⟨test⟩ of the cond succeeds, and the whole thing returns t. In other words, '(a b c)' and the value of x were the same, just as we thought!

However, suppose now that the value of x is '(a (b d))'. The first element of this list still matches the first element of '(a b c)', so match would be called again to work on '((b c))' and '((b d))'. This time both ⟨test1⟩ and ⟨test2⟩ would fail. So the whole cond fails, and returns nil as above, with no further evaluations of match.

This trick of getting a function to repeat itself on progressively simpler versions of its original inputs is known as *recursion*. In LISP, recursion is a very, very common programming technique. The effect here is to make the computer work down the two lists element by element, checking each time that the two corresponding elements are the same.

Now look at the following new version of our matcher. Its cond has one extra clause which specifies what to do if as it moves down the lists it finds that the current car of patt is an asterisk:

```
(defun match (patt sample)
   (cond ((and (null patt) (null sample)) t)
         ((equal (car patt) (car sample))
          (match (cdr patt) (cdr sample)))
         ((equal (car patt) '*)
          (cond ((equal (car (cdr patt)) (car sample))
                 (match (cdr patt) sample))
                (t (match patt (cdr sample)))))))
```

The asterisk is going to become what is called a 'segment operator': a symbol which can be inserted in the pattern list so that it will 'match' one or more elements in the sample list. For example:

(match '(a b * f) '(a b c d e f))

should succeed, because the segment operator should match everything in the sample list from c to e, inclusive. In order to achieve this, the matcher must, once it encounters the asterisk in the pattern list, ignore the current element in the sample list, applying itself again to the *same* pattern list and to the cdr of the sample list. This should continue until the element of the pattern list immediately following the asterisk is the same as the current element of the sample list:

(a b * f)	(a b c d e f)
(b * f)	(b c d e f)
(* f)	(c d e f)
(* f)	(d e f)
(* f)	(e f)
(* f)	(f)
(f)	(f)
()	()

Now let us forget about the boring A's and B's. Look at this:

(match '(* mother *) '(my mother really does hate me))

Weizenbaum's (1965) ELIZA program gave (intentionally) the impression of being a psychotherapist. If its 'patient' said anything at all about his/her mother, the program could detect it via a simple matcher similar in principle to the one we have just been looking at, and could then generate intelligent-seeming replies such as, 'Tell me more about your family.'.

I have shown you this in order to demonstrate the flexibility of LISP. One extra cond clause turned our matcher from an explanatory exercise of no practical use into a quite powerful tool. Once a LISP function or program has been written, extending its power and usefulness is usually a relatively simple matter. Furthermore, since a LISP program is composed of a large number of small, discrete functions, debugging is comparatively easy: a simple tracer can often isolate the error to a single function, where there may be only eight or ten lines to investigate rather than several thousand. It is hardly surprising that some 90% of the world's AI research is done using LISP.

A part of the flexibility of LISP comes from the fact that there is no distinction between functions and data. For example, there is a LISP function called nth, which selects and returns the *n*th element of any list. Suppose we had two lists l1 and l2, and that we wanted to know if the third element of one was the same as the ninth element of the other. We could do it like this:

(equal (nth 3 L1) (nth 9 L2))

The LISP evaluator will happily work out the two nth instructions in just the same way as earlier it worked out the *values* of a and b. Instead of the nth instructions, we could have put LISP expressions of arbitrary complexity as the arguments to equal. It does not matter – ultimately the evaluator will derive from those expressions returned values, which are then supplied as data for equal.

This means that a LISP list can contain not merely items of data or variables whose values are items of data, but also LISP functions which return items of data. This is an extremely powerful facility, largely freeing the programmer from the need for temporary variables whose sole purpose is to store intermediate values as computation proceeds.

In other words, much (usually most) of the knowledge stored in a LISP program is stored as functional rather than declarative knowledge: the program 'knows how to' derive a piece of data that it needs, rather than having the data explicitly represented somewhere as a 'fact'.

3.5   BUT THAT IS NOT THE ONLY WAY TO DO IT

That is the difference between 'functional' languages, of which LISP is one, and 'declarative' languages such as PROLOG. PROLOG stores facts, together with inference rules such as, 'a is true if facts b, c and d are true'. Given that rule, and given that facts b, c and d are indeed known to the machine, it can derive fact a.

In a similar way to that in which a LISP function can be divided into subfunctions, 'facts', b, c and d may in turn be inferences from simpler facts, and so on. In a PROLOG program the knowledge – and the complexity – are to be found in the declared rules and facts, rather than in any function which manipulates them. It is possible to regard PROLOG as a language having but one function: a sophisticated pattern matcher which can match its user's input 'question' through possibly long chains of inferences until the necessary underlying facts either are or are not found in the machine's memory. PROLOG then replies 'Yes' or 'No' to the original question.

The two styles of programming are very different in concept, and users accustomed to one style usually find the other extremely hard to follow. As a result there is a fierce argument going on between proponents of LISP and proponents of PROLOG. Well, more a shouting match than an argument: it is irrational even to make strict comparisons between the two languages. PROLOG is new and virtually unexplored; it may or may not prove capable of the demands likely to be made upon it. LISP, on the other hand, has been around for over thirty years and has a vast amount of expertise, not to mention software and programming techniques, to back it up.

One point of real similarity is that both languages started out as expressions of some formal system: LISP represented the mathematical notion of a function, and PROLOG represented Horn Clause logic: a subset of predicate calculus. Presumably in both cases the designers hoped that programs written in their new languages would be formally provable, rather than needing to be tested empirically under all likely input conditions. Unfortunately, the usual difficulties of mapping formal systems onto the real world intervened, and both languages now contain elements not accounted for in their original formalisms.

My personal view is that LISP will win, in the sense that it will remain the world's major AI language for the forseeable future. But every programming language has its advantages and disadvantages (LISP needs a lot of free memory in which to operate), and the wise programmer chooses the tool to fit the job.

3.6 LISP AND LISP ENVIRONMENTS

LISP being such a well-established language, many teams of researchers and even individuals have customized its top level (its user interface) so as to create convenient and helpful 'user environments'. Such things are particularly easy to do in LISP; for example, it is a trivial exercise to write a looping function which mimics the behaviour of LISP's own read-eval-print cycle. Once you run this function, you are effectively operating the normal LISP top level 'through' the function; so you can add all sorts of impressive facilities inside its loop.

Of the many (possibly over a hundred) such facilities which have from time to time been provided in various dialects of LISP, a few have become standard. The tracer and the stepper, which allow you to watch as evaluation of a program proceeds either at normal speed or under your control, are now so common that they are virtually part of the meaning of the word 'LISP'. So is the BREAK function, which when inserted into your program halts execution at that point and allows you to inspect the current 'state' of the program – usually you will want to know the current values of its variables. Most LISPs nowadays (except for the very tiny microcomputer versions) have some elegant method, such as a single keystroke, of accessing a sophisticated screen editor. And just before exiting from that editor you will be able to use a ZAP command to read your freshly-edited function back into LISP. One of LISP's big advantages, from the point of view of the program developer, is that it runs interpretively, which means that no compiling is necessary. So that having zapped and exited from the editor you can run your modified function straightaway.

After twenty-five years of development by widely-scattered groups, the term 'LISP' is a generic noun like 'cattle' rather than a proper noun.

Surprisingly, the differences between a function written in any one LISP dialect and the same function written in another dialect may be purely syntactic and only minor. But the user-interface – the environment you work in as you create your code – can be very different. In fact, there is a whole range of LISPs, from the LISP machine which requires a six-month study course before you can operate it, to InterLISP which can be so encyclopaedically helpful with its error-handling systems that some-times you wonder why it does not go away and write your program for you. Between the two extremes lie perhaps twenty or thirty different dialects of LISP, each with its own advantages and disadvantages for any individual user.

Of course, such a state of affairs is unbearably chaotic. Moving a perfectly healthy LISP program from one machine (and dialect) to another is always tedious, and often impossible. 'Implementation dependent' is the insult which LISP hackers always throw at each other's code – meaning that your program only works because of some obscure quirk in the dialect you are using.

Because of this, there is a trend now towards Common LISP. As its name implies, this will be (when it is finished) the dialect of LISP upon which everyone can agree. Current versions include all of the more commonly-used primitives and some of the less common ones. Each one is of maximal flexibility; for example, length will work on lists, as it normally does, but will also work on vectors or strings. Furthermore, functions such as member or assoc take an extra argument which specifies the test (normally eq) to be used. So in Common LISP you can look for those members of a list which do *not* contain some key pattern.

But Common LISP will only grow at the speed at which the LISP community can agree upon what is an essential part of LISP and what is not. Common LISP does not yet support object-oriented programming, which is an aesthetically delightful and astonishingly compact way of writing code. (It is also murderous to debug.) For a beginner, almost any LISP – even most of the microcomputer LISPs – will support months of happy hacking. They all contain the essential character of the language and are more than enough to learn on. But be warned: you will get hooked like the rest of us and you will want a bigger and better dialect in the end!

BIBLIOGRAPHY

The original version of LISP, known as LISP 1.5, is not used nowadays except as a demonstration of the mathematical basis of the language. Instead, there is a plethora of different dialects all of which have their own advantages and disadvantages. The major mainframe dialects are: MacLISP, InterLISP, UCI

LISP, and Franz LISP. Currently an attempt is being made to standardize on Common LISP, which may be your best bet if none of the books below covers the LISP on your particular machine. Common LISP is a subset of the major dialects; it will contain everything you need with which to learn the language, but may lack some of the more esoteric functions. Any of the following fvie books, three of them new and one a completely revised edition, will give you a good grounding in the principles of LISP.

Hasemer, T. (1984), *A Beginner's Guide to LISP*, Addison-Wesley, Wokingham, UK.

Touretzky, D. S. (1984), *LISP*, Harper and Row, New York.

Wilensky, R. (1984), *LISPcraft* , Norton, New York and London.

Winston, P. and Horn, B. K. P. (1984), *LISP*, Addison-Wesley, Reading, MA.

Narayanan, A. and Sharkey, N. (1985) *All Introduction to LISP*, Ellis Horwood Ltd.

REFERENCE

Weizenbaum, J. (1965), ELIZA – a computer program for the study of natural language communication between man and machine, *Communications of the ACM*, **9** (1), 36–45.

Section III

APPLICATIONS

The titles of the chapters speak for themselves. They present the most advanced areas of application of AI in language processing, speech processing, vision, robotics and expert systems. The chapters seem to share a similar pattern in the presentations:

- this is the topic;
- this is how you would do it with current computing techniques;
- this is why you need 'intelligence' applied to the solution;
- this is how AI is currently attempting to do it;
- these are the limitations.

Alan Ramsay presents a detailed account of the processing of English input in the typed form by computers. This rather strict interpretation of 'Natural Language Processing' stems from the historical attempt by AI people to separate various tasks into small modules in order to label them separately before dealing with the whole task.

Steve Isard and David Hogg present brief overviews of speech processing and vision, respectively. In these domains dealing with imperfections of collected data from the real world plays a major role.

Michael Brady presents a detailed presentation of the overall contribution of AI to the field of design and operation of robot manipulators.

Richard Forsyth presents an exposition of AI's success story so far in the form of self-contained and expert consultation systems.

4

Computer processing of natural language

ALLAN RAMSAY

In this chapter, we will outline the tasks that have to be performed in the course of language generation and processing, and we will discuss a number of theories about how these tasks might be performed. The chapter follows the standard AI approach of concentrating on understanding rather than generation, and on English rather than language in general or some other specific language. This is not to be taken as implying that understanding is more important or interesting than generation, or that English is particularly significant. It simply reflects the fact that the best developed techniques are those for understanding English. There will be some mention of the problems involved in generating decent English output, but nothing about either comprehension or generation in any other language. We will also sidestep the issue of how we convert between the signals (visual for text, auditory for speech) and the symbols of the language. Other chapters in this book deal with these tasks – our concern here is to relate the symbols, however they are manifested, to the information conveyed.

4.1   WHY STUDY LANGUAGE?

Most human beings spend a large part of their time talking to one another, or reading or writing. We communicate our needs and desires to one another; we convey information to each other; we even expend considerable effort on telling or reading stories – communicating with each other about things that never happened, involving people who never existed. Our birthright of language is among our most important faculties. It is what makes us human.

Our ability to communicate via language is one of the most useful things we know how to do. Without language we could not divide up a task and allocate some of its component subtasks to one person and some to another, except in the rigid, stereotyped ways that two birds might co-operate in building a nest or an army of ants might co-operate in attacking another such army. Without language we would not be able to teach one another about our experiences or discoveries. The only way we would be able to learn from someone else would be to watch their behaviour, try to understand its function and then mimic it. With language we can convey ideas directly from one person's mind to another, and we can explain where we got these ideas from, why we believe them to be true and what they can be used for. Many other species have signalling conventions, whereby specific actions or behaviours may be used to denote specific situations – danger signals, courtship dances, submission postures, etc.; but none seem to share our ability to combine signals in novel ways to denote novel concepts, and thus to tell each other about things which no member of the species has previously experienced.

Language use is also one of the most difficult things we know how to do. Consider the following story fragment, 'Jane wanted an ice-cream. She went and got her piggy bank, and shook it, but it was empty.' Compared with the task of understanding this, such 'expert system' problems as medical diagnosis, designing an office block or planning a genetic engineering experiment are trivial. Yet every one of us can construct a rich interpretation of this little story, without feeling that we have done anything at all clever or that we had to work very hard to do it. In this chapter, we will begin to sketch the processes and rule sets involved in understanding even a story fragment as simple as this. By the end of the chapter you should at least have a healthy respect for your own ability to use langauge.

Given that language is so useful, so uniquely human, and so difficult, it is hardly surprising that it has attracted an enormous amount of interest from AI researchers. Any program capable of generating and understanding unconstrained, fluent English speech or text will have to solve a large number of difficult problems which any mature English speaker appears to find easy. To write such a program, *we* will have to find out how these problems can be solved. Once we have done it, we will have a computer system which is far easier and more comfortable to use than anything which is currently available, at least for some tasks and domains. We will also have a rather better understanding of what we ourselves do when we are acting as language users.

4.2   TWO VIEWS OF LANGUAGE

Before we try to write language processing programs we have to get some reasonably clear idea of what language is and what we expect to have done when we have processed it. If we inspect the philosophical literature of the last 4000 years we will find that we are not the first people to have worried about this. We will also find that, for all the work that has gone into it, there is still very little agreement. Just about the only statement that would gain universal acceptance is something like: 'Language is to do with carrying ideas from one person to another via physically realized signals (i.e. noises, gestures and graphical marks).' What ideas are, how they relate to the signals that carry them, and how they relate to 'the world' are still very open questions. One of our tasks in writing natural language processing systems is to choose some answers to them.

We begin our discussion by contrasting two views of language. In the first, language is a complex system of rules which connect 'meanings' to particular choices of signals. In this view there is a hierarchy of levels of analysis, from the basic distinguishable signals up through word parts, then words, then syntactic structures, then interpretations of those structures, up to 'meanings'. A meaning is an abstract object of some sort, existing independently of any particular speaker/listener/writer/ reader, with some very close relationship with the way the world is or might be. For people who work within this paradigm, sentences and other linguistic constructs have meanings, which can be discovered by studying the way they are constructed out of basic symbols of the language (e.g. letters or distinguishable sounds). The function of a language processing system, from this point of view, is to apply a collection of rules which map meanings onto arrangements of symbols and vice versa. The language processing system is not expected to do anything with the meaning, it is simply supposed to extract it.

This view of language has a long history, with the most significant recent non-AI work being Tarski's 'verification conditions' theory of meaning, and the compositional semantics of Montague grammar. It can be seen as an attempt to answer the question, 'What is meaning?' The alternative view starts by asking a different question, namely, 'What is language for?' The most general answer we can come up with for this is, 'Language is used to get other people to do what we want them to.' What sorts of things can we get people to do by using language? We can do what is normally seen as the primary function of language, namely, we can persuade them to accept information that we think they should have. This is the information-carrying function of language – a means for conveying facts and theories from one person to another. But we can also get them to do all sorts of other things – to realize that we want them to convey information to us, to perform physical actions for us that we are unwilling or unable to do for ourselves, to change their own emotional states, to share our experiences. . . . From this point of view an analysis of language processing has to deal with the general relation- ship between the mental and physical states of the language producer, the particular combination of sounds that he/she produces, and the effects of this combination on the mental and physical states of the language consumer. Any aspect of the cognitive system of either participant which is relevant to the interchange is part of the language-processing system.

In the discussion below we will start from a position rather like the one you get by trying to answer the question 'What is meaning?' and we will look at the programs this leads us to develop. We will see how the rules which connect the various levels at which language may be analysed enable us to encode very complex relationships between entities in terms of sequences of choices from a basic set of symbols with realizations as physical symbols. These rules will be embodied in programs which can reconstruct the relationships and references from the sequence of symbols.

This discussion will show us how the basic information-carrying function of language may work, and how to write programs which extract the literal meaning of a piece of English text. Once we have this we will survey some AI attempts to show how this part of the language processing system interacts with the rest of the cognitive system. This work provides interfaces with the general knowledge of the participants, with their belief systems and with their general problem-solving skills, to produce more complex results than mere transmission of facts.

4.3   LANGUAGE PROCESSING IS A MULTI-LEVEL ACTIVITY

If we look at the way most animals use sounds and gestures to denote states of affairs, we see that they generally have a fixed set of signals, each of which denotes a specific state of affairs. A bird, for instance, will typically have one cry which means danger, one which means it is looking for a mate, one which means it is going to fight, and one which means that it accepts it has lost the fight it is having. There will be a direct, fixed mapping between the meaningful noises or dances or gestures it can make and the things it can want to denote.

In a human language there will also be a finite, fixed set of signals. Spoken English, for instance, makes use of about 50 distinct sounds, each of which may be characterized in terms of various options about how to produce noises – Should the tongue be in front of or behind the teeth? Are the lips open or shut when you start to make the sound? etc.? Written English uses 52 distinct graphical forms, which can be described by specifying the shape and orientation of each of their component strokes plus the relations between them (e.g. a T consists of a vertical line and a horizontal line, with the top of the vertical bisecting the horizontal one). English text input from a terminal keyboard also makes use of 52 distinct forms, with the descriptions this time consisting of patterns of electrical impulses. The difference between English and the calls of a seagull is that English can make these 50 or so recognized signals carry far more than 50 or so different messages, rather than just one per signal.

How is this done? To see what is going on, let us first consider what the seagull does when it makes a call, say its danger call. It makes a noise. What has this got to do with danger? Nothing – except that for all seagulls there is an immutable association between that noise and danger. This association is effectively arbitrary. There may, perhaps, be evolutionary reasons why a particular cry is associated with a particular message, but a seagull which hears a warning cry from another seagull is unlikely to be aware of why that particular cry denotes danger, it just knows that it does.

So the signalling conventions used by birds and animals make use of an ability to connect arbitrary signals to messages. Human languages extend this notion by associating combinations of signals with intermediate objects; which are then themselves grouped in combinations which denote further intermediate objects; which are in turn ..., until we come to a level where the particular combination of intermediate objects which we encounter actually denotes something of interest. We can make this clearer if we borrow from semiotics the notion of a *sign* as something consisting of a *signifier* and a *signified* (see, for example, Eco (1976)). This should not be confused with a *signal*, which is some physical stimulus, like a sound or a graphical mark. A signal can function as a signifier, but it is certainly not a sign. We will denote the relation between a signifier and a signified by writing the signifier above the signified, with a horizontal line between them, e.g.

$$\frac{\langle \text{sharp repeated note} \rangle}{\text{DANGER}}.$$

We can now illustrate the difference between the seagull's set of meaningful cries and a language like English. The seagull has a single set of signs, consisting of a particular type of cry as the signifier and a particular state of affairs as the signified, i.e.

$$\frac{\langle \text{sharp repeated note} \rangle}{\text{DANGER}} \qquad \frac{\langle \text{sustained loud cry} \rangle}{\text{MATING CALL}}.$$

In English, by contrast, anything which appears as the signified in some sign can function as the signifier in another. English consists of a series of layers of signs built on top of each other, e.g. for written English

(Combinations of) letters.

(Combinations of) word parts.

(Combinations of) words and endings.

(Combinations of) syntactic structures.

(Combinations of) basic meanings.

Overlaid meanings (connotations).

As mature English speakers we are able to recognize that combinations of letters (or basic sounds) denote word parts, combinations of word parts denote instances of words with suffixes, combinations of word instances denote syntactic constructions . . . . We are even able to use combinations of meanings to indicate further meanings, as when we attack a political measure by attacking its proponent's personality (using the sign 'unpleasant person'/'undesirable policy').

We will not worry about this final layer of sophistication for the moment. Our first task is to show how to write programs that can encode or decode the relationship between the levels from 'combinations of letters' to 'basic meanings'. We will start by considering techniques for relating pairs of descriptive levels, treating each pair in isolation. When we have seen how each piece of the overall job is done by itself, we will discuss how they might best be co-ordinated.

4.4 LEXICAL ANALYSIS

Since we are primarily interested in text rather than speech, and we are not concerned with how individual letters are recognized or generated, the lowest level with which we are concerned is where strings of letters are interpreted as words (for understanding), and where words are converted to strings of letters (for generation), i.e. with *lexical analysis*.

At first sight, it might seem that there was a simple 1–1 mapping between strings of letters and words – the sequence of letters D–O–O–R, say, corresponds to the word 'door'. This string of letters does not correspond to any other word, and no other string of letters corresponds to this word. All we need in order to deal with such a mapping is a simple data structure which enables us to record correspondences, e.g. a hash table, a binary search tree, or an association list. The easiest thing to use would be an association list, since this would allow us to use a single representation for finding the string corresponding to a given word and for finding the word corresponding to a given string. Such an association list would consist of a list of pairs, where the first element of each pair would contain a string of letters and the second element would contain all the other information about the word, e.g. its syntactic category and its meaning (however we express it). Thus an association list with an entry for the word 'door' might look like

[. . . [d–o–o–r [{category: noun}
                {meaning: movable plane used for separating rooms}]]
             . . .]

There are two problems with this simple-minded approach. The first, which we can do little about at this level of analysis, is that large numbers of words are ambiguous. By this we mean that the mapping from strings to words is 1–many. A given string can correspond to several different words. These words may be entirely unconnected, as with the words denoted by the string b–a–t, which can refer to flying rodents or to implements used in cricket or baseball for striking balls; or they may be connected in some way, e.g. they might have the same basic meaning, but different syntactic categories, as with the string h–e–l–p, where the corresponding word may be a noun or a verb. Whether they are related or not, they will cause problems when we come to deal with them later on, since the different versions will require different analyses. There is nothing we can do about them at the level of lexical analysis, since there is at this level nothing to distinguish them. We will simply have to keep multiple entries in our lexicon if we have strings that correspond to more than one word, and when we are interpreting such a string we will have to consider all its entries. There will be a corresponding problem in generation if we have several strings which correspond to identical words.

The other problem we face is that English uses a system of prefixes and suffixes to produce different versions of words, e.g. 'eating' is derived from 'eat' by adding the suffix '-ing'. Some of these endings are used to mark fairly minor changes in the way a word is used, e.g. in the above case the ending '-ing' indicates that the present participle form of the verb is being used. Others indicate radical alterations such as reversal of meaning ('qualify' → 'disqualify') or change of syntactic category ('qualify': verb → 'qualification': noun). It is up to the lexical analysis part of any natural language processing system to deal with these prefixes and suffixes, detecting them if the system is trying to understand text and adding them if it is trying to generate it.

In English, prefixes generally alter the meaning of the word to which they are attached by indicating something about the 'direction' in which it is to be applied. Adding 'in-' or 'im-' to the front of a word gives a feeling of inwardness ('inject', 'inside', 'implicit') or wrongness ('incomplete', 'inappropriate', 'immoral'), adding 'ex-' gives a feeling of outwardness ('expel', 'expatriate', 'explicit'), 'pre-' has a feeling of 'earlier than' ('prejudge', 'preemptive'). Unfortunately it is very hard to give a systematic account of what each prefix does. Vague notions about prefixes giving 'a feeling of the direction in which the meaning of a word is to be applied' are inadequate as a basis for programs which are to understand what is meant in a specific case. Thus although it would be possible to apply the techniques described below for the recognition of suffixes to the detection of prefixes, it is not at all clear what you would do with them once you had them. Most AI natural language systems have simply kept all necessary prefixed variants of words they knew about in their dictionaries. The relation between a word and a prefixed variant is regarded as something which can sometimes be *described* by referring to the common meaning of the prefix, but not *analysed* in terms of it.

Suffixes, on the other hand, generally mark precise facts about the way the word is being used in the current instance. Adding '-ing' to the end of a verb means that you are using its present participle form, adding '-s' to the end of a noun means you are using its plural form, adding '-er' to an adjective means you are using the comparative form. These are important facts which will be required at later stages of the analysis, e.g. by the syntactic and semantic systems, and must be recognized by the lexical analyser.*

There are only a small number of such 'feature marking' suffixes in English ('-ing', '-en', '-ed', '-s' for verbs, '-s' for nouns, '-er' and '-est' for adjectives and adverbs is just about the lot). If they were used simply by attaching them to the ends of words then it would be very easy to deal with them for both input and output. For output you would just attach them to the ends of words as required, as in 'eat' + '-ing' → 'eating'. For input, you would just look at the end of the word you were dealing with, see if it was a recognized suffix, and if so see if the string of characters you got by removing this suffix corresponded to a dictionary entry (this is to prevent you deciding that 'ring' ← 'r' + '-ing', while still allowing 'eating' ← 'eat' + '-ing'). Unfortunately, the act of attaching a suffix to a word may require you to make other changes to it. You may have to delete one or more final letters (as in 'change' + '-ing' → 'changing'), you may have to add letters or repeat them (as in 'bet' + '-ing' → 'betting', 'box' + '-s' → 'boxes'), or you may have to do both ('friendly' + '-er' → 'friendlier').

To see how to cope with this we have to consider exactly what

---

* There are a number of suffixes which *change* the syntactic category of a word, rather than merely noting special properties of the way it is being used in a given case, as in 'qualify' → 'qualification', 'Trotsky' → 'Trotskyite/Trotskyist', 'propaganda' → 'propagandize'. These, like prefixes, behave rather unsystematically, and few AI programs have attempted to take any account of them.

happens when a suffix is added. The rules which govern this are fairly complex, and yet are well known to us all. Any native English speaker would recognize that 'friendlyer', 'eatting', 'beting', 'boxs', and so on were incorrect, though most of us could probably guess what was meant in each case. Few of us could describe these rules in detail.

It is possible to write programs which can analyse words in terms of their roots and suffixes without going into great detail about these rules. The basic algorithm outlined above ('see if you recognize the ending, see if removing it gives you something else you recognize') can be adapted to work with a table of endings and replacements such as

Final characters	Replacements	Formal suffix	Example
-ing	-	-ing	eat → eating
-ing	-e	-ing	change → changing
-??ing	-?	-ing	hit → hitting
-ed	-	-ed	walk → walked
-ed	-e	-ed	hate → hated
-ied	-y	-ed	cry → cried
-??ed	-?	-ed	stun → stunned
-ed	-	-en	walk → walked
-ed	-e	-en	hate → hated
-ied	-y	-en	cry → cried
-??ed	-?	-en	stun → stunned
-en	-	-en	eat → eaten
-en	-e	-en	take → taken
-es	-	-s	box → boxes
-ies	-y	-s	cry → cries
-s	-	-s	take → takes

and similarly for -er and -est. Using this table we can try stripping recognized endings off words, *adding their replacements*, and then looking them up in the dictionary. There are a couple of points to note about the use of this table:

(1) We distinguish between the actual suffix and the intended one. This is most significant for the cases where an actual suffix of '-ed' denotes a formal suffix of '-en', since it may lead to ambiguous interpretations of a given character string (e.g. 'I was stunned' is structurally similar to 'I was beaten', and it is customary to regard the suffix on the verb in the two cases as being in some sense 'the same').
(2) Where we refer to an ending like '-??ed', we mean that the last two letters before the '-ed' are the same. Replacing this ending by '-?' amounts to removing the '-ed' and one of the repeated letters.

This is an extremely effective, but very simple, algorithm, which will cover a large number of instances of English word endings. It is inconceivable that there could be any algorithm which could deal with all the vagaries of the English suffix system (e.g. 'have' + '-s' → 'has', 'be' + '-ed' → 'was', 'bring' + '-en' → 'brought', etc.), so you will always need to keep a number of explicit dictionary entries for irregular endings.

This technique is fine for language understanding, even if it does seem rather rough and ready. It is thoroughly inadequate for generation. This is because our table contains information about what *may* happen when you add a suffix to a word, rather than a specification of what *must* happen. The table provides lists of options, each describing some combination of a terminal sequence of letters and a sequence which may replace them. It does not say anything about the circumstances in which any particular option will be chosen, apart from the implicit constraint that an option will only be chosen if its replacement string matches the final section of the root form of the word in question. For instance, suppose we wanted the '-s' forms of the words 'cry', 'stay', 'box' and 'eat'. If we simply use our table to find out what changes are possible we find that we have the following choices: 'crys', 'cryes', 'cries', 'stays', 'stayes', 'staies', 'boxs', 'boxes', 'eats', 'eates'. The table does not contain the knowledge we need if we are to choose the correct forms (i.e. 'cries', 'stays', 'boxes' and 'eats').

Probably the easiest way to organize our knowledge of how to add endings, rather than how to recognize them, is as a producton system, i.e. a set of IF . . . THEN . . . rules. Consider the following set of rules

IF   word and ending combine to produce non-standard form
THEN   look up dictionary entry for non-standard form.
IF   last letter of word is 'y' and previous letter is one of {r l s h} and first letter of ending is one of {a e i o u}
THEN   replace the 'y' by 'i' and add ending.
IF   last letter of word is 'e' and first letter of ending is one of {a e i o u}
THEN   remove the 'e' and add the ending.

It is not difficult (just tedious) to write down a set of rules of this form which will cover a large part of the English suffix system. The rules should be written down so that ones with more restrictive patterns should be tried first, with the rule which refers to non-standard forms always being the first one we look at. The major differences between this rule set and the table we used for recognizing endings are: (i) the rule set may contain conditions which depend on letters other than the final one in the word (e.g. to distinguish between 'bath' + '-s' → 'baths' and 'batch' + '-s' → 'batches'); (ii) the rule set makes use of letter classes such as {a e i o u} ('vowels') or {r l s h} ('liquid consonants'); and (iii) the rule set is used deterministically. When a rule whose conditions are met is found it is run immediately, and there is no chance of going back later to try another. This contrasts with our use of the table for recognition – when a table entry which may fit is found, we look in the dictionary to see if it actually produces a word, and if not we go on and look for another. Making a table for recognizing endings is easier than setting up a rule set for adding them, and probably runs more quickly, but contains less detailed information.

4.5   SYNTACTIC PROCESSING

A large part of language use is concerned with referring to things and to relationships between them. It would not be possible to use language for this if it consisted of nothing but a stream of unrelated words. Any utterance, any piece of text, must be split into groups of words which 'go together', and the significant relationships within and between these groups must be noted, before it is possible to make sense of it. To take a rather simple example, the sentence 'The tiger was eating the man' splits fairly naturally into three groups, namely, 'the tiger', 'was eating' and 'the man'. The internal properties of each group tell us that they refer, respectively, to a previously mentioned member of the class of objects called tigers, a continuous past action of the type known as eating, and a previously mentioned member of the class of objects known as men. The relationships between the groups tells us that the first entity referred to was performing the action on the second entity. We would know this much even if we did not know the meanings of the words 'tiger', 'eat' and 'man' – to see this, try to understand as much as you can of the sentence, 'The grudget was berolling the priddle.' You have got no idea what any of these words means, but you nonetheless know that there were two things, both of which were known to both you and the speaker/writer, and that the first was performing some action on the second (compare with, 'The priddle was berolled by the grudget').

In the nonsense words example above, the *pattern* of the words told us a lot about what the sentence would have meant, if only we had known the meanings of the individual words. The point becomes even clearer if we consider a sentence where all the words are meaningful, but the order is mixed up, such as, 'A was the eating man tiger'. Here all we can confidently infer about the meaning of the utterance is that it involves a man and a tiger, one of which is already known to us, and that one of them was eating the other. The problem is that once the structure of the sentence becomes confused, we cannot tell which words should be grouped together or what the relations between them are, so we do not know what to do with them.

The rules we use for analysing these structural relations are called the 'grammatical' or 'syntactic' rules of our language. They are extraordinarily complex, as we shall see, but as native speakers of whatever language is in question we all know all about them and all their most intricate details.

Unfortunately, as linguists, as natural language system builders, we know rather less about them. Linguists want to know about grammatical systems, both in general (What properties do all languages share?) and in particular (What are the syntactic rules of English/Serbo-Croat/ Navajo?), as a pure exercise in learning about language. System builders want to know about them because they do not want to write programs which cannot tell the difference between 'There are men eating tigers in the garden' and 'There are man-eating tigers in the garden'.

The problem is not just that we do not know the fine details of the grammar of English (or any other natural language). There is not even widespread agreement about the answers to such general questions as, what sort of things are grammatical rules, how much information can they be made to carry, or how used are they. In the following we will present one set of answers to these questions. The approach outlined below has been used in several successful natural language systems, but it is by no means the only possibility.

Most descriptions of natural language syntax make use of 'rewrite rules', i.e. formulae which say that some sequence of symbols may be rewritten as some other sequence. The simplest sort of rewrite rules, which are known as 'context free' (CF) rules, have a single symbol on the left-hand side (lhs) of some separator such as $\rightarrow$ and a sequence of symbols on the right-hand side (rhs). The following are typical CF rules:

(R1)   S $\rightarrow$ NP VP
(R2)   NP $\rightarrow$ determiner adjective noun
(R3)   VP $\rightarrow$ verb NP

Such rules are supposed to capture the constraints on what is acceptable in a language and what is not. We can use them either for synthesis or for analysis. To use them for synthesis we read them from left to right, saying that wherever we have an instance of the left-hand side of a rule we can replace it by the right-hand side. Thus starting with a string consisting of nothing but the symbol S, we can perform the following series of rewrites:

	S		
NP		VP	(by R1)
determiner adjective noun		VP	(by R2)
determiner adjective noun	verb NP		(by R3)
determiner adjective noun	verb determiner adjective noun		(by R2)

At this point we have expanded our initial string as far as we can – all the remaining symbols are 'terminal' symbols, i.e. we don't have any rules which have them as their left-hand sides. What we might have is a dictionary which contains instances of each of the classes referred to in the final string, so we can replace the category names by examples of the relevant categories, as in

The fat man ate a ripe tomato.
A young woman drives the large bus.
The green sausage watched a hot bath.

We can write a program to use a set of rewrite for generating grammatical sentences by basing it on the following algorithm:

(1) Given a sequence of symbols, find the first non-terminal.
(2) If you find one, find a rule which has it as its left-hand side and replace the occurrence of the symbol by the right-hand side of the rule. Go to (1).
(3) When all the non-terminals in the string have been replaced by terminals, replace each by a word of the appropriate sort.

This algorithm makes use of two global data structures, namely a set of rules and a dictionary. The set of rules might conveniently be represented as a list of two-element lists, where the first element of each list is the single symbol that appears on the left-hand side of some rule and the second element is the list of symbols that appears on its right-hand side, e.g.

```
[[ S        [NP VP]]
 [ NP       [determiner adjective noun]]
 [ VP       [verb NP]]]
```

Such a list of lists may easily be searched for a rule with a particular symbol as its left-hand side (simply walk along the list inspecting the first element of each entry). We can also use it for checking whether a symbol is terminal or not – if we look for a rule which has it as its left-hand side and we can't find one, then the symbol must be terminal.

The dictionary could also be represented as a list of two-element lists, this time with the terminal symbols appearing as the first elements of the lists, and exemplars of the categories named by these symbols appearing as the second elements, as in

[[determiner a] [verb ate] [noun bath] [noun bus] [verb drives] . . . .

This form has the advantage that it is more or less symmetrical – it is as easy to find a word belonging to a given category as it is to find out what category a given word belongs to. In either case, we simply walk along the list inspecting one component of each element until we find what we are looking for. We will find later on that the description of a word is rather more complicated than a simple atomic label, but it will do for the moment.

We can use sets of rewrite rules in the other direction, to find out how some sentence was constructed. The task here is to go from a sequence of words back to the symbol S, as in

the	beautiful	princess	rode	a	lightweight	bike	
determiner	adjective	noun	verb	determiner	adjective	noun	
	NP		verb	determiner	adjective	noun	(by R2)
	NP		verb		NP		(by R2)
	NP			VP			(by R3)
		S					(by R1)

In this sequence of rewrites, we have replaced each word by the name of the category to which it belongs, and then repeatedly found a rule whose right-hand side matched some substring of the current symbol sequence and replaced it by its left-hand side. This was not too difficult in the current case. If we have a large number of rules, possibly with similar right-hand sides, it can become very time consuming. It gets even worse if, as is often the case, there are words in the text which belong to more than one category. We will shortly look at some algorithms for finding appropriate sequences of rewrite rules fairly efficiently, but before that we will try to see why we want to do it at all.

We are *not* interested in grammar for its own sake. If grammar were not intimately connected with meaning, it would have only peripheral interest for us when we come to write language understanding systems. But it is. Each syntactic rule encodes some semantic relationship between the entities it deals with, so that the way we express relationships is by finding syntactic rules which encode them and which can be combined to produce a piece of text/an utterance; and the way we interpret such a thing is by recognizing the rules that were used in its construction, in order to be able to decode their significance. We recognize the differences in meaning in the following pairs of sentences by recognizing the significance of the differences in the ways they were constructed.

The tiger has eaten the lion.
The tiger has been eaten by the lion.

She is going to score a goal.
Is she going to score a goal?

The connection between grammar and meaning is crucial. A very large part of all research in linguistics (both general and computational) is concerned with grammar, trying to find out what sort of rules we use and how we use them. This research would not be nearly so important if the grammar did not carry a large part of the meaning. So when the debate about syntax starts to get technical and abstract, and apparently unrelated to anything interesting, remember: if we do not understand how the grammar works, we will not be able to extract the meaning.

4.6   TRANSITION NETWORKS

Work in AI and linguistics has produced a wide variety of grammars and programs for using them (such programs are known as 'parsers'. The process of trying to discover the grammatical structure of a piece of text or an utterance is known as 'parsing'). Most of the grammars include a set of rewrite rules (or something equivalent to one), though they are generally far more elaborate than the very simple set above, and they may not be the only rules in the grammar. We will concentrate here on one particular sort of grammar – the augmented transition networks, or ATNs, first described in Woods (1970) – and on parsing techniques associated with them. Grammars of this type have been widely and successfully used in language processing programs, but it should be remembered that there is not universal agreement that they are the best way to go.

Our original grammar was simple in both its content – it contained only three very simple rules – and its format. We might hope to improve it by simply adding more rules, to try to cover more cases. This would certainly help. We could try the following grammar.

S	→	NP VP
NP	→	determiner adjseq noun
NP	→	pronoun
adjseq	→	
adjseq	→	adjective adjseq
VP	→	vseq

$$
\begin{array}{ll}
\text{VP} & \rightarrow \text{ vseq NP} \\
\text{VP} & \rightarrow \text{ vseq NP NP} \\
\text{vseq} & \rightarrow \text{ verb} \\
\text{vseq} & \rightarrow \text{ auxiliary vseq}
\end{array}
$$

This is a bit more interesting. We have introduced new VP rules to cope with sentences like, 'The man ran', 'The dog ate the meat' and 'The man gave the woman a peach'. We have an NP rule which allows NPs to consist of a single pronoun like 'I', 'she' or 'they'. We have an interesting pair of rules which allows us to cope with the presence of any number of adjectives (including none) in the middle of an NP. This pair of rules says that an adjective sequence may consist of nothing, or of an adjective followed by an adjective sequence, which may itself consist of either nothing or an adjective followed by an adjective sequence, which may . . . Finally, we have introduced rules which say that where we simply had a verb in our original set of rules, we are now prepared to accept a verb sequence, i.e. a sequence of auxiliaries (words like 'is' and 'have') followed by a verb – note that a vseq is unlike an adjseq in that it cannot be empty, it must always end with a verb. With this set of rules we can cope with sentences like

I have given her a shiny new bicycle.
The old man had been eating a peach.
The unpleasant fat sweaty young man has died.

There is clearly still a lot that our grammar will not deal with, but we might hope that by simply adding more and more rules we would end up with a grammar which did cover all (and only) the legal sentences of English. How would we use it once we had it?

There are two basic techniques for using sets of rewrite rules for analysing the structure of a piece of text. These two mechanisms are the basis for nearly all the more powerful algorithms used with more substantial or sophisticated grammars, so it is worth looking at them in their simplest form as they apply to simple sets of CF rewrite rules like the one above.

Our first move is to reconstruct the rewrite rules as 'transition networks'. A transition network is a graph consisting of labelled nodes connected by labelled arcs. The labels on nodes are arbitrary, and are really only there for convenience. The labels on the arcs are important. They are the names of syntactic categories, such as 'noun', 'verb', 'NP', 'S', etc. We can rewrite our rule set as the following collection of transition networks

S: (a) —enter→ (b) —NP→ (c) —VP→ (d) —leave→ (e)

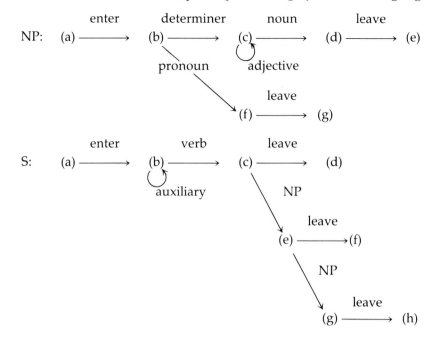

These networks are virtually equivalent to the set of rewrite rules, though they are rather more compact. They enable us to compress several rewrite rules into a single network (e.g. the VP network embodies all three VP rewrite rules), and they enable us to give very neat specifications of repeatable elements so that we no longer need the explicit rules for adjective sequences and verb sequences. How do we interpret a transition network?

The general shape of the networks, and the labels on the arcs, should be suggestive. Networks are things you try to cross by finding paths through them. Paths are sequences of arcs. ⟨enter⟩ and ⟨leave⟩ arcs have obvious interpretations – you enter a network via an ⟨enter⟩ arc and leave it by a ⟨leave⟩ arc. The labels on the other arcs correspond to the terminal and non-terminal symbols in the rewrite rules. The labels which correspond to non-terminals are themselves names of networks, so it is reasonable to suppose that you can cross one of these arcs if and only if you can find a route through the corresponding network. The other labels correspond to word classes. You can cross an arc with one of these labels if the next word in the text you are interested in is of the appropriate sort, and if it is you should move on to the next word.

The description of when you may cross an arc with a terminal label is completely neutral as to whether you are trying to do synthesis or analysis. For synthesis, 'the next word in the text you are interested in' (i.e. in the sentence you are generating) will be 'of the appropriate sort' if you make it so. Thus the description of how to interpret the networks can be construed as a recipe for constructing grammatical sentences, by interpreting the description of when a terminal-labelled arc may be crossed as an instruction to add a suitable word to the end of the partially constructed sentence. For analysis, finding out whether 'the next word in the text you are interested in is of the appropriate sort' is a matter of looking at it and seeing if it is. So we can also regard the description of what a network is about as a recipe for seeing whether, and how, some given piece of text is an acceptable sentence. We can sketch out a single algorithm which uses a set of networks to either construct or analyse a piece of text, as required.

To cross a network,
(1) Choose an ⟨enter⟩ arc, follow it to the node it leads into
(2) Choose an arc leaving this node.
   (2a) If this arc is a ⟨leave⟩ arc, you have done the job.
   (2b) If its label is the name of a network, try to find a route across this other network. If you manage it, cross the current arc and go to (2).
   (2c) The label on the arc must be the name of a syntactic category. If you are trying to synthesize a piece of text, add a word which belongs to the named category to the end of the partially constructed sentence and go to (2). If you are trying to analyse a piece of input text, inspect the next word. If it is the right sort of word, move your attention on to the next word in the sentence, cross the current arc, and go to (2).

This is a very sketchy sort of algorithm. Both the major steps require you to 'choose' some arc, without giving any guidance about which arc to choose if there are more than one or what to do if the choice turns out to be a mistake. Furthermore, steps (2b) and (2c) both contain instructions of the form 'if you manage to do . . . , then cross the current arc and go to (2)', without saying what you should do if you can't manage to do whatever was required. The problem is that this algorithm, like the vast majority of natural language parsing algorithms, is 'non-deterministic'. It contains decisions which have to be made on the basis of inadequate information, and which may turn out later to be wrong. It is very difficult to do anything about this. There simply is not generally enough information available locally at the time when a choice has to be made to guarantee that it will be made correctly. Wrong choices tend to lead to failures at the point where you are trying to do one of the 'if you manage to do . . . then cross the current arc and go to (2)' steps, but it can be extremely difficult to trace back to see exactly which of the many choices that have been made was the one that should be changed.

Non-determinism is a common phenomenon in AI. Decisions are constantly being made on the basis of inadequate information and revised in the light of subsequent investigation. Programs which behave like this have to be able to keep track of their decisions, in order to be able to go back and try alternatives when their first hypotheses turn out to be wrong. Some AI programming languages, e.g. PROLOG, have facilities for doing this built in, and with such languages it is straightforward to implement an algorithm like the one sketched out above – you simply keep making the first choice that comes into your head, letting the system keep track of what choices you made and where you were at the time, until you either finish successfully or you get stuck. If you finish successfully there is nothing more to be done, if you get stuck you just ask the system to 'backtrack' to the last situation in which you made a choice and start again from there with a different one.

If you are using a language which does not provide automatic back-tracking (or indeed if you are using one which does but you do not like the way it does it), you will have to keep track of where you were and what you chose to do yourself. For many problems of this sort it is customary to write recursive algorithms, using the recursion to save the information about where you had got to and what alternative decisions were available to you – a good simple example is the solution to the eight-queens problem. We have a problem using this technique with our outline parser, because the parser is already inherently recursive. Step (2b) says that it may be necessary, in the middle of an attempt to cross one network, to go and try to cross another (or indeed the same one, as in the sentence 'Eating people is wrong', which has a sentence as its subject). The two potential uses for recursion are incompatible – we cannot use it both for keeping track of situations and alternative decisions and for keeping track of how many networks we have piled on top of one another. If you want to implement this algorithm in a language which does not provide automatic backtracking, you will have to explicitly construct for yourself a stack of decision points (which must describe both the state the program was in when the decision was made and the alternatives that were available), and wind your way back through this stack when you get stuck.

The parser outlined above is of a type referred to by one of the following names – top down, goal driven, model driven, hypothesis driven. It has a high-level goal/model/hypothesis about the data it is supposed to be analysing, namely that it can be dealt with by finding a way through the S network, and it tries to verify that hypothesis by trying to find its way through lower level networks like ones for NPs and VPs, which may in turn involve it in trying to find ways through lower level networks, until it gets down to arcs with terminal labels which may be checked directly against the data. This may be contrasted with the following bottom up, or data driven, algorithm:

(1) Replace each word in the original string by its syntactic category.
(2) Starting at any chosen point in the string of symbols, find a network which can be crossed simply by matching labels on arcs in the network against symbols in the symbol string. If you manage it, replace the sequence of symbols that were matched by the name of the network and go to (2).

This algorithm is also non-deterministic. It includes an arbitrary choice – 'any chosen point in the string of symbols' – and a difficult subtask which it does not explain how to do – 'find a network which can be crossed . . . '. So again we will have to keep track of choices that were made in order to be able to backtrack when we find we can't 'manage it'. However, this time the algorithm is *not* itself recursive. There is never any need to investigate the possibility of crossing an embedded network, since any attempt to cross a network can only use symbols which are present in the current symbol string.

The bottom up algorithm may be difficult to follow. The following example may make it a bit clearer.

To parse 'He is watching the game' bottom up, first replace each word by its category name

He	is	watching	the	game
pronoun	auxiliary	verb	determiner	noun

Now choose a point in the string of symbols and find a network which can be crossed by matching labels on arcs in the network against symbols in the string starting at that point. We will start with the first word and the NP network – we can use the route (a)→(b)→(f)→(g). So we exchange the name of the network for the symbol that was matched

NP   auxiliary   verb   determiner   noun

and try again. This time we start with the fourth symbol, using the NP network again, and find that the route (a)→(b)→(c)→(d)→(e) works, so we replace the symbols that were matched (i.e. determiner noun) by the name of the network to get

NP   auxiliary   verb   NP

This time we start at the second symbol, using the VP network, and come up with the route (a)→(b)→(b)→(c)→(e)→(f). Replacing the matched symbols by the name of the network gives us

NP   VP

and now, starting with the first symbol and the S network, we get the route (a)→(b)→(c)→(d)→(e). Replacing the matched symbols by the name of the network gives us the string consisting of just S.

4.7 AUGMENTED TRANSITION NETWORKS

We now have two algorithms for parsing input text in terms of a grammar expressed as a set of transition networks. They are both non-deterministic, and they can both involve a lot of searching through the space of possibilities, with a lot of work either completely wasted or performed more than once. They are, however, the basis of virtually all systems which use an explicitly specified grammar. Kaplan's 'chart parser' provides a mechanism to ensure that work which was done successfully as part of an ultimately unsuccessful attempt is not wasted (Kaplan, 1973). Marcus (1980) describes an attempt to write the grammar as a deterministic program, and Riesbeck (1978) describes a program in which the sort of information usually used for syntactic analysis is incorporated directly in a program for constructing semantic interpretations. We shall not say much more about systems which do not use a separate parser to interpret the structure of input text in terms of an explicitly specified grammar. Such systems exist, and may in the future turn out to be the right way to go, but most current systems do contain a separate syntactic analysis phase using a grammar based on some elaboration of the idea of a set of rewrite rules.

Why do we need to elaborate on our basic context-free rewrite rules? In what ways are they unsatisfactory? What can we do to them to make them more satisfactory?

There are two major syntactic phenomena which are hard to capture with CF rules. The first of these phenomena is known as 'agreement'. This is where the internal structure of one component of the analysis depends on the internal structure of another. A common example in English is the fact that the 'number' of the subject of a sentence (i.e. whether it is singular or plural) must be the same as the 'number' of the verb, so that:

The girl is running down the hill.
The girls are running down the hill.
The girl runs down the hill.
The girls run down the hill.

are all acceptable, whereas:

> The girl are running down the hill.
> The girls is running down the hill.
> The girl run down the hill.
> The girls runs down the hill.

are not. An interesting example of the effect of number agreement in English comes in the following pair of sentences:

> The sheep is running down the hill.
> The sheep are running down the hill.

Inspection of the NP 'the sheep' in isolation does not tell us whether it is singular or plural – an oddity of the word 'sheep'. But because it has to agree with the verb, we can tell that it is singular in the first example, plural in the second. Note that we can only do this for NPs which are the subjects of the verb. In

> The girl sees the sheep.
> The girls see the sheep.

we have no clues about whether the sheep are singular or plural, whereas in

> The sheep are seen by the girl(s).
> The sheep is seen by the girl(s).

we can again make a judgement about how many sheep are involved. We have here a connection between the NP and VP parts of the S rule which is very hard to express using simple atomic symbols - just where and how are we going to express this (psychologically real) constraint?

The last two pairs of sentences introduce the other phenomon which is difficult to capture using simple rewrite rules like the above – the strong connections between various ways of writing things down. The sentences

> The old woman fixed the carburettor on his van.
> The carburettor on his van was fixed by the old woman.
> Did the old woman fix the carburettor on his van?

are extremely closely linked - indeed the difference in meaning between the first two is extremely unclear (see Foley and van Valin (1984) for an interesting discussion of this point).

There have been a number of attempts to extend the notion of a set of rewrite rules so that these phenomena can be neatly and compactly described. Most of them make use of 'feature sets' and 'movement rules' of one sort or another.

'Feature sets' provide subclassifications of the basic syntactic classes such as 'noun', 'verb', 'NP' and 'VP' in terms of specified properties like 'number', 'gender', 'tense' and 'transitivity'. Different grammars have different sets of features, and make use of them in different ways, but the basic idea is that you can get a concise description of agreement restrictions and other similar phenomena in terms of constraints on the values features may take. Typically, the constraints are either demands that two (or more) items on the right-hand side of a rule should have the same value for some specified feature, or that some right-hand side component of a rule should have a given value for a feature. Thus in one fairly well-known formalism (Pereira and Warren's (1978) direct clause grammar), we can express the fact that in English the subject of a sentence must agree with its main verb in number by the rule

S→NP (number = ?N, . . .), VP (number = ?M, . . .): M = N, . . .,

i.e whatever value the feature 'number' has for the NP must be the same as its value for the VP.

'Movement rules' allow us to specify connections between apparently different rewrite rules in terms of actions which 'move' right-hand side components of rules around. A typical example is the explanation of the relation between the active and passive forms of an ordinary transitive English sentence, say, 'He is writing it' and 'It is being written by him'. Most current grammars for English include a rule which says something like, 'The active form is transformed into the passive form by preceding the subject with the preposition "by" and moving it to a position after the verb, and moving the object to a position immediately before it'. Exactly what movements are allowed, how they are to be specified, and what their significance is has been the subject of much debate. The most developed theory is that of 'transformational grammar' (Akmajian and Heny, 1972; Chomsky, 1965), but there are now a number of serious competing theories, notably 'generalized phrase structure grammar' (Gazdar *et al.*, 1984) and 'systemic grammar' (Halliday and Martin, 1981). This is no place to go into a description of the details and relative merits of these various theories. We will simply look briefly at a particular formalism, namely, Woods' (1970) 'augmented transition networks' (ATNs), which has been used successfully in a number of computational language processing systems as a basis for implementing versions of all the above grammars.

Earlier, we argued that we could convert a set of context free rewrite rules into a slightly more convenient and compact form as a set of transition networks, for which we described two parsing algorithms. Transition networks are indeed a little more convenient than CF rewrite rules, but the improvement is not fantastic. Where they do begin to score is when we want to extend our notation so that it includes features and movements. We can 'augment' our simple transition networks by associating actions and conditions with arcs, so that before you are allowed to cross an arc you have to check not only that you have an entity of the right sort, but also that its associated conditions hold; and when you cross it, you don't just note what sort of arc it was, you also perform its associated actions. What sort of tests and actions are we thinking of?

The best way to think about them is as bits of program. Actions are bits of program which assign values to variables, conditions are bits of program that test values of variables. The only odd thing about them is the way variables (which are usually referred to as 'registers') behave. Each network has its own copy of all the registers that are going to be updated or inspected by actions or tests associated with its arcs. These local copies of registers behave rather like local variables in procedure bodies – you can do what you like to them within the context of one network and it will have no effect when you have crossed that network and returned to a higher level. There is one exception to this rule, and here there is a difference between the behaviour of registers and local variables: when you have crossed an arc in one network by crossing the lower level network associated with that arc, you can look back down to inspect (and perhaps copy, but *not* update) the values that specified registers had in the lower level network. Apart from this crucial facility, registers behave exactly like local variables, and tests and conditions are just pieces of program text in whatever language you like. Most implementations of ATN parsers have been written in LISP, so it is not surprising that most examples of tests and actions look a lot like bits of LISP. There is nothing very special about LISP in this context – so long as you get the behaviour of the registers right, there is no reason not to use BASIC, FORTRAN, or whatever else you like.

We can rewrite our S transition network yet again, using English as our 'programming language', to include tests and actions for checking number agreement –

	enter	NP	VP	leave	
S:	(a) ———→	(b) ———→	(c) ———→	(d) ———→	(e).

Test and actions:

(a) → (b):

(b) → (c):   Set register "NUMBER" to the value it has for the NP network.

(c) → (d):   Check that the value of the register "NUMBER" is the same as its value for the VP network.

(d) → (e):

We have put no restrictions on the tests and actions that may be associated with arcs, other than the global restriction that we must be able to specify them in our chosen programming language. It may be argued that they should be kept as simple as possible, with as much as possible being captured by the structure of the networks. This is attractive both theoretically and practically – theoretically because we want to keep our grammars, which are supposed to reflect some aspect of human linguistic competence, as clear as possible, and practically because simple objects are easier to design, construct and maintain than complicated ones. Some of the grammatical theories which have been embodied as ATNs do impose constraints on the range of allowable tests and actions, but the ATN formalism itself does not – if you really want to make them complicated you can.

The move from simple transition networks to augmented ones is going to require us to alter our parsing algorithms. The change is not enormous. We simply associate some program text with each arc of each network, and execute the associated program whenever we try to traverse an arc. This is easily done using a language like LISP or POP-11 which allows procedures to be treated as data structures, less easy in languages which do not. Whatever language we use for expressing our tests and actions, we will have to make sure that registers are treated correctly; this is usually done by maintaining an association list of register:value pairs for each network.

4.8   SEMANTICS

We have spent a lot of time so far looking at how we get from an input sequence of characters to a syntactic analysis of the words those characters make up. This is not what we actually want – we want to know what message the words carry. The reason we have spent so much time worrying about the syntactic structure of the word sequence is that it encodes such a large part of the message. Now that we have some idea of how to get at the syntactic clues, it is time to see how we can use them and what else we need to do.

We start by making a distinction between the explicit content of an utterance or piece of text and its implicit content. The explicit content, sometimes known as the 'propositional content', is that part of the meaning which can be obtained just by looking at the text/utterance in isolation from the context in which it was produced and from anything which precedes or follows it. It is commonly believed that this propositional content may be extracted by combining the meanings of the individual words according to the semantic rules associated with each syntactic rule. This belief certainly underlies all non-trivial computer systems for natural language processing – you may have to invoke other mechanisms to find out *why* somebody said something, or to *infer* things which they left unsaid, but before you get round to these more complex activities you will have to extract the propositional content.

We can illustrate these distinctions with some very simple examples. Consider the simple question, 'Do you know the time?'. The propositional content of this is that it is a yes/no question about the state of the listener's knowledge. In most situations where this question is uttered the message that the speaker is encoding is actually a request to be told the time. It may have other interpretations, e.g. as an expression of displeasure when both speaker and listener do know the time, and both know that the other knows it, and the listener is in fact late, but it very seldom functions as a disinterested question about a state of knowledge. For another simple example we can look at the story fragment we started the chapter with, about Jane's desire for an ice-cream. This story consists of a number of superficially unrelated statements – what have piggy banks got to do with ice-creams, why did she shake it, what are the consequences of its being empty? To interpret this story correctly we have to supply the answers to these questions from our general knowledge about the world. The writer of such a story *relies* on us to do so – stories (or textbooks) in which everything is spelled out in all its detail are excruciatingly boring, for both the writer and the reader. A substantial part of good writing is knowing how much to say and how much to leave out. Any program which is to understand reasonably unrestricted natural language will have to have access to the sort of general knowledge which we make use of when we process language. If it does not then people communicating with it will be forced to make explicit all the details that they usually leave out when communicating with other people, and (probably even worse) they will have to endure the machine stating every last obvious little fact, since it will not know what it can reasonably expect its partner to infer. We will return to the question of how to get the implicit content out of a piece of language when we have considered how to get its explicit content.

We have said several times that most of language use is a matter of expressing relations between entities. If this is so, propositional content should provide mechanisms for specifying entities and for stating relations between them. We will take the view that noun phrases are used for the first of these tasks, verb sequences (that is, sequences of auxiliaries and major verbs, *not* whole verb phrases) and prepositions for the second. This is a simplification. Apart from anything else, it is quite possible for relationships to function as entities – in 'My being late annoyed her', we have a relationship between a relationship (between actual and intended times of my arrival) and an entity (the person whose state of mind was altered). It is nonetheless a sensible place to start.

Noun phrases provide references, verb sequences provide relationships. A sentence (which will consist of noun phrases and verb sequences arranged appropriately) says that the relationship expressed by the main verb sequence holds between the entities referred to by the noun phrases.

There are two very important points to note about this. First, that the meaning of a sentence is being taken to be something which is constructed out of the meanings of its components, and second, that the way this meaning is constructed will depend on the way the components are arranged. To see the second point, consider the sentences 'He is lending her his tennis racket' and 'Is he lending her his tennis racket?' These are constructed out of very much the same components – 'he', 'her', 'his tennis racket' and 'is lending' – but because these components have been put together differently their meanings should be combined differently. Part of the overall message is the same – the particular relationships which are being asserted or questioned. Part is different – whether they are being asserted or questioned. These two points hold at all levels of analysis of propositional content – the basic meaning of a fragment of text is found by finding the basic meanings of its components and finding out what rule of combination of meaning is associated with the particular way the components are combined in the text.

This principle holds at all levels of analysis down to individual words.*

This means that the analysis of meaning will proceed by associating semantic rules with each of the syntactic rules in our grammar. We will discover the meaning of a fragment of text by discovering the meanings of each of its component parts, and then applying the semantic rule associated with the overall structure of the fragment to these lower level meanings.

This process clearly bottoms out when it gets down to the level of words. Since we are not going to try to explain how individual words come to mean what they do, we will have to provide them with 'meanings' explicitly. What the 'meaning' of a word, or of any higher level structure, looks like will depend on what sort of task we want our system to do and what our overall theory of meaning is. We cannot cover all the solutions people have proposed for this problem here – the best we can do is begin to sketch one approach, and follow this with some remarks on two more complete analyses.

We have assumed that NPs are used very largely for referring to

* There are some word parts – prefixes, components of words like 'explode' and 'implode', 'explain' and 'complain' – which carry part of the meaning of the whole word, but it does not seem possible to give a complete analysis of word meanings in terms of the meanings of their parts.

things. So the interpretation rules for NPs should be things which will enable us to find out what is being referred to. There are, roughly, two things we need to know in order to find out what somebody is referring to when they use an NP (or any other 'referring expression'). We need to know what sort of thing it is, and where to look for it. For a simple NP made up of a determiner, some adjectives, and a noun, it seems likely that the adjectives and the noun give us a general description of the sort of thing being talked about, and the determiner indicates where to look for it. General descriptions may be as simple as lists of required attributes, e.g. whatever is being referred to in the phrase 'a big red bus' must have the properties of being BIG (this one may be a bit tricky, since BIG is a relative concept: BIG for buses would be SMALL for mountains), RED and BUS-LIKE. Where to look can be more difficult. There are a number of *places* you can look for things – in the immediate environment, in the recently past conversation, in your general knowledge about the world; and there are a number of *ways* you can look for them – do you know there is only one, does it matter which you choose if there are more, do you have any guarantee that you are going to find one anyway. The particular ways in which English determiner types tell you where to look for things are rather complicated, but the following rules for interpreting NPs give at least a flavour of what is going on:

Semantic rule for (simple) NPs:
   Make a conjunction out of the descriptors associated with each adjective or noun in the NP. The referent of the NP is the object satisfying these properties which you will find if you look where the determiner tells you to.

Semantic rule for nouns or adjectives:
   Construct the descriptor (X is ⟨property⟩) where ⟨property⟩ is the class of objects denoted by the relevant noun or adjective.

Semantic rule for 'that':
   Look in the immediate environment for the required item.

Semantic rule for 'the':
   Look in the immediate environment or the recent conversation for a unique item of the required type.

Semantic rule for 'a':
   Look in the immediate environment or the recent conversation for some item of the required type OR do not go looking for one, just make a note that something of this sort is being talked about but it does not matter much which (or even whether there really is or could be one, cf. 'I'm going to tell you a story about a flying horse').

Using these rules, the 'meaning' of the phrase 'that big red bus' would be something like, 'To find the referent of this phrase, look in the immediate environment for an X such that (X is BIG) & (X is RED) & (X is BUS-LIKE) holds'.

We have here some (over)simple rules about how to construct the interpretation of a typical simple noun phrase. We have a mechanism for combining the meanings of the components into a description of how to find the referent, and we could extend this mechanism so that it incorporated the extra restrictions provided by things like prepositional phrases (as in 'the man with a parrot on his shoulder') and relative clauses (as in 'the man who stole my shirt'). Note that the interpretation of the NP is *not* its referent, it is the description of how to find the referent should you so desire. It is up to the semantic rule associated with the larger structure within which the NP is embedded to decide what to do with the description. In 'Tell me a story', the function of the determiner in 'a story' is to let you know that the speaker requires you to choose a concrete story from your personal repertoire of stories; in 'She told me a story' it indicates that although there was indeed some concrete story involved, you are not expected to know what story and there is no need for you to try to find out.

We will find similar, though probably more complex, rules for combining the meanings of verbs and NPs to give meanings for VPs, for combining the meanings of NPs and VPs to give meanings for Ss, and so on. As noted above, there are a large number of ways in which these rules can build meanings for complex expressions out of meanings for simple ones. Two particularly noteworthy approaches are described in Winograd (1972) and Schank (1973).

Winograd constructs his meaning descriptions in PLANNER, a PRO-LOG-like language in which expressions can function either as static descriptors of objects or as programs for finding objects that satisfy the descriptions. This is extremely convenient in view of our observation above that it is up to the larger expression within which an NP appears to decide how its meaning should be used. Sometimes it will be sensible for it to be used directly as a program for finding the required object in the real world – 'Give me that chocolate'. Sometimes it functions as a conversational marker, which may or not later get instantiated – 'I'd really love a chocolate', uttered in a situation in which there are no chocolates present. In Winograd's system (called SHRDLU) all meanings were expressions in this language. Sentence meanings were expressions which, when interpreted as programs, did things like try to construct a plan to achieve the speaker's goal (if the sentence was an imperative like 'Put the red block on the table'), try to find an answer to a question (if the sentence was in fact a question), or record a new fact in the system's model of the world (in response to declarative sentences like 'The blue block is behind the red one'). The particular sort of program that was constructed depended on the exact syntactic form of the sentence. But these programs were not necessarily executed – they were expressions, which could be the inputs into other meaning constructing programs, so that the embedded sentence in 'the man who stole my shirt' is not executed, it is added as part of the meaning of the NP, to be used as required later. The embedded sentence in 'I told you it was behind the red one' is not executed to record the fact 'At some past time it (whatever that refers to) was behind the red one (whatever that refers to)', it is itself used, as an expression, within the overall meaning of the sentence in which it is embedded. This notion of meanings as programs which can, but need not, be executed is an extremely powerful one.

The noteworthy point about Schank's work here is that he tried to isolate some small set of primitive actions and concepts in terms of which the meanings of all the verbs we use could be explained. He did not try to do anything particularly clever about the meanings of nouns and adjectives, but he did hope that he could find a set of primitives which he could use to analyse the meanings of all the verbs of English (perhaps of all languages). Part of the reasoning behind this was that, like Winograd and most other people in this area, he realized that he was going to have to do some further analysis once he had extracted the propositional content from his input text before he could hope to get at its actual functional meaning. If the propositional content was expressed in terms of a small set of primitives, the extra analysis was likely to be more uniform, possibly easier, than if each action had its own idiosyncratic structure which had to be fully understood before you could start to work with it. This work, which had a certain amount in common with some work on a theory of grammar called 'case grammar', was fairly successful. It is easy to scoff at any particular set of 'primitive concepts' which anyone proposes. Schank and his co-workers had a sensible goal in mind when they tried to specify their set of primitives, and they produced a number of significant programs using them.

4.9   THE FUNCTION OF THE UTTERANCE

We have now seen how to start extracting the literal content of an individual message. We can construct interpretations of 'Jane wanted an ice-cream' and 'Do you know the time?' which reflect their obvious surface meanings. The first makes a statement about the condition of some individual named Jane, namely that she was in a state which would have been more satisfactory to her if she had been in possession of something called an 'ice-cream'. The second is a yes/no question about the state of the hearer's knowledge of the time. We now need some account of how these literal interpretations are related to the effect that the speaker intends to have on the hearer – how the hearer is to link up all the meanings of the statements in the story fragment, how they are to realize that the person asking the question about the time really wants to be told what time it is, not whether the hearer knows it (but is not prepared to say).

These questions are sometimes – not always – taken to be outside the scope of linguistics. They are definitely *not* outside the scope of language processing systems. The solutions involve a study of general issues about memory organization, problem solving, common sense inference, interperson modelling – very general topics about cognitive processing in general. When you start to worry about how people *use* language, rather than about the internal rule systems which govern it as a self-contained system, you begin to find yourself drawn into studying the entire human cognitive system, with the daunting prospect that you will never be able to construct a complete language processing system until you have constructed a complete model of a human being. And in some ways this is right. Very down-to-earth everyday conversations require access to a substantial part of the knowledge and reasoning ability of the participants. Comprehension of large bodies of text which are designed to explore the limits of the available medium of communication must of necessity invoke everything you know about everything (James Joyce's *Finnegan's Wake* is a prime example, but there are many others more easily accessible to simple beings like you and me. Eco (1981) points out how much behind-the-scenes analysis goes on even when the most naive reader reads a Superman comic!). We have to tailor our expectations of how good our language processing program is going to be to our understanding of the limits of its real-world knowledge and reasoning powers.

Having made explicit all these caveats about just how much background knowledge is going to be required, let us have a brief look at some attempts to show how it might be organized and made use of. We may not yet be in a position to encode everything that is ever going to be needed, but it is at least worth looking at the ways people have suggested using it when we do have it.

The two areas in which some progress has been made are in accessing the knowledge required to fill in the 'obvious' missing links in what actually gets said, and in discovering how an utterance which is superficially one thing (say a statement, a question, an instruction) can function as another. Other issues, such as how a single body of text can be made to carry more than one message at a time, or different messages to different people, have not yet been seriously addressed in computational models.

Filling in unstated 'obvious' facts requires us to organize our knowledge in some way that embodies the difference between things which are obvious and things which are not. Things which are obvious in one context will be extremely unobvious in others, so what we are looking for is a mechanism by which things which are closely related to things we are already thinking about get somehow activated. We want, for instance, the fact that we are talking about obtaining things – ice-creams – which are usually obtained by purchasing them to immediately raise in our minds the question of money, so that the subsequent mention of piggy-banks, which are containers for money, can be easily assimilated. Probably the first description of an attempt to construct a computational model of how this works was Charniak (1972), which presents a model of how to deal with simple stories like the one about Jane and the ice-cream. In this model, each concept the program had was connected to a number of facts and rules which were liable to be significant in contexts in which the concept was mentioned. As the program proceeded through a piece of text, it would start forward chains of inference from each concept that was mentioned, establishing facts which could be inferred from what was said about the concept. So from the mention of 'wanting an ice-cream' it would start to generate facts like 'if you want something and you have not already got one, you may be able to get one by buying it from someone', and 'if you want to buy something you need money', and so on. Forward inference is a difficult thing to control, all you can really do is keep going for as long as you feel as though you are going somewhere and then stop. At this point you move on to deal with the next sentence in your story, which refers to piggy-banks, and start another chain of forward inferences. This one will spew out all sorts of statements, which will (you hope) include, 'Money is kept in containers' and 'If you need something and you know where it is kept you can try to get it from there'. At this point you can tie two of your inferred facts together – 'Jane needs money' and 'people who know where things they need are kept can go and get them' – to get an understanding of the causal links between the two parts of the story.

The notion that to understand how the components of a story are linked you have to try to reason about the things that get mentioned is extremely important. Unfortunately, the reasoning strategy (forward inference) that Charniak used turns out not to be all that successful – there are just too many things you can infer from any given starting point for this to be manageable. Schank and Abelson (1981) proposed a mechanism for collecting chunks of information that naturally go together into coherent structures, which could be invoked whole by the mention of critical key concepts. These structures, which they called 'scripts', are organized rather like stereotyped stories, with descriptions of all the participants that you would *normally* expect to find in a situation of the kind you are describing and of the actions you would *normally* expect them to perform. If you manage to invoke one of these frames, and to match the people in the story that you are actually telling to the people referred to in the frame, you can compress your story to the point where all you need to tell your listener about are the ways in which the events you are talking about were different from the ones in the script. It may be helpful for you to do a little more than this, e.g. you should probably throw in a few things which *are* in the script to reassure your listener that they are making use of the same script as you, and you may need to make use of more than one script in order to tell a single story, in which case you will have to give the listener some signal to indicate that you are changing scripts. Nonetheless, it does look like a mechanism which will enable the sort of inference required without leading you into wildly uncontrolled forward chains. There are some problems and unanswered questions – Where do scripts come from? How are they invoked? How do we know enough about what other people know to be confident about what scripts they have got? and so on – but they are the best proposal yet for a memory organization which will facilitate certain sorts of language processing.

The other area of progress in the use of background knowledge is in the processing of statements which appear to mean one thing but, in the context in which they are produced, actually mean another. This is a very wide topic indeed, which could be taken to cover issues such as lying by omission of relevant facts, the use of 'loaded terms' and 'leading' questions, etc. The particular aspect of all this that has been studied in AI is the interpretation of 'speech acts'. This work is concerned with trying to find out the function of utterances which have a surface appearance suggesting they mean one thing but in fact mean something else. These are not cases where the speaker is trying to mislead the hearer in any way. The problem is that simply mapping the structure of the sequence of words onto its propositional content does not convey the message that the speaker wanted to convey. The analysis of such things depends on the context in which they are uttered and the possible reasons the speaker might have had for producing them. Some examples:

'Do you know the time?'	Speaker does not know the time, believes that hearer does, wants to be told.
'Do you know the time?'	Speaker and hearer both know the time, both know that both know, hearer is late, speaker is expressing annoyance.
'The door's open'	Speaker has just heard a knock on the door and is inviting whoever knocked to come in.

'The door's open'   Someone has just come into the room, leaving the door open so there is a draught, and is being instructed to go back and close it.

The first two are, apparently, simple yes/no questions. Yet the first should be answered either with 'No, I'm sorry, I don't' or with a statement of what time it is. A simple 'Yes' is not an appropriate answer. The response to the second is something more like, 'Yes', I'm sorry, the train was cancelled'. An answer like, 'Yes, it's half-past three' (which would have been appropriate in the first case) would probably lead to a punch on the nose. The second pair of sentences are apparently simple statements of fact, to which the normal response would be to store them away for future reference. But in the situations described, they function as instructions to perform physical actions – entering the room, or going back across the room to shut the door. How do we discover what is meant by an instance of a sentence in a situation, as opposed to what the sentence means if we look at it in isolation?

This question has been addressed by a number of philosophers of language. Austin (1962) and Searle (1969) try to present conditions under which a sentence with some given surface form can function as some particular sort of act. Barwise and Perry (1983) try to deal with a slightly different aspect of the way context affects meaning, looking largely at the question of how the context contributes to the interpretation of referring expressions ('I', 'you', 'that box', 'the king of France') and relational expressions ('is running very fast', 'would have been more useful than it is'). The most significant AI work on interpreting the function of utterances is described in Allen and Perrault (1980) and Cohen and Perrault (1979). This work attempts to interpret the things people say by trying to find out what goals they might have which could be furthered by a listener's response to what was said. As an example we can take the simple 'Do you know the time?' question. The argument is that it is unlikely that the speaker really wants to know whether the hearer knows the time, because it is hard to imagine – in a normal, unloaded context – any real goal that the speaker could have which would be made easier to achieve by knowing whether some arbitrarily selected listener knows the time. It is, however, quite easy to imagine goals which would be facilitated by actually knowing what time it is. One way you can find this out is by asking someone who *does* know. But there is no point in asking someone who does not. Hence one way of furthering your real goal, which has knowing the time as a subgoal, is by finding someone who knows the time and asking them. So you pick someone out and ask them if they know the time, as a preliminary to actually asking them what it is. When they hear you ask this question, they think, 'Why did she ask me that, what good could it possibly do her? Ah, I know, if I say yes she's going to ask me what it is. Well to save her the effort, I'll tell her before she asks me'.

This explains the difference of interpretation of the questions in the two situations outlined above – in the second case, the hearer knows that the speaker does not need to be told the time in order to get on with whatever she was planning, since she already knows it, so she must have some other reason for producing the question. Furthermore, if the question had actually been a completely straightforward yes/no question (which is, I suppose, conceivable), then answering by stating what the time is is a satisfactory answer, since the fact that I *do* know the time can easily be inferred if I tell you what it is.

This work is concerned with the speaker's plans, which the listener must guess and, if she is so inclined, try to help with. It is couched in terms of the sort of plan descriptions introduced with the STRIPs planning algorithm (Fikes and Nilsson, 1971), an extremely important piece of AI research which is far outside the scope of this chapter on language. It is a very plausible explanation of how an utterance may be interpreted in the light of the context in which it occurs, but it does require the person (or system) doing the interpretation to perform an extremely difficult task – recognizing what the speaker might want to do which might be furthered by some response to the utterance. Sometimes it does feel as though you are doing this. When someone says something for which you are completely unprepared, you may think for a few moments before seeing what they could possibly want and tailoring your response accordingly, and if you cannot find any reason you may well say 'What do you mean? Why do you want to know?' To respond to an utterance by asking why it was made is to say that you cannot construct a more useful response until you know what goal your response is likely to help with. On other occasions, such as when a 'Do you know . . . ?' question is operating as a 'Please tell me . . . ' request, you probably do not have to go through the entire chain of reasoning because you have done it so often that you recognize what is going on straight away. Once the interpretation has become so habitual that there is no need to do any reasoning to arrive at it, it is perhaps better to say that one of the semantic rules associated with 'Do you know . . . ?' questions is 'This is a request for information'. Even so, we need some mechanism for distinguishing between 'Do you know . . . ?' questions which are to be interpreted as 'Please tell me . . . ' requests, and 'Do you know . . . ?' questions which are to be interpreted as 'Do you know . . . ?' questions ('Do you know how to bowl leg-breaks?'). And we still need the entire plan recognition and interpretation mechanism to deal with difficult cases like the second 'Do you know the time?', or either of the 'The door is open' examples.

4.10   PUTTING IT ALL TOGETHER

We have now seen, at least in outline, most of the pieces that we will need for a system for interpreting unconstrained natural language. We have not said very much about generation, but it is clear that anything we need for interpretation is going to have a counterpart in the generation process. Otherwise, how did it get into the text in such a way as to need to be extracted? We will finish with a few words on the problems of making a single interpretation system out of all of these pieces.

Earlier we drew a diagram showing layers of sign systems, with combinations of entities in one layer being used to denote entities in the next. This diagram indicates that we naturally think about language in terms of systems at different 'levels'. We do not just have a collection of interrelated systems, we have a hierarchy of interrelated systems. There is a net flow of processing from the bottom of the hierarchy, with the interpretation popping out of the top. An obvious way to implement a program that processed language at the various levels in this hierarchy would be to process it at the bottom one, pass the results of this on to the next, pass the results of this on to the one after, and . . . until you get to the top. Unfortunately, if we consider the following collection of groups of sentences, we see that it is often not possible to process language unambiguously at low levels without making use of high level information:

> The bats that live in South America are generally bigger than those that live in Britain.
> The bats that professional cricketers use are generally bigger than those used by amateurs.
>
> One of my greatest pleasures is watching old movies.
> One of my oldest friends is watching old movies.
>
> Bill hit John. Then he hit Peter.
> Bill hit John. Then Peter hit him.
> Bill hit John. He fell down.

In each of these examples there is a low level ambiguity which can only be resolved at a higher level. In the first case, we have a lexically ambiguous word – 'bats' – whose interpretation cannot be resolved until we understand the surrounding context. In the second we have two possible syntactic analyses, one of which would be obtained if we bracketed the sentence as [one of my . . .] [is watching] [old movies], and the other if we bracketed it as [one of my . . .] [is] [watching old movies]. The choice between the two forms cannot be made on the basis of syntactic information alone. It depends on the real world knowledge that pleasures cannot watch old movies, whereas friends cannot *be* activities such as 'watching old movies'. The final example illustrates how the intersentence task of pronoun de-referencing can require the use of both syntactic and semantic knowledge. In the first two cases, the most immediate reading of the pronoun is that it refers to the same person as the noun phrase in the corresponding position in the previous sentence. These two sentence pairs are equivalent to, 'Bill hit John. Then Bill hit Peter' and 'Bill hit John. Then Peter hit John', respectively. But in the third example this principle would lead us to 'Bill hit John. Bill fell down', which seems like such an unlikely story that we choose instead to read it as 'Bill hit John. John fell down'.

These examples show cases where the information available at one level of analysis is inadequate for completing the analysis at that level, no matter how hard you try. There are plenty of other instances where there is enough information for the analysis to be completed eventually, but where making use of higher level facts would lead to shortcuts. This problem has been inadequately dealt with in text processing systems. A number of mechanisms have been proposed in other areas of AI, notably in speech processing (Erman and Lesser, 1975; Woods, Kaplan and Nash-Webber, 1972), vision (Sloman *et al.*, 1978), and problem solving by constraint propagation (Stefik, 1981; Sussman and Steele, 1980), but there has been little successful work on how to use these mechanisms to co-ordinate the higher level components of language processing systems. To a large extent, the current typical AI natural language processing system is made of components whose internal control structures may be sophisticated mixtures of top-down and bottom-up processing, co-routining, hypothesis generation, and whatever, but whose communications with one another are driven almost entirely by low level components passing processed input on to high level ones, with very little information flowing back down to help guide low level decision making.

ANNOTATED BIBLIOGRAPHY

You will not get an adequate grounding in the techniques needed for computer processing of natural language without studying linguistics, computational linguistics and AI. The references below contain papers from all three fields. There are a large number of journals and conferences where results from general linguistics are reported. As far as computational linguistics is concerned, the most important sources are the *Journal of Computational Linguistics*, the International Conference on Computational Linguistics, and the European Conference on Computational Linguistics (all run by the Association for Computational Linguistics); two workshops on Theoretical Advances in Natural Language Processing were run in 1975 and 1978, and the proceedings of these contain a number of significant papers. The major sources for AI are the two journals *Artificial Intelligence* and *Cognitive Science*, the International Joint Conference on AI, the American Conference on AI, and the European Conference on AI.

Akmajian, A. and Heny, F. (1972), *An Introduction to the Principles of Transformational Syntax*, Prentice-Hall, Englewood Cliffs, NJ.

   Sound textbook introduction to transformational grammar as it was in 1972. The theory has undergone several changes since then, but this remains a good introduction.

Allen, J.F. and Perrault, C.R. (1980), Analyzing intention in utterances, *Artif. Intel.*, **15**, 143–78.

   Research paper on an AI attempt to understand 'indirect speech-acts', i.e. utterances whose surface form is not directly related to their meaning. This paper may be difficult to follow unless you know about AI theories of planning (Fikes and Nilsson, 1972; Nilsson, 1982).

Austin, J.L. (1962), *How To Do Things With Words*, Oxford University Press, Oxford.

   Philosophical discussion of how the meaning of an utterance depends on the situation in which it occurred. This is background reading – nothing directly computational is said.

Bach, E. and Harms, R.T. (eds) (1968), *Universals in Linguistic Theory*, Holt, Rinehart and Winston, New York.

   Collection of papers on syntactic theory. The most important of these for AI research has been Fillmore, 1968.

Barr, A. and Feigenbaum, E.A. (1981), *The Handbook of Artificial Intelligence*, Pitman, London.

   Useful survey of a number of fields of AI. Of particular interest here are the surveys of natural language processing and speech understanding, and of robot planning systems (as background for work on indirect speech acts). These both appear in volume 1. This book is *not* adequate as a stand-alone textbook. Its function is to give the reader a feel for AI research in various areas, and to point him/her to further reading.

Barwise, J. and Perry, J. (1983), *Situations and Attitudes*, Bradford Books, Cambridge MA.

   Important recent work in philosophy of language. Barwise and Perry try to reconcile the principles developed in formal semantics, particularly Montague grammar, with the observations made by people like Austin and Searle about the way meaning depends on context. This book is hard but good – again it is mainly background, though the computational implications are quite easy to spot.

Boguraev, B. (1979), Automatic resolution of linguistic ambiguities, Cambridge University Computer Laboratory Technical Report, No. 11.

   PhD thesis which attempts to make use of both semantic knowledge (the theory of 'preference semantics' presented in Wilks (1975)) and syntactic knowledge (in the form of an ATN grammar) for unambiguous analysis of input text. This is quite a nice piece of work, but it is not recommended to beginners.

Charniak, E. (1972), Towards a computational model of children's story comprehension, MIT AI Technical Report, No. 266.

Thesis on the use of background knowledge for filling in the gaps in stories. Important at the time, it may now be a bit dated – Schank and Abelson (1981) cover much the same ground, but with more experience of inference mechanisms to draw on.

Chomsky, N. (1965), *Aspects of the Theory of Syntax*, MIT Press, Cambridge, MA.

Seminal work on transformational grammar. Very important for an understanding of the framework within which computational (and non-computational) linguistics has developed over the last 20 years.

Clocksin, W.F. and Mellish, C.S. (1981), *Programming in PROLOG*, Springer-Verlag, New York.

Introduction to the programming language PROLOG. Cited here because it contains a clear description of a grammatical formalism, called 'direct clause grammar', and parsing algorithm for use with that formalism. See also Pereira and Warren (1980).

Cohen, P.R. and Perrault, C.R. (1979), Elements of a plan-based theory of speech acts, *Cogn. Sci.*, **3**.

An earlier paper on the ideas reported in Allen and Perrault (1980) on understanding indirect speech acts – again very interesting, but difficult to follow unless you know about AI planners (Fikes and Nilsson, 1971; Nilsson, 1982).

Colby, K.M. and Schank, R.C. (eds) (1973), *Computer Models of Thought and Language*, Freeman, San Francisco.

Useful, if slightly outdated, collection of introductory papers.

Eco, U. (1976), *A Theory of Semiotics*, Indiana University Press, Bloomington.

AI influenced account of how meanings can be layered on top of each other. There is no sophisticated analysis of how a program might make use of the theory presented in this book, but it is evident that any serious attempt to understand unrestricted natural language will have to deal with these issues.

Eco, U. (1981), *The Role of the Reader*, Hutchinson, London.

Applications of semiotic theory to literary criticism. This is a very interesting piece of work, but its applicability to computational theories of language processing is limited.

Erman, L.D. and Lesser, V.R. (1975), The HEARSAY-II speech understanding system, *Proceedings of the Fourth International Joint Conference on Artificial Intelligence*, 483–90.

Report on one of the speech understanding projects funded by the American Advanced Projects Agency in the early 1970s. The report in these proceedings is rather short.

Fikes, R.E. and Nilsson, N.J. (1971), STRIPS: A new approach to the application of theorem solving to problem solving, *Artif. Intel.*, **2**, 189–208.

Significant early report on AI planning and problem solving methods. I have cited it here because the techniques it describes are used in Allen and Perrault (1980) and Cohen and Perrault (1979), but it is interesting in its own right.

Fillmore, C. (1968), The case for case, in *Universals in Linguistic Theory* (eds E. Bach and R. T. Harms), Holt, Rinehart and Winston, New York.

Discussion of a theory of syntax which tries to account for the way that certain sentences appear to be ill-formed because of violations of what look like semantic constraints. This work has been frequently borrowed for AI natural language work.

Foley, W.A. and van Valin, R.D. Jr (1984), *Functional Syntax and Universal Grammar*, Cambridge University Press, Cambridge.

Alternative view of the way syntax works. This work is not couched in computational terms, and as far as I know there are no computer systems based on it. It is nonetheless of interest to computational linguists, particularly in view of the great efforts the authors make to cover a wide range of languages.

Gazdar, G., Klein, E., Pullum, G.K. and Sag, I.A. (1984), *Generalized Phrase Structure Grammar*, Blackwell, Oxford.

Recent contribution to syntactic theory, arguing that the syntactic properties of natural languages may be described using a more restricted theory than transformational grammar. It may be that more efficient or simpler systems may be built on the basis of GPSG than can be done using TG.

Halliday, M.A.K. and Martin, J.R. (1981), *Readings in Systemic Linguistics*, Batsford, London.

This is a collection of papers on a theory of grammar which describes syntactic phenomena in terms of combinations of choices made by the speaker. This theory is the basis of the syntactic analysis component of SHRDLU (Winograd, 1972), and has also been used in a number of language generation systems.

Kaplan, R. (1973), A general syntactic processor, in *Natural Language Processing* (ed. R. Rustin), Algorithmics Press, New York.

Comprehensible description of a parsing algorithm, 'chart parsing', which has been used by numerous people since Kaplan's original implementation.

Marcus, M. (1980), *A Theory of Syntactic Recognition for Natural Language*, MIT Press, Cambridge, MA.

PhD thesis describing a program which attempts to delay decisions about the form and function of the syntactic structure it is building until it has enough information to make the right choice. This work attempts to build on phenomena noted by linguists working within transformational grammar, and psychological observations. It is a very interesting piece of work, but the reader is advised to make up his/her own mind about how valid its claims to be psychologically plausible are.

Nilsson, N.J. (1982), *Principles of Artificial Intelligence*, Springer-Verlag, New York.

Useful, rather formal, textbook of AI techniques. Cited here as another way of getting hold of the background work on planning.

Pereira, F.C.N. and Warren, D.H.D. (1980), Direct clause grammar for language analysis – a survey of the formalism and a comparison with augmented transition networks. *Artif. Intel.*, **13**, 231–78.

Description of a mechanism for parsing making use of facilities built in to the programming language PROLOG. Clocksin and Mellish (1981) also describe this form of parsing.

Riesbeck, C.K. (1978), An expectation-driven production system for natural language understanding, in *Pattern Directed Inference Systems* (eds D. A. Waterman and F. R. Hayes-Roth), Academic Press, New York.

Description of one of a suite of programs written mainly by researchers at Yale University which attempt to model some of the more difficult aspects of language processing, such as using common sense to fill in the gaps in stories. Riesbeck's contribution is a program which identifies syntactic choices without building an explicit parse tree. Other related programs are reported in Schank (1975).

Rustin, R. (ed.) (1973), *Natural Language Processing*, Algorithmic Press, New York.

Collection of useful papers, mainly on computational techniques for syntactic processing (in either direction). It may be a little out of date now, but the descriptions of chart parsing and ATN parsing are as clear as you will find anywhere else.

Schank, R.C. (1973), Identification of conceptualizations underlying natural language, in *Computer Models of Thought and Language* (eds K. M. Colby and R. C. Schank), Freeman, San Francisco.

The first widely available appearance of Schank's theory that the entire structure of meaning can be built on top of a small collection of event types (about 15 primitive actions). This work is controversial, but extremely important.

Schank, R.C. (1975), *Conceptual Information Processing*, North Holland, Amsterdam.

A collection of papers describing programs which elaborate aspects of Schank's theories of conceptual primitives and memory organization.

Schank, R.C. and Abelson, R.P. (1981), *Scripts, Goals, Plans and Understanding*, Erlbaum, Hillsdale, NJ.

Discursive presentation of a collection of mechanisms for making use of shared background knowledge about stereotypical events. The work draws on computational systems described in Schank (1975) and on a number of plausible psychological considerations. It does not contain any direct presentations of programs, but its relevance for computational models is evident.

Searle, J.R. (1969), *Speech Acts: An Essay in the Philosophy of Language*, Cambridge University Press, Cambridge.

Background reading in philosophy of language about direct and indirect speech acts.

Sloman, A., Owen, D., Hinton, G., Birch, F. and O'Gorman, F. (1978), Representation and control in vision, *Proceedings of the Artificial Intelligence and Simulation of Behaviour/General Intelligence Conference*, Hamburg.

Brief report on a system for interpretation of messy line drawings. Cited here as an example of the use of complex control structures for dealing with problems with many levels of analysis.

Sparck Jones, K. and Wilks, Y.A. (1983), *Automatic Natural Language Parsing*, Ellis Horwood, Chichester.

This is a report on a recent workshop at which a variety of parsing algorithms were presented. Most of the papers are fairly accessible, and the collection as a whole gives a good indication of the current lack of consensus in the area.

Stefik, M. (1981), MOLGEN I and II, *Artif. Intel.*, **16**, 111–170.

　　Substantial report on a complex problem solver for planning experiments in genetic engineering. Cited here for the same reason as Sloman *et al.* (1978).

Sussman, G.J. and Steele, G.L. Jr (1980), CONSTRAINTS – A language for expressing almost-hierarchical descriptions, *Artif. Intel.*, **14**, 1–39.

　　Substantial report on the application of constraint propagation for problem solving in the field of electrical, electronic and digital circuits. Cited here for the same reason as Sloman *et al.* (1978).

Waterman, D.A. and Hayes-Roth, F.R. (eds) (1978), *Pattern Directed Inference Systems*, Academic Press, New York.

　　Collection of papers, mainly on 'expert systems'. Cited here for Riesbeck (1978).

Wilks, Y.A. (1975), A preferential, pattern-seeking semantics for natural language inference, *Artif. Intel.*, **6**, 53–74.

　　Description of an approach to natural language processing where semantic and pragmatic considerations, such as likely number and nature of the participants in some activity, are invoked early in the analysis to guide the later stages. Wilks' program is one of a number of attempts to do without an explicit phase of syntactic analysis, though Boguraev (1979) does employ a distinct parser in his program based on preference semantics.

Winograd, T. (1972), *Understanding Natural Language*, Academic Press, New York.

　　Seminal PhD thesis on integrated use of syntactic, semantic and pragmatic knowledge in a system for conducting natural language dialogues within a very restricted domain.

Winograd, T. (1983), *Language as a Cognitive Process*, Addison-Wesley, Reading, MA.

　　Textbook covering a number of important theories of grammar, and a number of parsing algorithms. This is an excellent book, though possibly rather heavy going for complete beginners without any support.

Woods, W.A. (1970), Transition network grammars for natural language analysis, *Commun. ACM* **13**, 591–606.

　　Rather dense presentation of Woods' formalism for expressing grammatical rules. This has been discussed in many places since then, including one of the papers in Rustin (1973) – the current paper is the first presentation I am aware of.

Woods, W.A., Kaplan, R. and Nash-Webber, B. (1972), The lunar sciences natural language information system: Final report, BBN Report No. 2378, Bolt, Beranek & Newman Inc.

　　Another of the American Advanced Research Agency funded speech analysis systems.

5

Levels of representation in computer speech synthesis and recognition

STEPHEN ISARD

The words 'Margaret Thatcher' are different from the words 'Britain's first woman Prime Minister', but they are equivalent in the sense that they refer to the same person. The word 'Thatcher' itself can be pronounced loudly or softly, with a high pitch or a low pitch, with an 'r' sound at the end by a Glaswegian or without one by a Londoner, and still all of these pronunciations count as the same word. A Scot pronouncing the 'r' sound at the end of 'Thatcher' will use the tip of the tongue in a way that an American would not, but the two pronunciations both count as 'r'.

The analysis of speech involves making classifications at a series of levels – Should this sound count as 'r'? Should this word count as 'Thatcher'? Should this phrase count as a reference to the Prime Minister? Generation of speech requires making a single choice from among the various equivalent forms at each level – What words should we use to refer to the Prime Minister? Should we put an 'r' sound at the end of 'Thatcher'? How should we make this 'r' sound?

5.1 INTRODUCTION

A spoken utterance can be described at a number of different levels. At the physical level, it is a sound wave, which can be described using a terminology of metres and seconds that can be applied equally to any human language, as well as to barking dogs, notes played on the clarinet, or leaves rustling in the wind. At the level of its significance to speaker and hearer, it might be a congratulation, or a polite refusal – terms which apply only to human linguistic acts, but which have nothing particular to do with sound. The same acts might be performed in writing or by gesture. We can view the job of the human speech perception system as that of turning the physical description present at the ear into the sort of description in terms of significance that we need in order to feel that we have really understood what has been said to us.

Intuition tells us that we pass through several intermediate stages on the way to full understanding. For instance, it is possible to know what words have been spoken to you, and still not grasp their point. There is a story about two psychiatrists who meet on the street. 'Hello,' says the first. 'Hmm,' thinks the second, 'I wonder what he meant by that.' It is also possible on occasion to make out the component speech sounds of words, but not the words themselves. This is the position of generations of English schoolchildren who have thought that they were singing a hymn about 'Gladly, the Cross-eyed Bear'.

Figure 5.1 sets out a series of levels of representation that are used by the computer speech synthesis and analysis systems to be surveyed here. The figure can be used as an outline of the material in the rest of the chapter. The boxes in Fig. 5.1 are the levels themselves and the upward and downward arrows are labelled with the names of the processes which compute the content of one level from that of another. Everything which follows is essentially an explanation of the terms which appear in Fig. 5.1.

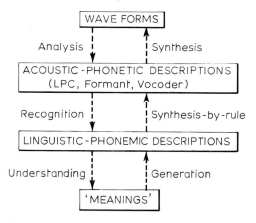

Fig. 5.1

Before launching in, however, it is worth noting that the conceptual framework summarized by Fig. 5.1 is derived from traditional linguistics and phonetics, and is in no sense the invention of workers in artificial intelligence. In fact, the contribution of artificial intelligence as such to the study of speech is somewhat controversial. The presence here of this chapter is justified not because it describes a branch of artificial intelligence, but because

(1) A full understanding of intelligence, artificial or otherwise, ought surely to encompass an understanding of speech.
(2) AI workers would like to include speech capacities in intelligent systems.
(3) The techniques and the overall approach described here, even if developed independently, can be seen to have a great deal in common with those used in some areas of AI, especially vision research, and one can at least express the pious hope that further developments might benefit from contact with AI.

With this caveat, we can begin filling in our outline.

5.2 LEVELS OF DESCRIPTION OF SPEECH

5.2.1 Wave forms

The most faithful representation that a digital computer can make of a physical speech event is simply a series of numbers representing the amplitude of the sound wave – the sound pressure detected by a microphone – at a series of successive instants. Such a series of numbers is known as a digitized wave-form, and 10 000 numbers per second is a typical sampling frequency for such a representation, while 12 bits per number is adequate for capturing the range of variation. The technology of passing back and forth between sound waves and digitized wave-forms stored in computers is well established.

Although a stock of messages could be stored as digitized wave-forms to be played out, there are a number of reasons for desiring a more abstract representation. The most important are:

(1) Digitized wave-forms consume a great deal of space. An utterance of 'Who's afraid of the big, bad wolf?' might last for about two seconds. At 10000 12-bit numbers per second, we need 240000 bits. Various of the acoustic coding techniques mentioned below might reduce this by a factor of between 5 and 10, say to 30000 bits. Stored as English text, it consumes only 272 bits.
(2) Short digitized wave-forms cannot be concatenated into perceptually satisfactory longer utterances. Gluing together the wave-forms of words recorded in isolation produces a jumbled effect, often giving the impression of several different voices, even when the words were spoken by the same person in the first place.
(3) We have no sort of 'distance measure' that can be applied for

purposes of recognition to unanalysed wave-forms in order to class utterances of the same word or phrase as closer together than utterances of distinct words or phrases.

5.2.2 Acoustic representations

In voiced human speech, e.g. normally produced English vowels, the sound created by the vibrations of the larynx is shaped by the upper portion of the vocal tract. The larynx might be vibrating at a rate of, say, 100 Hz (100 times per second) producing overtones at 200 Hz, 300 Hz, 400 Hz, . . . , that is, at all multiples of the larynx frequency. Depending on the shape given to the mouth by the positioning of the tongue, lips, jaw, etc., some of these overtones will be damped out, while others (close to the resonant or *formant* frequencies of the vocal tract) will pass through. In a typical neutral vowel, overtones in the regions of 500, 1500 and 2500 Hz (the 4th, 14th and 24th overtones) will pass through, together with slightly more damped versions of their immediate neighbours. If the larynx is vibrating at 200 Hz, then it will be the first and second overtones at 400 Hz and 600 Hz that will be favoured by the resonance at 500 Hz, and similarly for the higher resonances. Thus an analysis which displays the amount of energy in various frequency bands, in the speech range, up to, say, 4000–5000 Hz, can be used to class as similar two productions of the same vowel, one spoken in a high voice and the other in a low voice, although their displayed wave-forms would look rather different, the higher one repeating its basic pattern twice as frequently as the lower one.

The representation of speech as energy in a series of frequency bands is known as a 'vocoder' representation. Whereas a digitized wave-form has to represent that amplitude of the sound wave thousands of times per second, a vocoder representation, in which the energy in each frequency band is averaged over each hundredth of a second, is adequate to resynthesize a wave perceptually very similar to the original. A closely related form of representation tracks the formants over time. Trained speech scientists can often 'read' words and phrases from vocoder and formant displays.

A third form of representation, which has come into wide use within the past decade or so, because of the particularly efficient algorithms associated with it, is linear predictive coding, which derives its efficiency from the simplifying assumption that the vocal tract can be represented as an all-pole recursive digital filter. It can be shown that such a filter is equivalent, in acoustic terms, to a linked series of equal-length resonating tubes.

All of these forms of representation are essentially physical. They are language independent, exploiting only the redundancy given by the knowledge that the sounds involved come from a human vocal tract. As well as being more compact than wave-forms, they also have advantages with respect to (2) and (3) above. They are able to effectively separate out the contribution of vocal tract shape from that of larynx frequency. Distance measurements can then be defined which refer only to the characterization of vocal tract shape, and which begin to cluster sounds together in intuitively reasonable ways.

High quality resynthesis can be performed from descriptions in which the larynx frequency portion has been altered, but the remainder left unchanged. Systematic changes to duration and interpolations of vocal tract positions can also be performed in a manner not possible with wave-forms. This makes it possible to synthesize utterances by concatenating the *descriptions* of recorded words, or shorter units of speech, and avoid the 'jumpiness' that would be produced by concatenating the recorded words themselves. Techniques and hardware are available for passing back and forth between acoustic descriptions and waves.

5.2.3 Linguistic descriptions

The next level of abstraction is to associate linguistic entities, like words, syllables or phonemes (the 'basic sounds' of the language, corresponding roughly to the letters of the alphabet), with classes of acoustic descriptions. The problem is that the 'same' word, phoneme, etc. is pronounced differently by different speakers, and even by the same speaker on different occasions. The phoneme at the beginning of a word will look different when the word is pronounced in isolation and in continuous speech. There are also regular transformations that phonemes undergo in normal speech, such as the contraction of 'did you' into 'dija'.

Nevertheless, we are able to some extent to associate characteristic acoustic patterns with phonemes, and this association can be exploited both for recognition purposes, and in constructing artificial acoustic descriptions for purposes of speech synthesis. The nature of the correspondence between acoustic features and phonemes is a very live research issue.

For the purposes of this paper, I shall characterize as 'speech recognition' an enterprise which attempts to categorize a speech wave as a sequence of one or more linguistic entities. I will use 'speech analysis' for the production of acoustic descriptions, and reserve 'speech understanding' for attempts to go beyond linguistic description to 'meaning', in some sense. A large question from the point of view of speech research is whether recognition can be made significantly easier by embedding it in the context of understanding.

The term 'synthesis' is often employed for the creation of waves both from acoustic and linguistic descriptions. When the distinction needs to be made, 'synthesis by rule' is often used for the construction of artificial speech from linguistic input, and that is the terminology I shall adopt. 'Speech generation' will be reserved for the inverse of speech understanding, where one starts from some form of meaning representation. Many of the new tasks involved in extending back beyond the linguistic level are faced in the generation of printed text as well as spoken utterances, e.g. deciding whether some object is sufficiently prominent in the discourse to be referred to simply as 'it', or whether a fuller description is needed.

5.3 PROCESSES

5.3.1 **Recognition**

Extraction of phonemes from words or sentences is possible with 60–70% accuracy (Dixon and Silverman, 1977). In consequence quite good results can be obtained by applying phoneme recognition to the identification of words from a vocabulary chosen to avoid minimal phonetic distinctions, i.e. one not exhibiting pairs of words like 'written' and 'ridden'. However, considerable success in word recognition for vocabulary sizes of the order of 100 words has been achieved by the computationally simpler tactic of ignoring phonemes altogether and matching whole words against vocoder or linear predication templates (Sakoe and Chiba, 1978).

An initial difficulty raised by template matching is that the word to be recognized might be of a different length from the template that it is supposed to match. Simple linear scaling of the template to the length of the word is not the solution, since the constituent phonemes might take up different proportions of the total duration of the two utterances, and so acoustic events may still not line up properly even after scaling. This particular obstacle can be largely overcome by the use of dynamic programming (time warping) algorithms, which match each part of the template against each part of the target word, and which then look for the best match of an 'elastic template' against the word as a whole. With limited vocabulary sizes and suitable speaker training, recognition rates around 99% can be achieved. Furthermore, the algorithm can be extended to the recognition of sequences of words in connected speech by attempting matches of each template against each section of the input. Obviously, some care must be taken to limit the scope of the search. Bridle, Brown and Chamberlain (1982) present a technique for doing this, and for introducing grammatical constraints on possible sequences of words. NEC of Japan and Logica in Britain produce commercial connected word recognizers based on dynamic programming techniques.

5.3.2 Understanding

Speech understanding was the goal of the ARPA project (see Klatt (1977) for a review), in the sense that systems were to be judged on whether they *responded* correctly to their input, by giving the right answers to questions, rather than on whether they correctly identified all the words in the utterance. The project was launched on the assumptions that: (i) speech recognition should benefit from the constraints imposed by syntax, meaning and dialogue structure; and that (ii) to exploit these constraints it would be necessary to make knowledge sources interact in new and complex ways. The HARPY system (Lowerre, 1976), judged the most successful on the criteria established at the beginning of the project, provided confirming evidence for (i) but not (ii). In HARPY, the knowledge and constraints were all applied at compile time. First, phonetic constraints were used to reduce every sentence that the system might be called upon to recognize, to a set of possible sequences of roughly phoneme-sized acoustic segments. There were 98 different types of acoustic segment. The simple finite-state grammar of the system's language was then invoked to construct a huge network, each path through this network representing the acoustic segments of a possible sentence. Input sentences were broken into short pieces, each of which was scored according to how well it matched each of the 98 possibilities, and a highest-scoring-path through the network was found. No level of analysis between acoustic segments and whole sentences was used: sentences were treated, in effect, like giant words. HARPY responded correctly 95% of the time to continuous speech from five different speakers (three male, two female) using a vocabulary of about 1000 words. The vocabulary and set of allowable sentences were carefully chosen to minimize confusibility, so that some words appeared in only one of the allowable sentences. HARPY occupied about 200K 36-bit words on a DEC-10 computer and was judged capable of running in real time on a hypothetical machine executing 100 million instructions/sec.

The ARPA systems WHIM and HEARSAY were more complex and took on more ambitious tasks with theoretically more interesting techniques. Their very complexity makes it difficult to know whether their inferior performance by ARPA criteria was due to harder tasks, overall design or particular weak modules. One must also consider the possibility that, with hindsight, the ARPA criteria were not optimally chosen to foster the sort of work that the committee really wanted to see done.

5.3.3 Synthesis and generation

There are two main techniques in use for producing artificial speech. One (formant synthesis-by-rule) is to associate a formant pattern with each phoneme of the language, or perhaps several patterns with phonemes known to vary in consistent ways with the surrounding context. A pattern for an entire utterance is then constructed by interpolation. (This is somewhat of an over-simplification, but conveys the main idea.) With great attention to detailed measurements of natural speech, this technique can yield good phonetic results, as in the MITalk79 system (Allen, 1980) and the work of the JSRU in Britain. It is also used in the lesser quality devices now available for attaching to home computers.

The second technique, diphone synthesis (Dixon and Maxey, 1968) recognizes that the main difficulty in formant synthesis lies in capturing the way that the acoustic realization of a phoneme (a phone) is influenced by the other phonemes around it, producing different allophones in different contexts. It attempts to get round this difficulty by recording a natural utterance of each phoneme pair in the language, and storing an acoustic analysis of the portion from the middle of the first phone to the middle of the second. These middle-to-middle diphones are then glued together to form new utterances. Phonetic quality can again be very good.

Although pitch measurements and variations in phone length are largely ignored in recognition systems, they are important to naturalness and comprehensibility of synthetic speech, as well as conveying distinctions of syntax and meaning. There are two main approaches to calculating durations for phonemes, one that assigns 'intrinsic lengths' that are varied according to the surrounding context, and the other which takes into account the rhythmic structure of the sentence. Neither is yet ideal (see Isard, 1982). Pitch rules have been developed which can serve in simple cases.

MITalk79 is an example of a system for converting unrestricted English text into speech, a task involving not only synthesis, but an original analysis of the text to surmount the obstacles posed by English spelling, as well as to discover syntactic relations having consequences for pitch and duration. Somewhat paradoxically, full speech generation should be easier in some ways than synthesis from text, because the information sought by the text analysis stage should already be present in the generation system. That is, having constructed the sentence itself, it already knows whether 'read' should be pronounced as a present or past tense, and where the clauses and phrases end. Nevertheless, there are not as yet many examples of speech generation systems (see Young and Fallside (1980) for one).

5.4 DIRECTIONS FOR FUTURE WORK

5.4.1 Recognition and understanding

Speech recognition, with or without understanding, is still restricted to distinctly artificial conditions. There are many problems associated with background noise, especially of other speakers, and with catering for a variety of recording conditions, voices and dialects, where basic research still needs to be done before systems can move confidently out into the real world.

Template matching techniques cannot cope with arbitrarily large vocabularies. To extend beyond our present capabilities we need either methods for identifying a set of building-blocks, perhaps phones or diphones, out of which all words can be constructed, or ways of bringing in other sorts of knowledge, be it grammatical, semantic or whatever, to restrict the set of templates that need to be considered at any given moment. The appropriateness of a set of building-blocks will depend both on how easy they are to spot in the speech wave and on whether we can formulate rules that tell us how words will map onto them in various contexts, as when 'did you' turns into 'dija'. Some problems, for example the ability to cope with words not in the lexicon, or the ability to easily expand the lexicon to new words, can only be dealt with using building-blocks smaller than the word.

As the dynamic programming and pattern matching techniques are pushed to their limits, we may see a swing back towards research on how to use phonetic knowledge in speech recognition, or rather an attempt to apply the linguistic and psychological research that has continued in spite of styles in automatic speech recognition. It is possible that acoustic and psychological research will give us better sets of acoustic parameters, leading to more effective distance measures. Such parameters need to be capable of capturing the significant phonetic information in the face of a changing acoustic environment.

5.4.2 Synthesis and generation

Both formant synthesis and diphone synthesis can generate acceptable speech with proven practical applications, but we lack principles that would allow us to conveniently make changes to voice, dialect or speaking style. Additional work is needed at both phoneme and intonation levels to improve naturalness and intelligibility. We also need better ways of assessing the performance of synthesis systems.

To build formant synthesizers more easily for different voices and dialects, we need a better understanding of the principles of speech. In the short-to-medium term it seems likely that the drudgery of locating diphones in analysed speech can be largely automated, without too much advance in existing analysis techniques, making it easier to tailor this sort of synthesizer to speak in whatever way is desired. In the longer term, we can hope for principles for building the inherently more flexible formant synthesizers 'to order'.

The current active state of research on prosody ought to produce principles that can be used to make machines sound more as if they know what they are saying, for example, by rendering them capable of contrastive stress and the use of intonation to indicate pronoun reference. This will yield synthesis that is more comprehensible and less fatiguing to listen to. The ability to synthesize a variety of voices and dialects will render machine speech more practical in a number of areas, e.g. the classroom and speech prostheses.

ACKNOWLEDGEMENTS

This chapter is based on a paper prepared for a SERC Study Project on Architectures for Knowledge-Based Systems, December 1982. Chris Darwin's comments made the original paper less unreadable than it would otherwise have been.

ANNOTATED BIBLIOGRAPHY

Fallside, F. and Woods, W. (eds) (1985), *Computer Speech Processing*, Prentice-Hall, Englewood Cliffs, NJ.
Simon, J.C. (ed) (1980), *Spoken Language Generation and Understanding*, Reidel, London.
  Both of these collections arose from short courses on speech, at which specialists were invited to speak on their areas of interest. Some of the papers are introductory, others assume a knowledge of basic terminology. The papers on mathematical techniques assume a knowledge of calculus and complex numbers. A very wide range of topics is covered, from the low level properties of speech wave-forms to speculations on how people might use the meaning of what has been said so far to help decide the identity of the next word.
Linggard, R. (1985), *Electronic Synthesis of Speech*, CUP, Cambridge.
  A textbook which outlines the history of synthetic speech and then follows a discussion of the human speech production mechanism with a

careful development of the mathematical techniques used in modern systems. The mathematics is not always simple, but it is all there for a reader capable of following it.

Witten, I. H. (1982), *Principles of Computer Speech*, Academic Press, London.

This text covers all the topics introduced here, and more, in a systematic fashion. It starts of gently, but begins to assume some mathematics after the first two chapters. It contains a section on the sort of speech output devices that can be connected to home microcomputers.

REFERENCES

Allen, J. (1980), Speech synthesis from text, in *Spoken Language Generation and Understanding* (ed. J. C. Simon), Reidel, London, pp. 383–96.

Bridle, J.S., Brown, M.D. and Chamberlain, R. M. (1982), An algorithm for connected word recognition, *Proceedings of the Institute of Electrical and Electronic Engineers International Conference on Acoustics, Speech and Signal Processes*, May, 1982.

Dixon, N.R. and Maxey, H.D. (1968), Terminal analogue synthesis of continuous speech using the diphone method of segment assembly, *IEEE Trans. Audio Acoust.*, **16**, 40–50.

Dixon, N.R. and Silverman, H.F. (1977), The 1976 Modular Acoustic Processor (MAP), *IEEE Trans. Acoust. Speech Signal Process.*, **25**, 367–79.

Isard, S.D. (1982), Synthesis of rhythmic structure, *Proceedings of the Institute of Acoustics Conference*, Bournemouth, pp. E.1–E4.4.

Klatt, D.H. (1977), Review of the ARPA speech understanding project, *J. Acoust. Soc. Amer.*, **62**, 1345–66.

Lowerre, B.T. (1976), The HARPY speech recognition system, Ph.D. thesis, Carnegie–Mellon University.

Sakoe, H. and Chiba, S. (1978), Dynamic programming algorithm optimizating spoken word recognition, *IEEE Trans. Acoust. Speech Signal Process.*, **26**, 43–9.

Young, S.J. and Fallside, F. (1979), Speech synthesis from concept: A method for speech output from information systems, *J. Acoust. Soc. Amer.*, **66, 3,** 685–95.

6

Computer vision

DAVID HOGG

The field of computer vision is concerned with the design of computer systems to make sense of visual images. The purpose of this enterprise may be to gain some insight into the workings of naturally occurring visual systems, especially the human visual system, or it may be a technological one, for example, to provide visual capabilities in an industrial robot.

6.1 INTRODUCTION

The human visual system serves many purposes; for example, locating food, warning of danger, constructing artifacts, appreciating a landscape, navigating over unfamiliar terrain, etc. To these ends, our visual system must provide many kinds of information about the surrounding world and the objects within it; including, for example, three-dimensional (3-D) shape and position, identity, material construction, pliability, edibility, etc. How is it possible to infer these things from the time-varying pattern of light falling upon the retina? Writing computer programs to generate descriptions of this kind may shed some light on the mechanisms employed. (See Sloman (1982) for a discussion of the tasks of a general purpose vision system.)

On the technological front there are many applications for computer vision. For example, vision systems are being developed and used for robotics (see Brady, 1985), medicine, security, remote sensing and vehicle guidance. The range of applications broadens in line with the technology itself.

In a strict sense, computer vision would be concerned only with images analogous to the images formed within the eyes of natural vision systems. However, there are many kinds of non-visual images, obtainable in computer readable form, which pose similar problems in their interpretation; since like visual images, features of the image represent structures in the world. For example, many kinds of medical image are quite unlike visual images, having been formed in different ways (e.g.

X-ray computer tomography), yet the features of an image reflect under-lying anatomical structures in a patient.

Not only may the raw input to a computer vision system differ from that available to a natural vision system but some systems may already exceed the performance of natural systems for a small subset of tasks. For example, a computer vision system may be accurately calibrated in order to provide precise measurements of a scene (e.g. absolute 3-D position or distance). Clearly, though, in the majority of tasks, natural vision systems are vastly superior.

Designing computer vision systems is mostly concerned with writing computer programs to run on standard types of computer. However, the large amount of information which must be processed in some cases necessitates the use or design of non-standard kinds of computer. For example, interconnected arrays of processing elements are especially appropriate for image interpretation tasks. (See Hwang, 1983.)

6.2 THE VISUAL IMAGE

The input to a computer vision system is normally a discrete image composed of a matrix of integers from within a finite range, each of

Fig. 6.1 Machine part to be located.

which represents the light intensity over a small rectangular picture element known as a 'pixel'. Intensity values commonly range between 0 and 255, varying from the lowest intensity at 0 through intermediate levels to the highest intensity at 255. Another common case, known as a binary image, uses just two intensity levels of low and high intensity (0 and 1).

The amount of information contained within an image is a function of the number of pixels and the number of distinct intensity levels available. The choice of image resolution depends on the use for which the system is intended. For example, to determine the orientation and position of a machine part, like that shown in Fig. 6.1, for picking by a robot arm, it may be sufficient to obtain a 64×64 binary image under controlled lighting conditions (see Fig. 6.2). Whereas to recognize the people, trees and buildings shown in Fig. 6.3 would require many more pixels and intensity levels. To illustrate this point, Fig. 6.4 depicts a 64×64 binary image of the same scene in which there is almost certainly inadequate information to produce a useful description.

The information contained within a standard TV image would be adequately captured for most purposes by a 512×512 array of pixels and 256 intensity levels.

Fig. 6.2 64 × 64 binary image of machine part shown in Fig. 6.1.

Fig. 6.3 A typical outdoor scene.

Colour pictures are normally represented using three separate images, one to record the intensity of each component colour (i.e. red, green and blue).

To monitor the activity in a scene over time, a sequence of images must be analysed, and the rate at which these are selected is chosen to

Fig. 6.4 64 × 64 binary image of outdoor scene shown in Fig. 6.3.

ensure that important events do not occur between successive snapshots of the scene. In some cases, it is useful to treat a sequence of
snapshots of a scene as a single 3-D spatio-temporal image to simplify
some kinds of preliminary processing (e.g. Buxton and Buxton, 1983). A
collection of adjacent CT medical images of the human body may also be
combined in this fashion (e.g. Zucker and Hummel, 1981).

6.3   CURRENT TECHNIQUES

The current generation of applied computer vision systems are generally
inflexible and often require carefully controlled lighting and a restricted
environment; for example, an object of interest may have to be presented in isolation against a uniform background. The challenge is to
develop techniques leading to computer vision systems which perform a
wide variety of tasks working from images of everyday scenes.

An important stream of research is concerned with automating the
classification of images into one or more categories by examining small
numbers of measurements derived directly from each image (see Fu
and Rosenfeld (1984) for a discussion of this work). Deciding which
measurements are the most effective and the ways in which they should
be combined to make decisions are active areas of research.

Another approach is typified by work in the 'blocks world', in which
the task is to assign a consistent 3-D interpretation to line drawings of
blocks (see Boden (1977) for fuller discussion of work in this domain). In
this approach, the emphasis is on obtaining a description of the scene
by relating features of the image directly to properties of the scene and
exploiting various natural constraints within the blocks' micro-world to
determine a unique and consistent interpretation of features. Thus, for
example, line junctions in an image are related to vertices of blocks or
occlusions of edges by other blocks, and furthermore, there are many
constraints between the possible interpretations of adjacent junctions.

The remainder of this chapter examines a continuation of this spirit
towards the construction of general purpose computer vision systems in
which an explicit model (or theory) of the visual world plays a central
role in the design of systems and consequently in the interpretation of
images. Such a model might include general properties of the world like
the cohesiveness of matter and basic geometrical and optical principles,
through properties of generic classes of object such as the characteristic
shapes and material construction of man-made objects, to properties of
specific entities like the shape of a particular robot gripper. More ambitious models might include causal and functional relations between
objects, e.g. 'X supports Y', 'X turns Y', 'X restrains Y', etc.

6.4   REGIONS AND EDGES

A characteristic of physical entities is that the images of their visible surfaces tend to exhibit uniformities in texture, intensity, colour, etc. In attempting to interpret or explain an image the presence of such regularities may plausibly be associated with distinct and significant entities in the scene. Though it is easy to measure and represent intensity or colour, the description of texture, which is a more global feature, is more difficult.

Fig. 6.5 Computer generated segmentation of Fig. 6.3 into regions of aproximately uniform intensity.

Figure 6.5 shows regions of approximately uniform intensity, detected automatically from the image shown in Fig. 6.3; individual regions have been shaded with an exactly uniform intensity to distinguish them from neighbouring regions. Every pixel has been included in one of the regions to form what is known as a 'segmentation' of the image. In some cases it may be desirable to allow pixels to belong to more than one region or to none of the regions.

The correspondence between scene entities and regions is clear from Fig. 6.5, although there is not a simple one-to-one relationship. In some cases a scene entity gives rise to several regions and at other times a single region spans several scene entities. For example, the roughness of the grass bank seen in the centre of the picture, and the shadows formed by trees to the right of the picture, have each contributed to a division of the grass bank into several regions. On the other hand, the upper two flights of steps are crossed by a single region. Of course, for a general vision system it is hard to say formally what is meant by the expression 'significant scene entity', and so observations about the correspondence with image regions are bound to be vague. However, in some cases it may be possible to say precisely which are the significant scene entities and to evaluate segmentations of images accordingly.

In some applications, a segmentation of the image may be almost all that is required of a vision system. For example, appropriate segmentations of satellite images can be shown to demarcate land usage; features of the image within each region being used to identify the actual use to which the patch of land has been put (e.g. crops, buildings, water, roads).

However, for other applications a segmentation may be just a first step to obtaining a richer description of the scene. In this case, the next stage following on from segmentation into regions could be to associate regions with one another and with individual scene entities.

Intimately related to the regularities of an image are the local irregularities and it is not surprising that these have been studied in their own right. Local changes in intensity, colour, texture, etc., are related to underlying structure in a scene such as surface corners, changes in the

Fig. 6.6 Computer generated map of abrupt intensity changes in image shown in Fig. 6.3.

colour of a surface or the projected line along which one surface partly obscures another. Figure 6.6 depicts points of the image shown in Fig. 6.3 at which the intensity changes abruptly between neighbouring pixels.

Evidence has been found in natural visual systems for cells sensitive to local intensity changes (e.g. Hubel and Wiesel, 1968) and this has motivated considerable interest at the borders between the study of computational and natural vision systems (see Marr, 1982). Even if there were no evidence, there would be good reason to expect a visual system to make use of edges, whether it was natural or artificial.

6.5 DETERMINING VISIBLE SURFACE SHAPE

For many purposes the shape of an object must be sensed. The fact that humans seem able to form 3-D mental images for classes of object with widely varying shapes (e.g. rocks, trees, buildings) suggests that there is sufficient information in images, together with the properties of these generic object classes, to determine visible surface shape.

Binocular disparity, visual motion, texture, surface shading, surface contours and occluding contours have been shown to be valuable sources of information for determining the depth and orientation of visible surfaces (e.g. Horn, 1975; Marr and Poggio, 1979; Ullman, 1979; and in Brady, 1981 and Marr, 1982).

Binocular vision will serve to illustrate methods of this kind. Differences in the images formed by each eye in the human visual system give rise to the sensation of depth. These same differences have been exploited in computer vision systems to find the 3-D positions of visible surface features with respect to a pair of cameras.

Surface features must be identifiable and should appear at approximately the same position on the surface from both viewpoints. The problem of locating the surface features in three dimensions can be divided into two steps; namely, (i) identifying pairs of features, one from each image, which derive from the same surface positions, this is the 'correspondence problem', which also arises in motion perception; and (ii) computing the 3-D position of surface points, with respect to either of the viewpoints, from the 2-D position of corresponding image features and the viewing geometry.

General assumptions about the surfaces to be sensed are useful in constraining the search for correct correspondences between image features. For example, surfaces may be assumed to be continuous and reasonably smooth.

Computer implementations of binocular vision generally produce information about the locations of only a sparse array of points in the scene which happen to give rise to easily identifiable features in a pair of images. Those parts of visible surfaces from which there are no identifiable features are not directly located.

To be useful for most purposes, the sparse array of located points must be turned into a description of the shapes of the underlying surfaces. For example, to guide the path and orientation of a paint sprayer, a representation of the shape of the surface to be coated may be required. Knowledge of the 3-D position and shape of an object is important when the task is to grasp the object with a robot gripper.

In some applications it may be necessary to infer the overall shape of an unfamiliar object even though the surfaces on its reverse side are hidden from view. This would be useful in visually navigating a vehicle over a rocky landscape where the approximate positions and shapes of obstacles must be sensed.

The need to represent 3-D shape in a computer arises in areas other than computer vision. For example, computers are used in design to represent the shapes of products ranging from car bodies to shoes, in man-machine studies to represent the shape of the human body (see Badler, 1982) and in computer graphics.

One common technique is to partition surfaces into patches which may be represented individually in some concise form. For example, planar patches bounded by straight edges have been used extensively to represent complex shapes. The designer of a shape description of this form must decide first, where to place the seams between adjoining patches and second, what kind of patch descriptors to use (e.g. planar, parametric). For computer vision, the same thing can be done automatically for visible surfaces given the locations of at least some of their points.

6.6   OBJECT IDENTIFICATION

A general purpose vision system would be required to identify objects in a scene. One way in which this can be achieved is to match 3-D shape descriptions generated directly from the image against stored 3-D shape descriptions of familiar objects (provided as part of the *a priori* model of the world); the stored descriptions are normally referred to as 'models'. This recognition method should work whatever the orientation or position of the object with respect to the camera; other methods often treat different views of an object as distinct recognition tasks. Of course, a general purpose vision system may exploit both kinds of method.

Some kinds of variation within a class of objects may be accommodated using stored models which have variable numerical slots; the shape represented by the model depends on the values assigned to these slots.

In general, the main problem in identifying objects when several different types are known is the combinatorial explosion of ways of attempting to map image features into model fragments. The search somehow needs to be controlled. One way of minimizing this problem is to ensure that surface descriptions appear in a concise and canonical form, no matter how objects are viewed. Consequently, the placement of seams in piecewise descriptions of surfaces is important for recognition purposes.

In cases where it has been impossible to generate a reliable 3-D shape description of the scene because of ambiguities of the image, it may be possible to find evidence for invoking a particular stored 3-D model by examining 2-D features of the image directly (e.g. Brooks, 1981; Roberts, 1965). In other words, object specific information is used to interpret image features rather than general kinds of information about surfaces, as discussed above. However, when there is sufficient information to generate a reliable 3-D shape description without invoking object specific information, then it may be computationally advantageous to do so, even though the final objective may be to recognize a familiar object. The initial shape description will serve to index appropriate models from a potentially vast store of possibilities.

Figure 6.7 depicts a model for a walking person in which the overall shape is represented by 14 cylinders linked at the joints and free to articulate according to the values of eight numerical parameters. The general approach will be illustrated by considering a program (Hogg, 1983) which attempts to follow people walking through a scene in terms of this model. This program does not build 3-D descriptions for visible surfaces before invoking a stored model but rather matches 2-D image features predicted from the model against those found in the images.

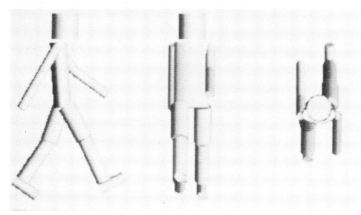

Fig. 6.7 An abstract model of human form.

Fig. 6.8 Single frame from an image sequence depicting a walking man.

The program examines snapshots of a scene at short intervals and locates the people it is following in each. One of a test sequence of images is shown in Fig. 6.8; the images in this sequence are taken at 1/25 s intervals and recorded at a resolution of 128 × 95 with 256 distinct intensity levels.

The program hypothesizes people walking through the scene by matching evidence in the local intensity discontinuities of the incoming sequence of images with discontinuities predicted directly from the abstract 3-D model for a person. The intensity discontinuities detected from the input image depicted in Fig. 6.8 are shown in Fig. 6.9.

As part of its output, the program superimposes a graphical reconstruction for each hypothetical person over successive images, from which mistakes are clearly visible (Fig. 6.10). The reconstructions are performed using standard graphical shading techniques (Newman and Sproull, 1979).

An interesting question about human vision is the extent to which information about specific classes of object mediates the preliminary analysis of images, or does it only become available once a rich description of visible surfaces has been formed? Could it be that knowledge is used in a strictly ordered fashion starting with the most general assumptions about the world and subsequently drawing on increasingly specific information? A possible answer is that it depends on the clarity of the images. Artistic images and images depicting scenes obscured by rain, fog or a clutter of objects may require that specific information about the

Fig. 6.9 Intensity discontinuities detected in frame shown in Fig. 6.8.

objects depicted be invoked before any sense can be made of the scene. Thus, when the world is unhelpful in one respect, e.g. fog or mist, it may be helpful in other ways, e.g. it contains only objects which conform to one's stored models.

Fig. 6.10 Computer generated reconstruction showing the program's 'hypothesis' about frame shown in Fig. 6.8.

6.7 LIMITATIONS

There are many limitations and possible stumbling blocks for the approach described in this chapter. Firstly, the *a priori* model of the world must be formulated explicitly by the programmer. There has been some progress in enabling a system to learn about the 3-D structure of specific kinds of object, but it is harder to understand how systems could acquire general visual expertise by observing the world over a period of time; for example, to develop the skills necessary to exploit binocular vision.

Throughout the history of computer vision there has been interest in self-learning systems based on network models (see, for example, Minsky and Papert, 1972). These systems could learn simple patterns but seemed to be limited in certain important ways. However, recently there has been renewed interest in this kind of approach (see Hinton and Anderson, 1981).

A second problem is that the available stock of 3-D representational techniques does not provide an obvious method for describing generic classes of object such as trees or Alpine landscapes (as opposed to mountain landscapes in other parts of the world). Indeed, a complete description of the range of shapes for a person would need to be considerably richer than the crude representation illustrated in Fig. 6.7.

A lot remains to be understood about how to combine information about a scene from different sources of information present in an image. For example, what happens if texture distribution and binocular disparity give rise to conflicting indications of surface shape?

ANNOTATED BIBLIOGRAPHY

Journals

IEEE Transactions on Pattern Analysis and Machine Intelligence. Edited by T. Pavlidis. IEEE-CS Press, New York.
  Contains a wide range of papers on computer vision.
Computer Vision, Graphics and Image Processing. Edited by L. G. Shapiro, N. Badler, H. Freeman, T. S. Huang and A. Rosenfeld. Academic Press, New York.
Artificial Intelligence. Edited by D. G. Bobrow and P. J. Hayes. North-Holland, Amsterdam.
  Occasionally contains papers on computer vision.
Image and Vision Computing. Edited by K. D. Baker. Butterworth Press, London.
Pattern Recognition. Pergamon Press, Oxford.
Pattern Recognition Letters. Edited by E. Backer and E. S. Gelsema. North-Holland, Amsterdam.

Books

Ballard, D.H. and Brown, C.M. (1982), *Computer Vision*, Prentice Hall, Engle-
wood Cliffs, NJ.
  A good introduction to the field of computer vision which includes
  descriptions of many of the available techniques with references.
Brady, J.M. (ed.) (1981), *Computer Vision*, North-Holland, Amsterdam.
  A special issue of the *Artificial Intelligence* journal containing a variety of
  papers, including several dealing with the determination of surface shape
  and the use of 3-D models.
Frisby, J. (1979), *Seeing: Illusion, Brain and Mind*, Oxford University Press,
Oxford.
  This book and Gregory's (next reference) are good introductions to
  human vision.
Gregory, R.L. (1966), *Eye and Brain: The Psychology of Seeing*, Weidenfeld and
Nicolson, London.
Hanson, A.H. and Riseman, E.M. (1978), *Computer Vision Systems*, Academic
Press, New York.
  A collection of papers dealing with computer vision.
Marr, D. (1982), *Vision*, Freeman, San Francisco.
  This book presents a 'framework for studying vision' in which computa-
  tional studies go hand-in-hand with biological studies of natural visual
  systems. A large part of the book deals with the description of local changes
  in images and the recovery of 3-D information about visible surfaces.

Conference proceedings

*International Conference on Pattern Recognition. Computer vision and Pattern Recog-
nition.* Originally known as 'Pattern Recognition and Image Processing'.

ANNOTATED REFERENCES

Badler, N.I. (1982), Modelling the human body for animation, *IEEE Trans.
Comput. Graphics Appl.*, **2**.
Boden, M.A. (1977), *Artificial Intelligence and Natural Man*, Harvester Press,
Brighton.
Brady, J.M. (ed.) (1981), *Computer Vision*, North-Holland, Amsterdam.
Brady, M. (1985), Artificial intelligence and robotics, *Artif. Intel.*, **26**, 79–121.
  Not much on vision, but provides a good context for someone wanting to
  see how vision would relate to robotics.
Brooks, R.A. (1981), Symbolic reasoning among 3-D models and 2-D images,
Artif. Intel., **17**, 285–348.
Buxton, B.F. and Buxton, H. (1983), Monocular depth perception from optical
flow by space–time signal processing, *Proc. Roy. Soc.* B, **218**, 22–47.
Fu, K.S. and Rosenfeld, A. (1984), Pattern recognition and computer vision,
IEEE Trans. Comput., **17**, 274–82.

Hinton, G.E. and Anderson, J.A. (1981), *Parallel Models of Associative Memory*, Erlbaum, Hillsdale, NJ.

Hogg, D.C. (1983), Model-based vision: a program to see a walking person, *Image Vision Comput.*, **1**, 5–20.

Horn, B.K.P. (1975), Obtaining shape from shading information, in *The Psychology of Computer Vision* (ed. P. H. Winston), McGraw-Hill, New York.

Hubel, D.H. and Wiesel, T.N. (1968), Receptive fields and functional architecture of monkey striate cortex, *J. Phys.*, **195**, 215–43.

Hwang, K. (ed.) (1983), Computer architectures for image processing, *IEEE Trans. Comput.*, **16**.

This is a special issue of *IEEE Trans. Comput.* containing several papers.

Marr, D. and Poggio, T. (1979), A theory of human stereo vision, *Proc. Roy. Soc.* B, **204**.

Marr, D. (1982), *Vision*, Freeman, San Francisco.

Minsky, M. and Papert, S. (1972), *Perceptrons*, MIT Press, Cambridge, MA.

Newman, W.M. and Sproull, R.F. (1979), *Principles of Interactive Computer Graphics*, 2nd edn, McGraw-Hill, New York.

A good introduction to the field of computer graphics.

Roberts, L.G. (1965), Machine perception of three-dimensional solids, in *Optical and Electro-Optical Information Processing* (eds J. P. Tippett *et al.*), pp. 159–98, MIT Press, Cambridge, MA.

Sloman, A. (1982), Image interpretation: The way ahead?, in *Biological and Physical Image Processing* (eds O. Braddick and A. Sleigh), Springer-Verlag, New York.

Ullman, S. (1979), *The Interpretation of Visual Motion*, MIT Press, Cambridge, MA.

Zucker, S.W. and Hummel, R.A. (1981), A three-dimensional edge operator, *IEEE Trans. Pattern Analy. Mach. Intel.*, **3**, 324–31.

7

Artificial Intelligence and robotics

J. MICHAEL BRADY

Since robotics is the field concerned with the connection of perception to action, Artificial Intelligence (AI) must have a central role in robotics if the connection is to be *intelligent*. Artificial Intelligence addresses the crucial questions of: What knowledge is required in any aspect of thinking? How should that knowledge be represented? and How should that knowledge be used? Robotics challenges AI by forcing it to deal with real objects in the real world. Techniques and representations developed for purely cognitive problems, often in toy domains, do not necessarily extend to meet the challenge. Robots combine mechanical effectors, sensors and computers. Artificial Intelligence has made significant contributions to each component.

7.1 ROBOTICS AND ARTIFICIAL INTELLIGENCE

Robotics is the *intelligent connection of perception to action*. The keywords in that sentence are 'intelligent' and concomitant 'perception'. Normally robotics is thought of as simply the connection of sensing to action using computers. The typical sensing modalities of current robots include vision, force and tactile sensing, as well as proprioceptive sensing of the robot's internal state. The capacity for action is provided by arms, grippers, wheels and, occasionally, legs.

The software of modern, commercially available, robot systems such as the IBM 7565 (Sacerdoti, 1975), the Unimation PUMA (Shimano, Geschke and Spaulding, 1984; VAL, 1980), and the Automatix cybervision (Franklin and VanderBrug, 1982; Villers, 1982) includes a wide variety of functions: it performs trajectory calculation and kinematic translation, interprets sense data, executes adaptive control through conditional execution and real-time monitors, interfaces to databases of geometric models and supports program development. It does some of these tasks quite well, particularly those that pertain to computer science; it does others quite poorly, particularly perception, object modelling, and spatial reasoning.

The *intelligent* connection of perception to action replaces sensing by perception, and software by intelligent software. Perception differs from sensing or classification in that it implies the construction of representations that are the basis for recognition, reasoning and action. Intelligent software addresses issues such as: spatial reasoning, dealing with uncertainty, geometric reasoning, compliance and learning. Intelligence, including the ability to reason and learn about objects and manufacturing processes, holds the key to more versatile robots.

Insofar as robotics is the intelligent connection of perception to action, AI is the challenge for robotics. On the other hand, however, we shall argue that robotics severely challenges AI by forcing it to deal with real objects in the real world. Techniques and representations developed for purely cognitive problems often do not extend to meet the challenge.

First, we discuss the need for intelligent robots and we show why robotics poses severe challenges for AI. Then we consider what is required for robots to act on their environment. This is the domain of kinematics and dynamics, control, innovative robot arms, multifingered hands and mobile robots. In Section 7.5, we turn our attention to intelligent software, focusing upon spatial reasoning, dealing with uncertainty, geometric reasoning and learning. In Section 7.6, we discuss robot perception. Finally, in Section 7.7, we present some examples of reasoning that connects perception to action, example reasoning that no robot is currently capable of. We include it because it illustrates the reasoning and problem-solving abilities we would like to endow robots with and that we believe are worthy goals of robotics and AI, being within reach of both.

7.2 THE NEED FOR INTELLIGENT ROBOTS

Where is the need for intelligent robots? Current (unintelligent) robots work fine so long as they are applied to simple tasks in almost predictable situations: parts of the correct type are presented in positions and orientations that hardly vary, and little dexterity is required for successful completion of the task. The huge commercial successes of robot automation have been of this sort: parts transfer (including palletizing and packaging), spot welding and spray painting. Automation has been aimed largely at highly repetitive processes such as those in major industrial plants.

But to control the robot's environment sufficiently, it is typically necessary to erect elaborate fixtures. Often, the set-up costs associated with designing and installing fixtures and jigs dominate the cost of a robot application. Worse, elaborate fixturing is often not transferable to a subsequent task, reducing the flexibility and adaptability that are supposedly the key advantages of robots. Sensing is one way to loosen up the environmental requirements; but the sensing systems of current industrial robots are mostly restricted to two-dimensional binary vision. Industrial applications requiring compliance, such as assembly, seam welding and surface finishing, have clearly revealed the inabilities of current robots. Research prototypes have explored the use of three-dimensional vision, force and proximity sensors, and geometric models of objects (Clocksin *et al.*, 1982; Faugeras *et al.*, 1982; Nakagawa and Ninomiya, 1984; Porter and Mundy, 1982, 1984; Trevelyan, Kovesi and Ong, 1984). Other applications expose the limitations of robots even more clearly. The environment cannot be controlled for most military applications, including smart sentries, autonomous ordinance disposal, autonomous recovery of men and materiel and, perhaps most difficult of all, autonomous navigation.

7.3   ROBOTICS PART OF ARTIFICIAL INTELLIGENCE

Artificial Intelligence is the field that aims to understand how computers can be made to exhibit intelligence. In any aspect of thinking, whether reasoning, perception or action, the crucial questions are:

(1) *What knowledge is needed?* The knowledge needed for reasoning in relatively formalized and circumscribed domains such as symbolic mathematics and game playing is well known. Highly competent programs have been developed in such domains. It has proven remarkably difficult to get experts to precisely articulate their knowledge, and hence to develop programs with similar expertise, in medicine, evaluating prospective mining sites or configuring computers (see Hayes-Roth, Waterman and Lenat (1983), Michie (1979) and Winston (1984) for a discussion of expert systems, and accounts of the difficulty of teasing knowledge out of experts). Among the many severe inadequacies of the current crop of expert systems, is the fact that they usually have limited contact with the real world. Human experts perform the necessary perceptual preprocessing, telling MYCIN, for example, that the patient is 'febrile 0.8'. Moving from the restricted domain of the expert, to the unrestricted world of everyday experience, determining *what* knowledge is needed is a major step toward modelling stereo vision, achieving biped walking and dynamic balance, and reasoning about mechanisms and space. What do you need to know in order to catch a ball?

(2) *Representing knowledge.* A key contribution of AI is the observation that knowledge should be represented *explicitly*, not heavily encoded, for example numerically, in ways that suppress structure and constraint.

A given body of knowledge is used in many ways in thinking. Conventional data structures are tuned to a single set of processes for access and modification, and this renders them too inflexible for use in thinking. Artificial Intelligence has developed a set of techniques such as semantic networks, frames and production rules, that are symbolic, highly flexible encodings of knowledge, yet which can be efficiently processed.

Robotics needs to deal with the real world, and to do this it needs detailed geometric models. Perception systems need to produce geometric models; reasoning systems must base their deliberations on such models; and action systems need to interpret them. Computer-aided design (CAD) has been concerned with highly restricted uses of geometric information, typically display and numerically controlled cutting. Representations incorporated into current CAD systems are analogous to conventional data structures. In order to connect perception, through reasoning, to action, richer representations of geometry are needed. Steps toward such richer representations can be found in configuration space (Lozano-Pérez, 1981, 1983a), generalized cones (Binford, 1981) and visual shape representations (Brady, 1982; Horn, 1982; Ikeuchi, 1981b; Marr, 1982).

As well as geometry, robotics needs to represent forces, causation and uncertainty. We know how much force to apply to an object in an assembly to mate parts without wedging or jamming (Whitney, 1983). We know that pushing too hard on a surface can damage it; but that not pushing hard enough can be ineffective for scribing, polishing or fettling. In certain circumstances, we understand how an object will move if we push it (Mason, 1982). We know that the magnitude and direction of an applied force can be changed by pulleys, gears, levers and cams.

We understand the way things such as zip fasteners, pencil sharpeners and automobile engines work. The spring in a watch stores energy, which is released to a flywheel, causing it to rotate; this causes the hands of the watch to rotate by a smaller amount determined by the ratios of the gear linkages. Representing such knowledge is not simply a matter of developing the appropriate mathematical laws. Differential equations, for example, are a representation of knowledge that, while extremely useful, are still highly limited. Forbus (1984) points out that conventional mathematical representations do not encourage qualitative reasoning, instead, they invite numerical simulation. Though useful, this falls far short of the qualitative reasoning that people are good at. Artificial Intelligence research on qualitative reasoning and naive physics has made a promising start but has yet to make contact with the real world, so the representations and reasoning processes it suggests have barely been tested (Bobrow, 1984; De Kleer, 1975; Forbus, 1984; Hobbs and Moore, 1984; Winston *et al.*, 1984).

Robotics needs to represent uncertainty, so that reasoning can successfully overcome it. There are bounds on the accuracy of robot joints; feeders and sensors have errors; and though we talk about repetitive work, no two parts are ever exactly alike. As the tolerances on robot applications become tighter, the need to deal with uncertainty, and to exploit redundancy, becomes greater.

(3) *Using knowledge.* Artificial Intelligence has also uncovered techniques for using knowledge effectively. One problem is that the knowledge needed in any particular case cannot be predicted in advance. Programs have to respond flexibly to a non-deterministic world. Among the techniques offered by AI are search, structure matching, constraint propagation and dependency-directed reasoning. One approach to constraint propagation is being developed in models of perception by Terzopoulos (1983), Zucker, Hummel and Rosenfeld (1977). Another has been developed by Brooks (1981, 1982) building on earlier work in theorem proving. The application of search to robotics has been developed by Goto, Takeyasu and Inoyama (1980), Lozano-Pérez (1981), Gaston and Lozano-Pérez (1983). Grimson and Lozano-Pérez (1984) and Brooks (1983). Structure matching in robotics has been developed by Winston *et al.* (1984).

To be intelligent, robotics programs need to be able to plan actions and reason about those plans. Surely AI has developed the required planning technology? Unfortunately, it seems that most, if not all, current proposals for planning and reasoning developed in AI require significant extension before they can begin to tackle the problems that typically arise in robotics, some of which are discussed in Section 7.5. One reason for this is that reasoning and planning has been developed largely in conjunction with purely cognitive representations, and these have mostly been abstract and idealized. Proposals for knowledge representation have rarely been constrained by the need to support actions by a notoriously inexact manipulator, or to be produced by a perceptual system with no human preprocessing. ACRONYM (Brooks, 1981; Brooks and Binford, 1980) is an exception to this criticism. Another reason is that to be useful for robotics, a representation must be able to deal with the vagaries of the real world, its geometry, inexactness and noise. All too often, AI planning and reasoning systems have only been exercised on a handful of toy examples.

In summary, robotics challenges AI by forcing it to deal with real objects in the real world. Techniques and representations developed for purely cognitive problems, often in toy domains, do not necessarily extend to meet the challenge.

7.4   ACTION

In this section, we consider what is required for robots to act on their environment. This is the subject of kinematics and dynamics, control, robot arms, multi-fingered hands and locomoting robots.

7.4.1   Kinematics, dynamics and arm design

The kinematics of robot arms is one of the better understood areas of robotics (Brady *et al.*, 1983; Paul, 1981). The need for kinematic transformations arises because programmers prefer a different representation of the space of configurations of a robot than that which is most natural and efficient for control. Robots are powered by motors at the joints between links. Associated with a motor are quantities that define its position, velocity, acceleration and torque. For a rotary motor, these are angular positions, angular velocities, etc. It is most efficient to control robots in *joint space*. However, programmers prefer to think of positions using orthogonal, cylindrical or spherical *Cartesian* coordinate frames, according to the task. Six degrees of freedom (DOF) are required to define the position and orientation of an object in space. Correspondingly, many robots have six joint motors to achieve these freedoms. Converting between the joint positions, velocities and accelerations and the Cartesian (task) counterparts is the job of kinematics. The conversion is an identity transformation between the joint space of 'Cartesian' arms (such as the IBM 7565) and orthogonal (x, y, z) Cartesian space. Cartesian arms suffer the disadvantage of being less able to reach around and into objects. Kinematic transformations are still needed to spherical or cylindrical Cartesian co-ordinates.

The kinematics of a mechanical device are *defined* mathematically. The requirement that the kinematics can be *efficiently computed* adds constraint, that ultimately affects mechanical design. In general, the transformation from joint co-ordinates to Cartesian co-ordinates is straightforward. Various efficient algorithms have been developed, including recent recursive schemes whose time complexity is linear in the number of joints. Hollerbach (1983) discusses such recursive methods for computing the kinematics for both the Lagrange and Newton–Euler formulations of the dynamics. The inverse kinematics computation, from Cartesian to joint co-ordinates, is often more complex. In general, it does not have a closed form solution (Pieper, 1968). Pieper (1968) (see also Pieper and Roth, 1969) showed that a 'spherical' wrist with three intersecting axes of rotation leads to an exact analytic solution to the inverse kinematic equations. The spherical wrist allows a decomposition of the typical six-degree-of-freedom inverse kinematics into two three-degree-of-freedom computations, one to compute the position of the wrist, the other to compute the orientation of the hand. More recently, Paul (1981), Paul, Stevenson and Renaud (1984), Feather-stone (1983), and Hollerbach and Sahar (1983), have developed efficient techniques for computing the inverse kinematics for spherical wrists. Small changes in the joints of a robot give rise to small changes in the Cartesian position of its end effector. The small changes in the two co-ordinate systems are related by a matrix that is called the Jacobian. Orin and Schrader (1984) have investigated algorithms for computing the Jacobian of the kinematic transformation that are suited to VLSI implementation.

If the number of robot joints is equal to six, there are singularities in the kinematics, that is, a small change in Cartesian configuration corresponds to a large change in joint configuration. The singularities of six-degree-of-freedom industrial robot arms are well catalogued. Singularities can be avoided by increasing the number n of joints, but then there are infinitely many solutions to the inverse kinematics computation. One approach is to use a generalized inverse technique using a positive definite $6 \times n$ matrix to find the solution that minimizes some suitable quantity such as energy or time (Kahn and Roth, 1971; Whitney, 1983). Another approach is to avoid singularities by switching between the redundant degrees of freedom (Fisher, 1984). Finally, if the number of joints is less than six, there are 'holes' in the workspace, regions that the robot cannot reach. Such robots, including the SCARA design, are nevertheless adequate for many specialized tasks such as pick-and-place operations. One important application of kinematics computations is in automatic planning of trajectories (Brady, 1983c).

Most attention has centered on open kinematic chains such as robot arms. An 'open' kinematic chain consists of a single sequence of links. Its analysis is reasonably straightforward. Much less work has been done on closed kinematic chains such as legged robots or multi-fingered hands. Although, in theory, the kinematic chain closes when the robot grasps an object lying on a work surface, it is usually (almost) at rest, and the kinematics of the closed linkage are ignored. More interestingly, Hirose *et al.* (1984) have designed a pantograph mechanism for a quad-ruped robot that significantly reduces potential energy loss in walking. Salisbury and Craig (1982) (see also Salisbury, 1982) have used a number of computational constraints, including mobility and optimization of finger placement, to design a three-fingered hand. The accuracy and dexterity of a robot varies with configuration, so attention needs to be paid to the layout of the workspace. Salisbury and Craig (1982) used the condition number of the Jacobian matrix (using the row norm) to evaluate configurations of the hand. This is important because the accuracy and strength of a robot varies throughout its workspace, and the condition number provides a means of evaluating different points. Yoshikawa

(1984) has introduced a *measure of manipulability* for a similar purpose. Attend to some object in your field of view, and consider the task of moving it to a different position and orientation. The movement can be effected by translating along the line joining the positions while rotating about some axis. The simultaneous translation and rotation of an object is called a screw, and screw co-ordinates have been developed as a tool for the analysis of such motions. Roth (1984) reviews the application to robotics of screw co-ordinates to link kinematics and dynamics.

The dynamic equations of a robot arm (see Hollerbach, 1983) consist of n coupled, second-order, differential equations in the positions, velocities and accelerations of the joint variables. The equations are complex because they involve terms from two adjacent joints, corresponding to reaction and Coriolis torques. One way to visualize the effect of such torques is by moving your arm, for example, opening a door or cutting with a knife. The motion of the forearm relative to the wrist generates a force not only at the elbow but, by the laws of Newtonian mechanics, at the shoulder. The faster you move your forearm, the faster you accelerate it, or the heavier the knife that you use, the larger the resulting torque at the shoulder. Conventional techniques have simplified dynamics by dropping or linearizing terms, or have proposed table look-up techniques. Recently, 'recursive' recurrence formulations of the dynamic equations have been developed that:

(a) compute the kinematics from the shoulder to the hand in time proportional to n;
(b) compute the inverse dynamics from the force and torque exerted on the hand by the world from the hand to the shoulder, again in time proportional to n.

The importance of this result is threefold:

(1) First, it suggests that a more accurate inverse plant model can be developed, leading to faster, more accurate arms. Friction is a major source of the discrepancy between model and real world. Direct-drive technology (Asada, 1982; Asada and Youcef-Toumi, 1984; Asada and Kanade, 1981) reduces the mismatch. In a direct-drive arm, a motor is directly connected to a joint with no intervening transmission elements, such as gears, chains or ball screws. The advantages are that friction and backlash are low, so the direct-drive joint is backdrivable. This means that it can be controlled using torque instead of position. Torque control is important for achieving compliance, and for feedforward dynamics compensation.
(2) Second, the recurrence structure of the equations lends itself to implementation using a pipelined microprocessor architecture, cutting down substantially on the number of wires that are threaded

through the innards of a modern robot. On current robots, a separate wire connects each joint motor to the central controller; individual control signals are sent to each motor. The wires need to thread around the joints, and the result is like a pan of spaghetti.

(3) Third, Hollerbach and Sahar (1983) have shown that their refinement of Featherstone's technique for computing the inverse kinematics makes available many of the terms needed for the recursive Newton–Euler dynamics.

Renaud (1984) has developed a novel iterative Lagrangian scheme that requires about 350 additions and 350 multiplies for a six-revolute joint robot arm. The method has been applied to manipulators having a general tree structure of revolute and prismatic joints. Huston and Kelly (1982) and Kane and Levinson (1983) have recently adapted Kane's formulation of dynamics to robot structures.

7.4.2 Control

Much of control theory has developed for slowly changing, nearly rigid systems. The challenges of robot control are several:

- *Complex dynamics*. The dynamics of open-link kinematic chain robots consist of n coupled second-order partial differential equations, where n is the number of links. They become even more complex for a closed multi-manipulator system such as a multi-fingered robot hand or locomoting robot.
- *Articulated structure*. The links of a robot arm are cascaded and the dynamics and inertias depend on the configuration.
- *Discontinuous change*. The parameters that are to be controlled change discontinuously when, as often happens, the robot picks an object up.
- *Range of motions*. To a first approximation one can identify several different kinds of robot motion: free space or gross motions, between places where work is to be done; approach motions (guarded moves) to a surface; and compliant moves along a constraint surface. Each of these different kinds of motion poses different control problems.

The majority of industrial robot controllers are open-loop. However, many control designs have been investigated in robotics; representative samples are to be found in Brady and Paul (1984), Brady *et al.* (1983), Paul (1981). They include optimal controllers (Dubowsky, 1984; Kahn and Roth, 1971); model reference control (Dubowsky and DesForges, 1979); sliding mode control (Young, 1978); non-linear control (Freund, 1982, 1984); hierarchical control (Salisbury and Craig, 1982); distributed control (Klein and Wahawisan, 1982); hybrid force-position control (Klein, Olson and Pugh, 1983; Raibert and Craig, 1983); and integrated system control (Albus, 1974). Cannon and Schmitz (1984) have investigated the precise control of flexible manipulators.

7.4.3 End effectors

Industrial uses of robots typically involve a multi-purpose robot arm and an end effector that is specialized to a particular application. End effectors normally have a single degree of freedom (Engelberger, 1980), parallel jaw grippers, suction cup, spatula, 'sticky' hand or hook. The algorithms for using such grippers are correspondingly simple. Paul's (1972) (see also Taylor, Summers and Meyer, 1982) centering grasp algorithm is one of the more advanced examples. Many end effectors have no built-in sensors. Those that do typically incorporate devices that give a single bit of information. The most common are contact switches and infra-red beams to determine when the end effector is spanning some object. The IBM 7565 is one of the few commercially available robot arms that incorporates force sensing and provides linguistic support for it.

Many tasks, particularly those related to assembly, require a variety of capabilities, such as parts handling, insertion (Whitney, 1983), screwing, as well as fixtures that vary from task to task. One approach is to use one arm but multiple single-DOF grippers, or multiple arms each with a single DOF, or some combination. One problem with using multiple single-DOF grippers is that a large percentage of the work cycle is spent changing grippers. This has inspired research on the mechanical designs that support fast gripper change. Another problem is that the approach assumes that a process can be divided into a discrete set of single-DOF operations.

Multiple arms raise the problem of co-ordinating their motion while avoiding collision and without cluttering the workspace. The co-ordination of two arms was illustrated at the Stanford Artificial Intelligence Laboratory in 1972 when two arms combined to install a hinge. One of the arms performed the installation, the other acted as a programmable fixture, presenting the hinges and other parts to the work arm. Freund (1984) has presented a control scheme for preventing collisions between a pair of co-operating robots. Whenever there is a possibility of a collision, one of the arms is assigned master status and the other one has to modify its trajectory to avoid the master.

In contrast with such end effectors, a human hand has a remarkable range of functions. The fingers can be considered to be sensor-intensive three- or four-DOF robot arms. The motions of the individual fingers are limited to curl and flex motions in a plane that is determined by the abduction/adduction of the finger about the joint with the palm. The motions of the fingers are co-ordinated by the palm, which can assume a

Fig. 7.1 The three-fingered robot hand developed by Salisbury and Craig (1982). Each finger has 3 degrees of freedom and is pulled by 4 tendons. The hierarchical controller includes 3 finger controllers, each of which consists of 4 controllers, one per tendon. Each controller is of the Proportional-Integral-Derivative type. (Reproduced from Salisbury, 1982.)

broad range of configurations. The dexterity of the human hand has inspired several researchers to build multi-function robot hands.

Okada (1979), described a hand consisting of three fingers evenly spaced about a planar palm. The workspace of the individual fingers was an ellipsoid. The three workspaces intersected in a point. Okada programmed the hand to perform several tasks such as tightening bolts. Hanafusa and Asada (1977, 1979) developed a hand consisting of three evenly-spaced, spring-loaded fingers. The real and apparent spring constants of the fingers were under program control. Stable grasps were defined as the minima of a potential function. The definition of stability in two dimensions was demonstrated by programming the hand to pick up an arbitrary shaped lamina viewed by a TV camera.

Salisbury (1982) (see also Salisbury and Craig, 1982) investigated kinematic and force constraints on the design of a tendon-driven three-fingered hand (see Fig. 7.1). The goal was to design a hand that could impress an arbitrary (vector) force in an arbitrary position of the hand's workspace. Four of the parameters defining the placement of the thumb were determined by solving a series of one-dimensional non-linear

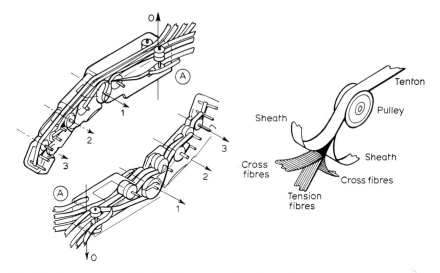

Fig. 7.2 The prototype Utah/MIT dextrous hand developed by Steven Jacobsen, John Wood and John Hollerbach. The 4 figures each have 4 degrees of freedom. (a)The geometry of tendon routing; (b) The material composition of tendons. (Reproduced from Jacobson *et al*. (1984), Figs 2(b) and 7.)

programming problems. A hierarchical controller was designed: PID controllers for each tendon; four such for each finger; and three such for the hand. To date, position and force controllers have been implemented for the individual fingers. A force sensing palm has recently been developed (Salisbury, 1984). It can determine certain attributes of contact geometries. The force sensing fingertips being developed for the hand will permit accurate sensing of contact locations and surface orientations. This information is likely to be useful in object recognition strategies and in improving the sensing and control of contact forces.

The Center for Biomedical Design at the University of Utah and the MIT Artificial Intelligence Laboratory are developing a tendon-operated, multiple-DOF robot hand with multi-channel touch sensing. The hand that is currently being built consists of three four-DOF fingers, a four-DOF thumb, and a three-DOF wrist (total nineteen DOF). Three fingers suffice for static stable grasp. The Utah MIT design incorporated a fourth finger to minimize reliance on friction and to increase flexibility in grasping tasks. The hand features novel tendon material and tendon routine geometry (Fig. 7.2).

7.4.4 Mobile robots

Certain tasks are difficult or impossible to perform in the workspace of a static robot arm (Giralt, 1984). In large-scale assembly industries, such as shipyards or automobile assembly lines, it is common to find parts being transferred along gantries that consist of one or more degrees of linear freedom. Correspondingly, there have been several instances of robot arms being mounted on rails to extend their workspace. The rail physically constrains the motion of the robot. More generally, the robot can be programmed to follow a path by locally sensing it. Magnetic strips, and black strips sensed by infra-red sensing linear arrays, have been used, for example in the Fiat plant in Turin, Italy.

More ambitious projects have used (non-local) vision and range data for autonomous navigation. Space and military applications require considerable autonomy for navigation, planning and perception. Mobile robots are complex systems that incorporate perceptual, navigation and planning subsystems. Shakey (Nilsson, 1969) was one of the earliest mobile robots, and certainly one of the most ambitious system integration efforts of its time. Later work on mobile robots includes Dobrotin and Lewis (1977), Everett (1982), Giralt, Sobek and Chatila (1977), Giralt, Chatila and Vaissett (1984), Harmon (1983a, 1983b), Lewis and Bejczy (1973), Lewis and Johnson (1977) and Moravec (1981, 1983, 1984).

All the robots referred to previously in this section are wheeled. This restricts their movement to (nearly) even terrain. Legged vehicles can potentially escape that limitation. The price to be paid for this advantage

Fig. 7.3 The six-legged robot developed by McGhee, Orin, Klein and their colleagues at the Ohio State University. The robot uses either an alternating tripod of support or wave gait. (Reproduced from Ozgumer, Trai and McGhee, 1984.)

Fig. 7.4 The quadruped robot built by Hirose, Umetani and colleagues at Tokyo Institute of Technology. The robot can walk upstairs, and can move forward in a crab gait. (Reproduced from Hirose *et al.*, 1984.)

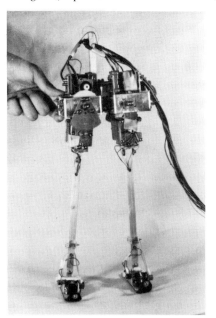

Fig. 7.5 The BIPER–3 walking robot built by Miura and Shimoyama at Tokyo University. See text for details (Reproduced from Miura and Shimoyana, 1984.)

is the extra complexity of maintaining balance and controlling motion. Following the photographic studies of Muybridge and Moayer in the late nineteenth century, a theory of locomotion developed around the concept of *gait*, the pattern of foot placements and foot support duty cycles. The Ohio State University hexapod, for example, has been programmed to use either an alternating tripod of support or 'wave' gait, in which a left–right pair of legs is lifted and advanced (Fig. 7.3) (Ozguner, Tsai and McGhee, 1984). Hirose's *et al.* (1984) quadruped robot (Fig. 7.4) employs a 'crab' gait, in which the direction of motion is at an angle to the direction the quadruped is facing.

Two generic problems in legged locomotion are moving over uneven terrain and achieving dynamic balance without a static pyramid of support.

The simplest walking machines employ a predetermined, fixed gait. Uneven terrain requires dynamic determination of foot placement, implying variable gait, Hirose *et al.*(1984) and Ozguner, Tsai and McGhee, (1984) analyse the constraint of balance, and use sensors in their choice of foot placement.

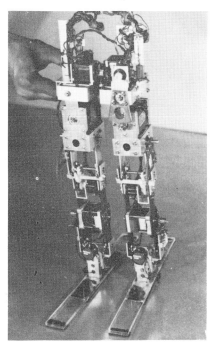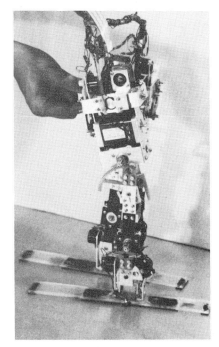

Fig. 7.6 The BIPER–4 walking robot under development at Tokyo University. BIPER–4 has a hip, knee and ankle joints on each leg. (Reproduced from Miura and Shimoyama 1984.)

Miura and Shimoyama (1984), Raibert and Tanner (1982) and Raibert, Brown and Murthy (1984) discuss the dynamic requirements of balance. Miura and Shimoyama report a series of biped walking machines. The first of these, BIPER-3 (Fig. 7.5) has stilt-like legs, with no ankle joint, and resembles a novice nordic skier in its gait. BIPER-3 falls if both feet keep contact with the surface; so it must continue to step if it is to maintain its balance. An ambitious development, BIPER-4, shown in Fig. 7.6, has knee and ankle joints. Stable walking of BIPER-4 has recently been demonstrated. Raibert considers balance for a three-dimensional hopping machine (Fig. 7.7). He suggests that balance can

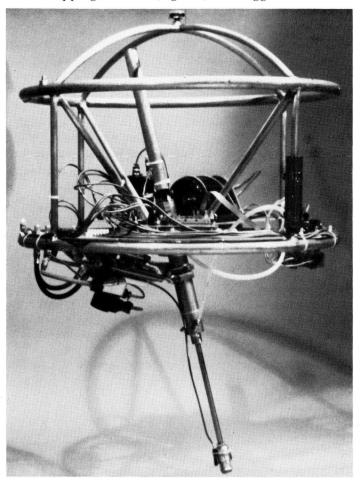

Fig. 7.7 The hopping machine developed by Raibert and his colleagues at Carnegie-Mellon University. (Reproduced from Raibert, Brown and Murthy, 1984.)

be achieved by a planar (two-dimensional) controller plus extra-planar compensation. His work suggests that gait may not be as central to the theory of locomotion as has been supposed. Instead, it may be a side-effect of achieving balance with coupled oscillatory systems. Raibert (1984) has organized a collection of papers on legged robots that is representative of the state of the art.

7.5 REASONING ABOUT OBJECTS AND SPACE

7.5.1 Task-level robot programming languages

Earlier, we listed some of the software features of modern, commercially available robot systems: they perform trajectory calculation and kinematic translation, interpret sense data, execute adaptive control through conditional execution and real-time monitors, interface to databases of geometric models and support program development. Despite these features, robot programming is tedious, mostly because in currently available programming languages the position and orientation of objects, and subobjects of objects, have to be specified exactly in painful detail. 'Procedures' in current robot programming languages can rarely even be parametrized, due to physical assumptions made in the procedure design. Lozano-Pérez (1983b, 1983c) calls such programming languages *robot-level*.

Lozano-Pérez (1983b, p. 839) suggests that 'existing and proposed robot programming systems fall into three broad categories: *guiding* systems in which the user leads a robot through the motions to be performed, *robot-level* programming systems in which the user writes a computer program specifying motion and sensing, and *task-level* programming systems in which the user specifies operations by their desired effect on objects.' Languages such as VAL II (Shimano, Geschke and Spaulding, 1984) and AML (Taylor, Summers and Meyer, 1982) are considered robot-level.

One of the earliest task-level robot programming language designs was AUTOPASS (Lieberman and Wesley, 1977). The (unfinished) implementation focussed upon planning collision-free paths among polyhedral objects. The emphasis of RAPT (Ambler and Popplestone, 1975; Popplestone, Ambler and Bellos, 1980) has been on the specification of geometric goals and relational descriptions of objects. The implementation of RAPT is based upon equation solving and constraint propagation. Other approximations to task-level languages include PADL Requicha, 1980), IBMsolid (Wesley *et al.*, 1980), and LAMA (Lozano-Pérez, 1976). Lozano-Pérez (1983c) discusses spatial reasoning and presents an example of the use of RAPT.

In the next section we discuss Brooks' work on uncertainty, several approaches to reasoning about space and avoiding obstacles, and synthesizing compliant programs.

7.5.2 Dealing with uncertainty

Consider the problem illustrated in Fig. 7.8. A robot has been programmed to put a screw in a hole. Will the program succeed? Each of the joint measurements of the robot is subject to small errors, which produce errors in the position and orientation of the finger tips according to the Jacobian of the kinematics function. The position and orientation of the screwdriver in the fingers is subject to slight error, as is the screw, box, and the lid on the box. These errors, we will call them the *base errors*, are independent of the particular task to be performed. They add up. Taylor (1976) assumed particular numerical bounds for the values of

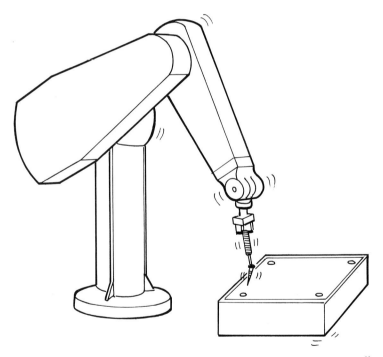

Fig. 7.8 Will the screw make it into the hole? The joint measurements are all subject to small errors, as are the placement of the box, the lid on the box, the orientation of the screwdriver in the hand and the orientation of the screw on the end of the screwdriver. When all these errors are combined, it can be quite difficult to guarantee that a task will always be carried out successfully.

the base errors, and used linear programming to bound the error in the placement of the screw relative to the hole.

Brooks (1982) worked with explicit symbolic (trigonometric) expressions that define the error in the placement of the screw relative to the hole. He applied the expression-bounding program developed for the ACRONYM project (Brooks, 1981) to the base-error bounds used by Taylor to deduce bounds for the errors in the placement of the screw relative to the hole. The bounds he obtained were not as tight as those obtained by Taylor, but were nearly so.

Brooks' approach had a substantial advantage over Taylor, however, and it is paradigmatic of the AI approach. The expression-bounding program can be applied with equal facility to the symbolic expression for the error and the desired size of the screw hole (the specifications of the insertion task). The result is a bound on the only free variable of the problem, the length of the screwdriver. The lesson is that it is possible to apply AI techniques to reason in the face of uncertainty. In further work, Brooks (1982) has shown how sensing might be modelled using uncertainties to automatically determine when to splice a sensing step into a plan to cause it to succeed.

7.5.3 Reasoning about space and avoiding objects

Robot-level programming languages require the programmer to state, for example, that the robot is to move the block B, whose configuration (position and orientation) R_S is to be moved to the configuration R_G. To ensure the robot does not crash into obstacles, the usual practice in robot-level languages is to specify a sufficient number of via points (Fig. 7.9) (see Brady, 1983c). In a task-oriented language, one merely says something like 'put B in the vice'. It follows that a crucial component of implementing a task-oriented programming language is automatically determining safe paths between configurations in the presence of obstacles. This turns out to be an extremely hard problem.

Lozano-Pérez (1983a) introduced a representation called *C-space* that consists of the safe configurations of a moving object. For a single object moving with six degrees of freedom (e.g. three translational and three rotational degrees of freedom), the dimensionality of the C-space is six. If there are m such objects, each of which can move, the dimensionality of C-space is $6m$. For example, for the co-ordinated motion of two three-dimensional objects, C-space is twelve-dimensional. In practice one can deal with 'slices', projections onto lower-dimensional subspaces.

Donald (1984) notes that there are two components of spatial planning systems. First, it is necessary to represent the problem, in particular, the obstacles. Second, it is necessary to devise an algorithm that can search

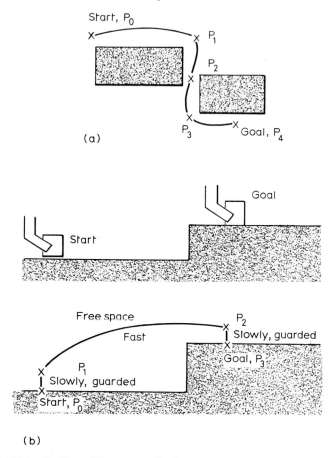

Fig. 7.9 (a) Point P_1, P_2 and P_3 are specified as via points to coax the robot through the narrow gap separating the two obstacles shown. (b) Via points can also be used to simplify trajectory planning. The two via points above the start and goal of the move assure that the robot hand will not attempt to penetrate the table as it picks up and sets down the object (Reproduced from Brady, 1983.)

for paths over the representation. Most work on spatial reasoning has used representations that approximate the exact polyhedral obstacles. Such representations may: (1) restrict the degrees of freedom in a problem; (2) bound objects in real space by simple objects such as spheres, or prisms with parallel axes, while considering some subset of the available degrees of freedom; (3) quantize configuration space at certain orientations; or (4) approximate swept volumes for objects over a range of orientations. Systems that use such representations may not be capable of finding solutions in some cases, even if they use a complete search procedure. An approximation of the obstacle environment, robot model or C-space obstacles can result in a transformed find-path problem which has no solution.

Lozano-Pérez (1981, 1983a) implemented an approximate algorithm for Cartesian manipulators (for which free space and C-space are the same) that tesselated free space into rectangloids, subdividing it as far as necessary to solve a given problem. The search algorithm is complete for translations, and illustrates the feasibility of the C-space approach. It works by alternately keeping the heading of an object fixed and rotating

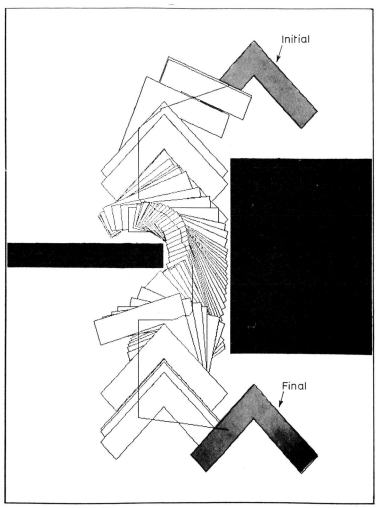

Fig. 7.10 A path found by the Brooks and Lozano-Pérez program. (Reproduced from Brooks and Lozano-Pérez 1983, Fig. 11(a).)

in place to alter the heading. Recently, Brooks and Lozano-Pérez (1983) reported an algorithm capable of moving a reorientable polygon through two-dimensional space littered with polygons. This algorithm can find any path of interest for the two-dimensional problem. Figure 7.10 shows an example path found by Brooks and Lozano-Pérez's program. Their attempts to extend the method to three dimensions 'were frustrated by the increased complexity for three-dimensional rotations relative to that of rotations in two dimensions' (Brooks, (1983b, p. 7).

Brooks (1983) suggested that free space be represented by overlapping generalized cones that correspond to *freeways* or *channels*. Figure 7.11 shows some of the generalized cones generated by two obstacles and the boundary of the workspace. The key point about the representation was that the left and right radius functions defining a freeway could be inverted easily. Given a freeway, and the radius function of a moving convex object, he was able to determine the legal range of orientations that ensure no collisions as the object is swept down the freeway. Brooks' algorithm is highly efficient, and works well in relatively unclut-tered space, but it occasionally fails to find a safe path when it is necessary to manouvre in tight spaces. Recently, Donald (1983) has proposed a novel channel-based technique.

Finally, Brooks (1983) has developed an algorithm that combines the

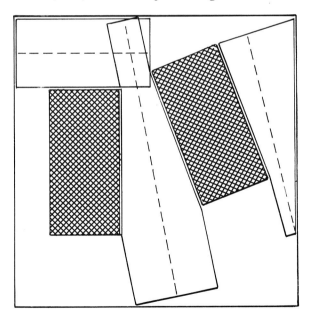

Fig. 7.11 A few of the generalized cones generated by two obstacles and the boundary of the workspace. (Reproduced from Brooks, 1983.)

C-space and freeway approaches to find paths for pick-and-place and insertion tasks for a PUMA. (The PUMA is a robot developed and marketed by Unimation Corporation from an original design by V. Scheinmann of the Stanford Artificial Intelligence Laboratory. It is popularly found in AI robotics laboratories.) Pick-and-place tasks are defined as four-degree-of-freedom tasks in which the only reorientations permit-

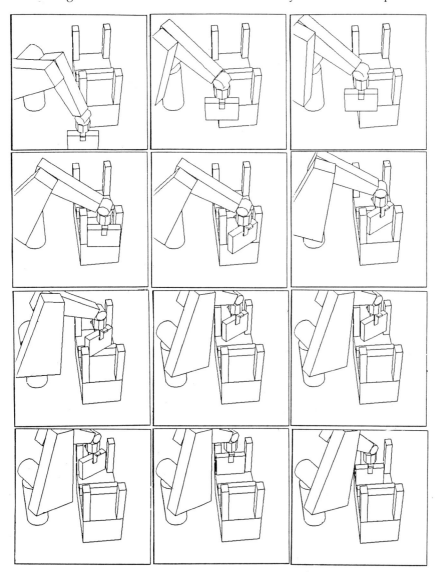

Fig. 7.12 An example of path finding for a PUMA by Brook's (1983) algorithm.

ted are about the vertical, and in which the found path is composed of horizontal and vertical straight lines. Figure 7.12 shows an example path found by Brooks' algorithm.

Brooks freezes joint 4 of the PUMA. The algorithm subdivides free space to find: (i) freeways for the hand and payload assembly; (ii) freeways for the upper arm subassembly (joints 1 and 2 of the PUMA); (iii) searches for the payload and upper arm freeways concurrently under the projection of constraints determined by the forearm. The subdivision of free space in this way is the most notable feature of Brooks' approach. It stands in elegant relation to the algorithms for computing inverse kinematics referred to earlier. It is assumed that the payload is convex, and that the obstacles are convex stalagmites and stalactites. It is further assumed that stalactites are in the workspace of the upper arm of the PUMA, not of the payload.

By restricting attention to a limited class of tasks, Brooks has designed an efficient algorithm that will not work in all cases. The advantage is that he does not have to contend with worst-case situations that lead to horrendous polynomial complexity estimates. For example, Schwartz and Sharir (1983) suggest a method whose complexity for r DOF is n^{2r}. For example, for two moving objects, the complexity is n^{4096}. Their algorithm is not implemented. Donald (1984) presents the first implemented, representation-complete, search-complete algorithm (at a given resolution) for the classical Movers' problem for Cartesian manipulators.

There has been a great deal of theoretical interest in the findpath problem by researchers in computational complexity and computational geometry. Schwartz and Sharir (1983), and Hopcroft, Schwartz and Sharir (1983) are representative.

7.5.4 Synthesizing compliant programs

Compliance is the opposite of stiffness. Any device, such as an automobile shock absorber, that responds flexibly to external force, is called compliant. Increasingly, compliance refers to operations that require simultaneous force and position control (Mason, 1983b). Consider programming a robot to write on a blackboard or on a softdrink can. One difficult problem is that the position of the end effector has to be controlled in arm co-ordinates which bear no relation to those of the task. But there is a greater problem to be solved. If one presses too hard, the surface and/or writing implement can be damaged. If not hard enough, the writing implement may leave the surface. The problem is that ideal planes and cylindrical surfaces only occur in mathematical texts. It is necessary to control the force exerted by the writing implement on the surface. Mathematically, the problem is overdetermined!

Easing up or pushing down on the pen may cause the tip position to vary too much, detracting from the quality of the writing.

An analysis of the forces that arise in inserting a peg into a hole led to the development of a spring-loaded device that can perform the insertion for tight tolerances at blinding speed. The device is called the Remote Centre Compliance (RCC) (Whitney, 1983). The RCC was an important early example of the use of force trajectories to achieve compliant assembly. Another example is scribing a straight line on an undulating surface. In that case, it is necessary to control position in the tangent plane of the surface, and maintain contact with the surface by applying an appropriate scribing force normal to the surface. Other examples of compliance include cutting, screw insertion, and bayonet-style fixtures, such as camera mountings. Clocksin *et al.* (1982) describe a seam-welding robot that uses the difference-of-Gaussians edge operator proposed by Marr and Hildreth (1980) to determine the welding trajectory. Ohwovoriole and Roth (1981) show how the motions possible at an assembly step can be partitioned into three classes: those that tend to separate the bodies to be mated; those that tend to make one body penetrate the other; and those that move the body and maintain the original constraints. Theoretically, this provides a basis for choosing the next step in an assembly sequence.

Trevelyan, Kovesi and Ong (1984) describe a sheep-shearing robot. Figure 7.13 shows the geometry of the robot and the 'workpiece'. Trevelyan, Kovesi and Ong (1984) note that 'over two hundred sheep have been shorn by the machine (though not completely) yet only a few cuts have occurred. This extremly low injury rate* results from the use of sensors mounted on the shearing cutter which allow the computer controlling the robot to keep the cutter moving just above the sheep's skin. Trajectories are planned from a geometric model of a sheep using Bernstein–Bézier parametric curves. The trajectory is modified to comply with sense data. Two capacitance sensors are mounted under the cutter just behind the comb. These sensors can detect the distance between the cutter and the sheep's skin to a range of approximately 30 mm. Compliance is needed to take account of inaccuracies in the geometric model of the sheep and the change in shape of the sheep as it breathes.

Robots evolved for positional accuracy, and are designed to be mechanically stiff. High-tolerance assembly tasks typically involve clearances of the order of a thousandth of an inch. In view of inaccurate modelling of the world and limitations on joint accuracy, low stiffnesses are

---

* Trevelyan informs the author that a human sheep shearer typically cuts a sheep over 30 times, and that serious cuts occur regularly.

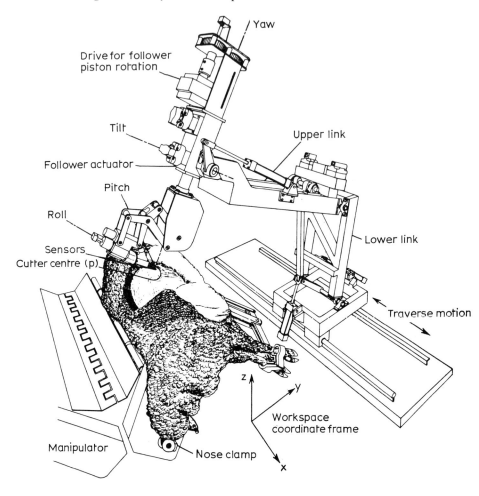

Fig. 7.13 The sheep-shearing robot developed by Trelyan and his colleagues at the University of Western Australia. A sheep naturally lies quite still while it is being sheared; indeed it often falls asleep. (Reproduced from Trevelyan, Kovesi and Ong 1984.)

required to effect assemblies. Devices such as the Remote Centre Compliance (RCC) (Whitney, 1983) and the Hi-T hand (Goto, Takeyasu and Imoyama, 1980) exploit the inherent mechanical compliance of springs to accomplish tasks. Such *passive-compliant* devices are fast, but the specific application is built into the mechanical design. The challenge is that different tasks impose different stiffness requirements. In *active-compliance*, a computer program modifies the trajectory of the arm on the basis of sensed forces (and other modalities) (Paul and Shimano, 1976). Active compliance is a general purpose technique; but is typically slow compared to passive compliance.

Mason (1983a) suggested that the (fixed number of) available degrees of freedom of a task could be divided into two subsets, spanning orthogonal subspaces. The subspaces correspond one–one with the *natural constraints* determined by the physics of the task, and the *artificial constraints* determined by the particular task. See Mason (1983b) for details and examples. For example, in screwdriving, a screwdriver cannot penetrate the screw, giving a natural constraint; successful screwdriving requires that the screwdriver blade be kept in the screw slot, an artificial constraint. Raibert and Craig (1983) refined and implemented Mason's model as a hybrid force-position controller. Raibert and Craig's work embodies the extremes of stiffness control in that the programmer chooses which axes should be controlled with infinite stiffness (using position control with an integral term) and which should be controlled with zero stiffness (to which a bias force is added). Salisbury (1980) suggests an intermediate ground that he calls 'active stiffness control'.

Programmers find it relatively easy to specify motions in positon space; but find it hard to specify the force-based trajectories needed for compliance. This has motivated the investigation of automatic generation of compliant fine-motion programs (Dufay and Latombe, 1984; Lozano-Pérez, Mason and Taylor, 1984). In Dufay and Latombe's approach, the geometry of the task is defined by a semantic network, the initial and goal configurations of parts are defined by symbolic expressions, and the knowledge of the program is expressed as production rules. Productions encode the 'lore' of assembly: how to overcome problems such as moving off the chamfer during an insertion task. Dufay and Latombe's program inductively generates assembly programs from successful execution sequences. The method requires that the relationships between surfaces of parts in contact be known fairly precisely. In general, this is difficult to achieve because of errors in sensors.

Lozano-Pérez, Mason and Taylor (1984) have proposed a scheme for automatically synthesizing compliant motions from geometric descriptions of a task. The approach combines Mason's ideas about compliance, Lozano-Pérez's C-space, and Taylor's (1976) proposal for programming robots by fleshing out skeletons forming a library of operations. The approach, currently being implemented deals head-on with errors in assumed position and heading. Lozano-Pérez, Mason and Taylor use a generalized damper model to determine all the possible configurations that can result from a motion. It is necessary to avoid being jammed in the friction of any of the surfaces *en route* to the goal surface. This sets up a constraint for each surface. Intersecting the constraints leaves a range of possible (sequences of) compliant moves that are guaranteed to achieve the goal, notwithstanding errors.

Programming by fleshing out skeletons is reminiscent of the *programmer's apprentice* (Rich and Waters, 1981). The similarities are that the computer adopts the role of junior partner or critic, programming is based on *cliches*, and design decisions and logical dependencies are explicitly represented so that the effects of modifications to a program can be automatically propagated through the program. The difference is that a *robot* programmer's apprentice works with rich geometric models. Lozano-Pérez has suggested that guiding can be extended to teach a robot plans that involve sensing, a large number of similar movements (for example, unloading a palette), and asynchronous control of multiple manipulators. The requirement that a system deal with rich geometric models also distinguishes the robot programmer's apprentice from earlier work in AI planning (Sacerdoti, 1975).

7.6   PERCEPTION

7.6.1   **Introduction**

The perceptual abilities of commercially available robots are severely limited, especially when compared with laboratory systems. It is convenient to distinguish contact and non-contact sensing. Contact, or local, sensing includes tactile, proximity and force sensing. Non-contact sensing includes passive sensing in both visual and non-visual spectral bands, and active sensing using infra-red, sonar, ultrasound, and millimeter radar.

Robot perception is only a special case of *computer* perception in the sense that there are occasional opportunities for engineering solutions to what are, in general, difficult problems. Examples include: arranging the lighting, controlling positional uncertainty, finessing some of the issues in depth computation, and limiting the visual context of an object. Appropriate lighting can avoid shadows, light striping, and laser range finding can produce partial depth maps, and techniques such as photometric stereo (Woodham, 1981) can exploit control over lighting. On the other hand, edge finding is no less difficult in industrial images, texture is just as hard, and the bin of parts is a tough nut for stereo. Motion tracking on a dirty conveyor belt is as hard as any other tracking problem. Representing the shape of complex geometric parts is as difficult as any representational problem in computer vision (Bolles, Horaud and Hannah, 1984; Brady and Asada, 1983; Faugeras and

Hébert, 1983; Faugeras, Hébert and Ponce, 1984). Existing commercial robot-vision systems carry out simple inspection and parts acquisition. There are, however, many inspection, acquisition and handling tasks, routinely performed by humans, that exceed the abilities of current computer vision and tactile sensing research.

The quality of sensors is increasing rapidly, especially as designs incorporate VLSI. The interpretation of sensory data, especially vision, has significantly improved over the past decade. Sensory data interpretation is computer intensive, requiring billions of cycles. However, much of the computer intensive early processing naturally calls for local parallel processing, and is well suited to implementation on special purpose VLSI hardware (Brady, 1983a; Raibert and Tanner, 1982).

7.6.2 Contact sensing

Contact sensing is preferred when a robot is about to be, or is, in contact with some object or surface. In such cases, objects are often occluded, even when a non-contact sensor is mounted on a hand. An exception to this is seam welding (Clocksin *et al.*, 1982). The main motivation for force sensing is not, however, to overcome occlusion, but to achieve compliant assembly. Force sensors have improved considerably over the past two or three years. Typical sensitivities range from a half ounce to ten pounds. Most work on force trajectories has been application specific (e.g. peg-in-hole insertion). Current research, aimed at developing general techniques for interpreting force data and synthesizing compliant programs, was discussed in the previous section. Kanade and Sommer (1984) and Okada (1982) report proximity sensors.

Touch sensing is currently the subject of intensive research. Manufacturing engineers consider tactile sensing to be of vital importance in automating assembly (Harmon, 1982, 1984). Unfortunately, current tactile sensors leave much to be desired. They are prone to wear and tear, have poor hysteresis, and low dynamic range. Industrially available tactile sensors typically have a spatial resolution of only about eight points per inch. Tactile sensors are as poor as TV cameras were in the 1960s, the analogy being that they are seriously hampering the development of tactile interpretation algorithms.

Several laboratory demonstrations point the way to future sensors. Hillis (1982) devised a tactile sensor consisting of an anisotropic silicon conducting material whose lines of conduction were orthogonal to the wires of a printed circuit board and which were separated by a thin spacer. Figure 7.14 shows some example touch images generated by Hillis' tactile sensor for four small fasteners. The sensor had a spatial resolution of 256 points per square *centimetre*. Raibert and Tanner (1982)

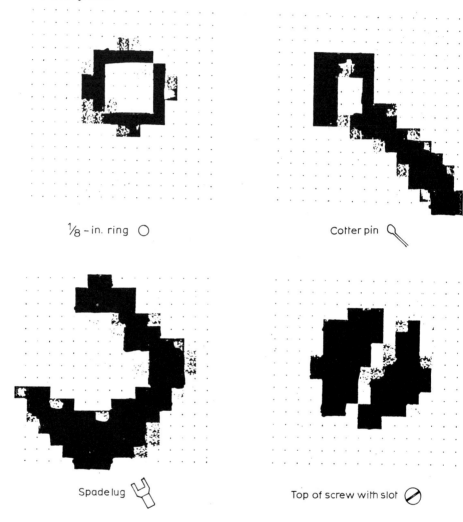

Fig. 7.14 Sample tactile images from the Hillis sensor. (Reproduced from Hillis, 1984)

developed a VLSI tactile sensor that incorporated edge detection processing on the chip (Fig. 7.15). This (potentially) significantly reduces
the bandwidth of communication between the sensor and the host
computer. Recently, Hackwood and Beni (1983) have developed a tactile
sensor using magneto-restrictive materials that appear to be able to
compute shear forces.

Little progress has been made in the development of tactile object

Physical layout

Pressure sensitive
elastic material

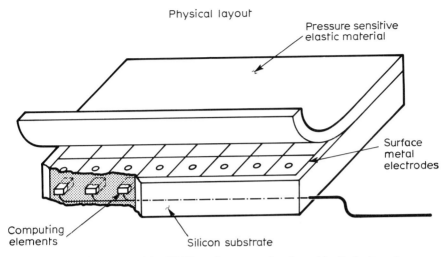

Surface
metal
electrodes

Computing
elements

Silicon substrate

Fig. 7.15 Architecture of the VLSI tactile sensor developed by Raibett and Tanner. A layer of pressure-sensitive rubber in contact with a VLSI wafer. Metalization on the surface of the wafer forms large sensing electrodes that make contact with the pressure-sensitive rubber through holes in a protective layer of SiO_2, the overglass. (Reproduced from Raibert and Tanner 1982.)

recognition algorithms. Hillis built a simple pattern-recognition program that could recognize a variety of fasteners. Gaston and Lozano-Pérez (1983) have built a program that constructs an interpretation tree for a class of two-dimensional objects. The program assumes that there are n discrete sensors, at each of which the position and an approximate measure of the surface orientation is known. They show how two constraints, a distance constraint and a constraint on the normal directions at successive touch points, can substantially cut down the number of possible grasped object configurations. Grimson and Lozano-Pérez (1984) have extended the analysis to three dimensions. Faugeras and Hébert (1983) have developed a similar three-dimensional recognition and positioning algorithm using geometric matching between primitive surfaces. Bajcsy (1984) has investigated the use of two tactile sensors to determine the hardness and texture of surfaces.

7.6.3 Non-contact sensing

Non-contact sensing is important for a variety of applications in manufacturing. These include:

(1) *Inspection*. Most current industrial inspection uses binary two-dimensional images. Only recently have grey level systems become

commercially available. No commercial system currently offers a modern edge detection system. Two-dimensional inspection is appropriate for stamped or rotationally symmetric parts. Some experimental prototypes (Faugeras and Hébert, 1983; Porter and Mundy, 1982) inspect surfaces such as engine mountings and airfoil blades.

(2) *Parts acquisition*. Parts may be acquired from conveyor belts, from palettes or from bins. Non-contact sensing means that the position of parts may not be accurately specified. Parts may have to be sorted if there is a possibility of more than one type being present.

(3) *Determining grasp points*. Geometric analysis of shape allows grasp points to be determined (Boissonat, 1982; Brady, 1982).

Active sensing has been developed mainly for military applications. Image understanding is difficult and requires a great deal of computer power. Forward-looking infra-red (FLIR), synthetic aperture radar (SAR), and millimeter radar imagery offer limited, computationally expedient, solutions to difficult vision problems. For example, FLIR shows hot objects (for example, a tank) as bright, simplifying the difficult segmentation of a camouflaged tank against trees. The algorithms that have been developed for isolating and identifying targets in natural scenes are restricted in scope. They do not generalize easily to manufacturing settings, where, for example, most objects are 'hot'.

Vision has the most highly developed theory, and the best sensors. Now one can get high-quality solid-state cameras. The rapid increase in the quality of solid-state cameras has been accompanied by the rapid development of image-understanding techniques.

Early vision processes include edge and region finding, texture analysis and motion computation. All these operations are well suited to local parallel processing. Developments in edge finding include the work of Marr and Hildreth (1980), Haralick, Watson and Laffey (1983) and Canny (1983). Developments in grouping include the work of Lowe and Binford (1982). Hildreth (1983) has developed a system for computing directional selectivity of motion using the Marr–Hildreth edge finder. Horn and Schunck (1982) and Schunck (1983) have shown how to compute the optic flow field from brightness patterns. (Bruss and Horn (1981) have developed an analysis of how the flow field can be used in passive navigation.) Brady (1983b, 1983c) and Brady and Asada (1983) have developed a new technique for representing two-dimensional shape, and have applied it to inspection.

The major breakthrough in vision over the past decade has been the development of three-dimensional vision systems. These are usually referred to as 'shape from' processes. Examples include: shape from stereo (Baker and Binford, 1981; Binford, 1984; Grimson, 1981; Nishihara and Poggio, 1984), shape from shading (Ikeuchi and Horn, 1981), shape from contour (Brady and Yuille, 1983; Witkin, 1981) and shape from structured light (Bolles, Horaud and Hannah, 1984; Clocksin *et al.*, 1982; Faugeras and Hebert, 1983; Porter and Mundy, 1982; Tsuji and Asada, 1984).

Most of these 'shape from' processes produce partial depth maps. Recently, fast techniques for interpolating full depth maps have been developed (Terzopoulos, 1983, 1984). A current area of intense investigation is the representation of surfaces (Brady and Yuille, 1984; Faugeras, Hébert and Ponce, 1984; Ikeuchi and Horn, 1981; Shirai *et al.*, 1984). Finally, recent work by Brooks (1981) discusses object representation and the interaction between knowledge-guided and data-driven processing.

7.7   REASONING THAT CONNECTS PERCEPTION TO ACTION

This final section is speculative. It presents three examples of reasoning and problem solving that we are striving to make robots capable of. The aim is to illustrate the kinds of things we would like a robot to know, and the way in which that knowledge might be used. The knowledge that is involved concerns geometry, forces, process, space and shape. The examples involve tools. They concern the interplay between the use or recognition of a tool and constraints on the use of tools. Reasoning between structure and function is particularly direct in the case of tools. Shape variations, though large (there are tens of kinds of hammer), are lessened by the fact that tools are rarely fussily adorned, since such adornments would get in the way of using the tool.

7.7.1   **What is that tool for?**

What is the tool illustrated in Fig. 7.16, and how is it to be used? We (reasonably) suppose that a vision program (Brady, 1984; Brady and Asada, 1983) computes a description of the object that, based on the smoothed local symmetry axis, partially matches a *crank*. The model for a crank indicates that it is used by fixing the end P onto some object O, and rotating the object O about the symmetry axis at P by grasping the crank at the other end Q and rotating in a circle whose radius is the length of the horizontal arm of the crank. Further investigation of the crank model tells us that it is used for increasing the moment arm and hence the torque applied to the object O. We surmise that the tool is to be used for increasing torque on an object O. We have now decided (almost) how the tool is to be used, and we have a hypothesis about its purpose. The hypothesis is wrong.

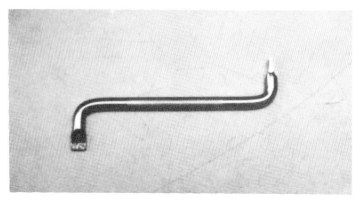

Fig. 7.16 What is this tool, and what is it for?

The one thing that we do not yet know about how to use the tool is how to fix it at *P* to the object at *O*. There are many possibilities, the default being perhaps a socket connector for a nut (as, for example, on a tyre lever). Closer inspection of the description computed by our vision program shows that the ends of the crank are screwdriver blades, set orthogonal to each other. Only screwdrivers (in our experience) have such blades. Apart from the blade, the tool bears some resemblance to a standard screwdriver, which also has a handle and a shaft. In the standard screwdriver, however, the axes of the shaft and handle are collinear. Evidently, the tool is a special-purpose screwdriver, since only screwdrivers have such blades.

Tools have the shape that they do in order to solve some problem that is difficult or impossible to solve with more generally useful forms. So why the crank shape? What problem is being solved that could not be solved with a more conventional screwdriver? Here are some screwdriver-specific instances of general problems that arise using tools:

- *Parts interface bug.* A part does not match the part to which it is being applied or fastened. For example, a wrench might be too small to span a nut; a sledgehammer is inappropriate for driving a tack. The screwdriver head may not match the screw (one might be Philips type). There is no evidence for this bug in Fig. 7.16 because the fastener is not shown.
- *Restricted rotary motion bug.* A tool that is operated by turning it about some axis has encountered an obstruction that prevents it turning further. This bug occurs frequently in using wrenches. A socket wrench solves it by engaging a gear to turn the wrench in one direction, disengaging the gear to rotate in the other. How is it solved more generally? There is an analogous *restricted linear-motion bug*, in

which a required linear motion cannot be performed because of an obstruction. Think of an everyday example involving tools (one is given at the end of the section).

- *Restricted-access bug*. As anyone owning a particular (expensive) kind of British car knows only too well, often the hardest part of using a tool is mating it to the corresponding part. Many tools have an axis along, or about, which they are applied. The most common version of the restricted-access bug is when the axis is too long to fit into the available space. In the case of screwdriving, this occurs when the screwdriver is restricted vertically above the screw. A short, stubby screwdriver is the usual solution to this problem.

Can the crank screwdriver also overcome restricted-access bugs? Of course. The geometric form of the crank screwdriver is necessary to solve this restricted-workspace problem, rather than being a torque

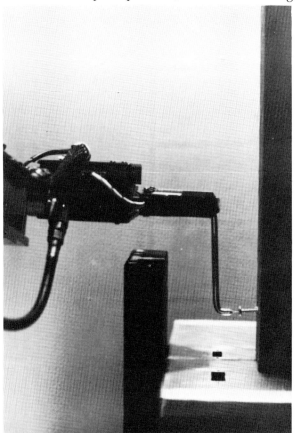

Fig. 7.17 An offset screwdriver overcomes the restricted access bug.

magnifier as initially hypothesized. In fact, the tool is called an *offset screwdriver*. Figure 7.17 illustrates its use.

Since I first presented this example, another solution to the restricted-access bug has been brought to my attention. Figure 7.18 shows a screwdriver whose shaft can bend about any axis orthogonal to it.

Why are the blades of an offset screwdriver set orthogonal to one another? Put differently, what bug do they help overcome? What would you need to know in order to figure it out?

No program is currently capable of the reasoning sketched above. Pieces of the required technology are available, admittedly in preliminary form, and there is cause for optimism that they could be made to work together appropriately. First, vision programs exist that can almost generate the necessary shape descriptions and model matching (Brady, 1984; Brady and Asada, 1983). There is considerable interplay between form and function in the reasoning, and this has been initially explored by Winston, Binford, and their colleagues, combining the ACRONYM system of shape description and Winston's analogy program (Winston *et al.*, 1984). To figure out that the crucial thing about the form is its ability to overcome a restriction in the workspace, it is necessary to be able to reason about space and the swept volumes of objects. This is the contribution of Lozano-Pérez (1981, 1983a, 1983b, 1983c), Brooks (1983b) and Lozano-Pérez, Mason and Taylor (1984). Forbus (1984) is develop-

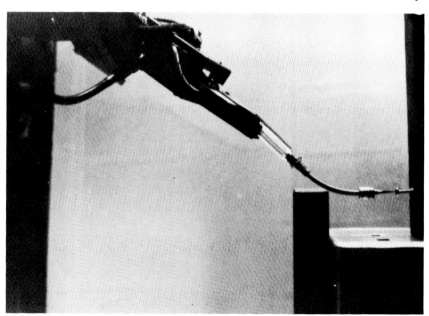

Fig. 7.18 A flexible screwdriver for solving restricted access bugs.

ing a theory of processes, a system that can reason about physical processes like water flow, heat and springs. This builds upon earlier work by De Kleer (1975) and Bundy *et al.* (1979). Notice that a system that is capable of the reasoning sketched above might be able to invent new tools, such as the flexible screwdriver. What is the difficult problem of realizing the flexible screwdriver design?

Answer to the problem: An example of a *restricted linear-motion bug*: Trying to strike a nail with a hammer when there is insufficient space to swing the hammer.

7.7.2 Why are wrenches asymmetric?

Figure 7.19(a) shows a standard (open-jawed) wrench. Why is it asymmetric? To understand this question, it is necessary to understand *how* it would most likely be judged asymmetric. This involves finding the head and handle (Brady and Asada, 1983), assigning a 'natural' co-ordinate frame to each (Brady, 1982, 1984), and realizing that they do not line up. Since the handle is significantly longer than the head, it establishes a frame for the whole shape, so it is the head that is judged asymmetric about the handle frame.

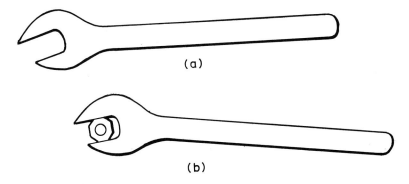

Fig. 7.19 (a) An asymmetric wrench. (b) How to use a wrench.

Now that we at least understand the question, can we answer it? We are encouraged to relate a question of form to one of function. What is a wrench for, and how is it used? It is used as shown in Fig. 7.19(b): the head is placed against a nut; the handle is grasped and moved normal to its length; if the diameter of the nut and the opening of the jaws of the wrench match, the nut (assumed fixed) will cause the handle to rotate about the nut. Nowhere is mention made of asymmetry. Surely, a symmetric wrench would be easier to manufacture. Surely, a symmetric wrench would be equally good at turning nuts. Or would it?

Recall that questions of form often relate not just to function, but to solving some problem that a 'standard', here symmetric, wrench could not solve. The main problem that arises using a wrench is the restricted rotary-motion bug. In many tasks there is an interval $[\phi_1, \phi_2]$ (measured from the local co-ordinate frame corresponding to the axis of the handle) through which the wrench can be rotated. The crucial observation is that a wrench is (effectively) a lamina. As such, it has a degree of freedom corresponding to flipping it over. Exploiting this degree of freedom makes *no difference* to the effective workspace of a symmetric wrench. It *doubles* the workspace of an asymmetric wrench, giving $[-\phi_2, -\phi_1] \cup [\phi_1, \phi_1]$. In this way, an asymmetric wrench partially solves the restriction rotary-motion bug. Perhaps this suggests how to *design* the head of a wrench, say by minimizing $[-\phi_1, \phi_1]$ subject to keeping the jaws parallel to each other. Perhaps it also suggests (for example, to Winston's (1980) analogy program) that other turning tools should be asymmetric, for analogous reasons. There are many examples, of course, including the offset screwdriver discussed in the previous section.

7.7.3 How to disconnect a battery

The final example in this section concerns a familiar AI technique: debugging 'almost-right' plans. A battery is to be disconnected. The geometry of the terminal is shown in Fig. 7.20(a). A plan, devised previously, uses two socket wrenches, one acting as a means of fixing the (variable) position of the nut, the other to turn the bolt. The socket wrenches are applied along their axes, which coincide with the axes of the nut and bolt.

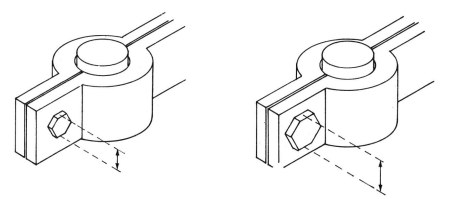

Fig. 7.20 (a) The geometry of a battery terminal. (b) Side View of the late model bolt.

A new model of the battery-laden device is delivered. The plan will no longer work because of two problems. First, there is an obstacle to the left of the head of the nut, restricting travel of the socket wrench along its axis. Using something akin to dependency-directed reasoning, truth maintenance or a similar technique for recording the causal connections in a chain of reasoning, we seek a method for adapting our almost-right plan to the new circumstance. There are a variety of techniques, one of which was illustrated in the offset screwdriver. That suggests bending a tool so that torque can be applied by pushing on a lever. In fact, socket wrenches have this feature built-in, so the first problem was easy to fix.

Unfortunately, the second problem is more difficult. The new model has a bolt that has a head which does not leave sufficient clearance for a socket wrench to fit around its head (Fig. 7.20(b)). We further reconsider the plan, adding the new constraints, removing those parts that were dependent upon being able to use the socket wrench (none, in this case). The next idea is to use a different kind of wrench, but this will not work either, again because of the insufficient clearance. The essence of the plan is to grasp either the nut or the bolt securely, and to turn the other. For example, we might secure the bolt and turn the nut. Several ways are available. The most familiar is to secure the bolt by grasping it with a needlenose plier. Different tools are required, but the functionality is equivalent at the level at which the plan is specified. Brady *et al.* (1984) and Connell and Brady (1985) report progress on a program to handle the problems described in this section.

7.8 CONCLUSIONS

Since robotics is the connection of perception to action, AI must have a central role in robotics if the connection is to be intelligent. We have illustrated current interactions between AI and robotics and presented examples of the kinds of things we believe it is important for robots to know. We have discussed what robots should know, how that knowledge should be represented, and how it should be used. Robotics challenges AI by forcing it to deal with real objects in the real world. An important part of the challenge is dealing with rich geometric models.

ACKNOWLEDGEMENTS

This paper is based on invited talks presented at the Annual Conference of the American Association for Artificial Intelligence, Washington, DC, August 1983, and the Quatrième Congres des Reconnaissance des Formes et d'Intelligence Artificielle, INRIA, Paris, January 1984. Many colleagues commented on earlier drafts or presentations of the material in this paper. I thank especially Phil Agre, Dave Braunegg, Bruce Donald, Olivier Faugeras, Georges Giralt, John Hollerbach, Dan Huttenlocher, Tomás Lozano-Pérez, Tommy Poggio, Marc Raibert, Ken Salisbury, John Taft, Dan Weld and Patrick Winston.

This report describes research done at the Artificial Intelligence Laboratory of the Massachusetts Institute of Technology. Support for the Laboratory's Artificial Intelligence research is provided in part by the Advanced Research Projects Agency of the Department of Defense under Office of Naval Research contract N00014-75-C-0643, the Office of Naval Research under contract number N0014-80-C-0505, and the System Development Foundation.

REFERENCES

Agin, G.J. (1980), Computer vision systems for industrial inspection and assembly, *Computer*, **13**, 11–20.

Albus, J.S. (1984), Integrated system control, in *Robotics and Artificial Intelligence* (eds L. Gerhardt and M. Brady), Springer-Verlag, Berlin, pp. 65–93.

Ambler, A.P. and Popplestone, R.J. (1975), Inferring the positions of bodies from specified spatial relationships, *Artif. Intel.*, **6**, 157–74.

Asada, H. (1982), A characteristics analysis of manipulator dynamics using principal transformations, in *Proceedings of the American Control Conference*, Washington, DC.

Asada, H. and Kanade, T. (1981), Design concept of direct-drive manipulators using rare-earth DC torque motors, in *Proceedings of the Seventh International Joint Conference on Artificial Intelligence*, Vancouver, BC, pp. 775–8.

Asada, H. and Youcef-Toumi, K. (1984), Development of a direct-drive arm using high torque brushless motors, in *Proceedings of the International Symposium on Robotics Research* (eds M. Brady and R. Paul), MIT Press, Cambridge, MA.

Bejczy, R. (1984), What can we learn from one finger experiments?, in *Proceedings of the International Symposium on Robotics Research*, Vol. 1 (eds M. Brady and R. Paul), MIT Press, Cambridge, MA.

Baker, H.H. and Binford, T.O. (1981), Depth from edge and intensity based stereo, in *Proceedings of the Seventh International Joint Conference on Artificial Intelligence*, Vancouver, BC.

Binford, T.O. (1981), Inferring surfaces from images, *Artif. Intel.*, **17**, 205–45.

Binford, T.O. (1984), Stereo vision: complexity and constraints, in *Proceedings of the International Symposium on Robotics Research*, Vol. 1 (eds M. Brady and R. Paul), MIT Press, Cambridge, MA.

Bobrow, D.G. (ed.) (1984), *Qualitative Reasoning about Physical Systems*, North-Holland, Amsterdam; also: *Artif. Intel.*, **24**, special volume.

Boissonat, J.-D. (1982), Stable matching between a hand structure and an object silhouette, *IEEE Trans. Pattern Anal. Mach. Intel.*, **4**, 603–11.

Bolles, R.C., Horaud, P. and Hannah, M.J. (1984), 3DPO: A three-dimensional parts orientation system, in *Proceedings of the International Symposium on Robotics Research*, Vol. 1 (eds M. Brady and R. Paul), MIT Press, Cambridge, MA, pp. 413–24.

Brady, M.D (1982), Parts description and acquisition using vision, in *Robot Vision, Proceedings of the Society of Photo-optical Instrument Engineers* (ed. A. Rosenfeld), Washington, DC, 1–7.

Brady, M. (1983a), Parallelism in vision (Correspondent's Report), *Artif. Intel.*, **21**, 271–84.

Brady, M. (1983b), Criteria for shape representations, in *Human and Machine Vision* (eds J. Beck and A. Rosenfeld), Academic Press, New York.

Brady, M. (1983c), Trajectory planning, in *Robot Motion: Planning and Control* (eds M. Brady, J.M. Hollerbach, T.J. Johnson, T. Lozano-Pérez and M.T. Mason), MIT Press, Cambridge, MA.

Brady, M. (1984), Representing shape, in *Proceedings of the Institute of Electrical and Electronic Engineers Conference on Robotics*, Atlanta, GA.

Brady, M. and Asada, H. (1983), Smoothed local symmetries and their implementation, in *Proceedings of the First International Symposium on Robotics Research*.

Brady, M. and Paul, R. (eds) (1984), *Proceedings of the International Symposium on Robotics Research*, Vol. 1, MIT Press, Cambridge, MA.

Brady, M. and Yuille, A. (1983), An extremum principle for shape from contour, MIT AI Memo 711, Cambridge, MA.

Brady, M. and Yuille, A. (1984), Representing three-dimensional shape, in *Proceedings of the Romansy Conference*, Udine, Italy.

Brady, M., Agre, P., Braunegg, D.J. and Connell, J.H. (1984), The mechanic's mate, in *Proceedings of the 1984 European Conference on Artificial Intelligence: Advances in Artificial Intelligence* (ed. T. O'Shea), Elsevier Science Publishers B.V., North-Holland, Amsterdam, pp. 681–96.

Brady, M., Hollerbach, J.M., Johnson, T.J., Lozano-Pérez, T. and Masow, T.M. (eds) (1983), *Robot Motion: Planning and Control*, MIT Press, Cambridge, MA.

Brooks, R.A. (1981), Symbolic reasoning among 3-D models and 2-D images, *Artif. Intel.*, **17**, 285–348.

Brooks, R.A. (1982), Symbolic error analysis and robot planning, *Int. J. Robotics Res.*, **1**, 29–68.

Brooks, R.A. (1983a), Solving the findpath problem by good representation of free space, *IEEE Trans. Syst. Man Cybernet.*, **13**, 190–7.

Brooks, R.A. (1983b), Planning collision free motions for pick and place operations, *Int. J. Robotics Res.*, **2**.

Brooks, R.A. and Lozano-Pérez, T. (1983), A subdivision algorithm in configuration space for findpath with rotation, in *Proceedings of the Eighth International Joint Conference on Artificial Intelligence*, Karlsruhe, W. Germany.

Brooks, R.A. and Binford, T.O. (1980), Representing and reasoning about partially specified scenes, in *Proceedings of the Image Understanding Workshop* (ed. L.S. Baumann), Science Applications, Tysons Corner, VA, pp. 95–103.

Bruss, A. and Horn, B.K.P (1981), Passive Navigation, MIT AI Memo 662, Cambridge, MA.

Bundy, A., Byrd, L., Luger, G., Mellish, C. and Palmer M. (1979), Solving mechanics problems using meta-level inference, in *Expert Systems in the Microelectronic Age* (ed. D. Michie), Edinburgh University Press, Edinburgh.

Cannon, R.H., Jr. and Schmitz, E. (1984), Precise control of flexible manipulators, in *Proceedings of the International Symposium on Robotics Research*, Vol. 1 (eds M. Brady and R. Paul), MIT Press, Cambridge, MA.

Canny, J.F. (1983), Finding lines and edges in images, in *Proceedings of the Third National Conference on Artificial Intelligence*, Washington, DC.

Clocksin, W.S., Davey, P.G., Morgan, C.G. and Vidler, A.R. (1982), Progress in visual feedback for arc-welding of thin sheet steel, in *Robot Vision* (ed. A. Pugh), Springer-Verlag, Berlin, pp. 187–98.

Connell, J.H. and Brady, M. (1985), Learning shape descriptions, MIT AI Memo 824, Artificial Intelligence Laboratory, Cambridge, MA.

Davis, L.S. and Rosenfeld, A. (1981), Cooperating processes for low-level vision: a survey, *Artif. Intel.*, **17**, 245–65.

De Kleer, J. (1975), Qualitative and quantitative knowledge in classical mechanics, MIT Artificial Intelligence Laboratory, AI-TR-352, Cambridge, MA.

Dobrotin, B. and Lewis, R. (1977), A practical manipulator system, in *Proceedings of the Fifth International Joint Conference on Artificial Intelligence*, Tblisi, USSR, pp. 749–57.

Donald, B.R. (1983), Hypothesising channels through free space in solving the findpath problem, MIT AI Memo 736, Cambridge, MA.

Donald, B.R. (1984), Local and global techniques for motion planning, MIT Artificial Intelligence Laboratory, Cambridge, MA.

Dubowsky, S. (1984), Model-reference adaptive control, in *NATO Advanced Study Institute on Robotics and Artificial Intelligence* (eds M. Brady and L. Gerhardt), Springer-Verlag, Berlin.

Dubowsky, S. and DesForges, D.T. (1979), The application of model-referenced adaptive control to robotic manipulators, *J. Dyn. Syst. Meas. Cont.*, **101**, 193–200.

Dufay, B. and Latombe, J.-C. (1984), An approach to automatic robot programming based on inductive learning, in *Proceedings of the International Symposium on Robotics Research*, Vol. 1 (eds M. Brady and R. Paul), MIT Press, Cambridge, MA.

Engelberger, J.F. (1980), *Robotics in Practice*, Kogan Page, London.

Everett, H.R. (1982), A computer controlled sentry robot: a homebuilt project report, *Robotics Age*.

Faugeras, O. and Hébert, M. (1983), A 3-D recognition and positioning algorithm using geometric matching between primitive surfaces, in *Proceedings of the Eighth International Joint Conference on Artificial Intelligence*, Karlsruhe, W. Germany, pp. 996–1002.

Faugeras, O., Hébert, M. and Ponce, J. (1984), Object representation, identification, and positioning from range data, in *Proceedings of the International Symposium on Robotics Research*, Vol. 1 (eds M. Brady and R. Paul), MIT Press, Cambridge, MA.

Faugeras, O., Hebert, M., Ponce, J. and Boissonat, J. (1982), Towards a flexible vision system, in *Robot Vision* (ed. A. Pugh), IFS.

Featherstone, R. (1983), Position and velocity transformations between robot end effector coordinates and joint angles, *Int. J. Robotics Res.*, **2**.

Fisher, W.D. (1984), A kinematic control of redundant manipulation, PhD Thesis, Department of Electrical Engineering, Purdue University, Lafayette, IN.

Forbus, K.D. (1984), Qualitative process theory , *Artif. Intel.*, **24**, 85–168.

Franklin, J.W. and VanderBrug, G.J. (1982), Programming vision and robotics system with RAIL, in *Proceedings of the Robots VI Conference*, Detroit, MI.

Freund, E. (1981), Fast non-linear control with arbitrary pole placement for industrial robots and manipulators, *Int. J. Robotics Res.* **1**, 65–78.

Freund, E. (1984), Hierarchical non-linear control for robots, in *Proceedings of the International Symposium on Robotics Research*, Vol. 1 (eds M. Brady and R. Paul), MIT Press, Cambridge, MA, pp. 817–40.

Gaston, P.C. and Lozano-Pérez, T. (1983), Tactile recognition and localization using object models: the case of polyhedra on a plane, MIT AI Memo 705, Cambridge, MA.

Giralt, G. (1984), Mobile robots, in *NATO Advanced Study Institute on Robotics and Artificial Intelligence* (eds M. Brady and L. Gerhardt), Springer-Verlag, Berlin.

Giralt, G., Chatila, R. and Vaisset, M. (1984), An integrated navigation and motion control system for autonomous multisensory mobile robots, in *Proceedings of the International Symposium on Robotics Research*, Vol. 1 (eds M. Brady and R. Paul), MIT Press, Cambridge, MA.

Giralt, G., Sobek, R. and Chatila, R. (1977), A multi-level planning and navigation system for a mobile robot: a first approach to HILARE, in *Proceedings of the Fifth International Joint Conference on Artificial Intelligence*, Tblisi, USSR.

Goto, T., Takeyasu, K. and Inoyama, T. (1980), Control algorithm for precision insert operation robots, *IEEE Trans. Syst. Man Cybernet.*, **10**, 19–25.

Grimson, W.E.L. (1981), *From Images to Surfaces: A Computational Study of the Human Early Visual System*, MIT Press, Cambridge, MA.

Grimson, W.E.L. and Lozano-Pérez, T. (1984), Local constraints in tactile recognition, *Int. J. Robotics Res.*, **3**.

Hackwood, S. and Beni (1983), Torque sensitive tactile array for robotics, *Int. J. Robotics Res.*, **2**.

Hanafusa, H. and Asada, H. (1977), Stable prehension by a robot hand with elastic fingers, in *Proceedings of the Seventh Symposium on Industrial Robotics*, pp. 361–8.

Hanafusa, H. and Asada, H. (1979), A robot hand with elastic fingers and its application to assembly process, in *Proceedings of the IFAC Symposium on Information Control Problems in Manufacturing Techniques*, pp. 127-38.

Haralick, R.M., Watson, L.T. and Laffey, T.J. (1983), The topographic primal sketch, *Int. J. Robotics Res.*, **2**, 50–72.

Harmon, L. (1982), Automated tactile sensing, *Int. J. Robotics Res.*, **1**, 3–33.

Harmon, L. (1984), Robotic traction for industrial assembly, *Int. J. Robotics Res.*, **3**.

Harmon, S.Y. (1983a), Coordination between control and knowledge based systems for autonomous vehicle guidance, in *Proceedings of the Institute of*

Electrical and Electronic Engineers Trends and Applications Conference, Gaithersburg, MD.

Harmon, S.Y. (1983b), Information processing system architecture for an autonomous robot system, in *Proceedings of the Conference on Artificial Intelligence*, Oakland University, Rochester, MI.

Hayes-Roth, P., Waterman, D. and Lenat, D. (eds) (1983), *Building Expert Systems*, Addison-Wesley, Reading, MA.

Hildreth, E. (1983), *The Measurement of Visual Motion*, MIT Press, Cambridge, MA.

Hillis, W.D. (1982), A high-resolution image touch sensor, *Int. J. Robotics Res.*, **1**, 33–44.

Hirose, S., Nose, M., Kikuchi, H. and Umetani, Y. (1984), Adaptive gait control of a quadruped walking vehicle, in *Proceedings of the International Symposium on Robotics Research*, Vol. 1 (eds M. Brady and R. Paul), MIT Press, Cambridge, MA.

Hobbs, J. and Moore, R. (1984), *Formal Theories of the Common Sense World*, Ablex, Norwood, NJ.

Hollerbach, J.M. (1983), Dynamics, in *Robot Motion: Planning and Control* (eds M. Brady, J.M. Hollerbach, T.J. Johnson, T. Lozano-Pérez and M. Mason), MIT Press, Cambridge, MA.

Hollerbach, J.M. and Sahar, G. (1983), Wrist partitioned inverse kinematic accelerations and manipulator dynamics, MIT AI Memo 717, Cambridge, MA.

Hopcroft, J.E., Schwartz, J.T. and Sharir, M. (1983), Efficient detection of intersections among spheres, *Int. J. Robotics Res.*, **2**.

Horn, B.K.P. (1982), Sequins and quills – Representations for surface topography, in *Representation of 3-Dimensional Objects* (ed. R. Bajcsy), Springer–Verlag, Berlin.

Horn, B.K.P. and Schunck, B.G. (1982), Determining optical flow, *Artif. Intel.*, **17**, 185–203.

Huston, R.L. and Kelly, F.A. (1982), The development of equations of motion of single-arm robots, *IEEE Trans. Syst. Man Cybernet.*, **12**, 259–66.

Ikeuchi, K. (1981a), Determination of surface orientations of specular surfaces by using the photometric stereo method, *IEEE Trans. Pattern Anal. Mach. Intel.*, **2**, 661–9.

Ikeuchi, K. (1981b), Recognition of 3D object using extended Gaussian image, in *Proceedings of the Seventh International Joint Conference on Artificial Intelligence*, Vancouver, BC.

Ikeuchi, K. and Horn, B.K.P. (1981), Numerical shape from shading and occluding boundaries, *Artif. Intel.*, **17**, 141–85.

Ikeuchi, K., Horn, B.K.P., Nagata, S. and Callahan, T. (1984), Picking up an object from a pile of objects, in *Proceedings of the International Symposium on Robotics Research*, Vol. 1 (eds M. Brady and R. Paul), MIT Press, Cambridge, MA.

Jacobsen, S.C., Wood, J.E., Knutti, D.F. and Biggers, K.B. (1984), The Utah/MIT dextrous hand – work in progress, in *Proceedings of the International Sym-*

posium on Robotics Research, Vol 1 (eds M. Brady and R. Paul), MIT Press, Cambridge, MA.

Kahn, M.E. and Roth, B. (1971), The near minimum-time control of open-loop articulated kinematic chains, *J. Dyn. Syst. Meas. Cont.*, **93**, 164–72.

Kanade, T. and Sommer, T. (1984), An optical proximity sensor for measuring surface position and orientation for robot manipulation, in *Proceedings of the International Symposium on Robotics Research*, Vol. 1 (eds M. Brady and R. Paul), MIT Press, Cambridge, MA.

Kane, T.R. and Levinson, D.A. (1983), The use of Kane's dynamical equations in robotics, *Int. J. Robotics Res.*, **2**, 3–22.

Klein, C.A. and Wahawisan, J.J. (1982), Use of a multiprocessor for control of a robotic system, *Int. J. Robotics Res.*, **1**, 45–59.

Klein, C.A., Olson, K.W. and Pugh, D.R. (1983), Use of force and attitude sensors for locomotion of a legged vehicle over irregular terrain, *Int. J. Robotics Res.*, **2**, 3–17.

Lewis, R.A. and Bejczy, A.K. (1973), Planning considerations for a roving robot with arm, in *Proceedings of the Third International Joint Conference on Artificial Intelligence*, Stanford, CA, pp. 308–15.

Lewis, R.A. and Johnson, A.R. (1977), A scanning laser rangefinder for a roving robot with arm, in *Proceedings of the Fifth International Joint Conference on Artificial Intelligence*, Tblisi, USSR, pp. 762–8.

Lieberman, L.I. and Wesley, M.A. (1977), AUTOPASS: an automatic programming system for computer controlled mechanical assembly, *IBM J. Res. Develop.*, **21**, 321–33.

Lowe, D.G. and Binford, T.O. (1982), Segmentation and aggregation: an approach to figure-ground phenomena, in *Proceedings of the Image Understanding Workshop* (ed. L. S. Baumann), Science Applications, Tysons Corner, VA, pp. 168–78.

Lozano-Pérez, T. (1976), The design of a mechanical assembly system, MIT, Artificial Intelligence Laboratory, AI TR 397, Cambridge, MA.

Lozano-Pérez, T. (1981), Automatic planning of manipulator transfer movements, *IEEE Trans. Syst. Man Cybernet.*, **11**, 681–98.

Lozano-Pérez, T. (1983a), Spatial planning: A configuration space approach, *IEEE Trans. Comput.*, **32**, 108-20.

Lozano-Pérez, T. (1983b), Robot programming, *Proc. Inst. Elec. Electron. Eng.*, **71**, 821–41.

Lozano-Pérez, T. (1983c), Spatial reasoning, in *Robot Motion: Planning and Control* (eds M. Brady, J. M. Hollerbach, T. J. Johnson, T. Lozano-Pérez and T. M. Mason), MIT Press, Cambridge, MA.

Lozano-Pérez, T., Mason, T. and Taylor, R.H. (1984), Automatic synthesis of fine-motion strategies for robots, in *Proceedings of the International Symposium on Robotics Research*, Vol. 1 (eds M. Brady and R. Paul), MIT Press, Cambridge, MA.

Marr, D. (1982), *Vision*, Freeman, San Francisco.

Marr, D. and Hildreth, E.C. (1980), Theory of edge detection, *Proc. Roy. Soc.*, B, **270**, 187–217.

Marr, D. and Poggio, T. (1979), A theory of human stereo vision, *Proc. Roy. Soc. B*, **204**, 301–28.

Mason, T.M. (1982), *Manipulator Grasping and Pushing Operations*, MIT Press, Cambridge, MA.

Mason, T.M. (1983a), Compliance and force control for computer control manipulators, *IEEE Trans. Syst. Man Cybernet.*, **11**, 418–32; reprinted in *Robot Motion: Planning and Control* (eds M. Brady, J. M. Hollerbach, T. J. Johnson, T. Lozano-Pérez and M. T. Mason), MIT Press, Cambridge, MA.

Mason, T.M. (1983b), Compliance, in *Robot Motion: Planning and Control* (eds M. Brady, J. M. Hollerbach, T. J. Johnson, T. Lozano-Pérez and M. T. Mason), MIT Press, Cambridge, MA.

Michie, D. (1979), *Expert Systems in the Microelectronic Age*, Ellis Horwood, Chichester.

Miura, H. and Shimoyama, I. (1984), Dynamical walk of biped locomotion, in *Proceedings of the International Symposium on Robotics Research*, Vol. 1 (eds M. Brady and R. Paul), MIT Press, Cambridge, MA, pp. 303–25.

Moravec, H.P. (1981), *Robot Rover Visual Navigation*, UMI Research Press, Ann Arbor, MI.

Moravec, H.P. (1983), The Stanford cart and the CMU rover, *IEEE Trans. Ind. Electron.*

Moravec, H.P. (1984), Locomotion, vision, and intelligence, in *Proceedings of the International Symposium on Robotics Research*, Vol. 1 (eds M. Brady and R. Paul), MIT Press, Cambridge, MA.

Nakagawa, Y. and Ninomiya, T. (1984), Structured light method for inspection of solder joints and assembly robot vision system, in *Proceedings of the International Symposium on Robotics Research*, Vol. 1 (eds M. Brady and R. Paul), MIT Press, Cambridge, MA.

Nilsson, N.J. (1969), A mobile automation: An application of Artificial Intelligence techniques, in *Proceedings of the First International Joint Conference on Artificial Intelligence*, Washington, DC.

Nishihara, H.K. and Poggio, T. (1984), Stereo vision for robotics, in *Proceedings of the International Symposium on Robotics Research*, Vol. 1 (eds M. Brady and R. Paul), MIT Press, Cambridge, MA.

Ohwovoriole, M.S. and Roth, B. (1981), An extension of screw theory, *Trans. ASME J. Mech. Des.*, **103**, 725–35.

Okada, T. (1979), Computer control of multi-jointed finger system, in *Proceedings of the Sixth International Joint Conference on Artificial Intelligence*, Tokyo, Japan.

Okada, T. (1982), Development of an optical distance sensor for robots, *Int. J. Robotics Res.*, **1**, 3–14.

Orin, D.E. and Schrader, W.W. (1984), Efficient Jacobian determination for robot manipulators, in *Proceedings of the International Symposium on Robotics Research*, Vol. 1 (eds M. Brady and R. Paul), MIT Press, Cambridge, MA.

Ozguner, F., Tsai, S.J. and McGhee, R.B. (1984), Rough terrain locomotion by a hexapod robot using a binocular ranging system, in *Proceedings of the International Symposium on Robotics Research*, Vol. 1 (eds M. Brady and R. Paul), MIT Press, Cambridge, MA.

Paul, R.P. (1972), Modelling, trajectory calculation, and servoing a computer controlled arm, AIM 177, Stanford AI Laboratory, Stanford, CA.

Paul, R.P. (1981), *Robot Manipulators: Mathematics, Programming, and Control*, MIT Press, Cambridge, MA.

Paul, R.C. and Shimano, B.E. (1976), Compliance and control, in *Proceedings of the Joint Automatic Control Conference*, pp. 694–9.

Paul, R.C., Stevenson, C.N. and Renaud, M. (1984), A systematic approach for obtaining the kinematics of recursive manipulators based on homogeneous transformations, in *Proceedings of the International Symposium on Robotics Research*, Vol. 1 (eds M. Brady and R. Paul), MIT Press, Cambridge, MA.

Pieper, D.L. (1968), The kinematics of manipulators under computer control, PhD Thesis, Department of Computer Science, Stanford University, Stanford, CA.

Pieper, D.L. and Roth, B. (1969), The kinematics of manipulators under computer control, in *Proceedings of the Second International Conference on Theory of Machines and Mechanisms*, Warsaw, Poland.

Popplestone, R.J., Ambler, A.P. and Bellos, I.M. (1980), An interpreter for a language for describing assemblies, *Artif. Intel.*, **14**, 79–107.

Porter, G. and Mundy, J. (1982), A non-contact profile sensor system for visual inspections, in *Proceedings of the Institute of Electrical and Electronic Engineers Workshop on Industrial Applications of Machine Vision*.

Porter, G. and Mundy, J. (1984), A model-driven visual inspection module, in *Proceedings of the International Symposium on Robotics Research*, Vol. 1 (eds M. Brady and R. Paul), MIT Press, Cambridge, MA.

Raibert, M.H. (1984), Special Issue on walking machines, *Int. J. Robotics Res.*, **3**.

Raibert, M.H. and Craig, J.J. (1983), A hybrid force and position controller, in *Robot Motion: Planning and Control* (eds M. Brady, J. M. Hollerbach, T. J. Johnson, T. Lozano-Pérez and T.M. Mason), MIT Press, Cambridge, MA.

Raibert, M.H. and Sutherland, I.E. (1983), Machines that walk, *Sci. Amer.*, **248**, 44–53.

Raibert, M.H. and Tanner, J.E. (1982), Design and implementation of a VLSI tactile sensing computer, *Int. J. Robotics Res.*, **1**, 3–18.

Raibert, M.H., Brown, H.B., Jr and Murthy, S.S. (1984), 3D balance using 2D algorithms?, in *Proceedings of the International Symposium on Robotics Research*, Vol. 1 (eds M. Brady and R. Paul), MIT Press, Cambridge, MA.

Renaud, M. (1984), An efficient iterative analytical procedure for obtaining a robot manipulator dynamic model, in *Proceedings of the International Symposium on Robotics Research*, Vol. 1 (eds M. Brady and R. Paul), MIT Press, Cambridge, MA.

Requicha, A.A.G. (1980), Representation of rigid solids: theory, methods and systems, *Comput. Surv.*, **12**, 437–64.

Rich, C.R. and Waters, R. (1981), Abstraction, inspection, and debugging in programming, MIT AI Memo 634, Cambridge, MA.

Roth, B. (1984), Screws, motors, and wrenches that cannot be bought in a hardware store, in *Proceedings of the International Symposium on Robotics Research*, Vol. 1 (eds M. Brady and R. Paul), MIT Press, Cambridge, MA.

Sacerdoti, E. (1975), A structure for plans and behavior, SRI Artificial Intelligence Center TR-109, Menlo Park, CA.

Salisbury, J.K. (1980), Active stiffness control of a manipulator in Cartesian coordinates, in *Proceedings of the Institute of Electrical and Electronic Engineers Conference on Decision and Control*, Albuquerque, NM.

Salisbury, J.K. (1982), Kinematic and force analysis of articulated hands, PhD Thesis, Department of Mechanical Engineering, Standford University, Stanford, CA.

Salisbury, J.K. (1984), Interpretation of contact geometries from force measurements, in *Proceedings of the International Symposium on Robotics Research*, Vol. 1 (eds M. Brady and R. Paul), MIT Press, Cambridge, MA.

Salisbury, J.K. and Craig, J.J. (1982), Articulated hands: force control and kinematic issues, *Int. J. Robotics Res.*, **1**, 4–17.

Schunck, B.G. (1983), Motion segmentation and estimation, MIT Artificial Intelligence Laboratory, Cambridge, MA.

Schwartz, J.T. and Sharir, M. (1983), The piano movers' problem, III, *Int. J. Robotics Res.*, **2**.

Shimano, B.E., Geschke, C.C. and Spaulding, C.H. (1984), VAL II: A robot programming language and control system, in *Proceedings of the International Symposium on Robotics Research*, Vol. 1 (eds M. Brady and R. Paul), MIT Press, Cambridge, MA.

Shirai, Y., Koshikawa, K., Oshima, M. and Ikeuchi, K. (1984), An approach to object recognition using 3-D solid model, in *Proceedings of the International Symposium on Robotics Research*, Vol. 1 (eds M. Brady and R. Paul), MIT Press, Cambridge, MA.

Taylor, R.H. (1976), The synthesis of manipulator control programs from task-level specifications, AI Memo 282, Stanford University, Stanford, CA.

Taylor, R.H., Summers, P.D. and Meyer, J.M. (1982), AML: A manufacturing language, *Int. J. Robotics Res.*, **1**, 19–41.

Terzopoulos, D. (1983), Multilevel computational processes for visual surface reconstruction, *Comput. Vision Graphics Image Process.*, **24**, 52–96.

Terzopoulos, D. (1984), Multilevel reconstruction of visual surfaces: Variational principles and finite element representations, in *Multiresolution Image Processing and Analysis* (ed. A. Rosenfeld), Springer-Verlag, New York.

Trevelyan, J.P., Kovesi, P.D. and Ong, M.C.H. (1984), Motion control for a sheep shearing robot, in *Proceedings of the International Symposium on Robotics Research*, Vol. 1 (eds M. Brady and R. Paul), MIT Press, Cambridge, MA.

Tsuji, S. and Asada, M. (1984), Understanding of three-dimensional motion in time-varying imagery, in *Proceedings of the International Symposium on Robotics Research*, Vol. 1 (eds M. Brady and R. Paul), MIT Press, Cambridge, MA.

VAL (1980), User's guide: A robot programming and control system, CONDEC Unimation Robotics.

Villers, P. (1982), Present industrial use of vision sensors for robot guidance, in *Robot Vision* (ed. A. Pugh), IFS.

Vilnrotter, F., Nevatia, R. and Price, K.E. (1981), Structural analysis of natural textures, in *Proceedings of the Image Understanding Workshop* (ed. L. S. Baumann), Science Applications, Tysons Corner, VA, pp. 61–8.

Wesley, M.A. *et al.* (1980), A geometric modelling system for automated mechanical assembly, *IBM J. Res. Develop.*, **24**, 64–74.

Whitney, D.E. (1983), The mathematics of compliance, in *Robot Motion: Planning and Control* (eds M. Brady, J. M. Hollerbach, T. J. Johnson, T. Lozano-Pérez and T. M. Mason), MIT Press, Cambridge, MA.

Winston, P.H. (1980), Learning and reasoning by analogy, *Commun. ACM*, **23**.

Winston, P.H. (1984), *Artificial Intelligence*, 2nd edn, Addison-Wesley, Reading, MA.

Winston, P.H., Binford, T.O., Katz, B. and Lowry, M. (1984), Learning physical descriptions from functional descriptions, examples, and precedents, in *Proceedings of the International Symposium on Robotics Research*, Vol. 1 (eds M. Brady and R. Paul), MIT Press, Cambridge, MA.

Witkin, A.P. (1981), Recovering surface shape and orientation from texture, *Artif. Intel.*, **17**, 17–47.

Woodham, R.J. (1981), Analysing images of curved surfaces, *Artif. Intel.*, **17**, 117–40.

Yoshikawa, T. (1984), Analysis and control of robot manipulators with redundancy, in *Proceedings of the International Symposium on Robotics Research*, Vol. 1 (eds M. Brady and R. Paul), MIT Press, Cambridge, MA.

Young, K.K.D. (1978), Controller design for a manipulator using theory of variable structure systems, *IEEE Trans. Syst. Man Cybernet.*, **8**, 101–9; reprinted in *Robot Motion: Planning and Control* (eds M. Brady, J. M. Hollerbach, T.J. Johnson, T. Lozano-Pérez and M. T. Mason), MIT Press, Cambridge, MA.

Zucker, S.W., Hummel, R.A. and Rosenfeld, A. (1977), An application of relaxation labelling to line and curve enhancement, *IEEE Trans. Comput.*, **26**, 394–403, 922–9.

8
The anatomy of expert systems

RICHARD FORSYTH

A human expert – a hospital consultant, a geologist, a chemical analyst, even a mere technical author – is usually someone we respect. Experts spend a long time studying and practising their skills and they do their jobs well. But the trouble with human experts is that they are scarce, they are not always reliable, they require payment, and in the long run, they die – taking much of their expertise with them. Many people, therefore, are interested in the idea of encoding expert knowledge in computer programs, to get the benefits without the drawbacks.

8.1 INTRODUCTION

The concept of the expert system arose in the 1970s when Artificial Intelligence (AI) researchers abandoned, or postponed, the quest for generally intelligent machines and turned instead to the solution of narrowly focused real-world problems. Thus the expert system is one of the first examples of applied AI, and expert systems techniques have spread out far beyond the confines of the research laboratories in which they were devised.

Already there are practical systems that can out-perform skilled humans at medical diagnosis, mass-spectrogram interpretation, classifying crop disease and much else besides. It is worth asking, therefore, how do they work?

Typically, an expert system is based on an extensive body of knowledge about a specific problem area. In general, this knowledge will be organized as a collection of rules that allow the system to draw conclusions from given data or premises – thereby letting it offer intelligent advice or take intelligent decisions.

This is the knowledge-based approach to systems design which represents an evolutionary change with revolutionary consequences. It replaces the tradition of

$$\text{data} + \text{algorithm} = \text{program}$$

with a new architecture centred around a 'knowledge base' and an 'inference engine', so that

$$\text{knowledge} + \text{inference} = \text{expert system}$$

which is clearly similar, but different enough in approach to have profound repercussions.

8.2   FEATURES OF EXPERT SYSTEMS

What exactly is an expert system? The field is too dynamic to lay down a rigid definition, but the following checklist of features should prove helpful.
(1) An expert system is limited to a relatively narrow domain of expertise.
(2) It should be able to reason with uncertain data (and unreliable rules).
(3) It must be able to explain its train of reasoning in a comprehensible way.
(4) Facts and inference mechanism are detachable: knowledge is *not* hard-coded into the deductive procedures.
(5) It is designed to grow incrementally.
(6) It is typically rule-based, containing numerous rules-of-thumb that express experts' judgemental processes.
(7) It delivers *advice* as its output – not tables of figures or eye-catching graphs.
(8) It makes money. (This is a performance requirement, to distinguish expert systems from other kinds of AI system.)
The key word is knowledge. Clearly, the objective of an intelligent problem-solving system (like yourself) is to cut out blind or random search. To do so a computer system has to exploit the same advantage that the human expert has over the novice – i.e. expertise or organized knowledge. Knowledge about facts, knowledge about rules of inference and knowledge about solution strategies.

8.3   THE ARCHITECTURE OF EXPERT SYSTEMS

We have said that an expert system contains an inference engine and a knowledge base. In fact, there are *four* essential components of a fully-fledged expert system:

(1) the knowledge base;
(2) the inference engine;

(3) the knowledge-acquisition module;
(4) the explanatory interface.

All four modules are critical. A knowledge-based system may lack one of them; but a truly expert system should not.

We will consider each of these four modules in turn, and explain how they work together. This entails a brief look at methods of representing knowledge, handling reasoning with uncertainty, inducing rules from examples and providing intelligible explanations to the user.

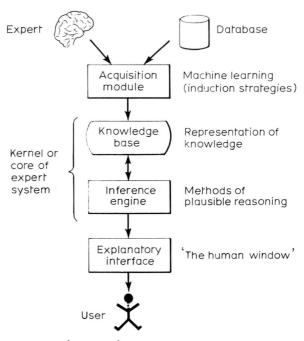

Fig. 8.1 An expert system framework.

8.4   THE KNOWLEDGE BASE

The two fundamental components of an expert system are the knowledge base and the inference engine. The knowledge base stores information about the subject domain; however, information in a knowledge base is not the passive collection of records and items that you would find in a conventional database. Rather it contains symbolic representations of experts' rules of judgement and experience, in a form that enables the inference engine to perform logical deductions upon it.

The two chief difficulties in developing a knowledge base are knowledge representation and knowledge acquisition.

The knowledge representation problem concerns the decision on how to encode knowledge so that the computer can use it. In general, the following elements must be represented:

- *Domain Terms*: the jargon used by experts in the field.
- *Structural Relationships*: the interconnections of component entities.
- *Causal Relationships*: the cause–effect relations between components.

The task of the knowledge engineer is to select appropriate means of storing such information symbolically. Four main methods have evolved:

- *Rules in IF–THEN Format*: the condition specifies some pattern and the conclusion may be an action or assertion.
- *Semantic Nets*: these represent relations among objects in the domain (e.g. horneblende is an igneous rock) by links between nodes.
- *Frames*: these are generalized record structures which may have default values and may have actions coded as the values of certain fields or slots.
- *Horn Clauses*: this is a form of predicate logic on which PROLOG is based and with the PROLOG system can perform inferences.

Early expert systems used the rule-based formalism almost exclusively, e.g. the MYCIN system (Shortliffe, 1976) for diagnosing blood infections. Here is a sample MYCIN rule.

IF:
    (1) the infection requiring therapy is meningitis, and
    (2) the type of infection is fungal, and
    (3) organisms were not seen on the stain of the culture, and
    (4) the patient is not a compromised host, and
    (5) the patient has been in a region where coccidiomycoses are endemic, and
    (6) the race of the patient is black or Asian or Indian, and
    (7) the cryptococcal antigen in the csf was not positive

THEN:
    there is suggestive evidence that the cryptococcus is not one of the organisms which might be causing the infection.

Rules are the predominant form of knowledge representation in expert systems. However, both MYCIN and PROSPECTOR (Gashnig, 1982), which are quoted (rightly) as rule-based systems, make use of other structures for background knowledge. In the case of MYCIN a 'context tree' is used to guide the course of the consultation. The precise structure of the tree varies with each consultation; and it is used to determine whether certain rules of inference (in the primary knowledge base) may or may not fire. In the case of PROSPECTOR a semantic net is

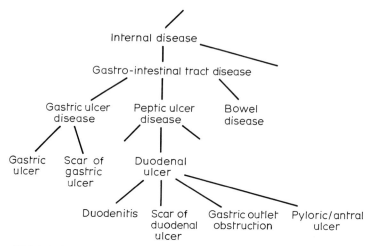

[This is just a small fragment of an ISA tree for internal medicine]

Fig. 8.2 Inheritance hierarchy.

employed to provide background geological knowledge. Net or tree-like structures are useful in setting up what are often called 'inheritance hierarchies' like that shown in Fig. 8.2 for a medical example. The arcs represent ISA links relating sets to supersets. Coding such knowledge in terms of a sequence of production rules would be simply clumsy.

Other significant expert systems have made use of record-like data structures known as frames to represent knowledge. Below is a frame that might appear in a hypothetical expert system for gambling.

Frametype:	Racehorse.
Name:	Fat Chance.
Age-in-years:	2.
Date-of-birth:	1983.
Owner:	Aga Khooker.
Last-Finish:	7.
All-Races:	[pointer to chain of race frames].
Form-Rating:	47. [out of 100]
Dam:	Mare's Nest.
Sire:	Speedy Gonzales.

Trying to encode this sort of information as rules would be tedious. Frames have the further advantage that they can contain default values and can also contain rules as entries – e.g. a rule for computing the form-rating from other data if it is missing.

Finally, the horn-clause form of logic has been brought to prominence by the popularity of PROLOG among certain AI workers. PROLOG

(Clocksin and Mellish, 1981) provides a flexible symbolic representation scheme that allows rules and facts to be coded in essentially the same way. For example, the clauses

mother (eve, cain).
father (adam, cain).

express simple assertions or facts in the database, while the clause

paternal_grandmother (X, Z):–
mother (X, Y), father (Y, Z).

expresses a relationship. It states that X is the paternal grandmother of Z if X is the mother of Y and Y is the father of Z. This relation can be treated as an inference rule that can be directly executed by the built-in theorem-prover, which searches the database. (Variables are in upper case and constants in lower case.)

The resolution-based theorem-prover built into PROLOG is not powerful enough, however, to serve as the inference engine of a full-scale expert system; so most expert system designers using PROLOG write a higher-level inference mechanism in that language. This means that the rules look more complex than the example above; for example, they may have weighting factors.

8.5   THE INFERENCE ENGINE

Inference is the process of deploying evidence in order to arrive at new conclusions. An inference mechanism consists of search and reasoning methods that enable the system to find solutions and, if necessary, provide justifications for its answers. There are two overall reasoning strategies – forward chaining and backward chaining.

Forward chaining involves working forward from the evidence (or symptoms) to the conclusions (or diagnoses). In a rule-based system it simply involves matching the IF conditions to the facts, possibly in a predetermined order. Forward chaining is easy to computerize, and is suitable in cases where all the data is going to be gathered anyway. Examples of such cases are when the data is generated automatically by an instrument or when a complete form has to be filled in as a matter of standard practice.

Backward chaining works from hypothesis to evidence. The system picks a hypothesis and looks for data to support or refute it. It can be programmed in a recursive manner, and typically leads to a more natural kind of dialogue in consultation-style systems. The problem of which hypothesis to investigate is not yet fully solved; and so, in practice, most systems use a mixture of forward and backward chaining.

For example, Naylor (1983) has developed the 'Rule-Value' method which decides what evidence to ask for next on the basis of how much it will reduce the overall uncertainty in the system.

Many expert systems allow for uncertainty in the facts obtained from the user and in the rules themselves. Shortliffe (1976), the inventor of MYCIN, devised an approximate reasoning scheme based on what he called 'Certainty Factors'. This has been criticized for being *ad hoc*, though it worked quite effectively in practice. Other systems have been based on Fuzzy Logic, which extends the operations of Boolean algebra to cover fractional truth-values intermediate between 0 (false) and 1 (true).

The most immediately appealing calculus of uncertainty, however, is probability theory. Most probabilistic expert systems follow the lead of PROSPECTOR and use Bayes's rule as the thread to tie together chains of uncertain inference. Bayes's theorem can be briefly stated as follows.

$$P(H : E) = P(E : H) \times P(H) / P(E)$$

This says that the probability of a hypothesis (*H*) given some evidence (*E*) is the probability of the evidence given the hypothesis times the probability of the hypothesis divided by the probability of the evidence. This may not seem a very staggering piece of mathematics, but it is easier to find out the proportion of chicken-pox patients who have spots, for instance, than the proportion of spotty persons who have chicken pox.

In fact most Bayesian systems work with odds rather than probabilities (at least internally) which allows them to employ an updating formula based on something called a 'likelihood ratio' (LR)

$$O(H : E) = O(H) \times LR(H : E)$$

stating that the odds in favour of the hypothesis given a piece of evidence are the odds on the hypothesis prior to that evidence multiplied by the likelihood ratio for that hypothesis given the evidence. Likelihood ratios can be calculated from two-way contingency tables (Forsyth, 1984). Below are a couple of frequency tables from Spiegel-

		Frequencies in percent (%)	
		not gallstones	gallstones
Sex	female	46	79
	male	54	21
Age	under 26	19	03
	over 25	81	97

halter and Knill-Jones (1984) relating age and sex to the hypothesis: Patient has Gallstones.

Clearly female patients over 25 are more likely to have gallstones than male patients of 25 or under. The question is: How much more likely? Bayes's rule provides a way to compute the answer to that question.

In this particular data set there were 57 patients who did have gall-stones and 1119 who did not. Taking sex as an indicator, the likelihood ratio of having gallstones for a female patient $LR(G : F)$ is 1.7154 and the likelihood ratio for a male patient $LR(G : M)$ is 0.3900. This says that the odds on the diagnosis of gallstones should be multiplied by 1.7154 once the doctor knows the patient is female (or by 0.39 if he is male). Age can be treated similarly. Thus evidence can be accumulated simply by multi-plication, or by addition if logarithms of the LR's are used. (Of course, the prior odds of having gallstones are pretty small; and merely being female is by no means enough to establish a diagnosis!)

The great attraction of Bayesianism is that it permits, indeed encour-ages, detailed statistical investigation. It does not have to rely on subjec-tive numerical estimates. Thus it heals the unfortunate breach between statisticians and knowledge engineers. Simple-minded Bayesianism has two serious disadvantages, however. In the first place the estimation of prior probabilities or odds (before any evidence is gathered) is problema-tical. It all depends on how you define the population you are interested in. Secondly, the various items of evidence must be independent, or if they are correlated some form of recalibration of LR's is required.

The first criticism loses some of its force if a large number of evidential indicators is considered. As the evidence piles up one way or the other, the effect of the prior odds is swamped. The second drawback is more fundamental, but in most practical systems (e.g. the HULK package) the knowledge engineer is warned during the rule-generation phase if two sources of evidence are highly correlated and given the opportunity to combine several associated variables into a single indicator. Generally speaking, correlated items of evidence should not be in separate rules but should be integrated into a single rule with a single likelihood ratio attached. For instance, it would be inadvisable in a weather-forecasting system to have one rule relating cloudiness to the probability of rain tomorrow and another rule relating humidity to the probability of rain tomorrow, since these two variables are strongly associated. It would be better to combine the two raw variables into some kind of 'dull-damp-ness' index.

8.6   THE ACQUISITION MODULE

Experts are notoriously bad at saying how they reach their conclusions, not because they wish to preserve trade secrets but because much of their 'intuition' lies buried beneath the level of consciousness. It has to be laboriously quarried out of the unyielding rockface of the human skull. So knowledge acquisition has come to be regarded as the main bottleneck in expert systems development.

One thing experts are good at, however, is criticism. (Aren't we all?) They can look at an example case and say what decision should have been taken and, if required, criticize a computer's suggested solution. So a good deal of attention has been devoted recently to developing software tools that allow an expert system to induce its own knowledge from pre-classified examples. Effectively, this power-assists the knowledge acquisition process.

Even if the system cannot do the whole job on its own – from a database of instances to a set of decision rules – it may be useful if it can refine its own knowledge base during a period of 'apprenticeship' or during use, i.e. by learning from its mistakes.

Another way of looking at induction packages is as ways of helping to make sure that the process of 'repaid prototyping' is indeed rapid. (We shall look in depth at various successful induction algorithms in Chapter 9.)

8.7   THE EXPLANATORY INTERFACE

One of the good things about MYCIN, PROSPECTOR and many classic expert systems was that they could justify their conclusions on request. Obviously when life-and-death or even profit-and-loss decisions are being handed over to the computer it is essential for the system to explain its reasoning. Here is a fragment of a session showing how MYCIN replies to a WHY? question posed by its user (who is a physician, not the patient, and will not accept diagnoses on trust without explanation).

Is meningitis a hospital-acquired infection?
** WHY
[2.0] This will aid in determining the organisms (other than those seen on cultures or smears) which might be causing the infection. It has already been determined that:
        [2.1] the infection which requires therapy is meningitis, and
        [2.2] organisms were not seen on the stain of this pending csf culture, and
        [2.3] the type of infection is bacterial, and
        [2.4] neurosurgery is not one of the relevant items from the history of this patient, and
        [2.5] the age of this patient is greater than 10 days.

Therefore, if:

> [2.6] the infection was acquired while the patient was hospitalized, then there is evidence that the organisms (other than those seen on cultures and smears) which might be causing the infection are e.coli (0.75), staphylococcus-coag-pos (0.3), pseudomonas-aeruginosa (0.3), klebsiella-pneumoniae (0.50
> – from [RULE545]

**

Note that this explanation facility is, in effect, a partial trace through the program's reasoning process, couched in medical-jargon English. Such explanations can be produced fairly easily and cheaply in rule-based systems (by regurgitating the rules being used and their predecessors) which is a point in favour of the rule-based encoding of knowledge.

Notice also that the conclusions have numerical weightings attached. These are, in fact, not true probabilities – although some systems do use probabilities. They are weightings which allow the system to deal with uncertainty in a consistent manner, and come up with an ordered list of likely diagnoses in the final analysis.

8.8   DEVELOPING EXPERT SYSTEMS

More and more organizations are finding that modest knowledge engineering projects can have useful payoffs. To decide whether a proposed application is likely to benefit from the knowledge-based approach to systems design, you should consider the following questions: (1) Is the problem diagnostic? (2) Is there no established theory? (3) Are the human experts rare? (4) Is the data 'noisy' or uncertain?

First, diagnostic problems do not only include medical diagnosis. Diagnosis of computer faults has also proved a happy hunting ground for expert systems designers. The kind of problem where the system must pick one from a finite list of potential answers is likely to prove suitable. Many categorization or forecasting tasks fall into this framework.

Second, domains where no established theory exists include company law, weather prediction and many branches of medicine. Skilled practitioners rely on knowledge and intuition because there are too many variables for a complete and consistent theory to have been worked out. On the other hand, if a formula already exists then there is no point in trying to approximate the solution using hundreds of rules of thumb.

Third, human experts are in short supply by definition if they are truly expert, but in some areas they are rarer than others. It is cost-effective to computerize skills that are in high demand before attempting more commonplace ones like image recognition, which pigeons can be trained to do very well and which yield less readily to automation than more intellectual abilities.

Fourth, the ability to handle unreliable and incomplete data is a very important feature of many expert systems. If the data is always reliable and clear-cut, this may not seem important; but we are often inclined to assume that our information is more certain than it actually is simply because computers have forced us in the past to pretend so. Now it is possible to be reasonably precise about uncertainty.

Once it is decided that developing a knowledge-based system is worthwhile, the question arises of what software to use.

There are four kinds of support software you might choose.

(1) *Shells*: standard inference mechanisms plus representation languages, e.g. MYCIN, ES/P Adviser, SAVOIR, SAGE.
(2) *AI Environments*: complete software environments for developing advanced systems, e.g. LOOPS, POPLOG, REVEAL.
(3) *AI Languages*: programming languages with specially good facilities for symbol manipulation, e.g. LISP, PROLOG, POP-11, SNOBOL4.
(4) *Conventional Languages*: The 'devil you know' wearing the 'emperor's new clothes', e.g. APL, BASIC, C, FORTRAN.

The expert system 'shell' is effectively an expert system with the specific knowledge ripped out. You are given an advice language (or equivalent) in which knowledge pertaining to your own application can be framed. The advantage of a shell is that it lets you get started quickly. The disadvantage is that you are likely to outgrow it. Most shells are essentially reconstructions of MYCIN's or PROSPECTOR's inference engine. You provide the knowledge. However, the shell designer cannot be expected to have foreseen exactly your problem. For that reason it is probably best to treat shells as learning tools that give you a chance to explore the field at relatively low cost and refine the ideas on what kind of expert system is actually needed.

One level down, are AI environments such as LOOPS (LISP Object Oriented Programming System). These software tools are more flexible than shells, but provide less in the way of pre-programmed inference mechanisms. LOOPS itself is based around LISP, but it includes a whole range of tools (editors, window managers, icon and mouse-control software, knowledge representation sublanguages and so on) to make the knowledge engineer's life easier. Both LOOPS and POPLOG are delightful systems to work with, and offer at the very least a significant increase in programmer productivity. The big disadvantage is that they are complex systems, too demanding for the average personal computer. Therefore you can develop systems which you cannot (yet) deliver to people with today's 8/16-bit desktop or portable microcomputers.

A good deal of mystique surrounds the first and second choice languages of AI researchers, namely LISP and PROLOG. Both have excellent facilities for creating and manipulating symbolic data structures, and both have proved their worth in AI research. But just because you get LISP, or PROLOG, on your micro and write a program in one of those languages, does not mean that you are somehow 'doing AI' or building an expert system. Both languages have good and bad features, and in their naked form (i.e. outside an AI support environment) do not get you very far along the road to knowledge engineering.

At the bottom level, it is worth reminding ourselves that expert systems can be written in any language you find convenient. There may be good reasons (efficiency of code, lack of necessity to retrain programming staff) for considering a conventional algorithmic language as the medium for your own knowledge engineering project. If you already have a large software base, at least you will be spared problems like trying to get a shell to communicate with your existing database (which can gobble up man-hours with a frighteningly voracious appetite).

8.9 SUMMARY

Expert systems represent a new approach to the design of software for intelligent decision support. Knowledge engineering is the name given to the methodology for building expert systems.

A typical expert system has four major components: (1) the knowledge base; (2) the inference engine; (3) the acquisition module; and (4) the explanatory interface.

The knowledge base consists of the information structures that encode the system's expertise. Usually, this is elicited from a human expert and reformulated in the computer's terms as a collection of rules, a network of facts or a frame-based structure. A knowledge base differs from a database in several ways: in particular, it is more active. That is, it contains rules for deducing facts that are not explicitly stored.

The inference engine uses the knowledge base and the facts of the case to derive new conclusions leading to a recommendation or diagnosis. Very often it can cope with missing or unreliable data by means of some form of approximate reasoning.

The acquisition module eases the knowledge acquisition process by testing proposed rules for inconsistency, redundancy and so forth. More advanced systems use inductive methods to create rules from examples, thereby generating new knowledge for themselves. This topic is covered in depth in Chapter 9.

The importance of an explanatory interface is that it allows the user to interrogate the system by posing HOW or WHY questions. HOW questions request the system to justify its own reasoning ('How did you reach that conclusion?'). WHY questions ask it to explain why it needs some piece of information ('Why are you asking me that?'). Both facilities make the system more usable.

More and more organizations are finding that knowledge engineering techniques allow them to tackle problems that could not be solved easily (or at all) with conventional methods.

ANNOTATED BIBLIOGRAPHY

Clocksin, W. and Mellish, C. (1981), *Programming in PROLOG*, Springer-Verlag, New York.

This was one of the first, and still one of the best, introductory PROLOG books on the market. The 'Edinburgh' dialect that it uses has become a *de facto* standard for the language as a result of the success of this textbook.

Forsyth, R. (ed.) (1984), *Expert Systems: Principles and Case Studies*, Chapman and Hall, London.

This book gives more detailed coverage of many of the topics discussed in the present chapter. Since I am biased, let me quote from the review in *British Book News*: 'The book is well written and anyone with a basic knowledge of computers wishing to learn more about expert systems will find it a useful introduction to the subject.'

Gashnig, J. (1982), PROSPECTOR: An expert system for mineral exploration, in *Introductory Readings in Expert Systems* (ed. D. Michie), Gordon and Breach, New York.

Gashnig was one of the authors of the influential PROSPECTOR system and this is a very clear description of how it works, with particular reference to its use of Bayesian reasoning and a discussion of how it was validated.

Harmon, P. and King, D. (1985), *Expert Systems: AI in Business*, Wiley, New York.

This is a very clear account, aimed at technical managers rather than programmers, of the state of the art in expert system design.

Hartnell, T. (1985), *Exploring Expert Systems on your Microcomputer*, Interface Publications, London.

An interesting do-it-yourself guide aimed at the non-specialist personal computer user.

Michie, D. (ed.) (1982), *Introductory Readings in Expert Systems*, Gordon and Breach, New York.

This book contains the Gashnig reference and a number of other interesting papers by key workers in the field of knowledge engineering.

Naylor, C. (1983), *Build Your Own Expert System*, Sigma, Wilmslow, Cheshire.

This popular book was the first to bring expert-system techniques to the home-computer enthusiast. It shows you, step-by-step, how to build up an expert diagnostic system in BASIC. Highly recommended as an entertaining introduction to the subject.

Shortliffe, E. (1976), *Computer-Based Medical Consultations: MYCIN*, Elsevier, Amsterdam.

Shortliffe invented the MYCIN system which has proved the most influential of all expert systems. It would not be exaggerating much to say that an expert system is a program that does something similar to what MYCIN did; to find out how . . . read this book.

Spiegelhalter, D. and Knill-Jones, R. (1984), Statistical and knowledge-based approaches to clinical decision-support systems, *J. Roy. Statist. Soc.*, **147**, 35–77.

This paper is interesting chiefly because it bridges the gap between statistical and knowledge-based approaches to clinical decision making. It uses a more sophisticated approach to Bayesian inference than is commonly employed in expert systems today.

Weiss, S. and Kulikowski, C. (1984), *A Practical Guide to Designing Expert Systems*, Chapman and Hall, London.

As the title implies, this is a practical guide for the expert system designer. One of the better knowledge-engineering guidebooks on the market.

FRONTIERS

One of the major bottlenecks of expert systems construction is the issue of knowledge extraction, which is costly and *ad hoc* in its present form. Automatic gathering of rules from experts, automatic generation of rules from examples and a form of adult learning seem to be necessary major components if expert systems are to become as successful as it is hoped they will be.

Richard Forsyth presents a chapter on machine learning which links into the earlier chapter on expert systems. He also raises the issue of the need for learning in intelligent systems in general. Machine learning has always been a cornerstone of attempts in cybernetics and early AI, but has been considered too difficult to tackle for a couple of decades. However, it seems to be enjoying a revival, both in orthodox AI in the form of systems for formula discovery in mathematics, and also within the new architecture initiatives as a basic mechanism for controlling computation in massive brain-like novel architectures. We seem to be in the same spiral as that encountered in cybernetics. That is, we now seem to have enough computational power to attempt building brain-like systems which also have a significant fraction of the computational power of the brain.

Ajit Narayanan, in his chapter, surveys these developments and seems to align himself with the researchers who believe that the dedication to the general purpose but sequential processing nature of our computing devices has blinded us to the possibilities offered in experimenting, not with programs to control a standard general purpose architecture, but with the design of new architectures for intelligent systems.

9

Machine learning

RICHARD FORSYTH

Machine learning, though neglected for the best part of 20 years, is one of the core problems of Artificial Intelligence (AI) because it is the key to so many other abilities. While mainstream AI concentrates on building 'adult' systems, there is a body of opinion which believes that problems like speech understanding and computer vision are so difficult that they can only be solved by building 'childlike' systems with the capacity to improve. After all, no one expects human babies to emerge from the womb and ask politely for a cup of tea (or even warm milk).

9.1 INTRODUCTION

A computer system may be said to learn if it improves its performance at a given task over a period of time without being reprogrammed. It is important to realize that this implies an agreed yardstick or standard against which the system can be measured. Therefore, in the absence of an agreed way of evaluating progress, it is meaningless to speak of learning.

Thus a learning algorithm attempts to do one or more of the following:

- cover a wider range of problems;
- give more accurate solutions;
- obtain answers at lower cost;
- simplify stored knowledge.

The last point assumes that simplification of stored knowledge is valuable, even if it does not result in better performance on the computer's task. This may be true if the system starts off with one set of rules and ends up with another equally effective set which happens to be more comprehensible to people, or simply more compact.

Machine learning can apply to many domains; but most successful learning systems have something in common: they fit into a classification framework. The objective of such systems is to look at some input data and classify or identify or interpret that data in some way. For example,

Input	Output
patient's symptoms	→ diagnosis tuberculosis
sonar signals	→ submarine 250 m below

Even within this paradigm, there are many important applications to be tackled, for example,

> given the weather readings for the last 7 days, predict whether a gust of over 60 knots will arise in the North Sea during the next 48 hours; given the drilling log of a test borehole, decide whether to drill an oil-well or not.

The exciting thing about machine learning is that it represents one more step away from programming (specifying how to do something) towards instructing (specifying what goals we want achieved).

9.2   A PARADIGM FOR LEARNING

Several methods of achieving automatic performance improvement have been tried. Two of the simplest – namely, rote learning and parameter adjustment – were pioneered by Arthur Samuel in his classic studies of machine learning using the game of checkers (Samuel, 1967). Even before that Rosenblatt and Selfridge, among others, had devised pattern-recognition systems with rudimentary learning capabilities (Rosenblatt, 1962; Selfridge, 1959).

Parameter adjustment is simply an optimization technique which has been extensively studied in the literature of applied mathematics. It hardly merits the title 'learning' (perhaps because it is relatively well understood!). Rote learning, with selective forgetting, can be effective enough in practice; but I discount it here because it is entirely uncreative. It is purely a storage compression technique, whereas the methods we consider are capable of generalizing and hence of learning the appropriate response in a situation not previously encountered.

Any system designed to create new knowledge and thereby improve its performance must include the following major components:

(1) a set of data structures that represent the system's present level of expertise (the Rules);
(2) a task algorithm (the Performer) that uses the rules to guide its problem-solving activity;
(3) a feedback module (the Critic) which compares actual results with those desired;

(4) the learning mechanism itself (the Learner) which uses feedback from the critic to amend the rules.

This is sketched diagrammatically in Fig. 9.1.

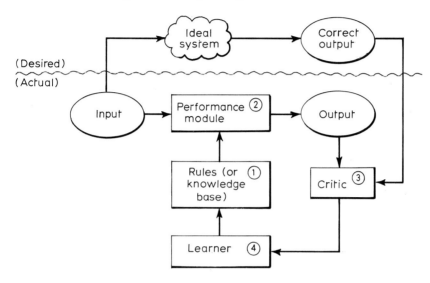

Fig. 9.1 Paradigm for learning.

Most current expert systems have a read-only knowledge base. A learning system, in contrast, has an erasable-programmable knowledge base. To keep things simple, we shall only consider tasks which can be reduced to input–output pairings so that the classification model makes sense, e.g. from symptoms to diagnosis, from game-state to appropriate move, and so on.

Obviously, although this chapter concentrates mainly on particular learning algorithms (module 4), the language or notation in which the system's knowledge is expressed (module 1) of crucial importance too.

9.3   THE DESCRIPTION LANGUAGE

Indeed the choice of representation to encode the system's knowledge is at least as important as the details of the learning algorithm. One of the most successful of recent 'discovery' programs, EURISKO (Lenat, 1982), owes its success largely to its highly flexible description language. All EURISKO's concepts and heuristics are expressed in a single format, as 'units'. Units are record-like structures that are manipulated by the discovery rules (other units). Simple syntactic changes in a unit are likely to lead to meaningful, and possibly valuable, new units. By contrast, small alterations in a conventional program or its data structures are likely to produce nonsense.

So before building a learning system it is vital to ensure that the description language is capable of expressing the kinds of distinction which will be needed. This is not a trivial problem.

It is convenient if the representation for the input data is the same as that for the descriptions (or rules) but this is not always the case. Some representations that have been used in practice are tabulated below.

System	Input formalism	Rule formalism
Perception	Feature vector	Weight vector
ID3	Feature vector	Decision tree
AQ11/INDUCE	Predicate calculus	Predicate calculus
LS–1	Feature vector	Rule-strings
BEAGLE	Data record	Boolean expression
EURISKO	'Units' (frames)	'Units' (frames)

A feature vector, as used in the Perceptron and other systems, is just an array of numbers. Each number characterizes the state of one attribute of the input.

The ID3 induction program (Quinlan, 1982) uses feature vectors for the input but a tree structure for the decision rules that it builds up. (An example is given later in this chapter.)

The series of programs devised by Michalski and his associates including AQ11 and INDUCE (Dietterich and Michalski, 1981) employ logical expressions in an extended predicate calculus notation to represent both input examples and class descriptions. The AQ11 program successfully induced a description from examples that enabled it to classify soybean diseases better than an acknowledged expert in agricultural biology.

LS-1 is a program that is described later in this chapter as an instance of a genetic learning algorithm (Smith, 1984). It was tested on a poker-betting task using simple feature vectors to represent the state of the game and fixed-length strings to represent production rules in a special language. These strings were manipulated by the pseudo-genetic operators and represented the system's expertise by controlling its betting decisions.

BEAGLE is another evolutionary learning program described later in this chapter. It uses 'flat-file' database records for its input examples and Boolean expressions, held internally as tree structures, for its rules.

Finally, EURISKO as mentioned above, which is one of the most impressive current discovery programs, uses framelike data structures called Units to represent practically everything in the system – including objects, concepts and heuristic rules. To show what a unit looks like, here is one of the concepts used by EURISKO in tackling a naval wargame (the Trillion Credit Squadron fleet design game) which it won.

Name:	Energygun.
Generalizations:	(anything, weapon).
Allisa:	(gameconcept, gameobj, anything . . . abstractobj, physicalobj, physgameobj).
Isa:	(defensiveweapontype, offensivewea- pon, physgameobj).
Myworth:	400.
Myinitialworth:	500.
Worth:	100.
Initialworth:	500.
Damageinfo:	(smallweapondamage).
Attackinfo:	(energygun-attackinfo).
Numpresent:	Nenergyguns.
USPpresent:	energygunUSP.
Defendsas:	(beamdefense).
Rarity:	(0.11 /19).
Focustask:	(Focusonenergygun).
Mycreator:	DLenat.
Mytimeofcreation:	4–June–81 16:19:46.
Mymodeofcreation:	(EDIT nucmissile).

Each field in the unit is called a 'slot' and describes one facet of the concept. For instance, The Isa slot says that an energy gun is a type of defensive weapon, among other things, and the Worth slot specifies its value, on a scale from 0 to 1000. It is important to note that rules and meta-rules can be described as units as well as concepts: this is one of EURISKO's strengths. (To describe EURISKO's mode of operation would take the whole chapter: it is a very complex system. In a nutshell, however, what it does is wander around its conceptual space making small alterations to its concepts and rules and seeing how well they work.)

From the variety of notations successfully used we can conclude that there is no one ideal representation language for machine learning problems. However, it is important that the representation used is adequately expressive for the task in hand.

9.4 LEARNING BY SEARCHING

Assuming that we can solve the non-trivial problem of devising a suitable description language, how do we automate the generation of accurate descriptions in that language?

One way of looking at the problem is as a search through the space of all possible descriptions for those which are useful in the current context. The number of syntactically valid descriptions is astronomical; and the more expressive the description language, the more explosive is this combinatorial problem.

Clearly, some way has to be found of guiding the search and thereby ignoring the vast majority of potential descriptions, or concepts, which are irrelevant to the purpose in hand.

Since search is a fundamental notion in AI, and since learning is usually considered as an unrelated topic, the idea of learning as a searching process is worth illustrating by an example. Let us suppose that we have a database of weather records and the task of the learning algorithm is to learn how to classify records on the basis of whether it rains the next day or does not. The machine must induce a rule for making this discrimination.

Assume further, for the sake of simplicity, that each record contains only four fields. These four variables are: rainfall in millimetres; sunshine in hours; wind (maximum gust) in knots; and pressure at noon in millibars. Thus a typical record from the 'training set' (the instances used in forming the rule) might be

rainfall   0;
sunshine   7.2;
wind   22;
pressure   1017;

rather a nice day, in fact!

The rules are composed by linking variable names and constants with the following operators.

Logical   AND, OR, NOT
Comparison   >=<

Thus the description language allows Boolean expressions such as

Sunshine<4 AND Pressure<1000

with brackets if necessary. This is a relatively simple description language, but it suffices for our imaginary weather-forecasting example.

Given the preceding training data and description language, the learning system can start with an initial description (which may be randomly created) and apply transformation operators to generate its successors. The successors are new descriptions for testing. The transformation operators may include generalization and specialization. The process is illustrated in Fig. 9.2.

Each description is a decision rule that can be evaluated according to

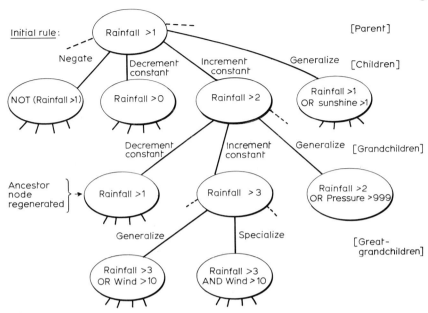

Fig. 9.2 Learning as a search. Here we are assuming that at each stage only the descendant with the highest evaluation score has its descendants generated by applying transformations such as: negate, increment constant, generalize, etc. The search defines a tree-like structure but the underlying *search space* has a network structure, as we see when the node Rainfall > 1 is encountered at two different levels of the search tree.

how well it distinguishes days followed by rain from days not followed by rain. One search strategy would be to generate successors only from rules that have a high evaluation score, i.e. effective rules.

The diagram shows that this process can be viewed as a search through a network where the nodes are descriptions (rules) and the links are transformations that modify descriptions and thereby generate new ones for testing. It is induction by machine.

Note that the search defines a tree-like structure, but the underlying search space is a network or graph, because repeated applications of the transformations can regenerate an ancestral rule. This corresponds to revisiting a node in the network, and there is an example in the diagram: 'Rainfall>1' appears at two different levels.

A number of searching methods have worked well with noise-free training instances (Langley, 1977; Mitchell, 1982). Dealing with 'noisy' data, however, is a more challenging problem. We shall restrict ourselves to looking briefly at a few systems that have had some success with noisy data.

9.5   PERCEPTRON-TYPE SYSTEMS

The earliest learning machines included a variety of trainable classifiers, which appeared in the 1950s, of which Rosenblatt's Perceptron attracted most attention (Rosenblatt, 1962).

Such systems were intended for automatic pattern-recognition tasks such as recognizing hand-printed letters of the alphabet or distinguishing between diseased and healthy blood cells. In general, they take their input descriptions as numeric vectors, and assign each data vector to one of two (or more) predefined classes. Most systems of this type use a weighting scheme whereby each feature in the data vector is multiplied by a coefficient and the products are added together. The result is then compared to a threshold (typically zero). During the training phase the weighting coefficients are adjusted in a systematic fashion according to the performance of the system on known examples.

The Perceptron is based on a simplified model of the human retina, as can be seen from Fig. 9.3.

To simplify matters we shall call all such systems Perceptrons, though strictly speaking the Perceptron is merely one of a large family of trainable classifiers that differ among themselves in significant respects (see Sklansky and Wassel, 1981).

As an illustration, imagine a Perceptron given the task of examining national flags and deciding whether the nation concerned is an Islamic

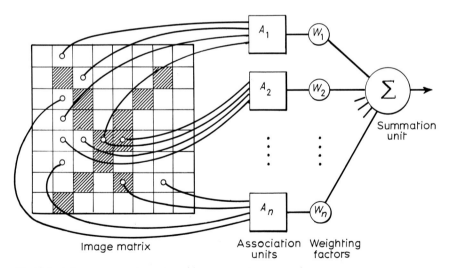

Fig. 9.3 A Perceptron. Association units combine single-pixel responses into group features. Each feature is weighted and the weighted sum is compared to a threshold to make the final class decision. But is it an *x* or a *y*?

country or not. The input data will be a coded description of a flag, and in the training phase this will be associated with the correct classification. The flags of Syria and Taiwan, for example, might be presented as follows.

[Feature	Syria	Taiwan	Coefficients]
Vertical bars	0	0	0
Horizontal stripes	3	0	0
Number of colours	4	3	0
Red	2	2	−1
Green	0	0	+4
Blue	0	1	−1
Gold	1	0	0
White	1	1	−2
Black	1	0	+1
Orange–brown	0	0	+1
Crosses	0	0	−1
Circles	0	1	0
Stars	0	1	−1
Moons	0	0	+2
[Category	+	−	]

Here the presence of various attributes has been numerically coded, so that Stars=1 means that there is one star in the flag, Green=0 means that the colour green is absent, Red=2 means that red is the dominant colour (covering more area than any other hue), and so forth. It will be noted that this is a rather impoverished description language. It does not, as it stands, convey any information about the relative positions of the various identifiable features (stars, crosses, etc.). You can see a lot more at a glance by looking at the flags of the two countries in Fig. 9.4, for instance, that Syria's flag has a golden eagle in the centre (which is not coded above). Nevertheless, feature vectors are simple to implement and adequate for many purposes.

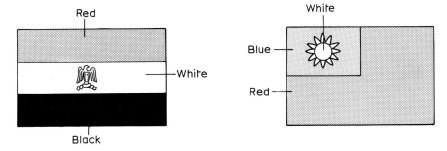

Fig. 9.4 Flags of Syria and Taiwan.

The task of the learning algorithm is to find a set of weights by which to multiply these numbers so that for Islamic countries the sum is positive and for others it is negative. A hypothetical set of such coefficients is shown above. It gives totals of −3 for Syria and −7 for Taiwan, so although it is going in the right direction, it is not yet correct on both these training instances. To improve the weight-set the Perceptron's error-correction strategy works as follows:

- If the output was positive but should have been negative, subtract all the input feature values from the corresponding weighting coefficients.
- If the output was negative but should have been positive, add all the input feature values to the corresponding weighting coefficients.

The process only adjusts weightings when a mistake is made. It can start from a random set of values and converge in a finite number of steps to the desired weightings – as long as the classes to be discriminated are 'linearly separable'. (This requirement effectively states that if the N features are envisaged as defining a shape in N-dimensional hyperspace, a hyperplane boundary can be drawn separating the region containing positive instances from that containing negative ones.)

There was a good deal of enthusiasm in the early 1960s for this kind of system. However, the Perceptron concept fell from grace with the publication of Minsky and Papert's (1969) book on the subject. They showed just how many interesting recognition tasks could not be performed by simple Perceptrons. For example, a Perceptron cannot in general be trained to recognize whether or not the left half of an image is the mirror image of its right half.

Perceptrons went out of fashion, but like so many scientific backlashes the reaction was overdone. Fortunately, a few dogged researchers continued to investigate learning algorithms of this kind. One such researcher is Igor Aleksander, now of Imperial College, London.

Aleksander and his colleagues have produced a practical recognition system called WISARD (Wilkie, Stonham and Aleksander's Recognition Device) which is a variation on the Perceptron theme using modern technology (Aleksander and Burnett, 1984). It operates on images containing 512×512 or 262 144 pixels and can make the rather subtle discrimination between a smiling and a frowning face in real time (i.e. at 25 frames a second from a TV camera). Its commercial potential in sorting and grading chocolates, eggs and other products visually by scanning a conveyor belt is already being realized.

WISARD is a trainable machine; and – unlike almost all recent AI systems – it is not a program running on a conventional computer, but consists of special hardware. It contains electronic components

(8 million bits of RAM) but not arranged as a computer system. This allows it to perform thousands of operations in parallel.

Another neurologically based approach to machine learning that requires special-purpose hardware is the Boltzmann machine (Hinton, 1985). This is based on a connectionist theory of how the brain works, so there are signs that the style of neural modelling that went out of fashion with the Perceptron is due for a revival. The revival depends on the fact that microelectronic circuits are becoming cheap enough for devices containing millions of processing elements to be feasible.

9.6   ID3

Quinlan's ID3 (Interactive Dichotomizer 3) embodies a different approach. It is not particularly robust in the face of noisy data, though it could be improved in this respect if it did not always seek a 'perfect' rule. The program works as follows.

(1) Select at random a subset of size W from the training set (the 'window').
(2) Apply the CLS algorithm (detailed below) to form a rule for the current window.
(3) Scan the entire database, not just the window, to find exceptions to the latest rule.
(4) If there are exceptions, insert some of them into the window (possibly replacing previous correctly classified examples) and repeat from step 2; otherwise stop and display the rule.

Note that this procedure actually throws away the latest rule and starts again from scratch on each cycle. The method of window selection is sometimes termed 'exception-driven filtering'. The need for a window arises because the main database may contain hundreds of thousands of cases and be too large to be processed (from disc) in an acceptable time.

The CLS algorithm (Hunt, Marin and Stone, 1966) is effectively a subroutine of the main program. The Concept Learning System (CLS) derives originally from work done by Jerome Bruner and other experimental psychologists in the 1950s and 1960s. It first appeared as a proposed model of what people do when given simple concept forming tasks, and only became a computer algorithm later on, due to Hunt and others. Thus it is a rare example of AI borrowing an idea from psychology, rather than the other way round.

CLS works by first finding the variable (or test or attribute) which is most discriminatory and partitioning the data with respect to that variable. Quinlan used an information-theoretic measure of entropy (surprise) for assessing the discriminatory power of each variable, but others have suggested different measures, e.g. the chi-squared statistic. Having divided the data into two subsets on the basis of the most discriminating variable, each subset is partitioned in a similar way (unless it contains examples of only one class). The process repeats recursively until all subsets contain data of one kind only. The end-product is a discrimination tree, which can be used later to classify samples not before encountered.

ID3 discrimination trees performed well on King–Rook/King–Knight and other chess end-game problems, where the data is clear-cut and free from noise. Really noisy data, however, such as weather records, leads it to grow very bushy decision trees which fit the training set but do not generalize to new examples. In the worst case it can end up with one decision node for every example!

ID3's main shortcomings are listed below:

(1) the rules cannot be probabilistic;
(2) two identical examples have no more effect than one;
(3) it cannot deal with contradictory examples (which are commonplace outside the rarified environment of chess end-games);
(4) the results are therefore highly sensitive to small alterations to the training database.

These objections would lose much of their force if ID3 stopped before it reached a subset with no counterexamples at all. To give an illustration, we return to our flag data, and the problem of telling Islamic from infidel nations by their flags. Figure 9.5 shows part of a hypothetical discrimination tree for this purpose. (N.B. This is not real data.)

The training set contains sixty-nine example flags, of which eleven are from Islamic countries (positive instances). At the top of the tree is the most predictive test, Green>1, which divides the data into those flags with green in them and the rest. The two boxes descending from the Yes and No branches show that this test partitions the data into two subsets: on the left are the twenty-six flags with green of which six are positive examples and twenty are negative; on the right are the flags without green, of which five are positive and thirty-eight negative examples. The partitioning continues down the leftmost branch with the next test, Moons>0, which divides the subset of green flags into those with a crescent- or moon-shaped icon of some sort (five cases) and the others (twenty-one cases). Of the five with green and one or more moons, only one is a negative instance. ID3 would go on and try to split up this very small subset, but with minor modifications it could be made to halt at that point. When the tree was later used in decision mode, it could classify a case where Green>1 and Moons>0 were both true as 'probably (80%) Muslim'.

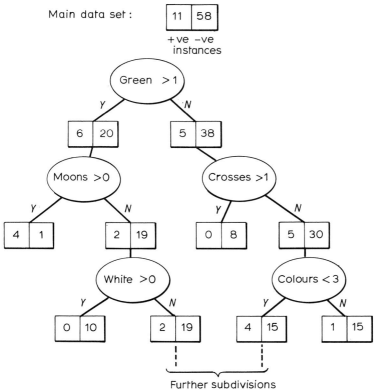

Main data set :

11 | 58

+ve −ve
instances

[Tests are in round boxes ; subset frequencies are in rectangular boxes]

Fig. 9.5 Partial probabilistic discrimination tree.

We also show some decision nodes where the process has gone down to a subset containing only one sort of data (0:10 and 0:8) which would be where ID3 normally terminates the subdivision.

Although a probabilistic ID3 (ID4?) would solve the problems outlined above, the system still has a major weakness. This is the poverty of its description language. Its rules are decision trees of a restricted kind in which each node is a test, which typically has only two branches. The tests can only be simple comparisons of a variable with a constant, e.g. Red>0 or Rainfall>12. This excludes compound tests of any kind, making use of logical or arithmetic operators. It also precludes comparison of one variable with another. Thus such innocent formulations as

Red>0 AND White<1

or even

Red>White

are simply inexpressible – though obviously they could be useful.

ID3 is relatively quick, but this efficiency is purchased at a cost. Clearly, a more expressive description language would make the tree-growing far more complex; but the poverty of its description language places the heavy burden of devising an effective set of descriptors squarely on the user. Any preliminary calculations or logical operations have to be incorporated in the descriptors before running the program. (ID3 is the basis of a package marketed as 'Expert-Ease' in the UK.)

9.7   GENETIC ALGORITHMS

When AI scientists look to nature for ideas on how to design self-improving devices, three systems catch their eyes – the nervous system, the immune system and the process of evolution.

The nervous system, especially the human brain, is a marvellously effective learning mechanism. But its operations are still shrouded in mystery. We do not yet understand it well enough to copy it. The body's immune response system can also be said to learn, in that it comes to distinguish self from other tissue. Over the course of a lifetime it learns to recognize millions of foreign proteins. Without its astonishing adaptability and reliability we would all quickly die. Yet it appears to be in essence a rote memory system: its powers of generalization are negligible.

That leaves the evolutionary process. It is certainly effective as a means of devising ever more advanced organisms, otherwise we would not be here contemplating it. It may be slow; but it can be speeded up in computer simulations. Above all, it is relatively well understood. It is simple enough for us to imitate with some hope of success.

Holland (1975) proposed a theoretical treatment of evolutionary adaptation which was largely ignored by the AI community at first. Now, however, some AI workers are starting to use genetic algorithms as the basis for effective learning systems. We shall look at one of them, described by Smith (1984).

Smith's LS-1 (Learning System 1) was tested on a number of tasks. One of these was learning to make bet decisions in the game of draw poker. The state of the game is represented by a small number of state variables, in effect a feature vector. The program can make one of four betting decisions: **BET HIGH, BET LOW, CALL** or **DROP**. This brings it into the classification framework, since it evaluates a situation and selects one of a limited number of alternatives as the appropriate response.

The knowledge was encoded as a list of stylized production rules. Each rule contained a pattern-template as its left-hand side, which could be matched against the game-state representation and the contents of working memory. Its right-hand side contained a list of actions which could deposit messages in working memory or initiate one of the four output responses. The system's main processing cycle is as follows.

(1) Randomly generate an initial population of M rule structures.
(2) Compute and save the performance score of each rule. If the overall average is sufficiently good, stop and display the rules.
(3) For each rule calculate the selection probability $p=e/E$ where e is its individual score and E is the total score of all M rules.
(4) Generate the next population of rules by selecting, using the selection probability distribution, and applying the genetic operators. Repeat from step 2.

Thus the expected number of offspring of any rule in the next generation is proportional to its success in the task being learned. This is the analogue of 'survival of the fittest'.

The genetic operators employed in step 4 are crossover, inversion and mutation. Crossover is a kind of mating in which, for instance, the rules ABCDE and VWXYZ might produce the descendant ABXYZ in the next generation. The inversion operation is rather like an internal crossover, and merely records elements so that the same items are not always close together.

Mutation is a background operator. It consists of making small random changes. It ensures that all parts of the search space (all descriptions in the language) are theoretically reachable; but, contrary to popular belief, it is not the primary means of generating new structures. (In simple terms, sexual reproduction is more effective than asexual reproduction.)

To allow these genetic operators to apply to the rule strings, Smith had to encode his rules as equal-length strings containing position-independent components. This is rather a severe restriction and makes it hard to devise a workable description language, and still harder to devise one that is intelligible to humans as well as the computer.

Nevertheless, his results were quite impressive. After 42 000 rounds of simulated poker betting (4200 generations) LS-1 was beating a hand-crafted poker program (in the betting phase) approximately 89% of the time. In addition, its decisions were in 100% agreement with a pre-defined set of poker 'axioms'. All evolutionary algorithms are essentially modified Monte Carlo methods, so it is perhaps fitting that one such algorithm should do so well in a gambling game. (This is a slightly simplified account of the evaluation, but it does not distort the fact that the system performed more than satisfactorily.)

The work of Smith and others has shown that Holland's ideas can serve as the basis for useful learning programs. The main disadvantage of genetic algorithms has been the constraints imposed on the form of rules, i.e. on the description language, so that the genetic operators can chop them up and resplice them without producing nonsense. We consider next another system with a biological flavour, which employs a somewhat less restrictive rule representation.

9.8 BEAGLE

BEAGLE (Biological Evolutionary Algorithm Generating Logical Expressions) is a computer system for producing decision-rules by induction from a database. As such, it addresses the problem – frequently side-stepped – of where the rules in a rule-based system come from.

BEAGLE works on the principle of 'Naturalistic Selection' whereby rules that fit the data badly are killed off and replaced by mutations of better rules or by new rules created by mating two better adapted rules. The rules are Boolean expressions represented by tree structures.

The original software (Forsyth, 1981) consisted of two PASCAL programs, namely HERB (Heuristic Evolutionary Rule Breeder) and LEAF (Logical Evaluator And Forecaster). Together they perform the task of classifying samples into one of two or more categories on the basis of a number of variables or features. HERB creates or modifies rules which LEAF then uses.

HERB requires three input files: a datafile, a payoff file and an old rule file (which may be empty). It produces as output a new rule file which is at least as good as the old one. The datafile contains the training set, for which the correct category membership is known. The user also has to furnish a payoff matrix which defines the value or cost of correct and incorrect classifications.

A rule is represented on file as a fully bracketed expression ended by a dollar sign, e.g.

$$((£4 \text{ GE } 15) \text{ OL } (£8 \text{ LT } £7)) \text{ \$}$$

which states that variable 4 (£4) should equal or exceed 15 or that variable number 8 should be less than variable 7 for the expression to be true.

Odd names like OL (for OR) were chosen to avoid clashing with PASCAL predefined symbols; but this description language is clearly not 'user-friendly', and in the latest version of BEAGLE the expression above would appear as

$$(\text{rainfall} >= 15) \mid (\text{morn:humidity} < \text{eve:humidity})$$

which names the variables and thus should be a lot clearer to the user.

LEAF is simpler than HERB. It merely takes a datafile in the same format as the training set and runs a rule file over it. It can be requested to print out, among other things, an ordering of cases from most likely to least likely YES. (The user determines what YES means under the circumstances.)

Note that the rules produced by HERB do not, in general, require extensive calculation and could in principle be applied by a person. Contrast this with, for instance, an SPSS discriminant function of ten coefficients each expressed to eight decimal digits of precision.

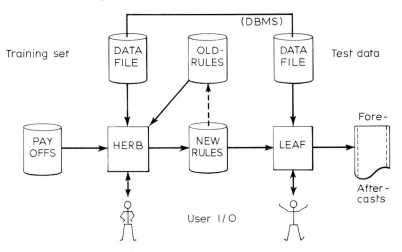

Points:
(1) Payoff file defines costs of various kinds of mistakes
(2) Initial old-rule file may be empty
(3) Rules are Boolean expressions
(4) LEAF is just one way of using the rules

Fig. 9.6 BEAGLE synopsis.

The BEAGLE learning algorithm consists of repeating the following procedure for a number of generations, where each generation is one run through the training data.

(1) Evaluate each rule on every sample according the payoff matrix, with a bonus to short rules.
(2) Rank the rules in descending order of merit and remove the bottom half.
(3) Replace 'dead' rules by applying the MATE procedure to a pair of randomly chosen survivors, thus recombining portions of good rules.
(4) Mutate a few randomly chosen rules (but not the top one) and apply procedure TIDY to all new rules – ready for the next generation.

The TIDY procedure cuts down on certain syntactic redundancies such as double negatives, constant expressions and so forth, leaving the pruned rule-tree with the same value but expressed more succinctly.

Obviously, this is based on a caricature of the 'Neo-Darwinian Consensus' in biology. Tests on hospital admissions (classing heart patients as fatalities or survivors) and on athletic physique (classing Olympic athletes as sprinters or distance runners) were carried out. It appears from the trials that the method works better than a standard discriminant analysis technique based on linear functions, and is quite robust in the face of noisy data. In addition, the rather naïve evolutionary theory embodied in the HERB program behaved in a gratifyingly lifelike fashion.

What typically happened was the appearance, and subsequent demise, of dominant 'species' of rule. Each type flourished for a while until quite suddenly supplanted by a new and superior line – usually a mutation of one of its own offspring. When this happened the extinction of the more primitive form was rapid and complete.

Here are the top two rules in one of the cardiac-patient tests after 111 and 1111 generations.

	Score
111:	
(137 OVER (£6 GT 53))	51
(135 OVER (£6 GT 53))	51
1111:	
(£6 GE (61 LESS £14))	69
(£6 GE (62 LESS £14))	69

The top pair in each case are obviously close relations (almost clones), while the newer pair are more distantly related to the older pair.

To interpret the rules, you need to know what variables are being measured. Variable number 6 (£6) is the patient's mean arterial pressure; variable 14 (£14) is the urinary output in millilitres per hour. The last rule says, in words, that if the mean arterial pressure is greater than or equal to the urinary output subtracted from 62 the patient will survive; otherwise not. This is just a superficial association in the data observed by the program, but a doctor could supply a deeper explanation. When the heart is failing, the kidneys pack up too, so it is a bad sign if the patient stops urinating. As for arterial pressure, we have become conditioned to think that high blood pressure is unhealthy; but a blood pressure of zero is even less healthy.

It is perhaps worth reflecting that biologists may be arguing over different evolutionary mechanisms without actually knowing the consequences of their rival theories. If this is indeed so, then the value of experiments like BEAGLE may in the long run be as tools for helping biologists refine competing hypotheses by building models and observing their behaviour. After all, it is notoriously difficult to predict the activities of complex systems even if they are of your own creation (children and brain-children alike).

9.9 CONCLUSIONS

It is hard to imagine machine intelligence without machine learning. After all, if someone repeats the same mistake over and over we call them stupid. Yet mainstream AI has for decades tried to build intelligent systems where all the contingencies facing the program, in effect, have to be anticipated and preprogrammed. The only surprising thing is how far this approach has gone (e.g. towards master-level chess-playing programs). This is a testament to the skill of AI programmers.

Nonetheless, effective machine-learning techniques have been devised. There has not been space to include them all (e.g. Winston, 1984) in this chapter, but enough has been said to show that AI workers need not handicap themselves by designing systems that cannot improve.

The age of the creative computer is about to begin.

ANNOTATED BIBLIOGRAPHY

Aleksander, I. and Burnett, P. (1984), *Reinventing Man: The Robot Becomes Reality*, Pelican, London.

Professor Aleksander was one of the workers who persisted with the neural-net approach to vision when it fell from fashion, and has recently designed a commercially successful adaptive image recognition device. This book describes it in a highly readable style.

Dieterich, T. and Michalski, R. (1981), Inductive learning of structural descriptions, *Artif. Intel.*, **16**.

Michalski and his team at the University of Illinois have devised a number of learning algorithms. This paper describes AQ11, among others, which learned to diagnose soybean disease from examples with a higher success rate than any human expert.

Forsyth, R. (1981), BEAGLE: A Darwinian approach to pattern recognition, *Kybernetes*, **10**.

This paper describes the BEAGLE evolutionary learning system in greater detail than the present chapter.

Forsyth, R. and Rada, R. (1986), *Machine Learning*, Ellis Horwood, Chichester.

Covers topics raised here in greater detail.

Hinton, G. (1985), Learning in parallel networks, *Byte Mag.*, **10**.

Geoff Hinton is the head of a team at Carnegie–Mellon University developing intelligent systems based on the Boltzmann machine – a highly parallel machine architecture modelled on the brain.

Holland, J. (1975), *Adaptation in Natural and Artificial Systems*, University of Michigan Press, Ann Arbor, Michigan.

This book analyses the adaptive properties of various abstract genetic algorithms, some of which have formed the basis for practical machine learning systems.

Hunt, E.B., Marin, J. and Stone, P. (1966), *Experiments in Induction*, Academic Press, New York.

This book describes the CLS algorithm, which formed the basis for Quinlan's ID3 learning strategy. It is an interesting example of a computer system inspired by psychological research. Usually it is the other way round: psychologists borrowing computer-science concepts.

Langley, P. (1977), Rediscovering physics with BACON-3, *Proceedings of the Fifth International Joint Conference on Artificial Intelligence*.

Langley's program is modelled on Francis Bacon's advice on how to conduct scientific research. It looks for regularities in physical data of the kind that led to discoveries, such as Boyle's Law, in seventeenth-century physics.

Lenat, D. (1982), The nature of heuristics, *Artif. Intel.*, **19**.

Douglas Lenat is the author of EURISKO, probably the most important learning system to date. This is a good account of how it works.

Michalski, R., Carbonell, J. and Mitchell, T. (eds) (1983), *Machine Learning*, Tioga Press, Palo Alto, California.

A useful source book, containing chapters by diverse authors, including Douglas Lenat and the editors.

Michie, D. and Johnston, R. (1985), *The Creative Computer*, Pelican, London.

A highly readable layman's guide to computer creativity which of course includes machine learning, since learning is the creation of new knowledge.

Minsky, M. and Papert, S. (1969), *Perceptrons*, MIT Press, Cambridge, MA.

This is the book that laid the Perceptron to rest by demonstrating what it could, and could not, do. As we have seen, however, the ghost of the Perceptron still haunts the AI laboratories of the world.

Mitchell, T. (1981), Generalization as search, *Artif. Intel.*, **18**.

A classic paper showing the connection between the two fundamental – and previously unrelated – AI topics of learning and search. The only problem with Mitchell's learning scheme is that it cannot cope with missing or incorrect training data.

Nilsson, N. (1965), *Learning Machines*, McGraw-Hill, New York.

An early textbook of the subject, still useful by virtue of its rigorous approach.

Quinlan, J.R. (1982), Semi-autonomous acquisition of pattern-based knowledge, in *Introductory Readings in Expert Systems* (ed. D. Michie), Gordon and Breach, New York.

This paper describes the ID3 program and some tests of it on chess end-game situations.

Rosenblatt, F. (1962), *Principles of Neurodynamics*, Spartan, London.

A book from the heady days when computers were still called 'electronic brains' with some ideas on how they might live up to that description. Rosenblatt was the author of the Perceptron concept.

Samuel, A. (1967), Some studies of machine learning using the game of checkers, II, *IBM J. Res. Develop.*

Another classic early paper in the field. Samuel invented several ways to get his checker-playing program to improve its performance, and it is fascinating to see how many modern ideas he anticipated.

Selfridge, O. (1959), Pandemonium: A paradigm for learning, *National Physical Laboratory Symposium on Mechanization of Thought Processes*, HMSO, London.

Even before the Perceptron, people were proposing models of learning loosely based on what goes on in the brain. Selfridge's was one of the first.

Sklansky, J. and Wassel, G. (1981), *Pattern Classifiers and Trainable Machines*, Springer-Verlag, New York.

For the mathematically inclined reader this book sums up what is —known about 'black box' approaches to learning, i.e. learning systems that do not have description languages that humans can understand, but rely on weighting vectors or other mathematical formulations.

Smith, S.F. (1984), Adaptive learning systems, in *Expert Systems: Principles and Case Studies* (ed. R. Forsyth), Chapman and Hall, London.

This chapter describes the LS-1 system that learned to make good betting decisions in poker using a genetic algorithm. The book contains two other chapters on machine learning.

Veve, S. A. (1980), Multi-level Counter-factuals for Generaliztions of Relational Concepts and Productions, *Arif. Intel.*, **14**.

Winston, P. (1984), *Artificial Intelligence*, 2nd edn, Addison-Wesley, Reading, MA.

Winston outlines a method of learning by amending structural descriptions expressed as semantic nets in his book. His methods are not considered further in this chapter, but they have had considerable influence on the field.

10

Memory models of man and machine

AJIT NARAYANAN

During the last 20 years or so, there has been an increase in the use of concepts taken from computer science for modelling psychological processes. This application of the computational metaphor is most clearly described by Boden (1979), who states that the computational metaphor can help the psychologist generate and test psychological hypotheses about the mind's content and functions. Boden then lists a number of computational concepts that have proved useful to psychologists, among which are: subroutine, recursive procedure, top-down and bottom-up processing, linear and parallel processing, and content-addressable memories. The aim of this paper is to survey one particular area of psychology to which the application of the computational metaphor is proving fruitful: memory. We shall see how psychologists have used the information-processing paradigm to explain various phenomena associated with human memory and how, more recently, various psychologists are rejecting this conceptual paradigm in favour of more hardware-oriented models.

10.1 THE TRADITIONAL USE OF THE INFORMATION-PROCESSING PARADIGM

The common view of human cognitive processing is that it proceeds in a linear, sequential fashion (Norman and Bobrow, 1976) through certain stages (Fig. 10.1). Details of the system vary from author to author, but the assumption is that processing proceeds from sensory transduction to final storage in long-term memory. Information from long-term memory is used in pattern recognition, and rehearsal processes can recycle material in short-term memory.

This model works in the following way. Physical signals – be they auditory or visual – are sensed by the system and transduced (i.e. linearly converted in the same way that a microphone picks up signals) to a form which can be stored in the sensory information store. Pattern recognition processes then attempt to identify the physical signal by

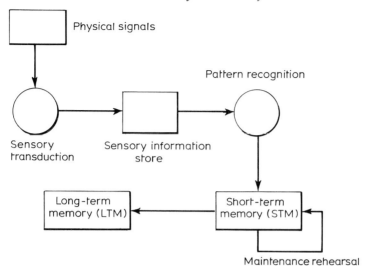

Fig. 10.1 Traditional linear sequential model of human memory.

matching the pattern of the sensory physical information against, typically, stored patterns in long-term memory. If a match is found, then
generally a symbolic identifier for that particular pattern – typically a
word or concept – is stored in short-term memory (STM). Without
maintenance rehearsal (i.e. without the subject maintaining an item in
his STM by, say, repeating it to himself), the symbolic item is lost after a
matter of seconds. The identifier may also enter long-term memory
(LTM) where it will be stored on a more permanent basis.

   This is obviously a simplistic account of what is essentially a complex
model, and the principles and components will be examined in greater
detail shortly. Another similar view of human memory comes from
Cohen (1969) (Fig. 10.2).

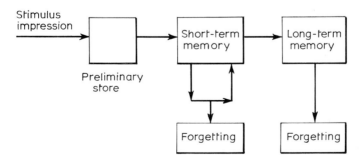

Fig. 10.2 Cohen's memory model.

The idea that memory may be viewed as a system of inter-related components (i.e. structurally) is not a new idea. James (1890) distinguished between primary memory, one that endured for a very brief period of time, and secondary memory, the knowledge of a previous state of mind. However, it is generally considered that the modern structural view of memory is due to Miller (1956), who used data to show that normal, adult, educated subjects can repeat back, in order, an average of only seven digits, letters or words immediately after presentation and irrespective of the different amounts of information each of these items conveyed. Also, we can check or code material in a form which allows more than the average seven individual items to be recorded. For instance, we could remember twenty words instead of seven if the twenty words included five words from four categories, such as animals, countries which have won the football World Cup, cities and weapons. As we listen to each word, we can categorize the item and, on recall, remembering the category names produce the instances to which they are related. In that paper, Miller developed the notion of the organism as an information-processing device, with a limited capacity for handling information but capable of overcoming these limitations by, for example, categorization.

However, it was Broadbent (1958) who introduced the notion of the organism as an information-processing device that explicitly contained an STM of limited capacity. While information was in this memory, rehearsal of this information and its transfer to more permanent store were possible. Without rehearsal, the information would be lost. Then in the late 1950s, Brown (1958), Peterson and Peterson (1959), and Sperling (1960) produced data which implied that there was a very STM for the aural and visual systems. If items were presented very briefly, under certain conditions there was rapid loss of the information. These experiments led to the postulation of buffer systems between the sensory systems on the one hand and STM on the other. However, certain models allow the LTM to play a part in the item recognition at the sensory stage (cf. traditional information-processing model presented earlier).

In addition, Tulving (1972) proposed a further division in the LTM, suggesting that in our LTM we have episodic knowledge and semantic knowledge. Episodic knowledge or memory concerns episodes peculiar to an individual, whereas semantic knowledge or memory concerns rules, facts and principles independent of the individual's existence. For instance, some of us will have knowledge on how to construct a Pascal computer program in that we remember the syntactic rules for doing so. This knowledge is independent of us; it is part of computer science. However, we each as individuals may have different memories or knowledge of how and when we acquired the knowledge – whether it was at school or evening class, whether it was taught to us or whether we read it. . . . This knowledge is more or less unique to us as individuals.

10.2   LOWER LEVELS OF THE PARADIGM

The above comments are consistent with the view that a human can be regarded as a symbol-manipulating or information-processing device and as such fit into a certain level of description and explanation. However, there is another, lower level of description still consistent with the application of the computational metaphor. At this level, the internal processes of the computer are used as paradigms for the human brain. For instance, multi-processor intercommunication techniques can be used as paradigm, for communication between units in the brain. Computer storage and retrieval processes at a 'physical' level can be used as paradigms for human memory storage and retrieval processes. This level of description is not at the most basic level, since the human brain and the computer brain are structured out of different building material. Rather, this kind of description assumes a common theoretical framework for examining the human mind and the computer 'mind'. Most frequently, the framework arises from regarding a human cognitive process and a computational process as consisting of recognizable states at a certain level of abstraction. The axioms of the theoretical system will require that the entity under examination be able to change from state to state and that the states of the entity be identifiable or recognizable.

Within this framework, it is possible to regard memory structure as a conceptualization imposed upon physical states, where one processor or many processors can control the use of the elements during input and output tasks. The computational metaphor here consists of adopting physical computer memory models and architectures as paradigms for human memory.

10.3   SOME CONCRETE EXAMPLES OF MEMORY MODELS

We shall now present some models. First, let us examine models which adhere closely to the traditional information-processing approach.

10.3.1   **HAM**

In 1974, Anderson and Bower (1974) proposed an architecture of a Human Associative Memory (HAM) system that is consistent with the traditional linear-stage theory of processing (Fig. 10.3).

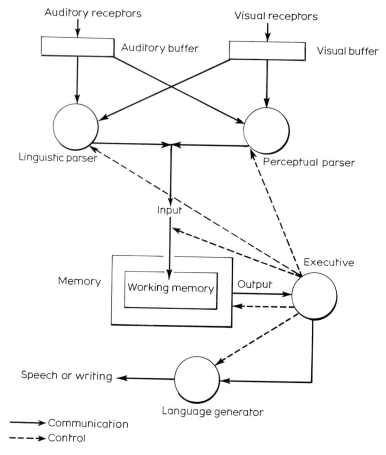

Fig. 10.3 The architecture of HAM.

HAM works in the following way. Auditory and visual receptors pick up physical signals which are stored in an auditory and visual buffer, respectively. Linguistic and perceptual parsers then attempt to identify and recognize the signals. Note that auditory information can enter the perceptual parser and that visual information can enter the linguistic parser. In this way, Anderson and Bower allow for cases where linguistic parsing is helped by visual clues and perceptual parsing is helped by auditory clues. The use of parsers evokes the idea of active rule-governed procedures for identification and recognition rather than simple passive pattern-matching. As a result of the parsing, an input compatible with memory representation of items is produced, and this input is then stored in working memory. An item in working memory may well be passed on to memory itself, and the memory components can themselves produce an output for the executive, or control mechanism, of the system to work on. The executive can then send items to the language generator which transforms the items into a form compatible with speech or writing. Note that the executive can control the operation of the parsers, the nature of the input, the working of the memory units and the language generator.

10.3.2 SHORT

SHORT (Gilmartin, Newell and Simon, 1976) is a computer program written in SNOBOL which represents a theory of how humans use STM and, to a lesser extent, how they use LTM and the various sensory-related buffers during common STM tasks (Fig. 10.4). In this figure, arrows 1, 2 and 3 represent the flow of information during implicit auditory rehearsal: X represents the process of recognition or perception, and this process has access to information in the LTM.

An auditory or visual item presented to the system is automatically registered in the appropriate sensory store: echoic memory or iconic memory. Research has shown that humans lose information very quickly from the sensory stores. Visual information persists for about 250 to 500 ms, or perhaps more, while auditory information lasts for at least 3 or 4 s. SHORT is constructed so that even after termination of the stimulus, a visual stimulus persists for 250 ms and an auditory stimulus for 3 s in their respective stores. When SHORT accesses a sensory store, part or all of that information is copied to the appropriate imagery store. An item is recognized if SHORT can find a match between a pattern of

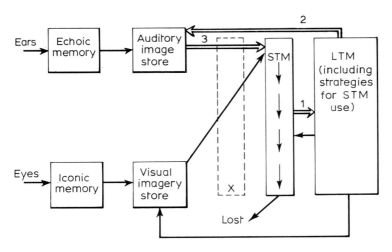

Fig. 10.4 The architecture of SHORT.

information in a store and a pattern previously stored in LTM. If such a match is found, a symbol denoting the corresponding entry in LTM is placed in STM. It is by means of pattern-matching that SHORT moves from the physical realization of auditory or visual stimuli to a symbolic representation which can then be manipulated.

STM is a linear array of eight cells organized as a queue. Each cell can hold a single symbol or chunk. In addition to symbols, cells can contain control information, such as symbols that indicate the status of some part of the system. Whenever a new symbol is placed in STM, the oldest one is bumped out and lost. Items can be retained in STM only by rehearsal, that is, by the system inserting a new copy of the item at the front of the STM. All searching or scanning in STM is from back to front, i.e from the oldest items to the newest.

Rehearsal consists of the following three steps:

(1) a symbol in STM is used to access a corresponding entry in LTM;
(2) stored at that entry in LTM is information about the symbol or chunk and its relation to other chunks, perhaps even programs for expressing the chunk via speech or script and for setting up a pattern in the imagery;
(3) finally, this pattern in imagery store can be re-perceived and a new symbol denoting it can be placed in front of the STM, thereby completing the process of rehearsal.

All the major processes in the model are timed so that SHORT carries out the same amount of processing as a human. For instance, SHORT can rehearse four single-syllable items per second.

10.3.3 Logogens

Next, let us describe John Morton's logogen model (Morton, 1970), which is probably the first real model to use the parallel processing metaphor.

Morton's functional model of memory is unusual on several counts. His model is functional in that he attempted to distinguish between brain processes on the basis of clearly identifiable functional criteria rather than structural criteria. Functional criteria include the logical nature of the code in which information is processed, the kinds of information that can interact, and the logical form of the processing operation.

One interesting result of adopting functional criteria is that Morton had no use for the distinction between STM and LTM in his model, since he believed that these terms only described differences in the interval between presentation and recall of information and did not refer to different storage systems. That is, Morton believed that 'short-term memory' and 'long-term memory' were separated only by the time that it took to recall an item from allegedly the one as opposed to allegedly the other when a stimulus was presented or when free recall was involved. Items presented recently would be recalled more quickly than items presented not so recently, but that did not mean there were two different memory systems.

Morton's model, known as the logogen model, was initially developed to account for performance in a variety of word recognition tasks. Morton assumed that when a verbal response was available, the same final unit operated to produce that response regardless of the source of the information that led to the response. So, if we read the word 'chair', or hear it spoken, or see the physical object, or if we are asked to complete the sentence 'I sat on a . . .', the same word is available as a response (and can be given overtly). The origin of the response is called a 'logogen' which is the part of the system that produces or leads directly to instructions being sent to the articulator (Fig. 10.5).

Let us now examine Morton's model in more detail. The sensory analysis systems, both visual and auditory, extract significant features from the stimulus. For instance, if the stimulus is the written word 'cat', the visual analysis system would extract information to the effect that there is an initial letter 'c', a second letter 'a', a final letter 't', that the

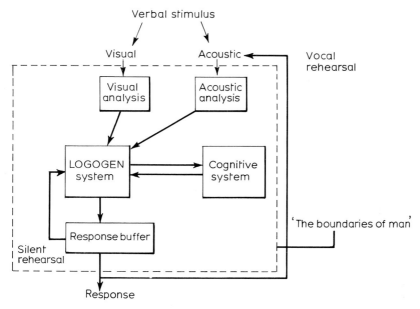

Fig. 10.5 The logogen model.

word is a three-letter word, and so on. If the stimulus is the spoken word 'cat', the acoustic analysis system would extract such acoustic information as 'one syllable word', and other auditory features would be identified. The information so extracted is fed to the logogen system, which consists of logogens. Each logogen is defined by its output which can be represented by a set of phonological features and by the sets of acoustic, visual and semantic attributes. A logogen can be understood as a word, for our purposes. The set of semantic attributes is the most important defining set. For instance, there would be two logogens for 'ball', even though the visual and acoustic attributes would be the same. One logogen would corrrespond to the meaning 'spherical object', and the other to 'social function for dancing'. If a logogen receives as an input an attribute which is a member of one of its defining sets, it acts as a counting device in that it is incremented. When the count reaches a certain threshold value, the appropriate response is made available.

For instance, if 'cat' were the visual stimulus, part of the output from visual analysis would consist of 'three-letter word'. The logogens for 'cat', 'dog' and 'cot' would all be incremented. If another part of the output were 'initial-letter c', the logogens for 'cat' and 'cot' would be incremented, but not the logogen for 'dog'. The response would be determined by the logogen in which the count first exceeded the critical, threshold value.

The power of the model arises from the assumption that the critical value of the count is not the same for all logogens. It is claimed that following the 'firing' of a logogen, its threshold is reduced, therefore leading to fewer sensory attributes being required to produce the response again. However, following this lowering of the value, the logogen stabilizes by slowly rising back to its critical value. It is suggested that the original critical value is never completely regained. The implications of these two claims are:

(1) the prior presentation of a word increases the likelihood of it subsequently being produced as an incorrect response, since fewer attributes are required to fire the logogen again and mis-identification of the stimulus becomes facilitated; and
(2) for high-frequency words, fewer sensory attributes will be required to produce the response than for low-frequency words, since the higher the frequency of usage of a logogen, the lower will be its initial value.

These claims are empirically verifiable.

The context (which can be of any kind) of a verbal stimulus has the same effect on the production of a response as the stimulus itself. For instance, the context of 'sot' in 'He is a drunken sot' consists of information gleaned from 'He is a . . . ', which in turn consists of the attributes 'noun', 'animate' and 'male'. All logogens whose semantic sets contain these items will be incremented accordingly prior to the word 'sot' being presented. These increments effectively reduce the amount of sensory information required to produce the response, since the attribute counts from the two sources, one being the context, the other the stimulus itself, are simply added together without regard to source. It is part of the function of the cognitive system to supply such contextual information to the logogen system, but for verbal information to act as a context, it must first have passed through the logogen system. So each logogen has two outputs: one goes to the cognitive system, the other to the response buffer.

With the first type of output, the cognitive system processes the information fed into it by the logogen system and sends signals back to the logogen system, thereby affecting the threshold values of logogens. The input to the cognitive system is semantic input. That is, it consists of the semantic attributes of logogens. However, the value of the count required to produce a semantic output to the cognitive system is lower than the value required to produce the second type of output to the response buffer. This is to account for the fact that sometimes it is necessary to obtain information from the subsequent context of a stimulus in order to recognize it, rather than the preceding context. So it is necessary to assume that the output of a logogen to the cognitive system occurs before the output to the response buffer, and that this information is then fed back into the logogen system after processing. More and more semantic information can be recirculated in this way as the subsequent context of the unrecognized stimulus is processed, until eventually the critical value of a certain logogen is reached and the phonological features of that logogen are output to the response buffer. An appropriate output to the response buffer in this case is caused by the full semantic description of an item provided by the cognitive system. So, for instance, when we come across 'It was a — that I sat upon', where the dash represents an unrecognized word, the semantic information from 'that I sat upon' can be recirculated back to the logogen system via the cognitive system, thereby leading to an increase in the count for 'chair' (as well as 'stool', 'bench' . . .).

The response buffer receives phonological features of triggered logogens and a response can then be said to be available. The system can then choose to output the response or not. The response buffer allows for the fact that when people are reading aloud, there is normally a gap between the eyes and the voice of up to five words in length. The response buffer is used for their temporary storage. Also, the system allows for 'silent rehearsal' of information output from the logogen system to be recirculated and fed back to the logogen system itself. Quick recirculation is useful when items presented to the system have to be recalled backwards, for instance. The response buffer has several properties:

(1) it has a limited capacity of items;
(2) it stores items temporarily;
(3) it stores items correctly when such items are initially placed in the buffer;
(4) when it is filled, it stays filled as long as the subject is paying attention to its contents.

If the subject decides to output an item from the response buffer phonologically, we then have a response sent out of the system. The acoustic properties of this response can then be fed back into the entire system, and here we have vocal rehearsal (e.g. an actor rehearsing the lines of a play). Note that the response buffer, which is similar to the STM component of the previous models, comes at the tail-end of the system.

In Morton's model, the cognitive system is the only part which has memory as part of its function. In the cognitive system will be syntactic and semantic rules, semantic information on the context so far encountered, and so on. Other parts of the system store information for varying lengths of time only as a by-product of their main functions. The logogen system is primarily a device for converting sensory information into semantic or phonological (language recognition), phonological information into semantic (silent rehearsal), and semantic information into phonological (speech production). Note that within the logogen system, there is no direct way of transferring information from one logogen to another.

10.4 CONCRETE EXAMPLES OF THE PARADIGM AT A LOWER LEVEL

Let us now briefly examine some lower level computational paradigms of memory (Winograd, 1976). According to the *sequential access* model, memory elements are stored in a built-in sequence, such as a series of locations along a physical storage mechanism, like a magnetic tape. The central processor can move along the sequence in any direction, but cannot 'jump' over any memory locations. For instance, if there is a certain item which is to be retrieved at the end of a tape, the read–write head of the mechanism must pass over all the intervening locations before reaching the desired location. The amount of time required to find or store an item depends strongly on how far that item is from the

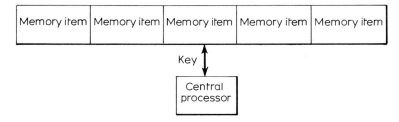

Fig. 10.6 Sequential access model.

current position being read, and retrieval time increases linearly with the amount of material stored (Fig. 10.6). Memory items are accessed by means of a 'key', which is some part of the memory item that uniquely distinguishes that memory item from other memory items.

This is the simplest memory access model available, but it is not a promising paradigm for human memory. One of the implications of this model is that humans who have a large number of items in their memory should take longer to recall arbitrary items than humans who have a small number of items in their memory, *ceteris paribus*.

According to the *random access* model, there is some device which can convert some element of the item (the key) into an address for a particular location in memory. The item can then be stored in that location directly (Fig. 10.7). Problems occur if two items have the same designated location (i.e. when 'collision' occurs), and there are several strategies available for overcoming these problems.

However, neither sequential nor random access models are considered powerful enough for representing memory organization and structure, mainly because of their reliance on passive elements. In both models, computer memory is regarded as consisting of individual elements which are nothing more than mailboxes. Models using active memory elements are considered to be much more promising. Most of

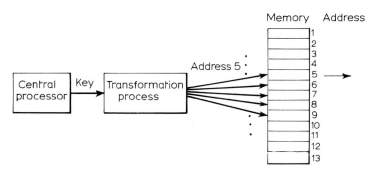

Fig. 10.7 Random access model.

the current research taking place in active memory centres around the notion of associative memory. There are two ways of looking at associative memory. The computer engineering approach refers to principles of memory organization and management and is commonly called content-addressable memory. The conceptual or logical approach refers to semantic representations of knowledge, usually by means of relational structure of semantic networks. We shall concentrate on the first approach, but our comments may sometimes mention the second.

10.5 SEMANTIC NETWORKS

It may be useful at this point to say a few words on semantic networks. The semantic net, developed by Quillian (1968) and others, was invented as an explicit psychological model of human associative memory. The concept of human associative memory is historically derived from Aristotle's so-called 'Classical Laws of Association'. In essence, these laws state that mental items such as ideas, perceptions, sensations and feelings are connected in memory under the following conditions:

(1) if they occur simultaneously ('spatial contact');
(2) if they occur in close succession ('temporal contact');
(3) if they are similar;
(4) if they are contrary.

Contemporary views of human associative memory generally use conditions (1) and (2) for storing or encoding information and (3) and (4) for recalling information. We then have the idea that memory is able to store representations of structured sequences, and information is searched for within memory on the basis of some similarity relating a key or search pattern to some item's pattern in the stored sequence. Given these introductory remarks, we can then say that a semantic network consists of a set of nodes, which represent objects or situations, and arcs or arrows, which represent the relationships between nodes and connect the nodes. Storage then consists of representing the item using nodes and arcs so that spatial, temporal and other forms of 'contact' or relation that objects, concepts or situations have with each other are clearly specified. Recall consists of identifying a node or relation in the network and following the arcs involved to recall the structure and content of the original sequence.

10.6 ASSOCIATIVE MEMORY AND CONTENT-ADDRESSABLE MEMORY

One way to look at associative memory is to imagine a collection of nodes, each of which represents a symbol or concept, physically linked together in a network. So this approach interprets the arcs of a semantic network to be wires capable of carrying signals, and each wire connects two nodes. Each memory element can process the signals received in some way and send out other signals. The most primitive type of association, called direct association, is formed when the representations of two or more items or events are brought together and stored in memory in direct physical (or logical) contact. Sensory experiences are associated if they occur simultaneously or within a short space of time.

In addition to direct associations, there may also be indirect associations, which occur at recall time. In this case, there must be two or more direct associations in memory which share common or identical items. For instance, we may have item 'a' associated with item 'b' directly, and item 'b' associated with item 'c' directly. Then we have an indirect association between 'a' and 'c' which may be found at recall or retrieve time.

Let us introduce a definition by Hanlon. Associative memory means a memory which is

> ' . . . a collection or assemblage of elements having data storage capabilities . . . which are accessed simultaneously and in parallel on the basis of data content rather than any specific address or location.' (Hanlon, 1966)

Another common term for associative memory is content addressable memory (CAM). CAM is a storage device that stores data in a number of cells that can be accessed on the basis of their content rather than by address location. Each memory element is active and communicates with the central processor. When something is desired from memory (e.g. the information associated with a single word), the processor sends out a message describing what is wanted – a key or cue – and each

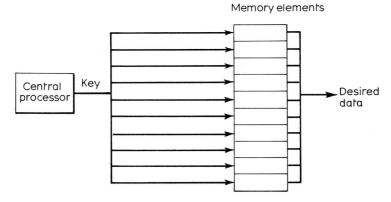

Fig. 10.8 General architecture for CAM.

element processes the description and decides whether it has the appropriate information. If so, it sends it back. For instance, the general architecture would be as given in Fig. 10.8. So, for instance, we could have the model as described in Fig. 10.9, which is similar to the architecture provided by Kohonen (1980). We could assume that at most one match will be found for any key. Every key word location contains a register for the word as well as a special combinatorial logic circuit which compares the key word, broadcast in parallel to all locations, with the stored contents.

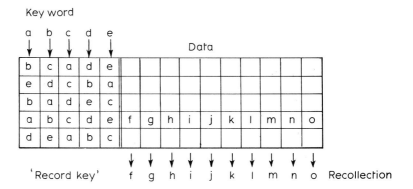

Fig. 10.9 Kohenen's CAM architecture.

10.7   IMPLEMENTING CONTENT-ADDRESSABLE MEMORY

Content-addressable memory can be implemented in either hardware or software. Software implementation is based on data-dependent memory mapping by means of programming techniques, whereas hardware implementation uses special hardward mechanisms for the storage and retrieval of data items. Let us consider software implementation first of all.

The simplest way to implement CAM by means of software is to use hash-coding. Symbolic names are translated into addresses of locations in such a way that the memory limitations of the computer are taken into account. Also, the hash transformation should ideally distribute the names evenly over the memory space so that the risk of collision is kept acceptably low. This method assumes that each data record of an association will have as a part a key of some type that can be input to the hash transformation. The address is calculated from the key and if the appropriate memory location is empty, the whole record, i.e. the data plus key, is stored at that particular address. The key needs to be stored so that, when retrieving, the system can check the input key against the

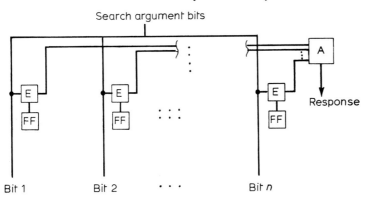

Fig. 10.10 Circuitry for CAM.

stored key in order to verify that the appropriate location has, in fact, been found. In cases of collision when storing, a record may be moved to some other location which has then to be searched for. Ideally, this other location, or reserve location, should be easily reached from the calculated address. One common method adopted to find a reserve location when collision occurs during storing (and retrieving) is the use of the next empty location following the calculated address. We can then say that the correct location is found on retrieval when the stored name agrees with that used as a search argument.

Now let us consider the simplest way to implement CAM by means of hardware. Assume that at word locations binary patterns with bit elements 0 or 1 are stored. The search argument is broadcast by means of a set of parallel lines, each one carrying a bit value, to the respective bit positions of all word locations. There will be built-in logical circuitry consisting of a logical equivalence gate at every bit position, and a many-input AND gate that is common to the whole location. The logic circuit will give a response if and only if the search argument agrees with the stored binary pattern (Fig. 10.10) (Kohonen, 1980). This diagram depicts a comparison circuit for one CAM word location, where 'FF' stands for 'bit-storage flip-flop', 'E' stands for 'logical equivalence gate', and 'A' stands for 'logical AND gate'.

10.8 SEARCHING CAM

The above implementation works very well when it is assumed that the entire search argument will always be presented. However, there may well be cases when a masked search is useful, i.e. when only a subset of the bits of the search argument is compared with respective bits in word memory. Those stored words which agree in the specified, or un-masked, bit positions with the search argument are read out.

The equivalence relationship can be unpacked as follows:

$$(x = y) = (x \times y) \text{ v } (\bar{x} \times \bar{y}),$$

where x and y denote the Boolean values of two binary variables:

    × stands for logical AND; v stands for logical OR
    ¯ stands for complement (negation).

That is, each logical equivalence gate would be constructed according to the above formula. For a masked search, each bit position is equipped with a match gate, plus some indication as to whether this bit is involved in the comparison or not.

10.9   CAM RESPONSES

There are several different strategies for handling responses from CAM. Let us assume that when something is desired from memory the processor sends out a message describing what is wanted – a cue – and each element processes the description as described above, sending back information if there is a match between search argument and stored word. We could then have separate data paths from each element to the processor, by means of which the processor and the memory elements communicate (Fig. 10.11). However, a more economical arrangement is to have a bus, which is a data path shared by all elements. Each element is able to read whatever is put on the bus by the processor, and if the element wishes to communicate with the processor, it puts a message on the bus as well (Fig. 10.12).

10.10   ACTORS AND DEMONS

So far, we have assumed a centralized processor which controls the retrieval of information and which then computes on the basis of the

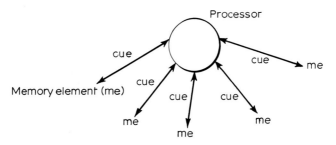

Fig. 10.11 'Star' configuration.

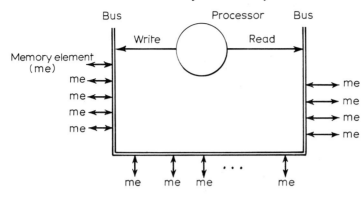

Fig. 10.12 Bus configuration.

information received. Norman and Bobrow (1976) proposed another method, called the actors and demons method, which constitutes a rejection of this assumption (Fig. 10.13). Their view is that the traditional linear sequence of processing stages is not an appropriate description of what happens. Instead they propose a large number of semi-independent procedures, called memory schemata, that analysze the data sent to them and return results to a common pool. A variety of procedures continually examine the data pool and operate on whatever data fill their

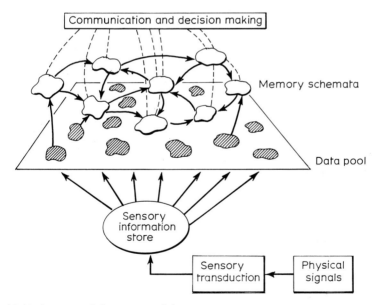

Fig. 10.13 Actors and demons model.

specifications. Some applicable procedure is automatically activated by the arrival of any new data. This is possible because of the ability of the memory schemata (demons) to extract features from the sensory data pool. Not only are the memory schemata active, but also they can communicate with one another (actors) without the need of an explicit control or executive mechanism.

Norman and Bobrow outline the following properties and processing principles of their system.

(1) There is a single, limited pool of resources from which processes must draw.
(2) Memory is constructed out of active units – schemata – that use the data available in a common pool, perform computations upon these data, and then send new results back to the common pool or to other schemata, and/or request specific information from other schemata. Schemata communicate with one another either directly or through the data pool.
(3) A schema consists of a framework for tying together the information about any given concept or event, with specifications about the types of inter-relations and restrictions upon the way things fit together. Schemata can activate procedures capable of operating upon local information and the common pool of data.
(4) Schemata can be invoked by the occurrence of data in the common database relevant to their operations, or by requests from other schemata or the central communication mechanism. A schema can request information from other schemata.
(5) There are no fixed memory locations in the head. Therefore, memory structures must refer to one another by means of descriptions of the information that they seek. Such references are context-dependent descriptions.

In Norman and Bobrow's system the general distinction between active processors and memory elements is blurred. Their system is much more distributed in that their large, active schemata can activate independent processing.

There are various implications of this model, some of which are as follows. We store information in memory as chunks of knowledge. For instance, our knowledge or memory of what is involved in, say, going to a restaurant and eating a meal could be represented by a memory schema. This is to interpret memory schemata at a high level of abstraction. We could easily interpret the schemata at a much lower level. For instance, we could have a memory schema that just identifies the right-hand vertical stroke of the letter N. We could imagine a hierarchical organization of schemata, with low-level schemata operating at the bottom-most level to extract important micro-features and passing the information on to the higher levels. Information flow can be in both directions as well as laterally. (More on this will appear later.) No matter how we interpret the schemata, the important point here is that each schema will have associated with it a processor which is responsible for that particular schema. Therefore, several schemata can work in parallel and can communicate with other schemata. Control of information-flow then becomes crucial if the system is not to sink into chaos, and the task of the communication and decision-making element in the model is to ensure that the system performs in a controlled manner.

Another important feature of this model is that it is both conceptually driven, or 'top-down', as well as data-driven, or 'bottom-up'. That is, the flow of information and control goes in both directions. Schemata can be controlled from above, they can also be 'triggered' by data existing in the pool, and they can alter data in the pool or call on other schemata.

10.11   THE METAPHORICAL REVOLUTION

Let us now examine some of the latest developments in the application of the computational metaphor to memory. Undoubtedly, the most important of these has been the lowering of the level of description. The latest models are characterized by the following properties.

(1) Such models are closely tied to a neurophysiological foundation.
(2) Such models use distributed memories which are an alternative to the 'spatial' metaphors of memory storage and retrieval presented above.
(3) Such models assume a distributed parallel processing system with no need for a central executive to co-ordinate processing.

The latest models begin with a consideration of the brain, how it works and how it is organized. The model builders then construct their memory theories. For instance, the McCulloch–Pitts model of the nervous system, in which the brain is approximated to a set of binary elements – abstract neurons which are either on or off – can be used. The Perceptron (originally developed by Rosenblatt (1961)) is a particular type of neuron and can be regarded as a threshold logic unit (TLU). The TLU has a number n of inputs, each associated with a real-valued weight that plays a role analogous to the 'synaptic strength' of inputs to a neuron. The total input to the TLU is an n-dimensional vector, a pattern of activity on its individual input lines. Each component of the input vector is multiplied by the weight associated with that input line and all these products are summed. The unit gives a value of 1 if this sum exceeds its threshold. Otherwise, it gives an output of 0. More formally, we can say that the output of a unit is the truth value of the expression

$$\sum (f_i \times w_i) > \theta,$$

where f_i is the activity on the ith input line and w_i is its weight, and θ is the threshold.

In the standard Perceptron scheme each input to the TLU is the output of a feature detector that responds to the presence of some feature in an input array. Much work was done on Perceptrons in the 1960s, the main task being to find a set of weights that would cause the Perceptron to respond if and only if a pattern of a particular type were present in the input array. The search for an automatic procedure, known as the Perceptron convergence procedure, that would automatically adjust the existing weights of a TLU whenever those weights would cause the Perceptron to give a wrong answer, was generally regarded as successful (Minsky and Papert, 1969; Nilsson, 1965). However, it had severe limitations for pattern-recognition models. For instance, it was found that Perceptrons could not cope with the exclusive-OR logical function. Despite their limitations, the Perceptron approach is still being adopted. The latest models tend to construct a type of neuron and various types of synaptic links between neurons to provide a physiological basis for the rest of their model.

Such models explicitly reject the idea that human memory is nothing more than a storage device, such as a filing cabinet, contemporary random-access memory, a library . . . The formulators of the latest models reject the assumption that information is stored in a particular place. In their view, information is stored 'everywhere'. Distributed memories retrieve individual memory traces from complex memory traces in the same way that a filter extracts individual frequency components from a complex acoustic waveform (Rumelhart and Norman, 1981). The filter can respond to whatever frequency it is tuned for, no matter how complicated the source. As long as the individual memory traces are sufficiently different from one another, there is no interaction among the stored traces. In these conditions, a distributed memory system can operate as a perfect storage and retrieval device. Storage is possible because each trace will be defined by its own pattern of activated memory elements. Links between activated elements will be formed at storage time. Retrieval is possible because at least a partial match of a search argument with a stored-memory trace will be sufficient to evoke the original pattern, since memory elements are interconnected and activating one element will activate others, and at most a total match will be required. However, the power of such models resides in one memory trace interacting with others. Thus, the system can allow for similar items of information to interact with each other so that common aspects are reinforced (by an increase in the appropriate synaptic strengths) and differing aspects are cancelled out.

Another way to put this is to say that instead of having one internal element or unit responding when, and only when, its particular item occurs, we now have each element or unit responding to many of the possible input items. If only one item is presented at a time, it will be represented by the pattern of activity of the internal units even though no individual unit uniquely specifies the input item. Instead of a single unit or element causing particular effects on other internal representations or on motor output, the pattern of activity of many units causes those effects. It now becomes unnecessary to have a separate higher-level unit that detects the pattern of activity and causes the appropriate effects.

Another claim made by the formulators of the latest models is that even though the computer operates with processing units capable of functioning in the order of tenths or hundredths of nanoseconds, the brain consists of processing units that operate in the order of milliseconds. Yet the brain can perform within those milliseconds processing feats that cannot be emulated in hundreds of minutes of computer time. The conclusion is that the brain accomplishes this feat through the simultaneous operation of many processing units. So, executives and sequentially organized stages of processing are rejected, and a distributed processing system is substituted. Complex computations are assumed to be carried out through the concurrent action of an enormous number of independent processing units, each carrying out its own simple computations or reacting only to its own local set of inputs.

The formulators of recent models argue for parallel processing on the grounds that humans have the ability to recognize items uniquely when given only a partial description of it. The item often 'just comes to mind', with no awareness of any deliberate searching. Moreover, we can do this with no prior warning of the description to come. The concept of CAM is obviously important here. This ability is difficult to program on a von Neumann machine. Such a machine accesses items by addresses, and it is hard to discover the address of an item from an arbitrary subset of its contents. So the von Neumann machine, which is based on the idea of a sequential central processor operating on the contents of a passive memory, is replaced by the idea of a large set of interconnected, relatively simple processors, which interact with one another in parallel via their own specific hardware connections. Changes in the content of memory are made by forming new connections or changing the strengths of old ones. This implies that the addressing mechanism is replaced by specific hardware connections. Items correspond to patterns of activity distributed over many simple hardware units, and the ability of an address to link one item to another is implemented by modifying the strengths of many different hardware connections in such a way that the pattern of activity corresponding to one item can cause the pattern corresponding to the other item. Thus, distributed representation appears to be a particularly appropriate method of coding for a highly parallel machine.

10.12 JUSTIFYING NEUROPHYSIOLOGY, DISTRIBUTION AND PARALLELISM

It should be noted that proposers of such models present a wide variety of arguments and evidence to justify the use of such properties in their models, and so our brief description of such arguments will not be complete.

The neurophysiological basis is argued for on the grounds that memory can be 'shifted' from one part of the brain to another. It appears as if parts of the brain can be reprogrammed neurophysiologically. Much research evidence is available which confirms this belief, and if memory models are to describe or explain memory adequately they must encompass the neurophysiological domain Also, more and more research is being done on functional specialization within the cortex. Anderson and Hinton (1981) claim that it is possible to distinguish about 50 different cortical areas, one of which, Area 17, is called the 'primary visual cortex'. However, this does not mean that the cortex can be easily subdivided into areas corresponding to different functions. Rather, it appears that such subareas of the cortex are connected together in complex ways – in series, in parallel and with potential loops. The point here is that a single cortical area containing many millions of neurons arranged and connected together will have significant implications for cognitive function. In addition, there appears to be considerable evidence to suggest that specified changes in synaptic connectivity store memory. Recent work on 'connection' machines, an instance of which is the Boltzmann machine (Fahlman, Hinton an Sejnowski, 1983, is based on this evidence.

The arguments for distribution are more contentious, and even if such arguments are accepted, there are at least two different ways in which distribution can be achieved. The more obvious one is to construct a distributed memory where each processor corresponds to a single node of the semantic network. Then the arcs of the network can be represented by hardware links, such as wires between units. The less obvious approach is to move up a level and say that each node of a semantic network corresponds to a particular pattern of activity over a large number of units. A node can then partake in many different patterns of activity. According to this approach, a node can now be interpreted as representing a concept, but the node also represents a pattern of activity at a lower microlevel. The implication is that interactions between concepts (i.e. links) are actually generated by many (perhaps millions of) simultaneous interactions at the level of their microstructures.

The arguments for parallelism are of two types. On the one hand, proposers of parallel models would appeal to empirical evidence concerning the existence of highly parallel hardware in the brain, especially in relation to vision and motor skills. Marr (1976) argued that human vision depends on many processes operating in parallel and that such parallel operations have been found to exist in the brain. Also, many neurophysiologists now accept that there is clear evidence of parallelism (and a degree of distribution) in the mammalian neocortex. On the other hand, various theoretical arguments can be proposed which purport to demonstrate that a parallel architecture, at least at the bottom micro-level, offers a much richer and more satisfactory model of human cognitive processes, such as those found in memory, than a purely sequential architecture. The implication here is that although we can simulate such parallel models on a von Neumann machine and at a certain level of description, this does not mean that the von Neumann concept is applicable at lower levels. It can also be argued that in certain areas, such as computer vision, a parallel architecture is more successful than a sequential architecture. That is, it may be acknowledged that for certain tasks, such as chess-playing and problem-solving, the sequential mode of operation corresponds closely to observations of how humans tackle these problems and also to verbal reports from those involved in the task. However, the claim is that there are unconscious processes which seem to demand the use of a parallel architecture.

All in all, the recent models which have the above three properties offer an alternative to the traditional, linear processing model of earlier years. Let us now examine two such models.

10.13 SPREADING ACTIVATION

McClelland and Rumelhart's Interactive Activation Model (IAM) (McClelland and Rumelhart, 1980) deals with letter (and hence, word) recognition. Reicher (1969) showed that when a string of letters is presented very briefly, subjects find it easier to recognize the letters if they form a word than if they form a nonsense string. Also, letter strings

forming non-words which nevertheless can be pronounced are intermediate in difficulty. McClelland and Rumelhart propose a model which
attempts to account for these findings. In so doing, they hope to shed
light on the knowledge that we use to identify and recognize words.
Among Reicher's findings there is the suggestion that perception of a
letter is helped by presenting it within the context of a word. It seems
that our knowledge of words can influence the process of perception.

IAM's basic idea is that when a string of letters is presented, appropriate letter detectors are activated. As the activations of letter detectors
grow stronger, word detectors are activated which then produce feedback so that the activations of the letter detectors are reinforced. Letters
in words are more perceptible since they receive more activation than
representations of either single letters or letters in an unrelated context.
IAM works for letters in either upper-case or lower-case type.

There are three basic assumptions to IAM:

(1) For visual word perception, there is a visual feature level, a letter
level and a word level. However, perceptual processing of any type
takes place within a system in which there are several levels of
processing, with each level representing a different level of abstraction. So, in addition to these three levels in visual perception, there
will be still higher levels of processing above the word level. IAM
thus presents just three layers of the system.

(2) Visual perception involves two kinds of parallel processing. First,
there is spatial parallel processing, which means that several letters
of a word (e.g. four) can be processed at the same time. Secondly,

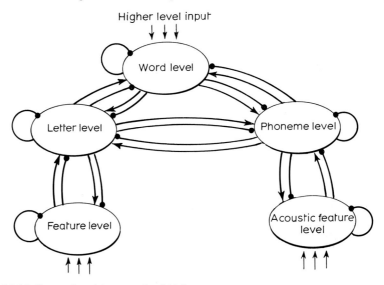

Fig. 10.14 General architecture for IAM.

processing takes place at several different levels at the same time. That is, processing at the feature level, the letter level, and the word level can occur simultaneously.

(3) Visual perception is interactive in that the information processing flow is both upwards (bottom-up) and downwards (top-down). However, one level can communicate only with its neighbouring level either above or below. Also, there is information processing flow within a level.

The general architecture of IAM (for both visual and auditory word perception) is given in Fig. 10.14. Visual input is fed into the visual perception processors and acoustic input into the acoustic feature processors. If we examine just the visual features, we find at this 'bottom' level that there will be processors designed to detect simple features of letters. For instance, if we assume that visual data must conform to a certain font, say,

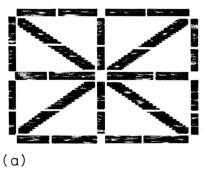

(a)

then any letter in the alphabet can be characterized according to the presence and absence of certain features. For instance, 'C' can be represented as

(b)

and 'L', 'M' and 'N' by

(c)

respectively, and so on. The example font has many different strokes, and we could have one processor per stroke at the bottom level. A presented letter will contain a number of different strokes, and all the corresponding processors will be activated. Strokes are defined not only by their shape but also by their relational position in the font.

Also, we could have feature detectors that look for larger features, such as the right-hand vertical stroke which occurs in 'A', 'B', 'C', 'H', 'J', 'M', 'N', 'O', 'Q', 'U', and 'W', for instance.

Communication proceeds through a spreading activation mechanism in which activation at one level spreads to neighbouring levels. The communication can be either excitatory or inhibitory. Arrows in the diagram represent excitatory activation, in which the recipient's level of activity is increased, and circular ends of connections represent inhibitory 'activation', in which the recipient's level of activity is decreased. Note that the intralevel inhibitory loop represents a kind of lateral inhibition in which incompatible units at the same level compete. For instance, if we have a feature detector which just scans for a full vertical right-hand stroke, if activated it can send inhibitory messages to feature detectors which look for a half vertical in the same position.

Also, the feature detectors can send both excitatory and inhibitory messages to the letter level. For instance, if a full right-hand vertical were detected, the unit responsible would send excitatory messages to the letter detecting processors for 'A', 'B', 'D', . . . and inhibitory messages to the 'P', 'C', and so on.

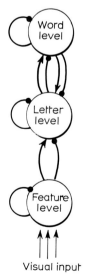

Fig. 10.15 Simplified IAM architecture.

Processors at the letter level operate by attempting to use the information fed to them by the feature detectors to identify the letter scanned. Letter detectors can send inhibitory messages to other letters and excitatory or inhibitory messages to feature detectors and word detectors (i.e. to neighbouring levels). For instance, when the letter detector for 'N' is activated by low-level feature detectors, it can send inhibitory messages to other letter detectors incompatible with 'N' (e.g. 'Z') and excitatory messages back to the feature detectors responsible for sending up the information in the first place to reinforce their levels of activity. Also, it can send inhibitory messages back to incompatible feature detectors to lower their level of activity, and it can send excitatory messages up to word detectors which contain the letter 'N'. In addition, inhibitory messages can be sent to word detectors that do not contain the letter 'N'. Word detectors, likewise, can, when activated, send inhibitory messages to other word detectors and excitatory and inhibitory messages back down to the letter detectors, thereby reinforcing or lowering their level of activity, respectively.

10.14   IAM'S ASSUMPTIONS

In their paper, McClelland and Rumelhart (1980) examine in some detail a simplified version of the above general architecture and even implement the model computationally (Fig. 10.15). Note in this figure that the interaction between the feature level and the letter level has been simplified, and acoustic input is ignored altogether. The authors then describe some of the assumptions of this model.

(1) Every relevant unit in the system is a node, and nodes are organized into levels. Nodes are identified according to the units they detect.
(2) Each node has associated with it a momentary activation value, a real number, which theoretically can vary from 1 to −1. Any node with a positive value is said to be active. In the absence of any inputs from its neighbours, all nodes are assumed to decay back to an inactive state, which may be zero or below. However, individual nodes will have their own rest value, determined by frequency of activation over a long period. For instance, nodes for high-frequency words will have higher resting values than those for low-frequency words. Each node will also have its own decay rate. A node's value is driven up or down, depending on the nature of the input (up for excitatory, down for inhibitory), but it can never go beyond the maximum and minimum theoretical values of 1 and −1, respectively. The authors formalize the model by providing the equations required to describe its behaviour. Essentially, the model is probabil-

istic in that it works on feature detectors reporting the probability that they have identified their respective features, and integration takes a running average of the activation of the node over previous time.

(3) The model operates in the following manner. We assume that the system is in a quiescent state. When a certain visual stimulus is presented, feature detectors start operating and send excitatory and inhibitory signals to the letter nodes. The values of certain letter nodes will rise above their resting level, whilst others, receiving inhibitory messages, will sink below their resting levels. The letter nodes in turn send excitatory messages to word nodes they are consistent with and inhibitory messages to word nodes they are inconsistent with. Also, within the letter level, various letter nodes will attempt to suppress each other for a given letter position. As word nodes become active, they too will compete with one another and send feedback down to the letter nodes. The idea is that the system will rapidly converge on the appropriate set of letters and the appropriate word, settling into a stable state in which the appropriate word and letter units are highly active and the remainder are not. Otherwise, no single set of letters will dominate over any other because of mutual inhibition. Superior recognition of pronounceable non-words over unpronounceable strings is now accounted for by the system having many word nodes active which almost fit the string. Such nodes reinforce the activity levels of the letter nodes, although the letter nodes will be inhibited also by words which do not contain the letter in that position. We can then say that pronounceable non-words are represented by distributed patterns of activity at the word level. Also, letters in words are more easily recognized than single letters, since reinforcing excitatory messages from a word will raise a letter's activity level above the level that the letter node would have reached alone.

The authors view their model as being similar to Morton's logogen system, but with several important differences. IAM is hierarchical, non-linear and interactive between the levels. Also, within a level, there is inhibitory interaction, and IAM incorporates certain dynamic assumptions.

10.15   INHERITING PROPERTIES

The second model we shall examine is Hinton's (1981) model for property inheritance. Although, strictly speaking, this is not a model in the same sense as the previous one we have examined, it is worth examining for two reasons.

First, instead of a different hardware unit corresponding to each node of the system, Hinton's model allows a node to represent or correspond to a particular pattern of activity over a large number of lower units. Thus, Hinton's model is of a more 'abstract' type in that it gives particular names (i.e. nodes) to particular distributed patterns of activity at a lower level. Second, Hinton's model demonstrates the advantages inherent in the use of a distributed representation and shows how simple connection machines may one day perform highly 'intelligent' tasks.

words on property inheritance. Suppose we are told that Clyde is an elephant. From this one simple fact, we immediately know a lot about Clyde which has not been explicitly mentioned. For instance, we know that Clyde is probably grey, has four legs, would not be a good pet for someone living in a basement flat, and so on. We would find it difficult to believe that all this knowledge about Clyde is stored explicitly with our recently acquired fact. Rather it appears that we have general knowledge about elephants. When we are told that Clyde is an elephant, this general knowledge is accessed by us and the general information about elephants is made available.

The importance of this example lies in the implications it has for AI. If an AI system is to serve as a model for human knowledge retrieval and store, it must exhibit comparable size, speed and flexibility. But although we can answer almost immediately what colour Clyde is, or whether he would be a good pet for a flat, it appears that a large amount of deduction and search is necessary. Yet humans with brains built from elements that are very slow by computer standards are able to answer such questions very quickly and with none of the apparent mental effort that one feels when, say, adding up a column of figures.

The property inheritance problem consists of finding a suitable way to represent a token (such as 'Clyde') and a type (such as 'elephant') so that the facts or properties associated with the type are inherited by the token. Two methods have been used.

(1) Duplicate all the information associated with the type and store it with the token. This approach is obviously space-consuming, and if new knowledge is acquired about the type, it must be added to all the tokens that exist.
(2) Use a pointer which allows a token to pick up its type so that whenever a question arises about a token which cannot be answered using the information stored at the token, the type can be inspected. We then develop the idea of token-type relationships that hold between adjacent levels of property inheritance trees. Every time a question is asked which cannot be answered at that level, the node's 'parent' or superordinate type is examined. If the question still

cannot be answered at that level, then the node's super-superordinate type is examined, and so on.

The second approach can be implemented using local representations in a parallel machine that needs specific hard-wired connections between the representations of types and tokens in order to allow property inheritance (Fahlman's NETL system (1979)). However, Hinton adopts a different approach, in that he codes type names and token names in such a way that they have certain patterns in common at a micro level. Any effects that are caused by the pattern for the type will automatically transfer to the patterns for the tokens (unless explicitly overridden). So property inheritance becomes automatic.

So, if we represent the system with the following three facts:

(1) has-legs (Ernie four);
(2) has-legs (elephant four);
(3) has-legs (person two);
and ask it to recall
(4) has legs (elephant ?);
(5) has-legs (person ?);

there would be no problem in retrieving the explicitly mentioned facts. But Hinton's system is such that if the following query were input

has-legs (Clyde ?)

the system would respond with 'four' even though there has been no explicit linking of 'Clyde' with 'elephant' at the observed level. Also, the query

has-legs (Bill ?)

would receive the answer 'two'. The reason for this is as follows.

10.16   INTELLIGENCE OR TRICKERY?

Examine the coding of the items below:

units	units	
000000	000000	0
111000	000000	elephant
000111	000000	person
111000	000111	Ernie
111000	111000	Clyde
000111	101010	Scott
000111	010101	Bill

Patterns of activity are used to represent the various objects. The states of the first six units code the type of object (elephant or person). The remaining six units are used to code a particular token by further specifying a type. The similarity between the patterns for a type and a token cause them to have similar effects, which then causes the appropriate generalization. So, the pattern for 'Clyde' contains the pattern for 'elephant', and the effects of this pattern are inherited by Clyde. Similarly, the pattern for 'Bill' contains the pattern for 'person'.

Hinton believes his system of distributed representations by-passes the property inheritance problem because the representation of the type is made to be a constituent of the representation for each token. Many sceptics just see his 'solution' as a clever sleight-of-hand, since it depends on the way the items are originally coded when presented to the system and the coding has to be done by a human operator. Nevertheless, it does show the potential of distributed, parallel machines with an underlying connectionist architecture.

10.17 CONCLUSIONS

There has undoubtedly been a change during the last few years in the psychologist's use or application of the computational metaphor. Whereas previously it was thought that the psychologist borrowed existing concepts and models from computer science to use as paradigms for, say, human memory models, it now appears that the psychologist is proposing as yet unbuilt and untested architectures and models for computer memory. There is even the suggestion in the latest models that the search for chips with more and more passive RAM may well be justified on technological grounds but scientifically speaking could well be wrong. That is, it could well be argued that if the brain does use parallel distributed structures, slow as these may be, computer scientists and engineers should study the organization of the brain and use that as a paradigm for computer memory, given the amazing efficiency and power of human memory. Thus, it appears as if the computational metaphor is being turned on its head. Perhaps we shall soon start talking of computer scientists, engineers and the AI community applying the 'neuropsychological metaphor' in their construction of computer memory models.

ANNOTATED BIBLIOGRAPHY

Hinton, G.E. and Anderson, J.A. (1981), *Parallel Models of Associative Memory*, Erlbaum, Hillsdale, NJ.

   This book will turn out to be a classic in the history of cognitive science. It contains some seminal papers by researchers who, although their models and ideas have not been fully worked out, *know* they're on the right track, and they attempt to convince the reader that getting the architecture worked out first is important.

Cofer, C.N. (1976), *The Structure of Human Memory*, Freeman, San Francisco.

This is a very useful and handy collection of articles by 'early' researchers in the area of human memory. Many of the articles give an accurate picture of how psychologists adopted computational concepts (sometimes too literally) when attempting to model memory.

Kohonen, T. (1980), *Content Addressable Memories*, Springer-Verlag, New York.

This book was one of the first to delve into the technicalities and theory of CAM. At the very least, it gives the reader an idea of how complex CAM is to build.

Cognitive Science, **9**, January–March 1985.

This is a special issue dealing with connection machines. The foremost researchers in the area (e.g. Feldman, Dell, Waltz, Rumelhart, McClelland and Hinton) have articles in this issue, and it describes developments made since 1981 (which was when the Hinton and Anderson book came out). It is compulsory reading for anyone wanting to discover more about the new architectures.

REFERENCES

Anderson, J.A. and Hinton, G.E. (1981), Models of information processing in the brain, in *Parallel Models of Associative Memory* (eds G. E. Hinton and J. A. Anderson), Erlbaum, Hillsdale, NJ.

Anderson, J.R. and Bower, G.H. (1974), *Human Associative Memory*, Wiley, New York.

Boden, M. (1979), The computational metaphor in psychology, in *Philosophical Problems in Psychology* (ed. N. Bolton), Methuen, London.

Broadbent, D.E. (1958), *Perception and Communication*, Pergamon, Oxford.

Brown, J. (1958), Some tests of the decay theory of immediate memory, *Quart. J. Exp. Psychol.*, **10**, 12–21.

Cohen, J. (1969), *Complex Learning*, Rand McNally, New York.

Fahlman, S.E. (1969), *NETL: A System for Representing and Using Real-World Knowledge*, MIT Press, Cambridge, MA.

Fahlman, S.E., Hinton, G.E. and Sejnowski, T.J. (1983), Massively parallel architectures for AI: NETL, THISTLE, and Boltzmann machines, *Proceedings of the 1983 Annual Meeting of the American Association for Artificial Intelligence*, Washington, DC.

Gilmartin, A., Newell, A. and Simon, H.A. (1976), A program modeling short-term memory under strategy control, in *The Structure of Human Memory* (ed. C. N. Cofer), Freeman, San Francisco.

Hanlon, A.C. (1966), *IEEE Trans. Electron. Comput.*, **15**, 509–21.

James, W. (1890), *The Principles of Psychology*, Henry Holt, New York.

Kohonen, T. (1980), *Content Addressable Memories*, Springer-Verlag, New York.

Marr, D. (1976), Early processing of visual information, *Phil. Trans. Roy. Soc.. B*, **275**, 483–524.

McClelland, J.L. and Rumelhart, D.E. (1980/81), An interactive activation model of the effect of context in perception, I and II, *Psychol. Rev.*, **88**, 5 and **89**, 1.

Miller, G.A. (1956), The magical number seven, plus or minus two. Some limits on our capacity for processing information, *Psychol. Rev.*, **63**, 81–97.

Minsky, M. and Papert, S. (1969), *Perceptrons*, MIT Press, Cambridge, MA.

Morton, J. (1970), A functional model of memory, in *Models of Human Memory* (ed. D.A. Norman), Academic Press, New York.

Nilsson, N.J. (1965), *Learning Machines*, McGraw-Hill, New York.

Norman, D.A. and Bobrow, D.J. (1976), On the role of active memory processes in perception and cognition, in *The Structure of Human Memory* (ed. C.N. Cofer), Freeman, San Francisco.

Peterson, L.R. and Peterson, M.J. (1959), Short-term retention of individual items, *J. Exp. Psychol.*, **58**, 193–98.

Quillian, M.R. (1968), Semantic memory, in *Semantic Information Processing* (ed. M. Minsky), MIT Press, Cambridge, MA.

Reicher, G.M. (1969), Perceptual recognition as a function of meaningfulness of stimulus material, *J. Exp. Psychol.*, **81**, 275–80.

Rosenblatt, T. (1961), *Principles of Neurodynamics: Perceptrons and the Theory of Brain Mechanisms*, Spartan, London.

Rumelhart, D.E. and Norman, D.A. (1981), A comparison of models, in *Parallel Models of Associative Memory* (eds G. E. Hinton and J. A. Anderson), Erlbaum, Hillsdale, NJ.

Sperling, G. (1960), *The Information Available in Brief Visual Presentations*, Psychological Monographs, 74, No. 11.

Tulving, E. (1972), Episodic and semantic memory, in *Organization of Memory* (eds E. Tulving and W. Donaldson), Academic Press, New York.

Winograd, T. (1976), Computer memories: A metaphor for memory organization, in *The Structure of Human Memory* (ed. C. N. Cofer), Freeman, San Francisco.

IMPLICATIONS

Sharkey and Brown open this section by providing us with a psychologist's view of Artificial Intelligence (AI) and Steven Torrance follows this with a philosopher's view. Both the following two chapters are mildly critical of AI and AI researchers.

Sharkey and Brown's chapter is a good example of a mixture of misunderstandings concerning what AI people do and justified requests for AI people to come up with some clear breakthrough in their endeavours. Their refutation of the analogy with flight and aerodynamics presented earlier in the *Introduction* mixes two self-contained and conflicting definitions of AI in order to show that they are inconsistent. We have already argued that finding a comprehensive definition of AI consistent with the practice of AI in itself is a research topic. However, where the contribution of psychologists such as Sharkey and Brown is needed is in their reminding us that we need to use a working definition of intelligence which is itself not circular. Their challenge is for AI to define intelligence without reference to a creature which exhibits intelligence. Taking up their challenge is not as simple as it seems, as AI is at the mercy of psychology which itself has no clear definition of intelligence. However, such clarity is not so central as it is to AI.

It is possible to produce a simple definition of intelligence arising from the existing work in AI which does not refer back to intelligent creatures. We know that intelligence requires the capability of having autonomous goal directed behaviour as well as ability to perceive the environment, represent it in internal representations and modify these representations in the light of experience. I am sure that we will discover clearer specifications of the requirements of intelligent existence as the work in AI progresses further.

Steve Torrance seems to attempt a partial definition of John Searle's position. The intention behind the earlier analogy between flight and intelligence to show that the claim that 'an artefact would have to have powers equivalent to the powers of the human brain' mistakenly assumes that AI is about replicating the mental states of the human brain. Artificial Intelligence is not about replicating human mental states, any more than building aircraft is about replicating birds. An aircraft is similar to a bird only in the respect that both have the capability of self-sustaining flight. An intelligent artefact would be similar to a human brain only in the respect that both can perform activities requiring intelligence.

The second mistaken claim is that 'biology matters'. This is analogous to the claim that the fact that birds are meat machines prevents flight being realized on any non-protoplasm artefact. In fact, as we have remarked, artificial flight is generally realized in artefacts whose material structure closely resembles that of 'old beer cans'.

Steve Torrance's objection to the artificial flight analogy seems to be that performance is an adequate criterion for deciding whether or not flight is taking place, whereas performance is not an adequate criterion for deciding whether or not understanding is taking place. This is the point which the 'Chinese room' experiment is designed to show. However, it then falls to the critics of performance as a criterion, to propose an alternative criterion by which one could establish whether or not understanding or equivalent mental processes are taking place. Searle seems to imply that biological make-up is, if not the criterion, the appropriate area in which to start looking.

To oppose Searle's position that 'biology matters' should not be taken as asserting the position that: 'Performance is all that matters.' What is crucial to the artificial flight analogy is not the performance of flight by aeroplanes, but rather that the study of aircraft flight has given us the scientific principles by which we can understand the flight of birds.

There seems to be no problem in asserting that a similar development will take place in such matters as human intelligent activity. This is most certainly not a claim that the simulation of a given human intelligent activity by a computer simply is all that there is to that activity. It is a claim merely that there are general principles underlying intelligent activity by both computers and humans.

Derek Partridge, in the final chapter, surveys the various social implications of AI. This is, unfortunately, something not taken very seriously by AI people up to now, while the effects of AI on society could be as great as that of the Industrial Revolution.

One of the many long-term effects of the Industrial Revolution has been the reduction in human society for the need of craftsmanship (the capability to do a manual task skilfully). As new, faster and, in some cases, even more accurate machinery has produced goods which replaced the craftsmen who produced goods prior to the Industrial Revolution, such people have moved to other areas of activity and have not passed on their skills to the next generation. Therefore, the skills which were the property of people have been taken away from them and invested in machines. On the surface, this would appear to be not a very bad idea. The burden of production has been put onto the machines. This relies on the machines always being available and people being available to improve the craft further without actually possessing the basics of the skill itself.

A parallel exists between the process of 'de-skilling' above, and the 'knowledge engineering' boom of expert systems, where intellectual skills of people such as doctors, lawyers, etc. are being invested in computer systems which, at some time in the near future, could play a similar role to that of their mechanical counterparts. This would result in a similar loss of skill in the intellectual craftsmanship as that which has resulted from the Industrial Revolution.

11

Why Artificial Intelligence needs an empirical foundation

NOEL E. SHARKEY AND
GORDON D. A. BROWN

In this chapter we discuss ways in which Artifical Intelligence (AI) and cognitive psychology interact within the new and growing discipline of cognitive science. We share with other cognitive scientists the assumption that it is useful to view the human cognitive system as computational. Within this common framework, however, different researchers adopt different approaches. The cognitive psychologist constructs theories and tests them by carrying out experiments with humans as subjects, while the AI researcher constructs and tests theories by implementing them as computer programs. Each discipline has its strengths and weaknesses, but we argue that their union creates a powerful methodology for the study of cognition. The chapter is divided into three parts. In the first, we examine some well-known definitions of AI and show that such definitions rely on intuitive notions of the human property of intelligence. This fact has implications for the ability of AI to produce explanations of human cognition. Second, we consider some of the problems in communication that result from the methodology-laden nature of cognitive modelling. In the third and final section, we provide two case histories of the successful co-operation of cognitive psychology and AI: schema theory and parallel spreading activation network theory.

11.1   ARTIFICIAL AND HUMAN INTELLIGENCE

We take as our starting point Minsky's (1968) definition of Artificial Intelligence (AI). Minsky defines AI as 'The science of making machines do things that would require intelligence if done by men.' This definition is not as useful as it seems at first glance. One problem is that it is not easy to define human intelligence. Indeed, Minsky's definition of AI brings to mind an operational definition of human intelligence: 'Intelligence is that which is measured by intelligence tests.' Even if we set aside this problem, however, the notion of 'requiring intelligence if done by men' is still problematic, because men can make machines do things in ways that bear no resemblance to the ways in which men do the same things. Consider the following example. We present a clever man with a problem of type X which we have been unable to solve ourselves. After a few moments of thought he comes up with a solution, and we are very impressed. Now the man tells us that during those moments of thought he was devising an algorithm which would guarantee a solution to any problem of type X. To demonstrate, he programs the algorithm into a computer on his desk. We then input several other problems of type X into the computer, and the program outputs the solution. Would we be impressed with the intelligence of the man or of the program?

In such a case, it might be said that the programmed solution was a product or reflection of the man's intelligence, even though the program had 'done something' which we considered to be a demonstration of intelligence in the man. We do not treat the program's behaviour as intelligent because we know that it was simply running through an algorithm that the man had produced. Because the program did not produce the algorithm itself, we know that the program was not solving the problem in the same way as the man, and so we do not want to describe its behaviour as intelligent. Of course, it could be claimed that in some sense the program was not really doing the same thing as the man. The program did not produce the algorithm following the same mental processes as the man.

The point we wish to make here is that any simple definition of AI (at least AI within cognitive science) should be extended so that it makes explicit reference to the notion of cognitive resemblance. In other words, it is not enough merely to write a program which mimics a piece of behaviour. The internal processing of the program should be as similar as possible, at some predefined level of description, to human internal processing on the same task. The attempt to produce programs with cognitive resemblance brings at least two major benefits. First, the human is the best model we have for AI. The study of human perform-ance can not only tell us what it is possible for a computational system to achieve, but it can also provide clues as to the best way to do things. Human errors, capacity limitations and mechanisms for forgetting com-bine to create the world's largest, most flexible and most efficient database and retrieval system. For these reasons, even engineers within AI who do not aspire to be cognitive scientists would be well advised to use humans as their model. Second, the attempt to imitate human cognition may enable us to refine our explanations of it.

There are some, however, who believe that we do not need to use the human as a model for AI (e.g. Yazdani, 1984). Furthermore, it has been argued that by creating non-human intelligences we can find good explanations of human intelligence (Sloman, 1984a, 1984b), and that a good explanation of human behaviour can be obtained simply by writing a program which exhibits the piece of behaviour to be explained (Hayes, 1984). In the next two subsections we argue against these positions in turn (although we do not argue against the position that the study of computational mechanisms can provide us with useful constraints on theories of human cognition).

11.1.1 The human as a model for Artificial Intelligence

We would like to discuss an analogy which we believe is very misleading. It has been said in certain AI circles that we did not need to use birds as a model when we were designing aeroplanes, so we do not need to use humans as a model when we are constructing Artificial Intelligence systems. For example, Yazdani (1984) states that:

> 'What is important is that the science of aerodynamics explains both bird flight as well as aircraft flight. In our view, the science of AI is comparable to that of aerodynamics when we consider the space of thinking objects.'

However, neither the analogy between aerodynamics and the discipline of AI, nor the analogy between flight and intelligence, can be maintained. Flight is the propulsion of an object through a three-dimensional observable space that we may call 'the air'. Thus, flight can be defined independently of flying objects. Flight can be, and was, observed independently of birds long before aeroplanes were ever thought of. It is the movement through air which a piece of paper, a feather or a leaf can do when picked up by the wind, and so there has never been a need to define flight as something which birds (or flying fish, or wasps) can do. Flight can be defined as travelling without contact with a planet's surface, that is, it can be defined without reference to any of the creatures which inhabit or move in the air.

We are now in a position to see the flaw in the analogy. Intelligence has never been defined in a way which is independent of those beings that we wish to call intelligent. There is no cognitive counterpart to travelling in the air. Our intuitive notion of intelligence is not something that is separable from humans (or at least animals). In other words, we cannot point to something outside of animals and say that it is intelligence in the way that we can point to something outside of birds or planes and say that it is flight. We cannot point to something and say it is thinking other than by comparison to humans.

To illustrate the problem further, let us make some substitutions within AI definitions. We begin with Minsky's definition of AI as '. . . the science of making machines do things that would require intelligence if done by men.' Substituting, as the analogy invites, 'birds' for 'men', 'aerodynamics' for 'AI', and 'flight' for 'intelligence', we get: "Aerodynamics is the science of making machines do things that would require flight if done by birds.' This seems strange, of course, because the reference to birds is simply redundant. We know what flight is, whether it is being done by birds or not. However, to take the reference to humankind out of Minsky's original definition would be to render it devoid of content. We can say that aerodynamics is the science of making machines fly (actually aerodynamics is the study of the behaviour of flow of air around objects, but we do not want to quibble about a definition), but not that AI is the science of making machines think, because we have an independent definition of flight but not of thought.

As yet another example, consider the version of the Turing test (1950) suggested by the analogy. The idea behind the Turing test is that if an interrogator decides wrongly that a machine is a person, then that machine is said to be exhibiting intelligence. Now, substituting again, we get: 'If an interrogator decides wrongly that a machine is a bird then that machine is said to be exhibiting flight.' Again there is redundancy in the statement, because there is no need to make any reference to birds at all. The machine is exhibiting flight when it is observed to be moving through the air without touching the ground.

We are not simply stretching an analogy too far. Rather, we are arguing against the claim, implicit in the analogy, that AI can be a part of cognitive science without making reference to psychological evidence. We do not wish to claim here that intelligence is only a property of organisms (in the way that Searle (1980) does). What we do claim is that no-one has satisfactorily defined something called 'intelligence' which exists independently of organisms. Such a definition, if it is possible, must be presented before the bird/plane analogy can be considered to be meaningful.

Similar arguments apply to Sloman's position. Sloman (1978, 1984a, 1984b) holds that there are no clear, shared criteria for the ascription of mind to a behaving system. Thus, he urges us to sidestep the question of criteria, and study instead ' . . . the space of possible minds' (Sloman, 1984a). This is, he explains, ' . . . a very richly structured space – not one dimensional, like a spectrum, not any kind of continuum. There will be not two but many extremes' (Sloman, 1984a).

However, Sloman still leaves us with the problem of deciding when we have, in fact, designed a possible mind. He says that we should make comparisons between behaving systems. However, to determine whether or not something inhabits Sloman's 'mind field', we can presumably only compare its behaviour with the behaviour of systems already inhabiting that space. But the question still remains as to how something is introduced into the space to begin with. In the absence of any independent definition of mind, systems can only be entered by being compared with humans. Sloman might say that a simple computational mechanism, like a thermostat, has only a little bit of mind, but he will still only be able to say how much mind a system has by comparing it with humans. Sloman must admit that we can only judge things to be mind-like to the extent that they exhibit human-like behaviour. Like Yazdani (1984), Sloman needs either an independent, non-trivial definition of mind, or he needs to take some account of cognitive resemblance. Only then can the comparison of behaving systems be carried out properly and scientifically.

It follows from our arguments so far that there are three different strategies that AI researchers could adopt. First, they could develop a definition of intelligence which does not make reference to humans (or animals if you like). This definition of intelligence would have to encompass what humans do and what machines may be able to do but without reference to either, as in 'flight is travelling without contact with the ground' (perhaps we should call this definition a definition of 'supergence'). However, the definition should be clear before the programming begins if researchers are to avoid severe problems of circularity.

Second, AI researchers could abandon attempts to investigate intelligence or thought and, instead, build automata or the like and call them something else. This would be pure engineering, but it could be useful to the cognitive scientist. For example, it is useful to be able to specify the minimum amount of knowledge required to perform some task. This can provide us with necessary boundary conditions for an account of some human performance. However, it would not itself be cognitive science, since cognition would not be the object of study. Rather, it would be useful to the cognitive scientist in the same way that mathematics and statistics are.

The third strategy is the most realistic one. The AI researcher can use as a model the source of our notion of intelligence, i.e. the human. In this way, our understanding of thinking may be extended. We suggest that AI researchers, even those who believe that they do not need to take account of psychological evidence, are really using their intuitions about themselves to develop their programs. Artificial Intelligence workers should recognize this fact, and take account of the evidence collected using the more objective methods of cognitive psychology.

11.1.2 **Artificial Intelligence as a model for the human**

We would like to make it clear that by studying only computational systems and their outputs we will not find adequate explanations of human behaviour. Contrary to this, it has sometimes been claimed that behavioural resemblance (mimicry) indicates that a program is a good explanation of some human behaviour. Hayes (1984) claims: '. . . an explanation is a good explanation just to the extent that the program when run does indeed exhibit the behaviour to be explained.' Our argument is that behavioural resemblance is simply not enough. Programs such as ELIZA (Weizenbaum, 1965) or PARRY (Colby, 1963) are not explanations of human behaviour, even though their output was sufficiently human-like to fool a lot of people. Marr (1977) notes that there is a problem when he complains that AI research: '. . . can degenerate into the writing of programs that do no more than mimic in an unenlightening way some small aspect of human performance.' We will argue that the only way to avoid this problem is to use the data from carefully controlled psychology experiments to help in the construction and validation of implementable explanations. Our argument will be that, since different mechanisms can give rise to the same behaviour, a simple comparison between systems exhibiting the same external behaviour will not necessarily amount to an explanation.

Sloman (1978) defends the notion that computer programs have explanatory power. He summarizes the objection to his position as follows:

> 'The persistent objector may now argue that the explanatory power of computer programs is doubtful, since even if a program does give a machine the ability to do something we can do, like understand and talk English, or describe pictures, that leaves open the question whether it does so *in the same way* as we do; so it remains unclear whether the program gives a correct explanation of our ability. The objector may add that it is clear that existing computers do not do things the way we do, since, at the physical level they use transistors and bits of wire, etc., whereas our brains do not . . . .'

However, Sloman (1978) does not think this is a serious problem. He says:

> 'It is all a matter of how much and what sort of detail of a process is described in answer to the question, "In what way did he do it?" That some very detailed description would be different in the case of a computer does not imply that there is no important level at which it does something the same way as we do. We don't say a Chinaman plays chess in a different way from an Englishman, *simply* because he learns and

applies the rules using a different language, so that his thinking goes through different symbolic processes. He may nevertheless use the same strategies.'

While this is, of course, correct, we only assume that the Englishman and the Chinaman use the same strategies when they play chess because of the (possibly unjustified) assumptions we make about the similarities between one human being and another. There is certainly no good reason to suppose that a computer and a human play chess in the same way just because they move pieces about on a board. In fact, Sloman himself only claims that the chess players *may* use the same strategies as each other. Thus, our main complaint is that while it is possible to find some level of description at which two behaviours are the same, it does not follow that our knowledge about the structure of one behaving system will explain the behaviour of the other. This is because the resemblance between the two systems may not be at what Sloman calls an important level (this is presumably the level at which we want to be able to describe the behaviour).

Sloman (1978) suggests a way to guarantee that a program performs some piece of behaviour in the same way as a human: 'Insofar as anything clear and precise can be said about "the way" in which a human does something (e.g. plays chess, interprets a poem, or solves a problem) the appropriate procedure can in principle be built into a suitable simulation, so that we ensure that the machine does it in the same way.' To say this is to admit the possibility that programs may produce human-like behaviour in quite unhuman-like ways.

Sharkey and Pfeifer (1984) have made the point that a program can mimic a piece of behaviour without necessarily being validated as an explanation of that behaviour (although it may be validated as a potential explanation of that behaviour). They explain this by introducing the notion of a HIDDEN TRANSFORMATION.

> 'Suppose we were to type four stories into four computer text files and summaries of the four stories into four more text files. This would give us a total of eight text files in all. Next we write a simple procedure called MATCH which checks to see if a piece of text typed at the terminal is the same as one of the stories in the story text files. If MATCH finds that the answer is "yes", it gives control to a second procedure called SUMMAR-IZE . . . which simply prints out the appropriate summary file. Now no one in their right mind would call this simple transformation a theory of text summarization. But suppose that we were to complicate things a little by making MATCH flexible enough so that a story would be recognized if the wording of a story being typed in was not exactly the same as the one in the text files. This could be done by making the specification of the original story less rigid. Suppose further that we were to scatter the story

summaries around a little more so that they were distributed in fifty files rather than in four. SUMMARIZE would now have to "assemble the summaries dynamically". In order to do all of this extra work MATCH and SUMMARIZE may need to call upon a number of other smaller subprocedures. For example, MATCH may now have a PARSER which in turn may have a LEXICAL-LOOKUP and a CONCEPT-DEINSTANTIATOR, etc. . . . See how much more impressive and difficult this hidden transformation is to understand. Let us stretch the illustration a little further. Suppose that a theorist has a good notion of what a program should output from a given input within certain degrees of freedom. If he is a clever and imaginative programmer he can then implement his theory as a hidden transformation. He could also incorporate a random element so that the program is not totally predictable, even to him.'

This example shows that there is no justification for judging the explanatory power of a theory by examining the performance of a program alone. Note that Sloman (1984a) says: 'It is even quite possible for the internal processes to be too rich to be revealed by external behaviour, so that in an important sense external observers cannot know exactly what is going on.' Thus, it will be difficult to discern the presence of hidden transformations just by looking at the behaviour of a program. What is more, even if a computer implementation turned out to be a good explanation of human cognition, the output from that program could not distinguish it from the set of possible hidden transformations; the output would be the same in either case.

It could, of course, be argued that programs are more likely to resemble human cognition if they are flexible (i.e. have the ability to solve a wide range of problems). However, a program containing many hidden transformations would be able to tackle tasks from many domains. In any case, as Bobrow *et al.* (1977) have said: 'Computer programs in general, and programs intended to model human performance in particular, suffer from an almost intolerable delicacy. If their users depart from the behaviour expected of them in the minutest detail, or if apparently insignificant adjustments are made in their structure, their performance does not usually change commensurately. Instead, they turn to simulating gross aphasia or death.' Even if flexibility was feasible at present, it would still not guarantee cognitive resemblance.

In summary, we have pointed out some of the general problems that researchers face if they attempt to assess AI programs without reference to psychological data. The performance of a program is very difficult to assess, and we have shown that the output alone is not sufficient to demonstrate that the program has explanatory power. If artificial behaving systems are to be used to explain other (e.g. human) behaving systems (cf. Sloman 1984a), then the two systems must be compared in terms of their cognitive architecture and processes, and not just in terms of their overt behaviour. One role of cognitive psychology is, of course, to discover the cognitive architecture and processes that under-lie behaviour. On the positive side, psychological evidence about human internal processing may, of course, support the claim that a program is a realistic model of actual human behaviour.

In the next section we discuss differences in the criteria that cognitive psychologists and AI researchers use to evaluate their progress, and we show that these differences can lead to the failure of communication between researchers in the two disciplines.

11.2 DIFFERENT METHODS, DIFFERENT MODELS

Miller (1978) explains the difference between AI and psychology in terms of 'theory development' and 'theory demonstration'. AI workers, on this account, believe that theory development is the most difficult and necessarily prior task, and that AI methodology is most appropriate to achieve this goal. Psychologists, in contrast, are more likely to have the attitude that an undemonstrable theory, or one that can be shown in the early stages of development not to be an accurate model of human cognition, is not worth developing. However, in reality both disciplines are involved with both theory construction and theory testing. For us, the major division between psychology and AI results from the adoption of different criteria for evaluating explanations.

We shall discuss ways in which the different assessment criteria of AI and psychology can lead to the development of different kinds of theories and models. This in turn may lead to failure of communication between the two disciplines. As researchers in each discipline examine the models generated within the other, they may find that the models are not assessable by the criteria of their own discipline. Worse, they may find that a model from one discipline would be rejected outright by the assessment criteria of the other. Eventually, distrust can set in, and work in what may now even be viewed as an opposing or competing discipline is suspected on principle or rejected out of hand.

Within both cognitive psychology and AI, the constraints on theory construction stem from the requirement that explanations be testable. However, the means of constructing and testing explanations are differ-ent for both disciplines, both in theory and in practice. Psychological research is often portrayed as the derivation of a model from a theory followed by the examination of that model to see what testable predic-tions it makes. The psychologist will then devise a method of testing the predictions experimentally. In contrast, AI research can be portrayed as the construction of a theory and the building of a computer implementation (equivalent to the psychologist's model) of that theory. The implementation will then be tested to see how well it performs on some task according to the specifications of the theory.

However, the reality for both disciplines is rather different. The psychologist has a range of techniques available for hypothesis testing. He/she has an armoury of tests of statistical significance, knowledge about the computational limitations of the machine that he/she will use. a significant result (that will be accepted by his/her peers), and an array of standard experimental techniques. The AI researcher has knowledge about the computational limitations of the machine that he she will use. He/she knows about the programming language, how large a program is practical, and he/she will want to achieve efficiency in the trade-off between use of space and use of processing. All of these factors interact to place constraints on the type of model or implementation which either researcher will in practice be able to test. No researcher will want to construct models or theories that they will not be able to test using the criteria of their own discipline.

11.2.1 Theory testing in psychology and Artificial Intelligence

In this section we will examine some of the problems with the test methodology of both disciplines. First, however, we shall clear up a confusion which, in our experience, many people have about what cognitive psychologists actually do. This confusion stems from a failure to recognize the distinction between common-sense psychology and scientific psychology. Cognitive psychologists do not coin their explanations of human action in terms of people's reasons for doing things. Rather, cognitive psychologists attempt to determine the mental structures and processes which humans use in performing various tasks such as reading and problem-solving. Like their counterparts in the physical sciences, cognitive psychologists formulate hypotheses and test them using objective measures under carefully controlled conditions. In contrast, common-sense psychologists attempt to explain individual human behaviour by reference to concepts such as motives and desires. The distinction between the two conceptions of psychology is an important one. If AI workers confuse or conflate the two then their scepticism about the value of psychology is understandable, for there are good arguments against the possibility of ever constructing a complete scientific common-sense psychology (cf. McGinn, 1979; Russell, 1984; Wilkes, 1984).

We will illustrate the difference between the two types of psychology with an example. Cognitive psychology does not seek to answer questions like 'Why did Mary read a book at 2:30 p.m. on Friday afternoon?'

Rather, it seeks to explain how it is that Mary is able to read at all, and what mental mechanisms Mary, *qua* human, possesses and uses as she reads. However, this is not to say that cognitive psychologists will not study things like emotions, feelings and desires. They may even study common-sense psychology, because it is used by people to interpret other people's behaviour (cf. Abelson, 1980). Cognitive psychologists, however, investigate these things in an attempt to understand how they can happen and what cognitive structures are involved in such happenings. The cognitive psychologist aims to discover the general laws and principles of human cognition rather than using particular emotions, etc. as explanatory concepts in themselves.

We now turn to a discussion of some of the methodological problems that accompany cognitive psychology. When a narrow approach to experimental psychology is adopted, concern with the use of inferential statistics and experimental methodology may come to overshadow the actual construction of large-scale cognitive theories (the reader with no knowledge of statistical methodology is referred to the simple account in Robson (1973)). Such preoccupation with methodology places severe constraints on the modelling and hypothesis-generation processes. These constraints, in combination with the fact that statistics are generally used to decide between hypotheses, can lead to a tendency we refer to as 'binary mindedness'. This is the tendency to consider, usually two, competing single-hypothesis models to the unwarranted exclusion of better alternatives. In the words of Black, Galambos and Reiser (1984), 'Cognitive psychologists are masters of hypothesis testing, but rank amateurs at discovering new hypotheses.' Black, Galambos and Reiser claim that cognitive and experimental psychologists have devoted most of their efforts to devising and refining their 'methods for verifying or disconfirming hypotheses.' They further suggest that: 'Hypothesis discovery seems to be somewhat disreputable within cognitive psychology.' They state that: 'Any study that creates more hypotheses than it eliminates is considered to be a bad study.'

This restriction of the number of hypotheses can be counterproductive. As Mynatt, Doherty and Tweney (1977) have shown experimentally, there is a human tendency to cling on to hypotheses once they have been generated, even when it would be more rational to abandon them for others. They recommend Platt's (1964) 'strong inference' strategy, which involves the generation of multiple hypotheses followed by the elimination of as many of them as possible.

A further consequence of the central role accorded to statistical analyses is the reckless postulation of processes at the expense of detailed specification of those processes. This occurs because a psychologist is able to make a prediction of the form, 'There will be an effect of X on Y', or 'The addition of B will cause A to have a larger effect on C' simply by asserting that some extra process will be required to do some task. To make the prediction, and test the model, it is not necessary to specify in detail exactly how the process is supposed to work. Consequently, the psychologist may end up proposing and testing a model which could never work in practice. This could never happen in AI, because AI theories must meet the criterion of implementability. We now discuss some of the advantages and disadvantages of the use of this criterion.

To say that a theory is implementable is simply to say that it can be expressed in the form of a computer program which will run successfully. If the human cognitive system is viewed as a computational system, it seems reasonable to require that any explanation of human behaviour should be expressible in the form of a program which could run on a computational system. For example, Hayes (1984) says that if a theory does not meet the criterion of implementability, it cannot be a satisfactory explanation: 'An acceptable explanation for a piece of behaviour must be, in the last analysis, a program which can actually be implemented and run.'

A consequence of aiming for an explanation which is implementable is that it will have to be specified in complete detail if it is to work as a computer program. It is this completeness of specification which often distinguishes an AI theory from a psychological theory. Lehnert (1978) holds that this is one of the major advantages of AI over psychology. She states that, 'The difference is analogous to instructing someone to multiply two numbers together, versus instructing someone to multiply two numbers together by means of a particular algorithm. By forcing ourselves to be concerned with the precise form of information in memory, and the precise operations manipulating that information, we can uncover significant problems that would otherwise be overlooked.'

There are many examples in psychology which illustrate Lehnert's point, e.g. models which refer to notions such as 'post-access checking' or 'orthographic spelling check'. As Kolers and Smythe (1984) put it: 'Many models of cognition, written in the spirit of the computational metaphor, make a tacit appeal in the end to the actions or operations of an agent external to the model itself, to some agent that attends, that selects, that decides, or even that knows.' (See Dennett (1978) for a discussion of homunculi within psychological explanations.) This difference in specificity leads AI researchers such as Hayes (1984) to point out that many psychological explanations 'do not make first base from an AI point of view' or are 'literally useless' or 'comically naïve'. It is true that psychological explanations are often not implementable, and this may be a valid criticism of psychology. However, we should point out that there can be good reasons for this. Artificial Intelligence researchers differ from psychologists in what they believe is 'allowable to know'. Artificial Intelligence researchers can produce an implementable explanation only by setting aside the requirement to test every step of the implementation. In cognitive psychology, it would not be permissible to do this, and so it will often not be possible to set up an implementation without going beyond the data available. If cognitive psychologists want to construct implementable theories, then they will have to go beyond the data and propose the existence of further mechanisms which have not been validated by observation.

We will now argue that, in the absence of such empirical corroboration, the detailed specification necessary to meet the implementability criterion is not only insufficient to guarantee a satisfactory cognitive explanation, but it may be positively misleading. We will also show how the methods of psychology can help overcome this problem.

There are at least two major problems with the idea that a running program must be a good cognitive explanation. The first of these is the use of what are referred to in AI circles as kludges. A kludge, according to Webster's dictionary, is 'A computer system which is made up of components that are poorly matched or were originally intended for some other use.' A kludge is essentially a means of patching up a mismatch between a theory and its implementation on a machine. Sharkey and Pfeifer (1984) explain a kludge as follows:

'A simple analogy would be of an architect who designs a perfectly elegant building only to find that several of the walls do not join at right angles. Now he has to have the builders put in wooden struts to fill in the gaps. These are the kludges. Worse still is that our architect finds that the struts look quite good and he now gives them a title "symmetrical pine dividers" and declares that they were an essential feature of his design. He may even begin to believe that they were part of his original design.'

Psychologists in cognitive science have similar problems when they do not have enough data to support all the details of a theory and have to invent some links in order to implement it. However, they can then submit these hypothesized links to a further empirical test. This ensures that the refinements they make to their models to permit implementability have a basis in the real world. A kludge within AI is more of a problem, especially as the only test of the implementation is that it runs. Since the kludge is added to get the implementation to run in the first place, it is not possible to use the run to test the validity of the kludge. Given this problem, we suggest that AI researchers should clearly mark the kludges in their programs. It will then be possible to return to the program at a later date and distinguish the theoretically motivated parts of the program from the kludges.

Another question we would like to raise here is this: At what point in implementation do we decide that there are too many patches to accept that the running program is actually a test of a theory? Psychology has its own criteria for deciding when a theory is not supported by the data. Perhaps similar criteria could be developed to decide whether an implementation supports a theory.

A second potential problem with the computer implementation of cognitive theories is the use of 'wishful mnemonics' (McDermott, 1976). This is simply a tendency among AI researchers to take their program function labels too seriously. It is usual to give a function in a program a mnemonic label to remind the programmer of its intended use. However, the programmer may then come to believe that the function is more than it really is, i.e. that it is what the label suggests. A simple example should make this clear. Imagine that we write a program that can do two different things. It either prints out a list, or stores it for later use. Now, suppose we call the two possibilities GOALS. We may then begin to think of these in the sense of human goals and begin to write functions which check the program's STATE OF DESIRE. This can be quite amusing as long as we know what we are doing. However, McDermott points out that it can be very misleading. He suggests that programmers should use function labels such as GOO34 instead of labels such as UNDERSTAND. If they do this, they will have to find good arguments to convince themselves and others that their programs have anything to do with the process of understanding.

In summary, implementation is not a panacea for all the ills of cognitive modelling. As we have seen, implementing a theory as a computer program can lead to serious problems, which are easily overlooked. We believe that experimental evidence is relevant to the construction of cognitive explanations, and so any link hypothesized in order to bridge the gap between a theory and its implementation should be tested empirically using human subjects. The continual refinement of implementation, experiment, implementation, and so on is necessary if we are to escape the problems of relying on implementability as the only criterion of explanatory adequacy. Of course, this should not be done in the overly constrained manner of the narrow version of psychology. Rather, we should take large sections of our theories and test various components, modifying as we go. This is rather like an electrician's approach to testing the wiring of a large installation. In combination with careful experimental practices, computer implementation can greatly increase the precision of any cognitive model.

11.2.2   Differences in the generality of explanations

A considerable amount of AI research involves the construction of large-scale systems and any one of these may encompass several of the subject areas of cognitive psychology (cf. Schank and Abelson, 1977 or Wilensky, 1983). This is one of the great advantages of AI which psychologists ignore at their peril. However, let us emphasize here that we are not suggesting that psychology is less general as a result of being more specialized. Rather, the fact is that psychology simply has a different kind of generality.

Sharkey and Pfeifer (1984) make this point in suggesting that one failure in communication between AI and psychology results from the fact that they section cognition differently to investigate it. There is a tendency within AI to model a tall 'vertical' section of cognition; one that includes several interacting mechanisms. In contrast, the tendency within cognitive psychology is to model a long 'horizontal' section; a single subprocess (or 'module'). For example, a psychologist may produce a model which is claimed to account for word recognition. This model may be general, in the sense that it is making claims about the processing of all of the words in the language. However, it lacks a different kind of generality if it does not specify the nature of the interaction between, say, word recognition and knowledge of the world. In contrast, an AI model of story understanding may make claims about the interaction of processes involved in word recognition, world knowledge, and thematic information. Nevertheless, it may only work with three or four carefully worded stories. These different conceptions of the notion of generality underlie many of the disagreements between workers in the two disciplines.

We suggest that differences in the sectioning of cognition arise as a result of the different methodological and assessment criteria. If an AI program is going to be assessed partly to the extent that it specifies interactions between cognitive modules, then, of course, there is an incentive to include as many modules as possible. The 'vertical' AI sectioning will also give rise to superficial resemblance to a wider range of cognitive functioning. In cognitive psychology, with its reliance on statistics, the explanations of mechanisms must hold for all the hypothesized applications of that mechanism. Thus, any model would be rejected out of hand if it made predictions that were only supported by performance on four specific examples.

Thus, different ideas about generality will influence the models produced by psychologists and AI workers. It is common practice in cognitive psychology to carry out close investigation of the subprocesses of cognition. One only has to glance through Neisser's (1967) book *Cognitive Psychology* to find the subject divided into topics such as iconic memory, short-term memory, visual buffers, long-term memory, and so on. Minsky (1975) has complained that this 'leads to attempts to extract more performance from fewer "basic mechanisms" than is reasonable'. However, many psychologists would claim that minimizing the number of 'basic mechanisms' is a good, parsimonious strategy. This is a clear illustration of the different conceptions of generality of the two disciplines. A further consequence of the psychologists' sectioning of cognition is that modularization leads to specialization with the result that, as Sharkey and Pfeifer have said, '. . . each subsystem in psychology is so fraught with its own technical difficulties that no one can put "Humpty" together again.'

In summary, we have suggested that the different notions of generality aimed at by researchers in cognitive psychology and AI lead to the modelling of cognition in different ways. It seems clear that the type of model the cognitive scientist should be aiming at will be general in both senses. Until such models are produced, however, the usefulness of each kind of generality should be recognized.

11.3   THE INTERACTION BETWEEN PSYCHOLOGY AND ARTIFICIAL INTELLIGENCE

In this last section we discuss ways in which cognitive psychology and AI can interact and have interacted within cognitive science. We would like to begin by discussing a myth, found even within cognitive science. The myth is based on the belief that trying to take account of the current psychological evidence while building an AI system is 'like trying to do weightlifting on quicksand'. Adherents to this belief might propose that it would be better to construct an AI system first, in a loose intuitive way, and then get the psychologist to test it later (cf. Miller, 1978). There are a number of things wrong with this argument.

First, it takes a long time to build a large AI system, and it may be completely wrong in principle at the outset. It may be the case that, using already existing knowledge, psychologists can look at the model and say that humans just do not operate in this way. The AI worker, especially if he/she has already invested time on his/her system, may now say that AI is a different discipline, and choose to ignore the psychological evidence. At this point we can forget about human resemblance or theory testing. This AI system has moved out of the realm of cognitive science into the realm of engineering.

Second, the AI theory and its implementation in its final state may not be coined in a way which allows psychological testing. This leads to difficulties for empirical workers within cognitive science, who are then faced with the problem of converting the AI model into a psychological process model in order to interpret their results and make psychological predictions. The first author of the present paper has had this problem with script research (Sharkey and Mitchell, 1985), where it was necessary to construct a new processing model to explain data and to run further experiments.

The reader may wonder why it is that most AI theorists do not base their models on sound psychological evidence. We have already discussed some of the factors that can inhibit interdisciplinary communication. However, we suggest that there are at least two other reasons. The first is that to the outsider the psychological literature seems like a highly technical mess. This is partly due to an inadequate knowledge of the experimentalists' jargon, and partly due to a lack of understanding of the subject matter of cognitive psychology. The second reason is that psychology is a subject in which a single experiment on its own is rarely decisive. Rather, a given experiment is generally offered as evidence in combination with the findings of experiments from other workers. A debate in the psychological literature is often rather like a case being tried by jury in a courtroom. Consequently, it can at times become a morass of caustic nit-picking over techniques and control. To some extent this is a healthy thing for a science, but many psychologists do get sidetracked and become more involved with techniques and methodology than with theory construction. Unfortunately, as we pointed out earlier, theory construction tends to be methodology-laden, and so too great an emphasis on methodology can inhibit interdisciplinary links.

The second reason why AI theorists do not use psychological evidence is that the data are often not relevant to their interests. Until recently, psychologists and AI researchers were not interested in the same kinds of things. Schank (1980) points out that he had this problem in the 1960s. We quote:

'. . . I developed an intense interest in making any representation I came up with as psychologically correct as possible. Unfortunately, psychologists were at this point very concerned with phenomena that could shed light on the validity of transformational grammars. This work did not provide much in the way of evidence one way or the other for the things I was interested in, so, since I was not trained to do the experiments myself, I had only my intuitions to rely on for psychological evidence . . . .'

With the emergence of cognitive science this position has changed considerably. Psychologists are now bringing their skills to bear on issues more relevant to AI. There is hope that the cognitive scientist of the future will be in a position both to construct and to assess AI models on the basis of his/her own psychological evidence. To demonstrate how the would-be cognitive scientist might go about getting involved in the kind of research programme we propose, we conclude this chapter by looking at two case histories where AI and cognitive psychology have interacted to produce explanations which neither of them could have produced alone.

11.3.1 Schemata and frames

The first case is that of schema theory, which originated within psychology in the work of the British psychologist, Sir Fredrick Bartlett, although the roots go back at least as far as Kant (1787). In the 1930s, Bartlett examined the ways in which people distort and reconstruct the memory of some event or story which they have previously heard or read. In one of his most famous studies (Bartlett, 1932) he used a story based on a North American Indian legend 'War of the Ghosts'. He gave this story to people to read and then tested their recall of it after various intervals of time. Bartlett was concerned with the systematic memory errors which non-Indians made in recalling the story (he had deliberately chosen a story which did not fit with the cultural conceptions of the people in his experiment). His subjects 'forgot' aspects of the legend which were incompatible with their knowledge. To account for his findings, Bartlett proposed that when people read a story they construct an abstract representation, or schema, of the story's general theme. This representation, he proposed, is affected by the reader's personal system of beliefs and emotions.

Clearly Bartlett was ahead of his time in some ways. Very little research was carried out on his notion of schema until some forty years later in the 1970s (e.g. Anderson, 1977; Rumelhart, 1975). It is difficult to pinpoint exactly why schema theories suddenly became so popular within the study of cognition, but it certainly had a lot to do with the interest shown by the AI community. In 1975, Minsky wrote an influential paper on the need for knowledge frames within AI, which he related, in numerous references, to the work of Bartlett (1932). However, Bartlett and Minsky differed in their purposes for studying schemata. As a psychologist, Bartlett wanted to examine the theoretical underpinnings of recall intrusions. Minsky, on the other hand, was concerned with questions about what knowledge an intelligent system needs, how the knowledge should be interrelated and how a computational system could use the knowledge efficiently.

Perhaps the most famous instantiation of the schema or frame idea came in the work of Schank and Abelson (1977). They were interested in how it is that readers can fill in the information needed to understand even the simplest text. For example, in order to understand the two sentences 'Jimmy sat down in the restaurant. The waiter took his order.' we need to have a lot of knowledge about restaurants. We need to know about the role of the waiter, and that 'ordering' refers to requests about food which is prepared in restaurants. Schank and Abelson referred to such social knowledge frames, or schemata, as 'scripts'. Scripts are essentially preformed packages of knowledge about stereotypical culture-bound events such as visiting a doctor or dentist, going to a wedding, catching a train and so on. The Schank and Abelson book described a language understanding program SAM (Script Applier Mechanism) which used scripts, and this excited interest among many psychologists (e.g. Bower, Black and Turner, 1979; Graesser, Gordon and Sawyer, 1979; Sharkey and Mitchell, 1985).

This interest arose partly because of the blending of procedural detail with the possibility of explaining psychological phenomena. However, the main interest was probably because the AI theory provided both a way of looking at the contents of schemata and a description of how they might be accessed in memory. This was something new which provided psychologists with the means of entry into research on knowledge structures which they had long needed.

The psychological research eventually fed back to the AI research and led to refinements in the theory as recounted by Schank (1982). (The interested reader is referred to a forthcoming book edited by Galambos, Black and Abelson which describes recent empirical developments and offers suggestions for refinements of the theory.) Schank was particularly interested in one finding from the Bower, Black and Turner (1979) study. Bower, Black and Turner had demonstrated that when people read a story about a visit to a dentist and a story about a visit to a doctor they were confused in their later recognition of which events were in which story. Bower, Black and Turner found that such confusions were located within similar scenes across different scripts. This led Schank to rethink the notion of a script.

Now, instead of saying that there is a paying scene in a restaurant script, a paying scene in a shopping script, and a paying scene in a getting-the-car-mended script, Schank has proposed that there is a general PAY scene in memory which each of these settings share. In his new theory, Schank (1979) proposes that, instead of scripts, we have many general scenes in memory which are dynamically assembled higher-level structures called MOPs (Memory Organization Packages). The end product of a call to a MOP resembles what used to be called a script. However, the new theory accounts for the memory confusions found in the Bower, Black and Turner study and also gives us a theory of reminding.

Thus, in the true spirit of cognitive science, we have a theory passing back-and-forth between two disciplines. A theory which originated in psychology and lay dormant for many years was revitalized by AI research. Intense psychological research then led to refinements within AI. The interested reader may also want to follow up some of the other programs and theories emanating from Schank and Abelson's group at Yale which have received attention from psychological experimentation. Examples include Riesbeck's (1975) ELI (e.g. Sharkey, 1983; Sharkey and Sharkey, 1983), Dyer's (1982) BORIS (e.g. Seifert *et al.*, 1984), Lehnert's (1978) 'plot units' (e.g. Reiser, Black and Lehnert, 1982), Schank's MOPs (e.g. Rieser, 1983) and TOPs (e.g. Seifert *et al.*, 1984), and Wilensky's (1983) 'goal configurations' (e.g. Sharkey and Bower, 1984).

11.3.2 Parallel spreading activation networks

The second case history we discuss is that of the parallel spreading activation network model. We begin in AI with Quillian's (1969) TLC (Teachable Language Comprehender), although we can trace the tradition of associationism back to Aristotle. Quillian's was the first attempt to use a network to model human long-term memory. The model was an attempt to simulate people's understanding of natural language in quite an extensive way, and we recommend the original article to our readers. We shall concentrate here on only the central component of the system: the memory network and the means of accessing information stored in it.

In Quillian's system, information in memory is made up of three types of data structure. First, there are concepts which refer to objects in the world such as fish, lawyers and donkeys. Second, each of these concepts has properties such as 'has fins', 'has lots of money', and 'is stubborn'. Third, there are associative links between the concepts. These links are formed such that memory is structured hierarchically. Take for example the category ANIMAL. One set of links below ANIMAL leads to MAMMAL, then BIRD, then down to ROBIN, and at the same level CHICKEN, OSTRICH, etc.

Now, to make the system economical in terms of storage space, Quillian only stored a property once in the network. For example, the property 'has skin' would be stored only once, with the unit ANIMAL. However, the system recognized that all of the concepts underneath ANIMAL in the hierarchy would also have skin. Similarly, rather than store the property 'has wings' with every bird, this property was stored only with the superordinate concept BIRD and was then inherited by each of the subordinates of BIRD. This idea of storing a property once, such that it is inherited by subordinates, is called 'the principle of strong cognitive economy'.

From the psychological point of view, perhaps the most important aspect of Quillian's model was the way in which it recognized input. If asked the question, 'Does a robin have wings?' a parallel search process would be initiated from both the concepts ROBIN and WINGS. If the search paths intersected the system could in principle answer 'yes', and otherwise 'no'. The search is called intersection search and the process is called spreading activation.

Now why this was so interesting to cognitive psychologists was that the system gave rise to very precise psychological predictions (which is an unusual characteristic of an AI model even today). These predictions were based on two fundamental parameters of the system. First, activation takes time to spread to the point of intersection. Second, since the system is hierarchical and operates on the principle of cognitive economy, it will take longer for activation to spread between distant than near concepts. Thus, for example, it should take longer for people to agree that a robin has wings than it would take them to agree that a bird has wings.

In fact this prediction was borne out with humans in an experimental investigation by Collins and Quillian (1969). They appeared to find evidence for hierarchical structuring and cognitive economy (on the assumption that activation took time to spread). The evidence indicated that it took approximately 75 milliseconds to spread activation from one concept to the next. This was interesting because it seemed that AI had come up with a theory of memory which had very strong psychological validity. However, the glory was quite short-lived. It was not long before other psychological investigations had found a number of flaws in the simple statement of the theory. We shall only briefly mention a few of these studies here as the idea is to give the reader a flavour of the work rather than to write a treatise on it.

Wilkins (1971) consulted category generation norms to compute the conjoint frequency of subjects and predicates for sentences like 'robins have wings'. Conjoint frequency is taken to be a reflection of the frequency with which words such as 'robin' and 'wings' occur together in written English. Wilkins found that conjoint frequency was a better predictor of verification time (i.e. the time to respond 'true' or 'false') than the time for activation to spread through a hierarchical structure. Similarly, Conrad (1972) showed that high conjoint frequency sentences were verified faster than low conjoint frequency sentences. Furthermore, Rips, Shoben and Smith (1973) found large within-category differences in verification time. People were much slower to verify that a pig is a mammal than to verify that a cow is a mammal. Also, there were cases in which the model predicted the reverse of what was found in the experiments. For example, it took people longer to verify that something was a mammal than to verify that the same thing was an animal even though animal is more distant in the hierarchy.

One way to preserve the original model was to drop the notion of cognitive economy in its strong form and to say that, although there is a fair amount of property inheritance, sometimes properties do get duplicated in memory. This is called 'the principle of weak cognitive economy' (Collins and Loftus, 1975). In addition, an assumption of differential link strength could account for the conjoint frequency effects. Stated simply, the links along which activation travel have different strengths and activation travels faster down stronger links. Thus, for example, concepts with a high conjoint frequency would have stronger links than concepts with a low conjoint frequency. Therefore, activation would intersect quicker for stronger links and thus verification time would be faster. Other more recent computational models of fact retrieval have taken such evidence into account, e.g. HAM (Anderson and Bower, 1973) and ACT (Anderson, 1976).

However, more recent experimental studies have led to further developments in memory modelling. In a series of sophisticated experiments, Ratcliff and McKoon (1981) demonstrated that activation did not take a measurable amount of time to spread. Their data indicated that activation spreads from a concept node to its neighbours almost instantaneously. This has led recently to a very sophisticated memory model called ACT* (Anderson, 1983) which takes all of these experimental factors, and many more, into account. There is not room to do justice to the model here since Anderson himself takes an entire book to do so, but it is recommended reading.

In this case history we have again seen how the interaction of AI and psychology can lead to an increasingly refined, computationally accurate, explanation of psychological phenomena. This is what should happen within cognitive science. It should perhaps be mentioned here that, although these case histories appear to report areas of research which are incompatible, Sharkey (cf. Sharkey and Mitchell, 1985; Sharkey, in press) has for some time been trying to combine the benefits of both of the approaches into a single psychologically plausible computational model, KAN (parallel spreading activation Knowledge Access Network). For an alternative to schema and associative network theories of memory see Morton (in press).

11.4 CONCLUSIONS

We have made the case in this chapter that, although psychology and AI each have a significant role to play in cognitive science, their union provides a powerful methodology for the study of cognition. On the one hand, psychologists can often get away with loose verbal descriptions of their models which would ' . . . not make first base from an AI point of view.' (Hayes, 1984.) We have argued that psychologists can gain a great deal of precision by implementing their theories as computer programs. On the other hand, AI could make great gains in the long run by building on a solid empirical foundation. At present, many AI theorists either believe (erroneously) that they are not using the human as a model or they believe that they do not need to take account of evidence from cognitive psychology. It has been argued here that there is a need for proper controlled human experimentation if AI is to have any kind of basis for its claim to be part of cognitive science.

We have also discussed ways in which different assessment criteria impede the interaction of AI and cognitive psychology. Problems with communication will remain until researchers recognize the strengths of the criteria adopted by both AI and cognitive psychology.

We adhere to the position, put forward by Sharkey (1982), that cognitive science must consist of three interacting parts which continually feed back to one another. These are:

(a) the construction of theory by whatever means available, e.g. intuition, imagination, formal reasoning, knowledge of people, knowledge of psychological evidence;
(b) theory evaluation by empirical testing using objective scientific methods; and
(c) careful computer implementation to ensure that the theory really is a possible explanation of human cognition.

11.5 ACKNOWLEDGEMENTS

We would like to thank Amanda Sharkey, Ajit Narayanan and Frances Watson for helpful comments on earlier drafts of this chapter.

ANNOTATED BIBLIOGRAPHY

Anderson, J.R. (1978), *The Architecture of Cognition*, Harvard University Press, Cambridge, MA.
    This is the third in a series of books in which John Anderson provides a large scale computational theory of human cognition, ACT* (pronounced

'Act Star'). The book is very wide-ranging in its coverage of experimental data and provides the reader with a detailed description of the ACT* computer simulation. Although we recommend this book to everyone interested in cognitive science, it should be pointed out that it is really rather technical. The beginner would be well advised to think of it as a challenge.

The Behavioural and Brain Sciences (Journal). Published by Cambridge University Press, Cambridge.

This journal frequently contains articles of interest to cognitive scientists. The papers are usually written by distinguished scientists and are accompanied by a large number of critical commentaries of the article, often contributed by members of different fields. The papers in this journal often reflect interdisciplinary links, and provide useful statements of important theoretical positions.

Cognitive Science (Journal). Published by Ablex Publishing Corporation, USA.

Cognitive Science contains relevant articles on AI and psychological theory. In particular, it publishes reports on psychologically relevant computer models. This is a high quality periodical we recommend as essential reading for anyone interested in cognitive science.

Russell, J. (1984), *Explaining Mental Life: Some Philosophical Issues in Psychology*, Macmillan, London.

This book, which is readable and not too technical, presents one view of what psychology should be about. The book contains useful chapters about the computational view of the mind, and discusses the position that important aspects of human experience are missed out by the computational approach.

Schank, R.C. and Abelson, R.P. (1977), *Scripts, Plans, Goals and Understanding*, Erlbaum, Hillsdale, NJ.

This is a very influential book in both psychology and AI. Schank and Abelson provide a unique view of language understanding. Really this is the first major attempt to provide an AI theory of how readers infer the links which make texts cohere. SPGU (as it is often called) is well worth a read for the beginner and specialist alike.

Sloman, A. (1978), *The Computer Revolution in Philosophy: Philosophy, Science and Models of Mind*, Harvester Press, Brighton.

Sloman provides an enthusiastic and accessible account of some of the ways in which AI can be used to change our way of thinking about ourselves. He is not primarily concerned with questions like: 'Can machines think?' or 'Are people machines?' Rather, he discusses AI as it can tell us about the human mind and shed light on long-standing philosophical problems.

REFERENCES

Abelson, R.P. (1980), In defence of common-sense representations of knowledge. Cognitive Science Technical Report, No. 6, Yale University, New Haven, CT.

Anderson, J.R. (1976), *Language, Memory and Thought*, Erlbaum, Hillsdale, NJ.

Anderson, J.R. (1983), *The Architecture of Cognition*, Harvard University Press, Cambridge, MA.

Anderson, J.R. and Bower, G.H. (1973), *Human Associative Memory*, Winston, Washington, DC.

Anderson, R.C. (1977), The notion of schemata and the educational enterprise, in *Schooling and the Acquisition of Knowledge* (eds R. C. Anderson, R. J. Spiro and W. E. Montague), Erlbaum, Hillsdale, NJ.

Bartlett, F.C. (1932), *Remembering*, Cambridge University Press, Cambridge.

Black, J.B., Galambos, J.A. and Reiser, B.J. (1984), Coordinating discovery and verification research, in *New Methods in the Study of Immediate Processes in Comprehension* (eds D. Kieras and M. Just), Erlbaum, Hillsdale, NJ.

Bobrow, D.G., Kaplan, R.M., Norman, D.A., Thompson, H. and Winograd, T. (1977), GUS, a frame driven dialog system, *Artif. Intel.*, **8**, (2), 155–73.

Bower, G.H., Black, J.B. and Turner, T.J. (1979), Scripts in memory for text, *Cogn. Psychol.*, **11**, 177–220.

Colby, K.M. (1963), Computer simulation of a neurotic process, in *Computer Simulation of Personality: Frontiers of Psychological Research* (eds S.S. Tomkins and S. Messick), Wiley, New York.

Collins, A.M. and Quillian, M.R. (1969), Retrieval time from semantic memory, *J. Verb. Learn. Verb. Behav.*, **8**, 240–7.

Collins, A.N. and Loftus, E.F. (1975), A spreading activation theory of semantic processing, *Psychol. Rev.*, **82**, 407–28.

Conrad, C. (1972), Cognitive economy in semantic memory, *J. Exp. Psychol.*, **92**, 149–54.

Dennett, D. (1978), *Brainstorms*, Harvester Press, Brighton.

Dyer, M.G. (1982), In-depth understanding: A computer model of integrated processing for narrative comprehension. Technical Report, No. 219, Department of Computer Science, Yale University, New Haven, CT.

Galambos, J.A., Black, J.B. and Abelson, R. (in press), *Knowledge Structures*, Erlbaum, Hillsdale, NJ.

Graesser, A.C., Gordon, S.E. and Sawyer, J.D. (1979), Recognition memory for typical and atypical actions in scripted activities: Tests of a script pointer + tag hypothesis. *J. Verb. Learn. Verb. Behav.*, **18**, 319–32.

Hayes, P.J. (1984), On the difference between psychology and AI, in *Artificial Intelligence: Human Effects* (eds M. Yazdani and A. Narayanan), Ellis Horwood, Chichester.

Kant, I. (1787), *Critique of Pure Reason*, 2nd edn, N. K. Smith trans., Macmillan, London, 1963. (Originally published in 1787.)

Kolers, P.A. and Smythe, W.E. (1984), Symbol manipulation: Alternatives to the computational view of mind. *J. Verb. Learn. Verb. Behav.*, **23**, 289–314.

Lehnert, W.G. (1978), *The Process of Question Answering*, Erlbaum, Hillsdale, NJ.

Marr, D. (1977), Artificial Intelligence – A personal view, *Artif. Intel.*, **9**, 37–48.

McDermott, D. (1976), Artificial Intelligence meets natural stupidity, *SIGART Newsletter*, **57**.

McGinn, C. (1979), Action and its explanation, in *Philosophical Problems in Psychology* (ed. N. Bolton), Methuen, London.

Miller, L. (1978), Has Artificial Intelligence contributed to an understanding of the human mind? A critique of the arguments for and against, *Cogn. Psychol.*, **2**, 111–27.

Minsky, M. (1968), *Semantic Information Processing*, MIT Press, Cambridge, MA.

Minsky, M. (1975), A framework for representing knowledge, in *The Psychology of Computer Vision* (ed. P. H. Winston), McGraw-Hill, New York.

Morton, J. (in press), Headed records: A framework for remembering and forgetting, in *Advances in Cognitive Science* (ed. N. E. Sharkey), Ellis Horwood, Chichester.

Mynatt, C.R., Doherty, M.E. and Tweney, R.D. (1977), Confirmation bias in a simulated research environment: An experimental study of scientific inference, *Quart. J. Exp. Psychol.*, **29**, 85–95.

Neisser, U. (1967), *Cognitive Psychology*, Appleton-Century-Crofts, New York.

Platt, J.R. (1964), Strong inference, *Science*, **146**, 347-53.

Quillian, M.R. (1969), The teachable language comprehender, *Commun. ACM*, **12**, 458–76.

Ratcliff, R. and McKoon, G. (1981), Does activation really spread?, *Psychol Rev.*, **88**, 454–7.

Reiser, B.J. (1983), Contexts and indices in autobiographical memory, Cognitive Science Technical Report, No. 24, Yale University, New Haven, CT.

Reiser, B.J., Black, J.B. and Lehnert, W.G. (1982), Thematic units in the writing of stories, Paper presented at the Annual Meeting of the American Educational Research Association.

Riesbeck, C. (1975), Conceptual Analysis, in *Conceptual Information Processing* (ed. R. C. Shank), North-Holland, Amsterdam.

Rips, L.J., Shoben, E.J. and Smith, E.E. (1973), Semantic distance and the verification of semantic relations, *J. Verb. Learn. Verb. Behav.*, **12**, 1–20.

Robson, C. (1973), *Experiment, Design and Statistics in Psychology*, Penguin, Harmondsworth.

Rumelhart, D.E. (1975), Notes on a schema for stories, in *Representation and Understanding* (eds D. G. Bobrow and A. Collins), Academic Press, New York.

Russell, J. (1984), *Explaining Mental Life*, Macmillan, London.

Schank, R.C. (1979), Reminding and memory organization: An introduction to MOPS, Technical Report, No. 170, Department of Computer Science, Yale University, New Haven, CT.

Schank, R.C. (1980), Language and memory, *Cogn. Sci.*, **4**, 243–84.

Schank, R.C. (1982), *Dynamic Memory: A Theory of Reminding and Learning in Computers and People*, Cambridge University Press, New York.

Schank, R.C. and Abelson, R.P. (1977), *Scripts, Plans, Goals and Understanding*, Erlbaum, Hillsdale, NJ.

Searle, J.R. (1980), Minds, brains and programs, *Behav. Brain Sci.*, **3**, 63–73.

Seifert, C.M., McKoon, G., Abelson, R.P. and Ratcliff, R. (1984), Memory connections between thematically similar episodes, Cognitive Science Technical Report, No. 27, Yale University, New Haven, CT.

Sharkey, N.E. (1982), The locus and control of script priming effects in reading, Unpublished doctoral dissertation, Exeter University, Exeter, UK.

Sharkey, N.E. (1983), The control of mundane knowledge in memory, Cognitive Science Technical Report, No. 20, Yale University, New Haven, CT. Also published by Comtex Corporation, New York, 1984.

Sharkey, N.E. (in press), A model of knowledge-based expectations in text comprehension, in *Knowledge Structures* (eds J. A. Galambos, J. B. Black and R. Abelson), Erlbaum, Hillsdale, NJ.

Sharkey, N.E. and Bower, G.H. (1984), The integration of goals and actions in text understanding, *Proc. Cogn. Sci.*, **6**.

Sharkey, N.E. and Mitchell, D.C. (1985), Word recognition in a functional context: The use of scripts in reading, *J. Mem. Lang.*, **24**, 253–70.

Sharkey, N.E. and Pfeifer, R. (1984), Uncomfortable bedfellows: Cognitive psychology and Artificial Intelligence, in *Artificial Intelligence: Human Effects* (eds M. Yazdani and A. Narayanan), Ellis Horwood, Chichester.

Sharkey, N.E. and Sharkey, A.J.C. (1983), Levels of expectation in sentence understanding, Cognitive Science Technical Report, No. 21, Yale University, New Haven, CT. Also published by Comtex Corporation, New York, 1984.

Sloman, A. (1978), *The Computer Revolution in Philosophy: Philosophy, Science and Models of Mind*, Harvester Press, Brighton.

Sloman, A. (1984a), The structure of the space of possible minds, in *The Mind and the Machine: Philosophical Aspects of Artificial Intelligence* (ed. S. Torrance), Ellis Horwood, Chichester.

Sloman, A. (1984b), Towards a computational theory of mind, in *Artificial Intelligence: Human Effects* (eds M. Yazdani and A. Narayanan), Ellis Horwood, Chichester.

Turing, A.M. (1950), Computing machinery and intelligence, *Mind*, **LIX**, 433–60. Reprinted in *Computers and Thought* (eds E. A. Feigenbaum and J. Feldman), McGraw-Hill, New York, 1963.

Weizenbaum, J. (1965), ELIZA – A computer program for the study of natural communication between man and machine, *Commun. ACM*, **9**, 36–45.

Wilensky, R. (1983), *Planning and Understanding*, Addison-Wesley, Reading, M.A.

Wilkes, K. (1984), Pragmatics in science and theory in common sense, *Inquiry*, **27**, 339–61.

Wilkins, A.J. (1971), Conjoint frequency, category size and categorization time, *J. Verb. Learn. Verb. Behav.*, **10**, 382–5.

Yazdani, M. (1984), Introduction: What is Artificial Intelligence?, in *Artificial Intelligence: Human Effects* (eds M. Yazdani and A. Narayanan), Ellis Horwood, Chichester.

12

Breaking out of the Chinese Room

STEVE TORRANCE

John Searle's critique of Artificial Intelligence (AI) is now well known, but the nature of his attack is often not clearly grasped. In this paper I discuss his 'Chinese Room' thought-experiment in the context of Alan Turing's 'Imitation Game'. It is particularly difficult to assess Searle's 'arguments against AI', simply because AI covers a multitude of sins. Indeed, the term 'strong AI' which is Searle's name for the position he is attacking, is rather inappropriate. A better name for the position might have been 'strong computationalism'. Outlined briefly the doctrine expresses the philosophical view that appropriately pro- grammed computers can possess genuine mental states, and that when we have such mental states, our brain is running similar such programs. But AI is the name of a research activity. It is neither a necessary nor a sufficient condition of being involved in the research activity of AI that one should assent to the philosophical doctrine which Searle calls 'strong AI', although it is perhaps true that a great many people who are engaged in the research activity do tend to favour that doctrine. But by attacking the doctrine under that name, Searle makes himself appear to be proposing by implication that the very activity of AI research, in the sense of writing programs which enable computers to simulate mental performances of various sorts, if not to replicate them, is itself disrepu- table or confused. This is unfortunate (and, I think, not Searle's intention).

12.1 INSIDE THE CHINESE ROOM

Searle (1980) considers the idea that a computer program could genu- inely be said to understand something. He argues as follows: Only machines which possess the causal powers of a human brain are capable of genuine thinking. A digital computer cannot in principle possess such causal powers, since such a machine is defined purely formally, in terms of the transformation of sets of symbols. Since programs are defined formally, they are not affected by the kind of hardware on which they may be implemented. It is this hardware-independence, frequently insisted upon by theorists in computer science and in AI, that Searle appropriates in his 'Chinese Room' argument.

Suppose that you had a program that could reproduce the behaviour of a native speaker of Chinese – that behaved in a way that was indistinguishable from some human being who genuinely did understand Chinese. We can imagine the program's performance to be as sophisticated as we like – quite convincing to other Chinese speakers, for instance. Defenders of what Searle calls the 'Strong AI' thesis would claim that, if the program generated all the behaviour appropriate to a native Chinese understander, then any system running that program would genuinely understand Chinese.

Since, by hypothesis, the nature of the program is not changed if we change the hardware, let us now imagine the program running, not on an electronic computer, but on a human one. Someone – a non-Chinese speaker – is sitting inside a room, and is presented with a series of characters which comprise a message in Chinese. Faithfully following the rules of the program, the person eventually produces, as output, an appropriate response to the message. (The human computer is, no doubt, many orders of magnitude slower than the electronic one, but this does not affect the argument, as a program is defined by the sequence of its operations, not by the nature of the physical mechanism that executes those operations.) Since the person inside the room clearly does not understand any Chinese merely in virtue of running the program, neither could it be true of a computer running the same program that, merely in virtue of that fact alone, it understood Chinese. In general, it cannot, says Searle, be a sufficient condition of some subject X's understanding something, that X be instantiating some program X.

A schematic illustration of Searle's argument is given in Fig. 12.1. Box A represents a human Chinese speaker, producing various textual outputs on the basis of various inputs. Box B represents some computer simulation of the textual input and output of this human speaker, which is judged to be as perfect as you like in purely performance terms. Adherents of strong AI will maintain that genuine understanding must be associated with Box B, as well as Box A, even though the textual input/output is generated by an electronic physical computational system, mediated through various levels of virtual machine, rather than a human physiological system. In opposition to this claim, Searle proposes Box C, which reproduces the performance of some underlying virtual machine of Box B, and therefore textual output at the top level which is indistinguishable from B and A (save in irrelevant respects, such as speed). But the understanding associated with Box C refers

A   B   C

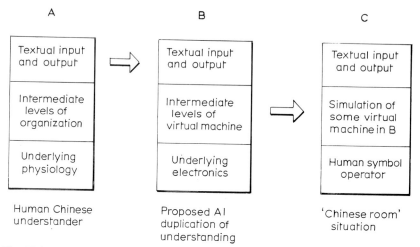

Fig. 12.1

solely to the human symbol operator's simulation of the virtual machine in B. Since the simulation by C of B is complete, the two are formally equivalent. Thus, if no (relevant) understanding can be attributed to the human operator associated with C, it would follow that no such understanding could be attributed to Box B.

12.2   TURING'S IMITATION GAME

In the background to Searle's discussion is the 'imitation game' propounded by Turing (1950) in his seminal paper, 'Computing Machinery and Intelligence'. Many myths seem to have grown up concerning that paper and what he was claiming in it, and concerning the Turing Test which is elaborated in it. I have seen or heard all of the following claims made: that 'Turing showed that any machine which could fool you into thinking that you were talking to a human being, would be intelligent'; that 'Turing defined the conditions under which a computer could be said to be conscious'; that 'Turing showed that, for any mental state S, if a computer successfully imitated the behaviour of a human being who was in state S, then the computer would also be in state S'; that 'Turing's imitation test consisted of a person trying to tell if he or she was talking to another person or to a machine'; and that 'Turing provided a test which has been passed already by several programs in the history of AI'; etc.

Each of these characterizations of Turing's views and the nature of his test, seems to me to be either misleading or false. Turing didn't explicitly purport to prove anything, or indeed to offer any direct theory of current notions of thinking, intelligence, consciousness, etc. He doesn't even talk much about intelligence or consciousness in his paper, except in the title. The test he devised was not one in which a subject had to tell directly between a human and a machine. And no currently existing program could conceivably pass the Turing test, by Turing's own conception of what it involved (although he may have been more optimistic than his own conception warranted).

Turing starts his paper by asking a question. He then spends much of the rest of the paper discussing another, rather different, question. His opening question is: 'Can machines think?' He immediately replaces this question by another which concerns a rather elaborate contest, which Turing describes in some detail. The test involves a game between three players, A, B and C. A and B sit together in a room, unseen by C, who converses with them by typewritten messages. A is a man, and B a woman; C's sex is immaterial. C has to identify which of his or her interlocutors is A and which is B. A's role is to confuse, and B's role is to help the interrogator C. (See Fig. 12.2.)

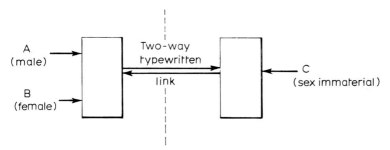

C's role : to assign identities to A and B
A's role : to maximize C's confusion
B's role : to minimize C's confusion

Fig. 12.2 Turing's imitation game

Turing's replacement to the question, 'Can machines think?' is: 'What will happen when a machine takes the part of A in this game?' Turing is extremely guarded as to the significance of such a replacement. But it is clear by innuendo, if not by explicit statement in his paper, that any machine (specifically any digital computer) which substituted for A smoothly enough not to affect the success in escaping identification by C, would be a machine to which it would be appropriate to ascribe thinking.

Turing does not, to my knowledge, discuss how his imitation game might be generalized. People have offered examples of variants of his test. For instance, it has been claimed that Weizenbaum's ELIZA passed the test (Weizenbaum, 1976), and that a paranoid simulation by Kenneth Colby and colleagues (see Colby *et al.*, 1972; Colby, 1981) also passed it. (Such claims were not made by the authors of either program, it is important to add.) But such programs are far too superficial to be taken as serious alternatives to Turing's own imagined test. It is clear that any Turing test program must be extremely robust, versatile and comprehensive, and must have, at the very least, a natural language processing ability far more sophisticated than is available on existing research, and must also have extensive reserves of common sense knowledge. Turing expressed the belief that such a program might exist by the end of the century. I think he was extremely optimistic.

12.3 PRODUCTIVE AND SUBJECTIVE MENTAL STATES

The question arises: What would any program which passed such a test show? That a digital computer could 'think'? Well, What is 'think' supposed to mean here? It is normally taken for granted that a being which thinks is, by definition, conscious, i.e. undergoes some sort of inner or subjective life. But only the crudest conception of what it is to be conscious could allow that the ability to pass a Turing test actually implied that some subjective awareness could be ascribed to the machine.

Perhaps Turing himself had such a crude conception. In his 1950 paper, he considered an objection to his test which said that a machine which passed the test would not be conscious. Such an objector, Turing said, would be forced into solipsism, since the existence of any human consciousness other than one's own is equally subject to doubt. But Turing's argument here is clearly fallacious since we have each got strong neurophysiological grounds for believing in the consciousness of other humans, whereas such neurophysiological grounds are precisely lacking in a digital computer, however convincing its external behaviour.

I believe that the grounds for thinking that the Turing test might suggest anything of any genuine psychological significance, are quite different. There is a class of mental properties which, unlike subjective states of consciousness, do not depend upon having a certain qualitative inner state of awareness but rather, it would seem, upon achieving certain results, or upon having certain abilities. I am thinking here of mental properties such as being able to solve various sorts of puzzles, or knowing how to diagnose blood disorders, as opposed to 'subjective' sorts of states, such as being conscious of a certain taste, or a certain feeling of giddiness. This is intended to provide a naïve, rough and ready distinction only, but one which suggests that the field of the

Mental may contain phenomena of two (at least two) radically different kinds:; things that we do with our minds, and things that go on in our minds.

Such 'productive' or 'performance-related' mental properties, as the former might be called, are clearly those that lie at the heart of research in AI, and for fairly clear reasons. A program which produced, for example, problem-solving behaviour would seem to be capable of getting a much more profound grip upon its respective domain of mentality, than would one which mimicked pain-reaction behaviour. A program which succeeded in detecting solutions to puzzles, or objects in an environment, or parsing an open class of natural language sentences, would clearly be succeeding in doing something mind-like.

Purists will insist that no actual mental activity is going on in such machines. But it does seem that something significant is happening. A pocket calculator may be performing only the simulacrum of calculation, but what it produces is not just the simulacrum of a result. And even if the result is not obtained 'in the way that we do it', there is still a clear relationship between the method used by the calculator and the methods we use. Further, whereas it seems easy to make a fairly clear distinction between the 'outer' (public) behaviour and the 'inner' (private) mental state in the case of pain and its associated behaviour, this doesn't seem so easy in the case of, say, calculation or learning, and their associated behaviours. What exactly is the inner experience which is supposedly hidden behind the facade of the public performance of learning? The subjective experience of learning? But that is not what gets the learning done, although it may be something which accompanies the learning.

Again, there are many mental attributes which seem peculiarly difficult to feign, at least in a settled, long-term way. One could perhaps go through one's life fooling everyone that one had severe arthritic pains. One would hardly live for an extensive period pretending one was an expert medical diagnostician (leaving certain sorts of rigging aside), if one, in fact, had no understanding about medicine; and again, it is difficult to see how one could successfully fool people into thinking that one was a superb chess player, if one could not really play the game at all.

A natural corollary of this reflection is that there are, in a sense, human variants of the Turing test – where, given certain extended behavioural displays, we would find it difficult to suppose that the relevant mental capacities were lacking in the human subjects concerned. (There are many non-mental capacities which are also like this: I once saw a cartoon in which an animal was running at speed to escape a predator, and joked: 'I'm only pretending I can run this fast!') These difficult-to-feign capacities seem to be particularly open to a behavioural analysis, as compared to the more 'hidden' sorts of properties which are often, in popular thinking at least, associated with the mind.

12.4   IS THE MIND A UNITY?

All these considerations are no doubt highly controversial. But I think they do give some weight to the idea that the Turing test may have plausibility when applied to certain sorts of mental states at least. There is a strong temptation to suppose that these 'productive' kinds of thinking – which are indeed instances of genuine mentality – are nevertheless somehow immanent or implicit in the associated behaviours. If computer programs can successfully provide a way of generating these behaviours – and no doubt that will be possible only by reproducing, in computational terms, some extremely complex set of internal structures and logical relationships – then surely this kind of mentality at least can be explained in a purely computational way, without reference to any inner seat of consciousness, or a transcendental Subject, or indeed to any of the details of neurophysiology which underpin the way such computational structures are actually realized in the case of human beings displaying such behaviours. Other kinds of mental state, on the other hand, may not be open to a similar computational account.

This cautious, conciliatory position leaves us with the following difficulty. If computational theory managed to explain the productive mental processes but not the other ones, then how would it account for the presumption that the mental is a unified field? It certainly feels as if our cognitive mental states form a unity with our qualitative sensations! This partial computational view would certainly seem to conflict with some powerful commonsense assumptions about the nature of our mind.

Well, it has become fashionable recently in philosophy of mind to criticize our pre-theoretical views of the nature of the mind – our 'folk psychology', as it is called – as incoherent and myth-ridden. Maybe this assumption that the mind forms a unity which must be explained in one single overarching way is one such myth. Or maybe we just have to say that some of our mental states rely upon the brain's properties as a computational device (and can therefore inhere in other computational devices), while other mental states rely upon non-computational features of the brain. A lot more needs to be said about all this, but there is no space to do so here.

Such difficulties apart, it certainly seems that the strong AI thesis is most convincing when applied to these 'productive' mental processes, as opposed to the qualitative or subjective processes. But Searle's Chinese Room argument is directed at showing that even cognitive mental states cannot be explained in computational terms.

12.5 CARBON CHAUVINISM AND CAUSAL POWERS OF THE BRAIN

A computer duplicating the behaviour of a native Chinese speaker might be very successful at generating the appropriate sentences. That is, it might possess whatever degree of productive capacity, judged in purely behavioural terms, one wished for. Yet, Searle claims, this in itself does not imply anything about its mentality. If a digital computer running the program really did possess the mental states appropriate to a native Chinese speaker, then so too would the human being operating the same program by hand, since the two 'machines' are formally equivalent. Yet the human inside the room does not understand Chinese at the outset (this is part of our supposition); and clearly would not acquire an understanding of Chinese simply through executing the operations of the program.

How then do we account for the existence of mental states? In Searle's view, mentality must be explained ultimately by reference to physiological properties, and specifically by reference to properties of our brain. In this way he runs counter to the AI tradition according to which the human brain is simply our bodies' mechanism for implementing the high-level functional organization on which the outward intelligent behaviours are in turn based. Of course, he has no detailed theory: he is just pinning his money on the eventual success of neurophysiology in giving detailed explanations of how the brain 'produces' thinking.

Searle's determination to oppose the computational view of thinking has seemed to many people to entail a certain sort of 'chauvinism' about mentality on his part – an arbitrary restriction of mind to carbon- or protoplasm-based organisms, as opposed, say, to silicon- or gallium arsenide-based ones. It was precisely such theoretical favouritism which led many critics of materialist philosophical theories of mind to adopt a functionalist approach to the mind.

But Searle is not really guilty of the 'carbon chauvinism' of which he has been accused: to make such an accusation is entirely to miss his point. Our mental states, Searle says, are caused by our physiological states. Any system with an equivalent causal base – with the same causal powers, to use his favourite phrase – will be equally capable of producing comparable mental states. No doubt there could be artificial systems which reproduce the relevant causal features of our physiologies, but although this would be a case of 'artificial intelligence', it does not involve the classical AI route to mentality associated with the Turing test.

12.6   FLAVOURS TO ARTIFICIAL INTELLIGENCE

I said earlier that AI covered a multitude of sins. There are many motivations for doing AI, many conceptions of what the point of the subject is, and many different sorts of claims that might be made on its behalf. I can think of at least three discernible orientations or 'flavours' to work in AI: a theoretical one, concerned primarily with shedding light on the nature of mentality; a technological one, concerned with getting computers to do various 'mind-like' things, without too much close attention to how nearly they reproduce the way that we did them; and a commercial one, concerned with generating marketable products.

Each of these types of AI has different characteristic conceptions about what might be involved in thinking or intelligence in computers, and on what the relevance of applying mentalistic notions to machines might consist in.

Commercial concerns are anxious to call their products intelligent on the slenderest of grounds, because this gets people to buy them. People who are concerned with the technical aspects of AI programming, on the other hand, are really interested only in issues of performance or productivity at the behavioural level. When they apply terms such as 'intelligence' or 'knowledge' to systems they might build or conceive they do not generally mean to make any serious philosophical or psychological claims (except, perhaps, when waxing philosophical as a form of relaxation). Clearly, there is a sense of 'intelligent' in which AI programs, or processes within them can, in a perfectly natural sense of the term, be said to exhibit intelligence.

Within the theoretical orientation towards AI (the cognitive scientists, the psychologists, philosophers, etc.) there are several different per-spectives. One possible role for theoretical AI is the production of computational models and simulations which help to explain, but are not intended to replicate, mental properties. Another role is the more long-term aim of building artificial systems which replicate deep proper-ties of human physiology rather than simply generating high-level behavioural simulations. Neither of these conceptions of AI need be damaged by Searle's arguments, which are really directed at the classical AI or 'functionalist' claim that in order to possess particular kinds of mental properties it is sufficient only that an entity instantiate certain computational structures, the physical basis or underlying architecture for these computational structures being irrelevant.

Unfortunately, many of the responses which have been made to

Searle have blurred the distinction between these different types of 'theoretical' AI. This is not surprising because many of the notions used in AI theoretical writing are eminently blurrable. For instance, it is easy to move from the idea of modelling aspects of a given property, to that of simulating that property, to synthesizing or replicating that property. There are a great many psychologistic terms, such as 'representation', 'learning', 'knowledge', 'interpretation', 'goals', etc., which are constantly used inside AI contexts, and where such usages are so clearly appropriate to what is being described, that it would be just cavilling to object that such applications are really metaphorical – just as it would be pedantic to point out that gas-stoves cannot really cook meals, since only people can. Nevertheless you cannot automatically assume that, because such ascriptions are natural, no further argument of any sort is needed to support the view that programs which 'learn', 'solve problems', 'interpret', etc., in these ways, must be subjects of genuine mentality.

12.7 LANGUAGE-MODELLING AND NEURO-MODELLING PROGRAMS

Of the numerous responses which have been made to Searle, I am going to concentrate on one or two which strike me as being particularly interesting. Space forbids anything like a representative survey. Here is one objection.

It has been supposed that you could counter Searle by modifying the imagined Chinese understanding program, so that it reproduced the relevant language-understanding behaviour by computationally duplicating the underlying neuronal states of the brain. Let us call the earlier version of the Chinese Room program the 'language-modelling' program, and this new version the 'neuro-modelling' program. Once we have introduced the latter, we have, surely, conceived of a simulation of thinking which not only reproduced the outward behaviour appropriate to a given mental process, but also the inner, physiological 'causal powers' demanded by Searle.

The problem with this objection – at least in its simpler forms – is that it is susceptible to the following dilemma. We are being asked to imagine a program which will have to contain an extremely detailed computational 'model' of the neuronal structure of a person's brain. But what sort of 'model' could this be? Like the earlier 'language-modelling' program, this program, if it is to be merely a program, must also in principle, be reproducible by a person shuffling symbols inside a room. But if the 'neuro-modelling' program merely provided an amazingly detailed symbolic representation of the structure of the brain, without duplicating the efficacy of the brain to generate the relevant psychological states, then the situation would be no better than before. It would be like having a car which contained under its bonnet, not an internal combustion engine, but a computer whose program faithfully represented the formal structure of an internal combustion engine, without having any corresponding power to communicate motion to the wheels, nor any mechanism to translate the computer's output signals into motion.

If, on the other hand, the program 'drove' some system which really did reproduce the relevant causal powers of the brain, then the program would no longer be playing a purely formal role – that is, it would no longer be merely a device for generating certain output symbols on the basis of certain input symbols, since it owed its efficacy to being causally embedded in a certain physical setting.

We have to imagine that this modified 'Chinese Room' program is, at the behavioural level, indistinguishable from the one in Searle's own example. That is, both are capable of generating identical textual outputs in Chinese that are in the view of competent judges, equally impeccable displays of understanding of the language. It will be noticed that, to concede to Searle that only the latter, 'neuro-modelling', program could provide an instance of genuine understanding, entails a rejection of automatic support for the Turing test as a criterion of mentality. But further, if one really presses the difference between the neuro-modelling program and the language-modelling program, one runs the risk of giving up the principle of formality of computational programs which lies at the very heart of the strong AI thesis, as Searle conceives it. (The possibility that this principle will indeed have to be given up is discussed below, in connection with some views of Aaron Sloman.)

12.8 PURE ARTIFICIAL INTELLIGENCE VERSUS EXOTIC ARCHITECTURES

There really does seem to be a tension here between two positions, which those who are sympathetic to 'strong AI' might wish to espouse. The first is a beautifully pure – almost Platonic, certainly Leibnizian – conception of computation emphasizing the abstract nature of the universal Turing machine: its power to produce a dazzling richness and diversity of effects from the most slender of bases. The trouble with this conception, however, is that, because of its abstractness, its richness can only be of a purely symbolic nature: it cannot effect any intervention in the real world, since, at this abstract level, its output can just as easily consist of marks on pieces of paper, as of electrical impulses capable of controlling other mechanisms. The second position involves a conception of computation which stresses the way that electronic computer systems can be embedded in all sorts of devices which may be used to interact with the real physical environment, or which may, in all sorts of ways, depend upon a particular physical embodiment of abstract computational patterns in order to have the particular properties which are being claimed for it.

Searle's 'Chinese Room' argument is not as effective against claims made on behalf of this latter conception of a computational mechanism, since it is no longer possible to suppose that a person inside a room moving around bits of paper can reproduce exactly the characteristics of such a machine. If, for example, it is claimed that it is an integral part of such a machine that it has robotic sensorimotor appendages which interact with objects in a real environment, and if, further, it is claimed that certain mental states may attach to the system as a whole, where this is taken to include its sensorimotor components, then it is no longer relevant for Searle to argue that a human buried inside the robot's recesses, who stands in for the electronic computational engine as a generator of the purely formal elements of the program, would not be a subject of the relevant mental states. Searle would need to base his argument on grounds other than merely an appeal to the lack of causal powers of a purely symbolic computational engine, since the device, as we would now be considering it, would no longer be one which had been abstracted away from any such causal powers.

We started in the relatively pure realm of the Turing test and the purely abstract Turing machine which seemed to go hand-in-hand with its appeal, where we were trying to assess whether it would be safe to accord intelligence or mentality to a program which decoded and generated strings of symbols. Once we leave these relatively clear cases, however, and look instead at the more exotic cases of computational simulations of the brain, it becomes difficult to keep a clear view of the issues. It is possible to imagine a wealth of examples ranging from creations which are thought to be not far over the horizon of the current state of the art, for instance the parallel connectionist or 'Boltzmann' architectures which are now being discussed, and which may be capable of reproducing certain deep aspects of particular mental properties such as vision or learning (see Hinton, 1981, cited in Boden, 1984; and Feldman and Ballard, 1982); through a wealth of speculative kinds of creations, to half or totally imaginary beings which may serve to unhitch any intimate associations that may still remain in certain old-fashioned minds between mentality and our peculiar human physical makeup.

12.9   THE LIMITED SCOPE OF SEARLE'S ARGUMENT

It would be pointless to deny the abstract possibility of success in producing genuine-but-artificial mentality by some means at some point in the future, or to deny that, at the very least, a host of various kinds of artificial mentalities are describable within the space of the scientifically conceivable, even if they were never to be practically realizable. Such possibilities have little to do with the majority of current research programmes, which operate at a much less spectacular leave. But also such possibilities are not in any way denied by Searle's 'Chinese Room' argument.

It is important to stress, therefore, that Searle's primary arguments against 'strong AI' are not arguments against the possibility of artificial intelligence as such. That is, his arguments are not denying that there might one day be artefacts with genuine minds, or systems possessing genuine mentality, in which computation might play a central role in generating causal processes within the overall system.

Nor, indeed, are his arguments intended to deny the potential success of intelligent behavioural simulation by existing computational methods to any arbitrary degree of success, where such behavioural simulation is distinguished clearly from actual mentality or intelligence. His arguments have a very limited target: a particular, highly circumscribed, but widely believed claim made on behalf of AI. (But see, for example, Dreyfus (1979) for a much wider critique of the claims of AI.)

Yet AI, as a research programme, or as a general 'ideology' concerning how to approach the study of the realm of the mental, does not stand or fall with such a claim. When Searle delivered his Reith Lectures there was a certain amount of agonizing in both the quality newspapers and computer press, about how Searle was encouraging a new wave of ill-will towards AI research, which had so recently regained (in the UK) official favour after the dark days following the Lighthill report. As it should by now be clear, any such apprehension was founded on a quite radical misunderstanding of the nature of Searle's argument. There were others who said that Searle was to be commended for puncturing the pretensions of people who were making heady predictions about the capabilities of the coming generations of expert systems and 'intelligent' machines.

But Searle's arguments imply nothing about how actual AI systems currently under development are likely to perform, since they do not touch the issue of performance at all, being rather about the interpretation of such performances.

12.10 SLOMAN'S 'WEAK STRONG AI'

As I said at the beginning of this paper, although there is a widespread feeling among AI disciples that Searle's 'Chinese Room' argument must be wrong, there seems to be little agreement as to where exactly the error lies. I'd like, therefore, to discuss some interesting remarks made by Aaron Sloman in recent papers (Sloman, 1985a, 1985b), where he suggests that the Chinese Room argument may be correct, but that it does not, as Searle thinks, demolish the essence of the 'strong AI' position. Thus Sloman suggests that Searle's central claims can be conceded without any need to give up the basic points espoused by supporters of strong AI.

Sloman's point turns on the claim that there is a crucial difference between the situation where a certain collection of computational operations is performed by a human being, as in the Chinese Room, and the situation where those same operations are executed by an automatic, 'mechanical' device, such as an electronic computer. (As we shall see, the difference is not as crude as that.) Sloman's arguments suggest that those who claim that mental processes result from computational processes, might nevertheless wish to deny that a computational process has really taken place, in the fullest sense of the word, if the operations are performed by deliberate human actions.

Such a claim would constitute a much weaker 'strong AI' thesis than the one which is attacked by Searle, but it would be strong enough to make it possible both: (a) to argue that appropriately programmed computers might possess genuine mental states; and (b) to appeal to such programs as providing explanations for those same mental states in us.

To summarize Sloman's position: imagine some computational process C which supposedly 'generates' a given mental process M, in the sense that certain computing devices, when instantiating C, will be the subjects of the mental process M. Sloman suggests that there are important constraints upon the conditions under which that process M will result from the instantiation of C. If, for example, the various operations of C are performed by a human being, then the mental process M will not result. If, on the other hand, the operations are performed on a device designed to switch automatically between the various constituent operations of C, then the mental process M may well result. (Our brains, Sloman is presumably implying, are just such automatic devices.)

12.11 WHAT ARE THE RELEVANT KINDS OF COMPUTATIONAL PROCESSES?

Is there any justification for driving a wedge in here? Sloman's argument is based on a difference in the way that the operations of the relevant computational process C are causally related to the program when those operations are performed by a human being (or a group of human beings), and when they are performed by a computer. In the former process the program acts merely as a guide to what the human agents actually do; in the latter case the causal link is (typically) much more direct: the program drives or controls the computations.

It is very tempting to suppose that Sloman is making the difference between the two sorts of cases depend merely upon a question of reliability or dependability – as if he were suggesting that human-mediated computations do not count as computational processes in the true sense of the term, because human beings are relatively unpredictable. In comparing an electronic calculator to a person operating the program of such a calculator, for example, Sloman writes: 'The person would be subject to a much richer variety of possible interrupting, diverting, or distracting influences, including purely internal influences like suddenly remembering an unfinished task, or hating the person who asked the arithmetical questions' (ibid., p. 29).

Clearly, however, one could imagine a superbly reliable human being, who is supremely dedicated to the task of performing a set of operations with total accuracy. Would this not fulfil Sloman's criterion of a case of a computational process which was driven by the program, rather than merely guided by it? (The process might be performed more reliably this way than it would if executed by an extremely cranky and unreliable computer!) What if this highly reliable (almost moronic, perhaps, but still human) agent were put inside the Chinese Room performing the appropriate computational operations? Wouldn't Searle's argument apply at least in this type of situation?

But this is, I think, to misunderstand Sloman's point, which is aimed at differentiating: (i) instances of a computational process C where the operations relate causally in a relatively straightforward way to the device which is performing them; from (ii) instances in which those operations are seated in some extremely complex set of further processes.

When humans perform computations their performances are embedded in an extremely rich operational environment: the multifarious sets of purposes, motivations, beliefs, expectations and so on, that make up an individual human being's psychological constitution (on any view of how that psychological constitution is to be explained). Humans are excluded from the set of relevant computing devices, on Sloman's view, not because they are inherently unreliable, but because they are inherently far too operationally rich. Many 'merely computational' instantiations of process C (i.e. ones which are not performed by humans) will also be far too rich to qualify as appropriate instances for generating the appropriate mental states – for instance, cases where the primary program for C is itself embedded in, or conditioned by, some highly convoluted set of secondary, or *n*-ary, processes (a case of this might be a robot inside the Chinese Room – the robot might possibly understand many things, but clearly not Chinese, which is the mental property under discussion)!

Evidently, the distinction which Sloman is seeking to make here is neither simple to characterize nor sharp – but it may be a quite genuine one for all that. But are there any grounds for granting that it is a significant one – apart from the desire to insulate the strong AI thesis from Searle's attack? My feeling is that something quite important does underlie the distinction, but I would approach it from a rather different direction.

12.12 MENTAL PROCESSES NEED REAL SUBJECTS

One question which arises in relation to Searle's Chinese Room case is: 'Who is supposed to be the subject of the putative Chinese understanding?' Searle assumes that, if the program were to generate mental states like understanding, those states would have to belong to the person inside the room who is performing the operations. His assumption is based upon the fact that there is no other (relevant) person around. One type of response to Searle (the so-called Systems Response) consisted of saying that it is not the person in the room who would understand Chinese, but 'the system as a whole'. I will not here discuss Searle's highly dismissive counterblast to this suggestion. Rather, I would like to give arguments of my own for being strongly suspicious of the suggestion that one mentality could somehow be constituted by another quite separate mentality.

The reason, it seems to me, why there cannot be any other subject in the Chinese Room besides the symbol operator is that any such subject would be altogether too contingent upon the symbol-operator's own subjecthood. One person's mental organization cannot depend upon the mental organization of another person in the way that would be implied by such a situation. The supposed Chinese-understanding subject would be far too transitory to be a real subject: it would come and go with the starting and stopping of the symbol-operator's work; it would have no real biography, its 'memories' would be ersatz memories, its plans and purposes ersatz purposes.

In order to talk of genuine mental states you have to be able to talk of a person in whom those mental states inhere – a person with some kind of coherent history and at least some of the range of other personal qualities that we normally attribute to ourselves – perceptions, beliefs, desires, sensations, pains, a 'point of view', situation in a physical and social environment, etc., etc. To the extent to which these features are absent from our supposed model of a person, we progressively impoverish our notion of personhood. That is why it is so implausible to suppose, as adherents of the Systems Response do, that the mental property of understanding Chinese might be attributed to so abstract and ethereal an entity as 'the system as a whole' (see Torrance, 1984).

These considerations relate to Sloman's discussion of appropriate kinds of computational processes for generating mental states in the following way. Accept, for a moment, the strong AI claim that at least some mental processes are computational in the sense under discussion. Sloman would be right that not any old way of producing an appropriate set of computations would suffice to generate any such mental state. Mental states might be computational, but they do not just appear from nowhere and fade away. They must be the mental states of SOMEONE. And I could not generate the mental states of someone else – not because I am inherently too unreliable, or because the causal connections between the computational operations were too remote or were mediated by independent causal conditions (although both these things may be true) – but because one person cannot be constituted out of some other person's psychological organization. (Subject to certain qualifications which do not affect the present issue) there can be no sub-personal persons.

So one person (or group of persons) performing certain formal operations would be a quite inappropriate computational device for 'realizing' the mental life of another person. But it could well be, for all that, that there are other computational devices which are appropriate for such an end, where the components which perform the underlying processes do so in an impersonal, 'mechanistic' way. Presumably the brain consists of such impersonal components (although, of course, in what sense, and to what extent, if any, it is a computational device is a different matter).

Thus Sloman is perhaps justified in supposing that a version of strong AI might be supportable even if one concedes the soundness of Searle's central argument. Nevertheless, it may turn out to be an even weaker form of 'strong AI' than Sloman envisages. For if I am right, not merely would one have to ask for some quite tough constraints on what would count as an appropriate computational realization for any given mental states, one would also have very tough constraints on what would count as mental states. One would not, for example, expect mental processes (such as understanding a passage of text, or solving a problem, or calculating a sum) to occur in isolation. Mental states occur in minds, and surely (I can only argue persuasively here) minds must have a far greater degree of complexity, multifacetedness, coherence, autonomy and persistence than is often currently claimed by supporters of strong AI.

12.13 CONCLUSIONS

I will briefly summarize some of the strands of my discussion.

(1) The Turing test throws into relief a distinction between two kinds of mental process: 'productive' and 'subjective' processes. Productive mental processes seem to be more susceptible to a computational realization, because somehow the mental process seems to be made manifest in the behavioural performances, and in the results of those performances.

(2) Searle tries to show that, as against this, all that can be duplicated in any purely computational realization of such a mental process, is the productivity, and not the mentality. His 'Chinese Room' argument seems to provide a striking way of showing this, by stressing the purely formal nature of computation.

(3) The problem of evaluating Searle's argument is made more difficult by the multiplicity of claims made on behalf of AI by members of the AI community and others. They have mistaken the nature of Searle's criticism of AI, which is more limited than might be thought.

(4) Sloman's arguments suggest that Searle's critique of strong AI can be neutralized by adopting a more limited notion of what counts as a computational process. But Sloman's way of showing this may need to be revised, or supplemented by appealing to a principle of non-embeddibility of subjects.

It would follow from this discussion that Searle has not, after all, succeeded in showing that no version of the 'strong AI' position is worth considering. What I have not done here is given any argument to show that some particular version of strong AI must be true. Maybe such a demonstration is impossible (at least for now). Certainly most supporters of the AI 'paradigm' rely upon persuasive arguments and an accumulation of suggestive evidence, rather than demonstration.

What I have suggested is that the AI paradigm possesses plausibility, at least in relation to certain mental properties, like 'learning', 'understanding', 'problem-solving', and so on. It seems to me, however, to be much less plausible in relation to so-called states of consciousness.

It might be argued that, if all that AI could do was to reproduce mental productivity without the consciousness, then very little would hinge upon the question of whether what a computer displayed was genuine understanding, learning, problem-solving, etc., or only simulations of those phenomena. If you had a machine or an organism which 'gave all the behavioural signs of being in pain' then you might well think that, on ethical grounds, it was important to determine whether or not it was the sort of thing that was capable of actually being in pain, (I discuss this and related issues in Torrance, forthcoming). On the other hand, a machine which gave a perfect behavioural replication of understanding, would not necessarily excite such nagging doubts. Given that the performance really is up to scratch, there does not seem to be the same ethical motivation for worrying about whether 'real' mental states are there. And it is not at all clear that, were one to persist in such worries, one would be making a lot of sense.

12.14 ACKNOWLEDGEMENTS

I have benefited from discussions with colleagues at Middlesex Polytechnic, the Cognitive Studies Group at Sussex University, and elsewhere. In particular, I would like to thank Margaret Boden, Aaron Sloman, Blay Whitby and Masoud Yazdani. This paper has also benefited from research done while I was in receipt of a grant from the Nuffield Foundation.

ANNOTATED REFERENCES

Block, N. (1978), Troubles with functionalism, *J. Phil.* Reprinted in *Readings in the Philosophy of Psychology*, Vol. 1 (ed. N. Block), Methuen, London.

Ned Block produced a thought experiment in this article which is an interesting precursor to John Searle's Chinese Room. Block gives a powerful defence of the 'qualia' objection, as it has come to be called, to functionalist or computationalist accounts of mind. Block's paper is discussed, and related to Searle's arguments, in the introduction to Torrance (1984).

Block, N. (ed.) (1980), *Readings in the Philosophy of Psychology*, 2 Vols, Methuen, London.

An excellent and extensive anthology of key papers in the philosophy of mind and cognitive science, with first-rate introductions to different topic areas.

Boden, M.A. (1984), What is computational psychology?,*Proceedings of the Aristotelian Society*, Supplementary Volume, pp. 17–35.

In this paper Margaret Boden gives an account of how principles governing a computational approach to psychology might be suggested by work of David Marr, Geoffrey Hinton and others, in computer vision.

Colby, K.M., Hilf, F.O., Weber, S. and Kraemer, H. (1972), Turing-like indistinguishability tests for the validation of a computer simulation of paranoid processes, *Artif. Intel.*, **3**, 199–221.

This is one of several reports by Kenneth Colby and colleagues of the Parry project for modelling paranoid conversational behaviour. Transcripts of the conversations with computer 'patients' were interleaved with transcripts of conversations with human patients, and qualified doctors failed to tell the 'real' from the 'fake' cases.

Colby, K.M. (1981), Modeling a paranoid mind, with open peer commentaries, *Behav. Brain Sci.*, **4**, 515–33.

A more recent discussion of the Parry research.

Dreyfus, H. (1979), *What Computers Can't Do: A Critique of Artificial Reason*, rev. edn, Harper and Row, New York.

This is one of the most extensive philosophical critiques of the theoretical presuppositions of AI. The crux of Dreyfus's argument is that AI techniques of knowledge representation may produce superficially successful results in certain domains which lend themselves to such treatment, but that human cognition is too creative or 'open' to respond in general to an AI treatment.

Feldman, J.A. and Ballard, D.H. (1982), Connectionist models and their properties, *Cogn. Sci.*, **6**, 205-54.

This is a discussion of some issues surrounding non-Von Neumann computer architectures, which are playing an increasingly important role in AI research.

Hinton, G.E. (1981), Shape representation in parallel systems, *Proceedings of the Seventh International Joint Conference on Artificial Intelligence*.

Geoffrey Hinton is a leading researcher into connectionist architectures, and their use for modelling vision and learning.

Searle, J.R. (1980), Minds, brains and programs, with open peer commentaries, *Behav. Brain Sci.*, **3**, 417–57.

This was the original source of Searle's 'Chinese Room' argument, published with a commentary by 28 discussants, together with Searle's replies.

Searle, J.R. (1984), *Minds, Brains and Science*, The 1984 Reith Lectures, BBC Publications, London.

Searle dealt with the 'Chinese Room' problem in his second lecture. The lectures as a whole aimed to present a materialistic view of the mind which was compatible with some of the key features traditionally ascribed to mentality, and which did not commit the errors of an approach guided by AI or 'cognitivism.'

Sloman, A. (1985a), Strong strong and weak strong AI, *AISB Quart.*, No. 52, 26–32.

This paper provides an interesting response to Searle's critique of 'strong AI' by claiming that Searle's argument is probably sound, but is directed at an uninteresting position that no defender of AI would really be concerned to support.

Sloman, A. (1985b), What enables a machine to understand?, *Proceedings of the Ninth International Joint Conference on Artificial Intelligence*.

In this paper certain themes raised in Sloman (1985a) are developed. The author suggests that primitive notions of semantics may be ascribable to computers – even when not running 'AI' type programs – and that richer semantic notions may be gradually built up via the construction of progressively more complex systems.

Torrance, S.B. (1984), in Editor's Introduction, *The Mind and the Machine*, Ellis Horwood, Chichester.

This is a collection of papers from a conference on philosophy and AI held in London in 1983, which combines theoretical discussions with summaries of recent research in various fields of AI.

Torrance, S.B. (forthcoming), Ethics, mind and artifice: some remarks on the scope and limits of the AI paradigm, in *AI for Society* (ed. K. S. Gill), John Wiley, Chichester.

This paper compares the narrow AI claim that certain categories of mental process are computationally realizable, with the wide claim that all mental states are so realizable. The two positions turn out to be different both in plausibility and in ethical significance.

Turing, A.M. (1950), Computing machinery and intelligence, *Mind*, **LIX**, 433–60. (Reprinted in E. Feigenbaum and J. Feldman (eds) (1963) *Computers and Thought*, McGraw-Hill and A. R. Anderson (ed) (1964) *Minds and Machines*, Prentice Hall, Englewood Cliffs, NJ.)

One of the central documents of AI theory, by a key figure in the history of computing science. This article should perhaps be taken rather as a manifesto than as a rigorously argued defence of a clearly articulated position. Nevertheless, it has been a highly influential article.

Weizenbaum, J. (1976), *Computer Power and Human Reason*, Freeman, San Francisco. (Reprinted 1984, Penguin.)

Joseph Weizenbaum is the originator of one of the most famous 'products' of AI, the ELIZA program, which (in one version) simulates a psychotherapist. But Weizenbaum is also one of the foremost critics of the 'artificial intelligentsia', as he calls it.

13

Social implications of Artificial Intelligence

DEREK PARTRIDGE

In this chapter I shall explore some of the possible social implications of Artificial Intelligence. This material is of necessity highly speculative and the reader should bear this in mind, perhaps assigning to my prognostications a credibility that lies somewhere between that of 'what the stars say', and a theoretical physicist's prediction of the details of an undiscovered quark.

13.1 INTRODUCTION

Some readers might point out that 'the computerized society is here, now – we can just look around and see the social effects'. This is true to some extent, but we are concerned with the computerized society in which AI is playing a leading role. All of the current hoopla about expert systems notwithstanding, AI is not yet a major force in practical applications of computers. And it will not be for quite some time. But the time of AI will come, and the social effect will be cataclysmic.

The questions that confront us are: What will be the nature of these drastic changes engendered by AI? What is at the end of the road, Paradise Regained, or an Orwellian nightmare? Most likely neither, I think, but certainly the potential for both tendencies is present.

So can we identify and separate the potential for social enrichment from the potential for adverse effects, and foster the former whilst stomping on the latter? Probably not, at least not with any real precision, but we must try. Technological changes can be very fast whilst social ones are typically slow. A motivation for predicting the future is then to initiate social changes long before they are really needed.

For example, if a greatly increased leisure time is identified as an effect of AI technology then we must plan for it and begin to foster social changes such as greatly increased leisure opportunities. If society is somewhat reoriented before the full technological impact, then there is every hope that the resultant change will be a benefit to society. Whether any major change to the infrastructure of society is a bane or a blessing is, to some extent, a matter of opinion anyway. In such cases we can look at both sides of the question, and I shall attempt to do this. Other potential impacts of AI technology are generally agreed to be socially undesirable and we shall look at ways of avoiding them.

But, in summary, the actual effects of massive AI presence in society are highly debatable – all that we can be sure of is that they will be large effects. Some of the more agreed bad possibilities we must plan to avoid, and the good ones we should encourage both in the strictly technological sense and within the society that must mesh with the envisaged technological change. The value of many forecasted changes is highly debatable and the debates should continue.

As an introductory example of an important and contentious, multi-faceted, social implication of AI, let us take up the issue of AI and employment.

13.2   INCREASED LEISURE OR HIGHER UNEMPLOYMENT?

Will the AI boost to automation in general lead to good news or to bad? Will we have increased leisure to enjoy? 'AI could be the Westerner's mango tree' (Boden, 1983). Artificial Intelligence 'can free us not only from drudgery but for humanity . . . people both in and out of work will have time to devote to each other, which today they do not enjoy. Friendship could become a living art again.'

Schwartz and Grossman (1983) echo this sentiment in conclusion to their report for the National Science Foundation on the 'Next Generation of Robots'. On the social impact of industrial robots they state that we can take satisfaction in the robot takeover of hazardous, repetitive, and menial tasks and their general contribution to productivity. But some cautionary reflections are suggested. 'The gradual unfolding of the enormous potential of artificial intelligence can be expected to affect profoundly the fundamental circumstance of human existence. Today's robotic developments exemplify this . . . it will progressively reduce the labour used in industrial production, ultimately to something rather close to zero.' If society can respond appropriately to this deep change, we may profit in the manner foretold by Aristotle: 'When the loom spins by itself, and the lyre plays by itself, man's slavery will be at an end.' Although Dugan (1985) asserts that 'watching TV and going shopping are clearly now the major cultural activities in the United States' and, I suspect, that Europe is not significantly different in this respect. Whilst not wishing to pass any value judgements on what people do with their spare time such observations do not seem to provide a basis for confidence in Boden's particularly attractive prediction.

On the other hand, with the Protestant Work Ethic firmly entrenched in much of western society and the social stigma attached to unemployment (perhaps fostered by governments striving for 'full employment' and cognizant of the fact that high income tax rates combined with social security payments can make unemployment a viable financial strategy), non-employment on a grand scale could give rise to a deep social malaise, as Boden also observes.

Additionally, Boden comments that the effect may be more pronounced with men than with women; for women, in general, have, of necessity, adjusted to the role of performing the demanding and vital 'work' of homemaking whilst being classed as unemployed. Also the 'caring' professions, which are likely to be AI resistant, are dominated by women. Such employment is automation resistent; it is also the class of employment that can be expanded (almost) indefinitely whilst other types of human employment are shrinking.

Nilsson (1984) explores how AI is likely to affect employment and the distribution of income. A first question is whether AI, as a component of automation in general, will diminish or increase the need for human labour. 'There are', as Nilsson says,'many more or less reasonable arguments on both sides of this issue', but Nilsson is of the opinion that there are important distinctions between AI and previous technologies and that leads him 'to the conclusion that the total amount of human labour used to produce our goods and services will decline markedly'.

Noting that most people in the world presently consume very little, Nilsson cites Albus (1983) who is of a contrary opinion *vis-à-vis* AI and unemployment. Albus states:

'The world is filled with need. It is premature to worry about robots eliminating work as long as there exist such overwhelming problems as providing food, clothing, shelter, education, and medical care for millions of people living in desperate poverty.'

Nilsson observes that although this potential for employment is large, it is also finite.

Nilsson thus turns to consider the social implications of unemployment (by which he means 'that people's time will not be spent predominantly working for an income') – a social phenomenon that may be a result of automation in general, but one that will perhaps be significantly magnified by the practical applications of AI. As an approach to allaying the economic fear posed by unemployment Nilsson favours Albus' suggestion of separating income from employment. Then it is proposed that most of our income will be derived from a return on capital investment – a national incentive scheme will allow us all to become capitalists, not just the wealthy minority.

Next, he deals with the sociopsychological fear of unemployment: employment can be psychologically beneficial quite apart from the income that it generates. Although it is clear that humans need such beneficial activities, it is not clear that they must be tied to the production of income. The fear of losing a job may be much more the fear of losing economic rewards rather than psychological ones. Thus if separate economic support is available through other means, the problem of finding fulfilling and psychologically rewarding activities for all those people that desire them should not be too difficult.

But, needless to say, a workable system of economic support, independent of employment, is not just around the corner. In addition, massive unemployment problems due to the successful application of AI are also not imminent. Nilsson's point is that such a future is quite feasible and a new socioeconomic system will become necessary. Thus it is not too early to be concerned with this problem. Governments need to be rethinking the goal of 'full employment', developing automation-resistant 'human service' jobs, etc.

The pace of technological change is accelerating while socioeconomic changes are very slow; the only hope is to predict the social impacts of AI, in a general sense at least, and then initiate the exploration of potential socioeconomic remedies as soon as possible in the hope of being somewhat prepared when the real effects are felt. The decrease in employment opportunity must be accommodated in a non-disruptive fashion. 'Shrinking of the workweek and a compensating increase in income derived from non-employment sources, such as stock ownership and transfer payments, should proceed in step.'

13.3 THE COMPUTER'S IMAGE AND THE HUMAN'S VIEWPOINT

Let us now consider a related phenomenon – that of computer literacy. A computer literate person has a reasonable appreciation and understanding of the scope and limitations of computers. Needless to say, the vast majority of people, even in the computerized societies, are not computer literate. Is that a problem? Many people are not automobile literate either, yet such people typically manage to use cars effectively to achieve their goals.

But cars are not computers. Further than that they are not even in a vaguely similar class of 'tools'. Cars serve a relatively narrow function – largely that of transportation – and a person can, and usually does, successfully limit the influence that this transportation tool exerts on his or her life. That is not to say that cars do not exert a significant influence on the structure of western society, but when compared to the potential influence of intelligent computers the difference must be reckoned in orders of magnitude. There is not any *one* use, or clase of uses, for intelligent computers; they have the potential to permeate *every* aspect of our lives.

The above argument illustrates an assumption that appears to be almost axiomatic in all discussions of the social implications of AI, or indeed just of computers: the AI, or computer, revolution will be more disruptive in almost every respect than other superficially similar epochs in the history of man. I tend to support this assumption but I will list some subsidiary presuppositions:

- First, some of the most important problems still await technical solutions – presumably the solutions will eventually arrive, but perhaps not.
- Second, there is a question of sufficient resources both human and material – the former we can do something about, the latter we will just have to make the best use of what we have got, but AI system development is not very demanding in this respect.
- Third, there is a question of time; it is quite possible that more immediate problems such as overpopulation or global nuclear pollution will arise, take priority, and consume most of humanities attention and resources.

Thus one can challenge the basic assumption from three standpoints: intellectual, material and temporal. Nevertheless, I believe that AI's impact will be enormous. In addition, it is difficult to foresee its influence doing anything else but keep on growing – it will not be an immediate shock to the foundations of society but a continually growing, compelling force for social change.

The major consequences of the lack of understanding of even the basics of computer technology (i.e. that humans specified, and designed the programs that are directly responsible for the behaviour of the computer) is detrimental to society. This general lack of understanding causes a failure to question where and how computers are used, and the reliability of what the computer generates. Hence many ill-considered and poorly designed applications of computers constantly inflict some human programmer's inadequate understanding of the situation on our lives. The all-too-common manifestation of a poorly conceived and executed example of computerization is the human response to all justified complaints: it is an apology that takes the general form of, 'I'm sorry but the computer doesn't allow us to do that'.

The failure to properly evaluate potential applications of computer technology is often the result of the misconception that computerization is, by definition, a good thing. And this itself is due to the association of computers with modernization and progress – these latter two concepts give rise to so many of the phenomena that blight our lives. I am reminded of the way that persons whose goal is to make money by replacing countryside and old buildings by new buildings are called developers – and development is, of course, always a good thing! And if that is a slight exaggeration, it is certainly true that the burden of disproof lies with the opposition – i.e. development is a good thing unless proven otherwise. So, too, with computers as a means for modernization, proposed computerization should be costed out carefully, and not just in immediate financial terms, before we buy into it. The last, and not wholly separate, aspect of computer illiteracy concerns the degree of credibility to be assigned to the information that a computer generates.

Computers are machines and thus not subject to the biases and prejudices that distort human information processing and decision-making – computers are objective in some absolute sense. In addition, computers are driven by purely logical mechanisms that are open to inspection thus computer-generated results must be totally rational and logical; they must be the 'truth'. Unfortunately (or is it fortunately?), the most utter rubbish and prejudice-saturated nonsense is as easily generated from logical mechanisms as by any other means. The use of a logical basis in no way guarantees correct and true conclusions. In fact, quite the contrary is the case. Simple classical logic is singularly ineffectual in the empirical world of incomplete and poor quality information. A major quest in AI is to find logics that are powerful enough to be effectively applicable to the real world (see Turner, 1984).

Thus computers are, in general, no more infallible than you, or I, or the persons who programmed them. In straightforward numerical applications, such as accounting, a computer is likely to be more accurate than a human being, but only to some degree that is dependent upon the quality of the program. No commercial program has ever been *proven* to be correct (a sad practical fact that computer scientists are working hard to remedy). Thus errors are part and parcel of even the most straightforward computer applications. But we can determine if any computer-produced answer is indeed correct or incorrect (by independently working through the appropriate calculation). Thus the computer-generated balance of one's bank account is either correct or incorrect; its correctness is not a matter of degree, nor is it open to debate by a panel of differently biased experts in the field. So the credibility even of non-AI computer applications is open to question. Now consider how AI aggravates this already non-trivial problem.

The answers or information that an AI system will produce (such as a plan for financial investment, or a medical diagnosis) are typically not simply correct or incorrect. Adequacy is the criterion to apply, and the general adequacy of an AI system's performance is neither quickly nor easily decidable. The reliability and value of an AI computer application is thus an exceedingly awkward problem – as are similar questions when applied to naturally intelligent systems (i.e. you, I and them). The social danger then is that the average person is reluctant (perhaps because of a feeling of ignorance with respect to computers) to subject computer systems to the same degree of scrutiny that he or she might well apply to an unknown person. As computer systems begin to replace or assist man's intellectual functions, circumspection and caution should be the overriding considerations.

'That's all very well', you might say, 'but how can I hope to evaluate an object whose functioning is a total mystery to me?' One answer is education; we must improve the general level of computer literacy in advance of the proliferation of computers in our society. But such a programme, which is already underway within the school system, if successful will generate another class of social problem: it will widen the generation gap. Perhaps this is inevitable if we accept that technological progress (there's one of those loaded words again), even if not necessarily a good thing, is here to stay. Better than the permanent division of society into computer illiterate and literate, a computer élite, a priestly class that controls the destiny of the masses, we might opt for general computer education and tackle the widening generation gap problem as well. Generation gaps are, after all, not peculiar to computerization. Again the automobile created a rift between the drivers and the non-drivers. But the argument here is, as it so often is, an argument that computerization is happening so fast and the results will be so all encompassing that any comparison with earlier technological revolutions is not valid – a difference of degree will produce a difference in kind. As I have said, that a basic premise of much of the 'computerized society' writing, and one that the reader must not dismiss lightly.

An opposite opinion is given by Chace (1985), he claims that AI will be the means whereby computers become just another tool – 'The computer is, when all is said and done, a tool, no more than a tool.' Artificial Intelligence will form the interface between man and computer, an interface that hides all of the details and presents the potential user with exactly the outward appearance that he finds most comfortable to work with. I have grave doubts about this optimistic opinion, and they will be discussed below, but first I shall present a general overview of the manner in which AI is expected to impact on society.

13.4   THE IMPACTS OF INTELLIGENT COMPUTERS

The purpose of this section is to survey the likely technological uses of AI before we discuss the possible repercussions on society. In general, AI addresses the problem of constructing computer systems to perform functions that would normally be considered to require an intelligent being. From our current perspective it is immaterial whether AI is mechanistically similar to humans, or whether it is aimed at surpassing rather than just emulating human performance. The point is that AI, if successful, will perform functions that were hitherto the special preserve of humanity – perhaps the last feature that sets the human race apart.

A number of commentators have cast the AI revolution as the next in a series, from Copernicus to Darwin, that has continually forced us to reappraise our place in the great scheme of things – and always with the result that we are not so special as we had previously thought ourselves to be. Clearly a profound societal change, but for better or for worse? Again it is a matter of opinion, and if it is seen as inevitable then we should be planning to minimize the adverse effects when the time comes.

A second major role of AI in society, and one that is seen as not so potentially disruptive, is for AI systems to augment rather than replace human intelligence – a co-operative venture between man and machine to achieve goals that are otherwise unattainable. If one views the potential of AI as having all of the capabilities of human intelligence plus some extras, then the machines will not need any assistance – which is not to say that they will not be sufficiently socially astute to use human help just to allay our feelings of inadequacy. On the other hand, there are some strong indicators which suggest that human intelligence and machine intelligence are likely to be rather different. If current research in AI is any guide to the future (and I am not sure that it is), then the partnership to super intelligence might be comprised of the global knowledge and broad association abilities of human beings, together with the exhaustive rigour and depth of machines in limited domains.

Closer to the present, one definite area of AI success is that of expert systems: computer systems that promise to outperform human experts in certain very limited areas of application. A very few such systems are already in use: configuring VAX computers and diagnosing pulmonary dysfunctions in real applications environments, for example. Many more such expert systems are being designed and tested in research laboratories and in AI software companies throughout the world. Many people who are in a position to know, confidently predict a wealth of such AI software within the next few years.

The immediate social impacts of expert systems will perhaps be on the experts that they replace or assist, as discussed above. The effects on the society of users of such inanimate expertise is hard to gauge. It is claimed that replacing human–human interaction by human–machine interaction can lead to nothing other than deleterious social consequences. It is also claimed (not by the same people) that man–computer communication can be both effective and satisfying for the human communicant who may feel overawed and subtly intimidated by the presence of a high-powered human expert whose valuable time is being consumed. As usual there are two sides to the argument.

Another type of confidently expected AI system is the natural language system – a computer that will possess some understanding of, say, English in the same way that you or I do. Some systems will serve as interfaces between the human user and a computer system that he wishes to use. Thus you will be able to direct your computer in English (mostly likely typed rather than spoken to begin with) to solve some problem that you may also specify in English. Dialogues in English as the medium of communication with computers may come to replace either monologues in PASCAL or BASIC (the user-constructed program which is just telling the computer how to solve some particular problem), or dialogues in say PROLOG and English if you are lucky enough to have an interactive environment (you communicate in a programming language and the computer replies in English).

A significant breakthrough in natural language processing could suddenly make computer technology readily available to everyone – most people today have neither the time, patience, nor motivation to go through the agony of learning a programming language and all the pedantic restrictions attendant on its successful use. Natural language interfaces are currently available for certain uses, for example, the querying of a database. But such natural language systems are very limited and totally static. That is to say, they are only usable in a small number of well-defined applications in which the fairly small class of allowable utterances is specified in advance. General and flexible natural language communication with computers is a future event; it is also the event that will alter the face of computers for the majority of potential users.

Having briefly looked at the general form of the threatened AI invasion and at the current situation in commercial AI, let us gaze further into the future at the hopes and the fears that are associated with the AI computer revolution – first the bad news.

13.5　THE THREATS OF ARTIFICIAL INTELLIGENCE

It is time to temporarily wear the hat of foreboding and to look at some of the worst that AI portends.

13.5.1　The misanthropic man

As intelligent computers supply more and more of our informational needs in the comfort of our own homes, we can forsee a drastic reduction in human–human interaction. As the need to communicate with fellow beings atrophies we can predict a similar decline in general ability to do so. Television, a relatively trivial source of private gratification when compared to the potential of AI systems, has arguably already reduced the general level of competence in social intercourse. A society of misanthropes is (apart from a contradiction in terms, perhaps) difficult to construe as anything other than a forecast of a negative implication of AI.

13.5.2　Big Brother is a natural language processing system

By combining our earlier discussion of the potential of AI for natural language processing, and the degree to which people's lives may be controlled by interaction with intelligent systems, discussed immediately above, we can see the pivotal role that natural language interfaces might play in shaping society.

In natural language, meaning is a slippery concept: a statement in English is typically open to a variety of interpretations – subtle, and not so subtle. A natural language processing system will be biased, intentionally or not, to the interpretations of its designers. In a totally non-trivial manner a natural language system can impose its own world view on any human who needs to use it as an interface to some other system (e.g. a database of information, or a history teaching system). A monopoly of natural language processing can impose a uniform structure (perhaps with the best of intentions) on all our dealings with computers, which could be the majority of our dealings. The computer élite controls the interfaces: certain things can be done and certain things cannot, so the system tells us – Big Brother is looking after us.

I have consciously over-dramatized, I think. But combine the above scenario with the popular belief the correctness and lack of bias associated with machines (a belief in that might well grow as AI systems improve), then it looks even more likely; the reader should recall the optimism of Chace, described earlier.

With the best will in the world a too casual attitude to natural language interfaces (and AI systems, in general) can lead society into a trap that will be difficult to get out of. Perhaps this is just an extreme case of the well-known phenomenon that an ill-considered exploitation of technological advances can lead to an unfortunate dependence.

Again I will argue that the AI version is particularly insidious for it can strike directly at the core of humanity – at intelligence and humanness –it is not restricted to some peripheral capability such as the weight of steel that can be lifted or the speed with which we can get from A to B.

Weizenbaum (1976) rails at the thoughtless enthusiasm with which all things artificially intelligent are pursued in some sectors of society. In particular, he cites the *New York Times'* proposed data bank of current events. Weizenbaum argues, 'Of course, only those data that are easily derivable as by-products of typesetting machines are admissible to the system. As the number of subscribers to this system grows, and as they learn more and more to rely on [it] . . . how long will it be before what counts as fact is determined by the system?' Then along comes AI 'Soon a supersystem will be built, based on the *New York Times'* data bank (or one very like it), from which "historians" will make inferences about what "really" happened, about who is connected to whom, and about the "real" logic of events.' He concludes, 'There are many people now who see nothing wrong in this.'

Weizenbaum also addresses the tricky problem of the morality of pursuing AI research that has potential for adverse social effects as well as some obvious benefits. The 'listening typewriter' is one of his examples: the social benefit of a device that will type out spoken English is arguably but plausibly real, yet the same device could automatically monitor and transcribe telephone conversations, for example – such an application is less plausibly in the interests of society. Tying this sort of problem together with the vast military funding that AI research has enjoyed for many years leads directly to some awkward decisions from which society could directly benefit or suffer, or both.

13.5.3 The trouble with almost-intelligent computers

A final aspect of the socially injurious potential of AI that I want to consider concerns almost-AI systems. A truly artificially intelligent computer system presumably has all the 'good' characteristics of human intelligence, a minimum of the 'bad' ones (like limited attention span – I shall return to this general possibility), and then perhaps something extra. Whilst I am not claiming that such a system would not have profound effects on society both good and bad, I wish to draw attention to the problems associated with computerization before it attains this lofty goal – if it ever does. Those are the implications of AI in the immediate and foreseeable future.

How does an almost-intelligent system behave? That is an open question and perhaps largely one of definitions anyway. For our current purposes we need only consider the potential effects on society of computer systems that are credited with being intelligent when, in fact, they fall far short of it.

Boden (1977) draws attention to the 'plausibility tricks' in natural language systems, such as Winograd's SHRDLU program: 'SHRDLU's dialogue ends with the deceptively friendly response "YOU'RE WEL-COME!" and the dialogue as a whole is carefully composed by the programmer to hide SHRDLU's ignorance *even of blocks and pyramids'*, which is this program's specific area of expertise. I have elsewhere (Partridge, 1986) described this tendency – the ELIZA syndrome – of human beings to attribute to programs far more intelligence than they actually possess (by any reasonably objective measure) as soon as the program communicates in English phrases. It is difficult for most people to resist the temptation to assume that when a computer generates its output in English the computer system also understands the English in the same deep sense that a human being does when generating the same utterances.

The potential troubles that will arise from continual and wholesale overestimation of the capabilities of almost-AI systems hardly needs elaborating. To begin to forestall this potential social hazard Boden suggests, 'that the limits of individual programs should be made as clear as possible to users, and plausibility tricks used sparingly, if at all.' This is a reform that I support, but I have grave doubts as to the possibility of adhering to this corrective measure even if everyone agrees to it. Again, my doubts are fully explained elsewhere (Partridge, 1986), the crux of the problem is that determination of the scope and limitations of an AI program can be very difficult even for the system designer – recall that solutions to AI problems are typically not correct or incorrect, but highly debatable. Add to this the very likely possibility that any moderately sophisticated approach to AI is going to involve self-adaptive mecha-nisms – i.e. non-trivial machine learning – and the chances of assessing the limitations of an AI system look to be depressingly slim.

Now I am beginning to touch upon the questions of whether 'full-blown' AI systems are really a practical possibility; this is not quite the question under consideration here, but it does have important social significance.

Conventional software has caused, and is still causing, a lot of prob-lems with respect to its reliability and predictability – a set of problems collectively known as 'the software crisis'. Artificial Intelligence software, due to the above-mentioned extra characteristics, appears to hold a lot of promise for substantial escalation of the current predicament. It is true that means for effectively dealing with the special difficulties posed by AI software may well be found. The software crisis itself, although far from having passed, is being increasingly fettered; its effects on society, are continually being reduced in severity by advances in software engineering techniques, advances such as structured programming. Thus there is every hope that we shall eventually learn to manage and control complex, self-adaptive systems. Or will we?

Intelligent behaviour is, almost by definition somewhat unpredictable and many intelligent decisions are, as I have already said, very hard to evaluate. So almost-intelligent computers are a rich source of potential social problems, and it is not clear that truly intelligent ones will be any less trouble in this respect. I doubt if society as a whole will be ready to relinquish control to the ministrations of some benevolent super-AI machine. The alternative is to develop some means of evaluating the reliability of AI systems (and, worse, evaluating almost-AI systems). Currently no one has much idea of how to do this. But once again, we need to think about solving this problem before the technological breakthroughs force us to use *ad hoc* and inadequate evaluation and control procedures.

In a limited form this problem is already being tackled in the research on expert systems. When an expert computer system generates a result (e.g. a medical diagnosis) and the human experts disagree or are surprised, then the system's output must be evaluated. The current strategy is to build an 'explanation' component into the system so that it can 'explain' its surprising response, which might be surprising because of an unknown system error, or because of human misjudgement or ignorance. It is of the utmost importance to be able to distinguish between these two possibilities. Although a built-in explanation capability is one approach to this particular problem, it is far from a general solution.

13.5.4 The trouble with truly intelligent systems

Having spent some time considering the dangers inherent in almost-AI systems I wish to consider briefly a common assumption about the 'ideal' AI system. A number of commentators assume that we either could not, or could choose not to, build AI systems that include the dubious accoutrements of human intelligence such as emotions (Boden, 1977) or inefficiency (Chace, 1985) – the former assumption is still largely a question of faith, it is the latter one that I wish to challenge.

It is not at all certain that any reasonable degree of intelligence is constructable without some of the undesirable characteristics of human intelligence just emerging as epiphenomena. Hofstadter (1979) makes this case *vis-à-vis* AI and emotions, whilst Boden (1977) claims that no one is likely to choose to build emotions into an AI system. The point is that they may have no choice if such emotions just appear when AI systems reach a certain level of complexity.

An analysis of the information that an AI system will have at its disposal (i.e. typically incomplete and unlimited) and the limited processing resources that must nevertheless generate timely results suggest that 'pure' AI is unlikely, if not impossible (see James and Partridge, 1973).

A final source of social problem that AI may engender is then some mechanical analogue of the problems that inevitably accompany human intelligence: problems such as, lack of attention, forgetfulness, anger, personal dislike, etc.

Let us now dwell on the more hopeful prospects for the AI computer revolution.

13.6   PARADISE REGAINED?

In generalities, the hopeful possibilities associated with a proliferation of AI throughout society rest upon the apparent ease with which man's most powerful attribute, intelligence, can be duplicated, tailored to suit specific needs, and distributed to wherever it is needed or to whomever requires it. Cheap intelligence, on tap so to speak, clearly has unlimited potential to alleviate many social ills, if used wisely.

More optimistic than most, Michie and Johnston (1985) boldly offer AI as a necessary feature of man's future.'With it [AI], our future looks brighter than we can imagine. Without it, we may have no future at all.' That is a fairly unequivocal statement. It is based upon some fundamental assumptions that I have already questioned: first, that 'human-like' AI systems will be achieved; and second, that such systems will be understandable to the extent that we can accurately assess the credibility of the information they generate.

I am a good deal less sanguine than they about the validity of the second assumption, but they, in fact, go further along this path. They argue that the necessity for AI is to provide crucial assistance in understanding, and thus controlling and managing our ever more complex technologies. Weapons technology and strategies for national defence, for example, will certainly be advanced beyond the limits of human understanding. But the technological advances will continue and thus our only hope for complex system management will be human intelligence and AI, in co-operation. Using a development of the 'explanation' component of expert systems, mentioned earlier, AI will provide a 'human window' through which people will be able to 'see', at an appropriate level, the workings of otherwise opaque, complex systems.

The happier applications of AI supplement human understanding, according to Michie and Johnston, and will result in the taming of 'poverty, hunger, disease, and political strife' – that is all clearly, 'a good thing'.

13.7 THE CUSTOMIZATION OF MASS PRODUCTION

An artificially intelligent system should be able to respond appropriately to each human being that interacts with it; good AI systems will treat individuals as individuals. In this respect AI offers the possibility of restoring personal service and yet retaining the general benefits of mass production. This aspect of AI systems is often highlighted in arguments for intelligent computer aided instruction (ICAI). The promise of individualized instruction benefits the bright and the backward.

One basic system, say a mathematics tutor, can be cheaply mass produced – one copy for each student – but that just appears to be the mass production that we have all come to know and, if not love, at least tolerate. The new twist that good ICAI will bring is a sophisticated machine learning ability. Consequently, each copy will adapt to the specific student who happens to be using it; it should be responsive to his/her strengths, weaknesses, general level of competence, and preferred style of interaction. Better than this, each copy of the system should build up and subsequently have access to a 'model' of each student that has interacted with it. Thus the ICAI will, through repeated interaction. get to 'know' individual students and can thus treat each as an individual by activating the appropriate model as soon as the student is identified.

So good AI applications, of which the above-described ICAI is just one example, hold the promise of customized mass production: a wealth of cheap expertise and assistance in all fields of human endeavour that also embodies a sensitive treatment of people as individuals. The reader should notice that the adjective 'good' as a qualification on the type of AI system is the operative word here. No such 'good' ICAI yet exists, and the many less-than-good ones serve to fuel the arguments for the detrimental effects of AI. But having already sounded the warnings associated with AI systems that do not make the grade, we should now focus on the potential of 'good' systems without allowing current inadequacies to obscure the vision.

Whilst using ICAI as an example of potentially beneficial AI, I can continue with this particular application area to illustrate a rather different propitious aspect of AI. The above-described ICAI can be viewed as using a machine to replace or augment the typical human role, without really altering that role. Another promise of AI is to be able to offer some service to society but in a somewhat different and improved style when compared to the average human expert in the field. The AI paradigm may be different: it may be the paradigm of the best human expertise, or it may be a totally new and even better paradigm that was born out of disembodied intelligence.

An example of this approach to intelligent systems in ICAI is the LOGO project of Papert (1980). Papert has a vision of education for the future, a paradigm in which children become creatively involved in exploring possibilities; discovery and excitement replace discipline and suffering. As Boden (1977) points out, 'educational methods based on the pedagogical philosophy of LOGO-turtle might well change a child's (or adult's) way of thinking about "failure".' A change from passive defeatism to a positive incentive to improve. By implementing such new paradigms as an AI system they can be explored and developed before any major commitment is made. Artificial Intelligence allows us to explore and evaluate theories of, for example, education of a complexity that has hitherto been impossible. We are no longer restricted to the set of necessarily simplistic theories that the average human mind can readily grasp (but beware of the trap of passive acceptance).

This last example moves us into the realm of using AI to change and improve man's conception of himself and thus generate a somewhat different society – clearly potential for a benign influence of AI.

13.8   MAN'S REFLECTION IN THE COMPUTATIONAL METAPHOR

I wish to defend the view that the computational metaphor is not, as Weizenbaum (1976) suggests, necessarily 'profoundly humiliating'. I have already discussed the situations when Weizenbaum might be correct and they centre around overestimating the capabilities of almost-AI systems. But quite the opposite possibility arises with good AI that is used wisely.

Boden (1984) provides an eloquent defence against Weizenbaum's charge. The crux of the plea is that the concept of 'mechanism' and hence the computational metaphor is far wider than most people realize; it is, in fact, wide enough to embrace any aspect of humanness that we care to name (provided, that is, that we do not employ a double standard, demanding from the mechanism proof of some quality that we ascribe to humans on the basis of little more than hearsay).

It is thus only an impoverished view of the concept of mechanism that leads one to the mistakenly depressing conclusion that if AI fulfills its promises then man is merely a machine. And currently, if one proclaims that there are no obvious limits to AI then one is at least tacitly also disseminating the view that man is merely a machine. This view is dehumanizing and can only lead to harmful social effects.

Clearly, I do not support this line of argument. The false step is the failure to dissociate oneself from the nineteenth-century interpretation of machines. Despite the occasional, ill-considered, public relations announcement to the effect that AI has given us a basic understanding of human intelligence that just needs a few years of filling-out, AI researchers tend to be continually impressed by the complexity and subtleties of the human machine; they are not blasé at all.

There is a history of overambitious and – given the benefit of hindsight – ridiculous, predictions from the doyens of AI that the detractors, such as Weizenbaum (1976) and Dreyfus (1979), are fond of quoting. The point is that at the time the predictions were thought to be quite reasonable – what was thought to be nearly implementable then, we would not now attempt. While other disciplines start small and scale up, AI, so far, has a history of scaling down – respect for the complexity and subtleties of human intelligence just keeps on growing.

The humanist's reaction against mechanistic theses stems from an antiquated and bankrupt view of machines. Artificial Intelligence offers the means to enrich the implications of a mechanistic philosophy. The social benefit will then derive from the realization that there may be nothing dehumanizing in the admission that we are products of a mechanistic universe. Lumsden and Wilson (1983), for example, defend the mechanistic implications of their gene-culture coevolution theory of humanity against a similar attack from the humanists. These authors argue that an understanding of the physical basis for moral thought and consideration of its evolutionary meaning will put us in a better position to choose ethical precepts and the forms of social regulation needed to maintain those precepts. In addition, they see a necessity for such close self-examination and manipulation of values in a world growing steadily more complicated and dangerous.

Artificial Intelligence can help to undermine the 'kneejerk' reactions that all too often arise when humanity is referred to in terms of machines and mechanisms. A series of such reactions can, for example, be found within the sequence of books, intriguingly titled: *Beyond Reductionism* (Koestler and Smythies, 1969); *Chance and Necessity* (Monod, 1971); and *Beyond Chance and Necessity* (Lewis, 1974).

Blasting off into the future once more we can look at this general argument in the specific context of the household robot – a popular but distant realization of the fruits (or just one of the pits?) of the AI revolution. What will be the effect on the human household of having a mechanical menial domiciled with them? Any attempt at an answer has first to present some presumptions about the robot's capabilities and character. Let us assume that this is truly an AI robot and is capable of running a home with much the same basic capabilities of a human homemaker. As for its character, there might be roughly three options:

(1) the emotionless, feelingless, cold, efficient, rational automaton – let us call it the Spock model;
(2) a robot with all the human characteristics of love, hate, boredom, lack of interest, failure to pay attention, devotion to the family, etc. – the human model; and
(3) a version that has all of the good human qualities such as, caring, sensitivity to others, efficiency, industry, etc., and none of the bad ones – the optimum model.

I would suggest that the human model has little to recommend it in terms of potential social benefit (no slight on *Homo sapiens* in general is here intended, in fact, some of my best friends are human). The possibility of more-or-less beneficial social effects really rests with the Spock versus the optimum model.

Is the influence of the optimum model on the family members likely to be more beneficial (or less disruptive) than that of the Spock model? This question leads us on to the fundamental problem of whether to maintain a clear line between people and machines (even truly intelligent machines). If the demarcation is established and maintained then perhaps the efficient and emotionless Spock model is preferable. However, I suggest that this line of demarcation will of necessity become fuzzy in places, and hence the more laudable human characteristics that the optimum model exhibits the better.

My belief is that such clear choices will not be open to us – in the same way that we cannot make an internal combustion engine that does not generate heat. It is also my belief that the machine–human identity problem can and should be avoided for the foreseeable future. That is not to say that no one will develop neuroses based on such an identity, but that such neuroses will not be a major social problem if we recognize the possibility and tackle it properly.

An analogous situation, which does not cause major social problems, despite some individual ones, is the relationship between some humans and their pets, particularly dogs – 'man's best friend'. These two situations are perhaps superficially similar but the AI will be so much closer to humanity than a dog can be (objections to the contrary of indignant dog-owners notwithstanding) a difference in degree becomes in effect a difference in kind, you may argue. And you might be justified. Again we return to the fundamental point of whether AI will occasion just another degree of difficulty with respect to social problems or does it open up the possibility of totally new problems? We must accept that the latter alternative might prove to be the reality.

The social effects of AI are profoundly ambiguous. Artificial Intelligence can be grossly misused – the effects will be disastrous – but it can instead be used wisely to the general benefit of society. All new technologies contain both possibilities; we can misuse the most well-intentioned inventions. Far from being an exception, AI is, perhaps, more open to misinterpretation and abuse than most things, and the resultant social disruption hardly bears thinking about. But consider the implications we must – and without loss of time. The potential benefits of AI are also both dramatic and seemingly unlimited. It is thus imperative to continually be considering the possible options and to attempt to foresee the future in order to gain the best chances of reaping a maximum of benefits with a minimum of harm.

Perhaps Milton had an inkling of all this three hundred years ago. Coming out clearly on the positive side for AI as a force in society, he wound up his version of the human predicament with:

> . . . and now thou hast avenged
> Supplanted Adam, and, by vanquishing
> Temptation, hast regained lost Paradise,
> And frustrated the conquest fraudulent.
>   . . .
> A fairer Paradise is founded now
> For Adam and his chosen son, whom thou,
> A Saviour, art come down to reinstall,
> Where they shall dwell secure, when time shall be,
> Of tempter and temptation without fear.

> *Paradise Regained*, Book IV
> 1671

ANNOTATED BIBLIOGRAPHY

Albus, J. (1983), The robot revolution: An interview with James Albus, *Commun. ACM*.
   This interview with one of America's leading robotics researchers is focused on social questions. Albus does not believe that widespread automation will lead to unemployment. He claims that there is no historical evidence that rapid productivity growth leads to loss of jobs; 'productivity will never saturate', he states.

Boden, M.A. (1977), *Artificial Intelligence and Natural Man*, Basic Books, New York.

> A different book on AI, it stresses and examines in detail programs (such as ELIZA and Parry) that may shed light on the understanding of human nature. This book also contains an extensive argument for AI as an antidote to the dehumanizing influences of natural science.

Boden, M.A. (1983), Artificial Intelligence as a humanizing force, *Proceedings of the Eighth International Joint Conference on Artificial Intelligence*, pp. 1197–8.

> A position paper for a panel discussion on AI's impacts on human occupations and distributions of income. The Nilsson article referenced below was developed from his contribution to this same panel discussion.

Boden, M.A. (1984), AI and human freedom, in *Artificial Intelligence, Human Effects* (eds M. Yazdani and A. Narayanan), Ellis Horwood, Chichester.

> A 1978 paper reprinted in a book which is a collection of articles that together address many aspects of the interactions between AI and other human endeavours: medicine, law, education, etc. Boden's contribution is founded on the idea that AI is based on mechanisms of hitherto unexplained power and complexity. Hence any comparison with human qualities and abilities should elevate our outdated concept of mechanism rather than degrade our view of humanism.

Chace, W.M. (1985), Intelligence, artificial and otherwise, *AI Mag.*, **5**, 22–5.

> An article by an eloquent humanist on the possible impacts of AI, he argues that AI is not to be feared. For a number of reasons he does not see AI fully emulating human intelligence anytime in the twenty-first century. He sees AI as offering us just another tool, like the hammer or the knife; a tool to help us achieve our goals.
>
> The *AI Magazine*, published by the American Association for AI, is a good source of social comment that does not typically get into journals. The *AISB Quarterly* is another such source that is published in the UK.

Dreyfus, H.L. (1979), *What Computers Can't Do*, Harper and Row, New York.

> A landmark in AI despite the AI community's attempts to ignore it. He makes a lot of good points about the oversell in AI but unfortunately he also employs a number of highly dubious, if not downright fallacious, arguments to support his contentions. It is entertaining and instructive if read with circumspection.

Dugan, C. (1985), Letters to the Editor, *AI Mag.*, **5**, 10–11.

> Dugan's letter is a response to the Nilsson article (referenced below) in which he claims that certain caveats must be applied to the Nilsson view. Most importantly, the increased productivity that AI may bring is also likely to increase the rate at which we are contaminating our planet.

Hofstadter, D.R. (1979), *Godel, Escher, Bach: An Eternal Golden Braid*, Basic Books, New York.

> Perhaps the best AI book ever! It is a tangled web of insights on minds and machines and almost everything else. It can be read on many levels. Whatever your interest in AI, Hofstadter has something thought provoking to say about it – although you will have to disentangle it from everything else.

James, E.B. and Partridge, D. (1973), Machine intelligence: The best of both worlds?, *Int. J. Man Mach. Stud.*, **4**, 23–31.

A paper that argues from both psychological data and the nature of information in the empirical world that the inaccuracies and errors of human intelligence may well be a part of machine intelligence also. There are a number of reasons to believe that error-free, logical processing cannot be a basis for intelligent behaviour.

Koestler, A. and Smythies, J.R. (1969), *Beyond Reductionism, New Perspectives in the Life Sciences*, Beacon Press, Boston.

A collection of papers arguing for a more global view of scientific results. Specifically, this book attempts to provide a refutation of, in Koestler's words, 'the four pillars of unwisdom': that biological evolution is the result of nothing but random mutations; that mental evolution is the result of nothing but random tries preserved by reinforcements; that man is a passive automaton controlled by the environment; and that the only scientific method is quantitative measurement.

Lewis, J. (1974), *Beyond Chance and Necessity*, Garnstone Press, London.

A collection of philosophical arguments designed to promote the view that man cannot be explained and understood in purely reductive materialist terms. In particular, this collection was organized to oppose the specific views of Monod (referenced below).

Lumsden, C.J. and Wilson, E.O. (1983), *Promethean Fire, Reflections on the Origin of Mind*, Harvard University Press, Cambridge, MA.

A popular account of the authors' theory of gene-culture coevolution. They argue that although there is a biological explanation for all aspects of our 'humanness' there is an interaction between genes and culture that in no way undermines our cherished qualities, such as free will.

Michie, D. and Johnston, R. (1985), *The Creative Computer: Machine Intelligence and Human Knowledge*, Viking, London.

An unashamedly optimistic description of the potential of AI to improve the human lot. In my opinion, it does gloss over some very awkward problems *en route* to the good things that AI may offer society.

Monod, J. (1971), *Chance and Necessity*, Knopf, New York.

An argument, based on the author's Nobel-prize-winning work in molecular biology, for the idea that 'The cell is a machine. The animal is a machine. Man is a machine.' For Monod this is perhaps an unpleasant idea but one for which there is hard proof, and hence it is an idea that we must learn to live with – but remember that a major part of the problem may be due to our impoverished conception of machines.

Nilsson, N.J. (1984), Artificial Intelligence, employment and income, *AI Mag.*, **5**, 5–14.

A lengthy article discussing, in full, many of the possibilities, relevant to employment and income, that an AI revolution might generate.

Papert, S. (1980), *Mindstorms: Children, Computers, and Powerful Ideas*, Basic Books, New York.

A small, cheap paperback in which Papert expounds his theories of education with special reference to the use of computers. In Papert's view, computers are typically misused in the education of children. Computers should facilitate a child's exploration of some unknown domain – the emphasis being on active exploration rather than the avoidance of mistakes.

Partridge, D. (1986), *Artificial Intelligence: Applications in the Future of Software Engineering*, Ellis Horwood, Chichester.

I argue that AI programs tend to lack the necessary characteristics of practical software – i.e. reliability, robustness, transparency. I also claim that AI software and more conventional software are essentially different, and that AI software development should not be forced into the conventional software engineering paradigm, a new development methodology is needed, and many basic problems (such as that of machine learning) need to be solved before we will see the full potential of AI in practical software.

Schwartz, J.T. and Grossman, D. (1983), The next generation of robots, in *The First-Year Outlook on Science and Technology 1982*, National Science Foundation, Washington, DC, 20550, pp. 75–85.

This report discusses the inadequacies of current industrial robots, primarily their lack of flexibility. It suggests that self-adaptive robots that can operate effectively in a flexibly-fixtured environment are a necessary future development. The authors make some comments about the societal effects of the widespread use of such robots.

Turner, R. (1984), *Logics for Artificial Intelligence*, Ellis Horwood, Chichester.

This slim volume surveys the non-standard logics that may be of use in AI. All such logics tend to be underpowered for anything but gross simplifications of AI problems. It is thus not surprising, as the author points out, that a sound and complete formal basis is not usually to be found in a substantial AI project. The hope is that development of the current ideas on non-standard logics will result in formalizations that are adequate for AI.

Weizenbaum, J. (1976), *Computer Power and Human Reason*, Freeman, San Francisco.

This book was begun as an attempt to repeat Dreyfus' argument, 'but do it right'; it turned out to be something rather different. Rather than argue about the technological limitations of AI, Weizenbaum argues that certain types of AI research should not be pursued because they are immoral or 'obscene' – a difficult argument to make, but one that is well worth attempting.

Index

Abelson, R.P. 18, 29, 100, 107, 109, 277, 281, 284–86, 289–93
Acoustic coding 113
ACRONYM 141, 155, 172
ACT 288
Actors 242–44
Advice 187
Aerodynamics 4, 263, 264, 269, 270
Agin, G.J. 176
Agre, P. 177
Agreement 89–91
Akmajian, A. 91, 106
Albus, J. 145, 176, 317, 333
Alexander, I. 214, 223
Algorithms
  acoustic signal processing 114
  dynamic programming 116
  human intelligence 268
  machine learning 205, 206, 208, 214, 215, 218–20
  natural language processing 77, 78, 81, 87–89
  psychological investigations 278
  spatial planning 142, 155, 157, 158, 160
  tactile interpretation 165
  versus heuristics 15–17, 23, 24, 26, 27
Allen, J.F. 102, 106, 118, 121
Alpha-beta pruning 21
Alvey Report 5, 6
Ambiguity 75, 104
Ambler, A.P. 153, 176, 183
AML 153
Analogy 20–22, 174
Anderson, J.A. 134, 136, 248, 257
Anderson, J.R. 229, 230, 258, 288–90, 292
Anderson, R.C. 284, 290
Animal communication 70, 72, 73

APL 196
AQ11 208
Architecture 187, 203, 240, 249, 257, 304, 305
Aristotle 238, 286, 316
ARPA 117
Artificial intelligence
  adequacy of systems 321, 326
  definition 3–5, 13–16, 27, 28, 263, 267–70
  languages 33, 34, 37, 41, 59–61, 87, 196
  non-determinism 87–89, 141
  relationship to psychology 275–78 281–88
  relevance to robotics 137–39, 155, 175
  social implications 264, 315–33
  speech processing 112, 113
  sponsorship 5, 8, 325
  strong view 306, 307, 310, 311
  theories 275, 276, 278, 280
Asada, H. 144, 164, 168, 169, 172, 173, 176, 177, 179, 184
Association lists 74, 75
Athletic physique 222
Auditory information see Sounds
Augmented transition networks 83, 91, 92
Austin, J.L. 102, 106
Autonomous navigation 139, 149
AUTOPASS 153

Bach, E. 106, 107
Backer, E. 134
Background 126
Backtracking 16, 19, 34, 87
Backward chaining 191
BACON 26
Badler, N. 130, 134, 135

Bajcsy, R.   167, 176
Baker, H.H.   168, 176
Baker, K.D.   134
Ballard, D.H.   135, 305, 313
Barr, A.   6, 16, 28, 106
Barrett, R.   42, 47
Bartlett, F.   284, 290
Barwise, J.   102, 106
BASIC   49, 92, 196, 323
Battery   174, 175
Baumann, L.S.   184
Bayes theorem   192, 193
BEAGLE   208, 220, 221, 223
Bejczy, R.   149
Beliefs, 27
Bellos, I.M.   153, 183
Beni, G.   166, 179
Binford, T.O.   140, 141, 168, 176, 177, 185
Binocular disparity   129, 134
Biology   263, 264
BIPER   151, 152
Birch, F.   109
Birtwistle, G.M.   25, 28
Black, J.B.   277, 285, 286, 290–92
Block, N.   312
Blocks world   126
Bobrow, D.   134, 140, 175, 226, 243, 244,
     259, 274, 290
Boden, M.   7, 126, 135, 226, 258, 305, 312,
     316, 317, 326–28, 330, 334
Boguraev, B.   106
Boissant, J.D.   168, 176, 178
Bolles, R.C.   164, 169, 177
Boltzmann machine   215, 248, 305
BORIS   286
Botany   13
Bower, G.H.   229, 230, 258, 285, 288, 290,
     292
Bradshaw, G.L.   26, 29
Brady, J.M.   122, 129, 135, 140, 142, 145,
     155, 156, 168, 169, 172, 173, 176–79,
     182, 185
Braffort, P.   29
Braunegg, D.J.   177
Bridle, J.S.   117, 121
Broadbent, D.E.   228, 258
Brooks, R.A.   131, 135, 141, 154, 155, 157,
     158, 160, 172, 177
Brown, C.M.   135
Brown, G.D.A.   263
Brown, H.B.   152, 183

Brown, J.   228, 258
Brown, M.D.   117, 121
Bruner, J.   215
Bruss, A.   177
Bruynooghe, M.   20, 28
Buffers   36, 39
Bundy, A.   173, 178
Burnett, P.   214, 223
Burstall, R.M.   42, 47
Buxton, B.F.   126, 135
Buxton, H.   126, 135
Byrd, L.   178

C   42, 196
Campbell, J.A.   22, 28
Cannon, R.H.   145, 178
Canny, J.F.   168, 178
Carbon chauvinism   301
Carbonell, J.G.   29, 224
Cardiac patients   222
Caring professions   317
Cartesian manipulators   142, 157, 160
Case grammar   98
Categorization   228
Cause and effect   18, 25, 140, 189
Centre for Biomedical Design   148
Chace, W.M.   321, 324, 327, 334
Chamberlain, R.M.   117, 121
Charniak, E.   7, 16, 20, 28, 100, 106
Chatila, R.   149, 179
Chess   16, 216, 272, 273, 299
Chiba, S.   121
Chinese room   264, 294, 295, 300–09, 311
Chomsky, N.   91, 107
Chouraqui, E.   20, 28
Classification   126, 130, 132, 134, 138, 194,
     205–07, 212, 218
Cliches   164
Clocksin, W.   42, 47, 107, 139, 161, 165,
     169, 178, 191, 198
CLS   215
Cofer, C.N.   258
Cognitive economy   287, 288
Cognitive psychology   13, 14, 275–77, 279,
     281–84, 289
     see also Psychology
Cognitive science   8, 13, 14, 26, 168, 270,
     271, 279, 286, 288
Cognitive systems   235, 236, 278
Cohen, J.   227, 258
Cohen, P.R.   102, 107

Colby, K.M. 107, 109, 272, 290, 298, 312, 313
Collins, A.N. 288, 290
Collins, J.S. 42, 47
Colmerauer, A. 42
Colour 125, 127–29
Combinatorial explosion 131, 210
Common LISP 62, 63
Common sense 276, 277
Compilers 37–39, 41, 42, 45, 61
Compliance 138, 139, 160–63, 165
Computational metaphor 226, 229, 232, 257, 278, 330
Computer aided design 140
Computer literacy 318, 319, 321
Configuration space 140
Connectionist machines 215, 248, 255, 257, 305
Connell, J.H. 175, 177, 178
Conrad, C. 287, 290
Consciousness 296–98, 300, 311
Constraint propagation 141
Contact sensing 165–67
Content 93, 94, 100, 102
Context free rules 80, 84, 91
Contexts 18, 189, 250
Control 142, 145
Copernicus 322
Coriolis torque 144
Cox, P.T. 20, 28
Craig, J.J. 143, 145, 146, 163, 183, 184
Cybernetics 203

3-D vision 122, 123, 126, 129–32, 139
Dahl, O.J. 28
Darwin, C. 322
Data structures 36, 38, 43, 74, 81, 93, 140, 197, 206, 208
Data types 37, 42
Databases 34, 44, 137, 188, 197, 208, 216, 220, 323
Davenport, J.H. 15, 24, 28
Davey, P.G. 178
Davis, L.S. 178
Davis, R. 24, 28
de Jong, P. 27, 28
De Kleer, J. 140, 173, 178
Debugging 37, 39, 49, 59, 62, 174
Declarative languages 33, 46, 60
Demons 242–44
Dennet, D. 278, 290

Dependency directed reasoning 141
Des Forges, D.T. 145, 178
Descriptive languages 208–10, 217–20
Diagnostic problems 195, 207
Dialects 119, 120
Dictionaries 76, 79, 81
Dietterich, T. 208, 223
Diphones 118–20
Dixon, N.R. 116, 118, 121
Dobrotin, B. 149, 178
Documentation 40, 42, 45–47
Doherty, M.E. 277, 291
Donald, B.R. 155, 158, 160, 178
Dowson, M. 20, 28
Dreyfus, H.L. 306, 313, 331, 334
Dubowsky, S. 145, 178
Dufay, B. 163, 178
Duggan, C. 316, 334
Dyer, M.G. 286, 290
Dynamic programming 116, 117, 119
Dynamics 142, 144

Eco, U. 73, 99, 107
Edges 129, 168
Editors 38, 39, 40, 44, 45, 61
Education 10, 329, 330
Eisenstadt, M. 9, 47
ELI 286
ELIZA 9, 59, 63, 272, 296, 326
Emotions 327, 328
Engelberger, J.F. 178
English 70, 72–75, 78, 80, 84, 89, 91, 113, 114, 118, 272, 323, 326
Entropy 215
Erman, L.D. 105, 107
Errors 284, 320, 327
EURISKO 207–09
Everett, H.R. 149, 178
Evolutionary learning 208, 218–20, 222, 223
Expert–Ease 218
Expert systems
  architecture 187
  characteristics 187, 188, 196
  computer aided instruction 9, 329, 330
  domains 6, 186, 187, 195, 322
  explanatory interface 194, 195, 327
  impact 265, 323

inference engines   188, 191–93, 197
knowledge bases   188–91, 197, 207
shells   44
Explanation   26, 187, 188, 194, 195, 197,
    327, 329

Fahlman, S.E.   248, 256, 258
Fallside, F.   119–21
Faugeras, O.   139, 164, 165, 167–69, 178
Featherstone, R.   142, 145, 179
Feature sets   90–92
Feedback   206
Feigenbaum, E.   6, 7, 16, 28, 29, 106
Feldman, J.   7, 305, 313
Fiat car plant   149
Fikes, R.E.   103, 107
Fillmore, C.   107
Finite state grammar   117
Fisher, W.D.   143, 179
Fixtures   138, 139
Flags   212–14, 216
Flight   4, 263, 264, 269, 270
Foley, W.A.   108
Forbus, K.D.   140, 172, 179
Formant synthesis   118, 120
Forsyth, R.   7, 192, 198, 203, 220, 223
FORTRAN   42, 92, 196
Forward chaining   191
Frames   18, 20, 101, 140, 189, 190, 197, 284,
    285
Franklin, J.W.   137, 179
Freeman, H.   134
Freund, E.   145, 179
Frisby, J.   135
Fu, K.S.   126, 135
Functional languages   60
Functions   49, 51–56, 58–61
Fuzzy logic   192

Gait   151
Galambos, J.A.   277, 285, 290
Garbage collection   37
Gashnig, J.   189, 198
Gaston, P.C.   167, 179
Gazdar, G.   91, 108
Generalization   206, 218
Generalized cones   140, 158
Generalized phrase structure grammar   91
Generate and test   23
Genetic learning   208, 218–20
Geometry   138–40, 147, 148, 153, 161, 163,
    164, 169, 174

Gerhardt, L.   178, 179
Geschke, C.C.   137, 153, 184
Gibson, J.   33, 40, 42, 47
Gifford, D.   15, 28
Gilmartin, A.   231, 258
Girault,   148, 149, 179
Goals   102, 286
Gordon, S.E.   285, 290
Goto, T.   141, 162, 179
Graesser, A.C.   285, 290
Grammar   80–84, 89, 91, 93, 98, 117, 119
Graphical reconstruction   132
Gregory, R.L.   135
Grimson, W.E.L.   167, 168, 179
Grossman, D.   316, 336

Hackwood, S.   166, 179
Halliday, M.A.K.   91, 108
HAM   229, 230, 288
Hanafusa, H.   146, 179
Hanlon, A.C.   239, 258
Hannah, M.J.   164, 169, 177
Hannah, P.   164, 169, 177
Hanson, A.H.   135
Haralick, R.M.   168, 179
Hardware   214, 215, 226, 240, 241, 247,
    249, 255, 294
Hardy, S.   40, 47
Harmon, L.   149, 165, 179
Harmon, P.   198
Harmon, S.Y.   179
Harms, R.T.   106, 107
HARPY   117
Hasemer, T.   33, 63
Hash coding   240
Haugeland, J.   29
Hayes, P.J.   13, 28, 134, 269, 278, 289, 290
Hayes-Roth, F.R.   109, 110, 139
HEARSAY   117
Heart disease   222
Herbert, M.   165, 167–69, 178
Henry, F.   91, 106
HERB   220–22
Heterarchy   27
Heuristics   13, 15–19, 21–25, 27, 28, 208
Hewitt, C.   20, 27, 28
Hi-T hand   162
Hidden transformations   273, 274
Hierarchy   26, 27
Hildreth,   161, 168
Hilf, F.O.   312
Hillis, W.   166, 167

Hinton, G. 109, 134, 136, 215, 223, 248, 254–58, 305, 313
Hirose, X.X. 143, 150, 151
Hirschberg, D. 29
Hobbs, 140
Hofstadter, D.R. 328, 334
Hogg, D.C. 131, 136
Hogger, C.J. 17, 28
Holland, J. 218, 219, 224
Hollerbach, J.M. 142, 144, 145, 148, 177, 182, 183, 185
Horaud, P. 164, 169, 177
Horn, B.K.P. 63, 129, 136, 140, 168, 169, 177
Hsuang, T.S. 134
Hubel, D.H. 129, 136
HULK 193
Hummel, R.A. 126, 136, 141, 185
Hunt, E.B. 215, 224
Huston, X.X. 145
Hwang, K. 123, 136
Hypothesis testing 276, 277

IAM model 249–54
IBM7565 137, 142
IBMsolid 153
ICOT 8
ID3 208, 215–18
Identification 130, 131
Ikeuchi, K. 140, 169, 184
Images 126–28, 196
Implementability 278–80, 282, 289, 331
    see also Testability
Income 317, 318
INDUCE 208
Induction 194, 203, 210, 215, 220
Industrial revolution 264, 265
Inference 60, 99–101, 187, 189
Inference engine 188, 191–93, 197
Information processing paradigm 226, 228, 229, 236
Inheritance of properties 25, 190, 254, 286
Inoyance, T. 141, 162, 179
Instruction set 44
Integration 15, 16, 24
Intelligence tests 268
Intelligent behaviour
    evaluation 327
    goal of AI 16, 21, 25, 28, 322
    guided 263
    heuristics 21
    learned 50

modelling 14
    programs 268, 269, 272–74, 296, 300
    theories 26
Intelligent tutoring systems 9, 329, 330
Interactive activation model *see* IAM
INTERLISP 40, 62
Interpreters 37–39, 61
Intonation 120
Intuition 21, 194, 195
Invention 173
Isard, S.D. 118, 121
Islamic flags 212–14, 216

Jacobsen, S. 148
James, E.B. 328, 335
James, W. 228, 258
Japan 7, 8, 33
Johnson, T.J. 149, 177, 182, 183, 185
Johnson-Laird, P.N. 8
Johnston, R. 224, 328, 329, 335
Joint space 142
Joyce, J. 99
JSRU 118
Judgement 188
Just, M. 290

Kahn, 143, 145
KAN 288
Kanade, T. 144, 165, 176
Kane, T.R. 145
Kant, I. 284, 290
Kaplan, R. 89, 105, 108, 110, 290
Katz, B. 185
Kelley, F.A. 145
Kieras, D. 290
Kinematics 141–46, 160
King, D. 198
Klatt, D.H. 117, 121
Klein, E. 108, 145, 149
Kludges 279
Kluzniak, F. 17, 28
Knill-Jones, R. 193, 199
Knowledge
    acquisition 188, 194, 197, 203
    bases 186–88, 197, 207
    common sense 72, 94
    creation 206, 207
    engineering 139, 193, 197, 265
    episodic 228
    functional 60
    grammatical 119
    memory 228, 244

minimum requirement   271
organization   100
real world   104
representation   139–41, 189, 207–09,
   218, 284, 285
semantic   105, 119, 228
transfer   50
visual interpretation   132, 169
Koestler, A.   331, 335
Kohonen, T.   240, 241, 258
Kolers, P.A.   278, 290
Kornfeld, W.A.   27, 28
Koshikawa, K.   184
Kovesi, P.D.   161, 162, 184
Kowalski, R.   17, 28
Kraemer, H.   312
Kulikowski, C.   199

Laffey, T.J.   168, 179
LAMA   153
Land usage   128
Langley, P.   26, 29, 211, 224
Latombe, J.C.   163, 178
Law   10
Leading questions   101
LEAF   220, 221
Learning   16, 70, 134, 138, 194, 203–23,
   305, 311, 326
Lehnert, W.G.   278, 286, 290, 291
Leisure   315, 316
Lenat, D.B.   24, 28, 139, 207, 224
Lesser, V.R.   105, 107
Levison, D.A.   145
Lewis, J.   331, 335
Lewis, R.   149, 178
Lexical analysis   74, 76
Libraries   40, 42, 44, 163
Lieberman, L.I.   153
Lighthill Report   5, 6, 8, 306
Linear predictive coding   114, 116
Linggard, R.   120
Linguistics   40, 80, 83, 99, 105, 112, 119
Light intensity   123, 124, 127–29, 132
Linnaeus   13
LISP
   ATN parsers   92, 93
   list processing   48–50, 52–63
   LOOPS system   196
   microcomputers   197
   POPLOG system   41–43, 196
   primitives   33
   user-modelling   27

Lists   48, 56, 74, 75
Loaded terms   101
Loftus, E.F.   288, 290
Logic   17, 18, 61, 189, 190, 208, 320
Logica   117
LOGO   330
Logogen   232–36, 254
Lonquet-Higgins, C.   8
LOOPS   196
Lowerre, B.T.   117, 121
Lowry, M.   185
Lozano-Perez, T.   140, 141, 153, 155, 157,
   158, 163, 164, 167, 172, 177, 179, 182,
   183, 185
LS-1   208, 218, 219
Luger, G.   178
Lumsden, C.J.   331, 335

Machine learning   16, 70, 134, 138, 194,
   203–23, 326
MACSYMA   15, 16, 24
Manipulability   143
Manufacturing processes   138, 329
Marcus, M.   89, 108
Marin, J.   215, 224
Marr, D.   129, 135, 136, 140, 161, 168, 182,
   249, 258, 272, 290
Martin, J.R.   91, 108
Mason, T.M.   140, 160, 163, 177, 182, 183,
   185
Mass production   329
MATE   221
Mathematics   14, 15, 21, 22, 140, 142
Maxey, H.D.   118, 121
McCarthy, J.   9, 26, 29
McClelland, J.L.   249, 250, 253, 259
McCorduck, P.   7
McCulloch-Pitts model   245
McDermott, D.   7, 14, 16, 20, 28, 29, 280,
   290
McGhee, R.B.   149, 151, 182
McGinn, C.   276, 290
McKoon, G.   288, 291
Meaning   71, 72, 74, 75, 82, 83, 95, 97, 101,
   102, 115, 117, 118
Means-ends analysis   18, 19, 22
Mechanistic philosophy   330, 331
Medicine   10, 122
Mellish, C.S.   42, 47, 107, 178, 191, 198
Melzak, Z.A.   17, 29
Memory
   active   237, 238

associative 238, 239
  content addressable 238–42, 247
  errors 284
  functional 232
  human associative 229
  iconic 282
  long term 226–28, 231, 232, 282
  organization packages 285
  primary 228
  reminding 285
  rote 218
  shemata 243, 244, 245
  scripts 101
  secondary 228
  short term 227–28, 231, 232, 282
  structural model 228, 229, 232
  working 219
Mental states 294, 296, 298, 300, 301, 309, 310
Messick, S. 290
Michalski, R.S. 29, 208, 223, 224
Michie, D. 8, 139, 178, 182, 198, 224, 328, 329, 335
Microplanner 20
Military applications 139, 325
Miller, G.A. 228, 259
Miller, L. 14, 29, 275, 282, 290
Milton, J. 333
Minsky, M. 3, 8, 9, 18, 29, 134, 214, 224, 246, 259, 267, 270, 282, 284, 291
Minimax strategy 22
Misanthropy 324
MIT Artificial Intelligence Laboratory 148
MITalk79 118
Mitchell, D.C. 283, 285, 288, 292
Mitchell, T.M. 211, 224
Miura, H. 150, 152, 182
Mnemonics 280
Moayer, 151
Mobile robots 147–51, 153
Models
  computational 13, 14, 17
  concept learning 215
  evolutionary 223
  geometric 137, 139, 140
  heterarchial 27
  human 268, 271
  language 303, 304
  mathematics 25
  memory 226–28, 233, 236, 237, 245, 247, 254
  neurophysiological 303, 304

personal interaction 99
  psychological 276–83, 288, 289
  role in AI 13, 14, 17, 26, 27, 52
  story understanding 100
  vision 126, 130, 131, 133, 134, 212
Monod, J. 331, 335
Montague, W.E. 290
Montague grammar 71
Monte Carlo methods 219
Moore, R. 140
MOPS 285
Moravec, H.P. 149, 182
Morgan, C.G. 178
Morton, J. 232, 233, 236, 254, 259, 288, 291
Moses, J. 15, 29
Motion 129, 168
  see also Mobile robots
Movement rules 90–92
Mundy, J. 139, 168, 169, 183
Murthy, S.S. 152, 183
Mutation 219, 222
Muybridge, 151
MYCIN 139, 189, 192, 194, 196
Myer, J.M. 184
Mynatt, C.R. 277, 291
Myrhaug, B. 28

Naive physics 140
Nakagawa, Y. 139, 182
Narayanan, A. 10, 28, 203
Nash-Webber, B. 105, 110
Natural language
  generation 74, 81, 86, 104, 116
  processing 9, 70, 76, 80, 323, 324, 326
  understanding 74, 78, 82, 86, 89, 98, 99, 102, 104
Naturalistic selection 220
Navigation 139, 149
Naylor, C. 7, 192, 198
NEC 117
Neeham, R. 8
Neisser, U. 282, 291
NETL 256
Neurophysiology 14, 26, 212, 245, 248, 249, 257, 298, 300, 301, 303, 304
Nevatia, R. 184
Newell, A. 8, 231, 258
Newman, W.M. 132, 136
Nilsson, N.J. 17, 22, 24, 29, 103, 107, 108, 149, 182, 224, 246, 259, 317, 318, 335
Ninomiya, T. 139, 182
Nishihara, H.K. 168, 182

Noisy data   211, 216, 222
Non-determinism   87–89, 141
Norman, D.A.   226, 243, 244, 246, 259, 290
Nygaard, K.   28

Object-oriented programming   25, 62
O'Gorman, F.   109
Ohwovoriole, M.S.   161, 182
Okada, T.   146, 165, 182
Olson, K.W.   145
Ong, M.C.H.   139, 161, 162, 184
Optimization   206
Orin, D.E.   143, 149, 182
Orthographic spelling check   278
O'Shea, T.   9, 47, 177
Oshima, M.   184
Owen, D.   109
Ozgumer, F.   149, 151, 182

Pada, R.   223
PADL   153
Palmer, M.   178
Papert, S.   134, 136, 214, 224, 246, 259, 330, 335
Parallel processing   215, 232, 247–50, 256, 257
PARRY   272
Parsers and parsing   83, 86, 87, 89, 92, 230
Partridge, D.   326, 328, 335, 336
Parts access bug   170
Pascal   34, 42, 228, 323
Patch descriptors   130
Pattern matching and recognition
  AI methods   20, 22, 141
  LISP   57–60
  machine learning   206
  memory   230
  PROLOG   34, 60
  speech   116, 119
  vision   26, 130–34
Paul, R.   142, 145, 162, 176–79, 182–85
Pavlides, T.   134
Pearl, J.   20, 29
Perception   138, 149, 164
Perceptron   208, 212, 214, 215, 245, 246
Pereira, F.C.N.   91, 108
Pereira, L.M.   20, 28
Perrault, C.R.   102, 106, 107
Perry, J.   102, 106
Peterson, C.R.   228, 259

Peterson, M.J.   228, 259
Pfeifer, R.   142, 273, 279–82, 292
Philosophy   10, 40, 263, 330, 331
Phonemes   115–18, 120
Phonetics   112, 119
Pick-and-place   143, 159
Pieper, D.L.   183
Pitch   118
Pixels   123, 124, 127, 129, 212, 214
PLANNER   97
Planning   103, 143, 149, 155, 164, 174, 175
Platt, J.R.   277, 291
Poggio, T.   129, 136, 169, 182
Poker   219
Polya, G.   16, 17, 29
Ponce, J.   165, 178
POP-2   42
POP-11   33, 34, 40–43, 93, 196
POPLOG   33, 40–42, 44–47, 196
Popplestone, R.J.   42, 47, 153, 176, 183
Porter, G.   139, 168, 169, 183
Post access checking   278
Prefixes   75, 76
Prendergast, K.   9
Price, K.E.   184
Probability   192, 195, 216, 217
Problem representation   20, 21
Procedural languages   42, 46
Procedures   93, 153
Production rules   140, 218
Programmer's apprentice   164
Programming environments   33, 35, 36, 39–41, 46, 61, 62, 196
PROLOG
  compared with PLANNER   97
  declarative languages   60
  expert systems   191, 196, 197
  inefficiency   19, 20
  microcomputers   197
  natural language   323
  pattern matcher   34, 60
  predicate calculus   17, 61, 189, 190
  primitives   33
  POPLOG system   41–44, 46
  search mechanism   34, 87
  theorem prover   191
Pronunciation   111, 115, 254
Property inheritance   190, 254, 286
Prosody   120
PROSPECTOR   189, 192, 193, 196
Protestant work ethic   317

Pruning   22, 24
Psychology
   cognitive   13, 14, 267–79, 281–84, 289
   concept learning   215
   evidence   270, 274
   memory models   238, 257
   relationship to AI   40, 257, 263, 277, 278, 282, 283, 285–89
   speech recognition   119
   theory testing   276, 277, 280
Pugh, A.   145, 178
Pullum, G.K.   108
PUMA   137, 159, 160
Purposes   27

Qualitative reasoning   140
Questions   94, 101–03, 117
Quillian, M.R.   238, 259, 286, 291
Quinlan, J.R.   208, 215, 224

Raibert, M.H.   145, 152, 153, 163, 165–67, 183
Ramsey, A.   42, 47
RAPT   153
Ratcliffe, R.   288, 291
Recursion   56, 58, 87, 142, 144
Registers   92, 93
Reicher, G.M.   249, 250, 259
Reiser, B.J.   277, 290, 291
Romote sensing   122, 128
Renaud, M.   142, 145, 183
Requicha, A.A.G.   183
Resolution   17, 191
Restricted access bug   171, 172
Restricted motion bug   170, 173, 174
REVEAL   196
Rewrite rules   80–85, 89–91
Rich, C.R.   164, 183
Rich, E.   9, 20, 29
Riesback, C.K.   89, 109, 286, 291
Rips, L.J.   287, 291
Riseman, E.M.   135
Roberts, L.G.   131, 136
Robinson, J.A.   17, 29
Robotics
   algorithms   17, 142, 158–60, 168
   arms and hands   124, 126, 140–44, 146–48
   challenge for AI   138–41, 155
   compliance   160–64
   contact sensing   165–67

   control   142, 145
   household applications   331, 332
   industrial applications   149, 316, 317
   legs   143, 148–53
   programming   142, 153, 154, 164
   reasoning   154–59, 169, 172, 173
   software   137, 138
   tool use   169–75
   unemployment   316, 317
   vision   122, 124, 126, 164, 167, 168
Robson, C.   277, 291
Roots of words   77
Rosenblatt, F.   206, 212, 224, 245, 259
Rosenfeld, A.   126, 134, 135, 141, 178, 185
Roth, B.   142–45, 161, 182, 183
Rules
   expert systems   187–89, 195, 197, 206
   grammatical   80–85, 91
   linguistic   71, 72, 80–85, 91
   machine learning   208, 209, 211, 215, 220, 221
   memory   230, 236
   movement   91
   production systems   78, 79, 189
   PROLOG   60, 191
   rewrite   80–85
   semantic   93, 96, 97, 103, 236
   stories   100
   syntactical   80–85, 91
Rumelhart, D.E.   246, 249, 250, 253, 259, 284, 291
Russell, J.   276, 291, 293
Rustin, R.   109

Sacerdoti, E.   137, 164, 184
Sag, I.A.   108
Sahar, G.   142, 145
SAINT   15
Sakoe, H.   121
Salisbury, J.K.   143, 145–48, 163, 184
SAM   285
Samuel, A.   206, 225
Satellite images *see* Remote sensing
Sawyer, J.D.   285, 290
SCARA   143
Schank, R.C.   8, 18, 29, 97, 98, 100, 107, 109, 281, 283–86, 291, 293
Scheinmann, V.   159
Schema   267, 284, 285, 288
Schmidt, E.   145, 178
Schrader, W.W.   143, 182

Schunk, B.G.   168, 184
Shwartz, J.T.   160, 184, 316, 336
Screwdrivers   170–75
Scripts   18, 100, 101, 283, 285
Search
  AI methods   19, 20, 22, 24, 28, 141
  algorithms   155
  combinatorial explosion   131, 210
  memory   241, 246, 287
  PROLOG   34, 191
  random   187
  rule induction   210, 211, 219
  speech recognition   117
  visual identification   131
Searle, J.R.   5, 102, 106, 109, 263, 264, 270,
    291, 294–96, 300–11, 313
Segmentation   127, 128
Seifert, C.M.   286, 291
Sejnowski, T.J.   248, 258
Selfridge, O.   206, 225
Semantic networks   140, 163, 189, 197,
    238, 239, 248, 249
Semantic rules   96, 97, 103
Semantics   93, 105, 119, 234, 235, 236
Semiotics   73
Sensing   137–39, 165–68
Sexual reproduction   219
Shakey (robot)   149
Shape   129–31, 134, 140, 168, 169, 172
Shapiro, L.G.   134
Sharir, M.   160, 184
Sharkey, A.J.C.   292
Sharkey, N.E.   263, 273, 279, 281–83, 285,
    286, 288, 291, 292
Sheep shearing robot   161, 162
Shells   196
Shimano, B.E.   137, 153, 162, 183, 184
Shimoyana, I.   150, 152, 182
Shirai, Y.   169, 184
Shoben, E.J.   287, 291
SHORT   231, 232
Shortliffe, E.   189, 192, 198
SHRDLU   97, 326
Simon, H.A.   26, 29, 231, 258
Simon, J.C.   120
SIMULA   25
Signals and signs   70–74, 229, 231
Silverman, H.F.   116, 121
Simulation   3, 25, 140, 264, 294, 295
Skills   195, 264, 265
Sklansky, J.   212, 225

Slagle, J.R.   15, 24, 29
Sloman, A.   40, 42, 47, 109, 122, 136,
    269–74, 292, 293, 304, 307, 308, 310, 313
Smith, E.E.   287, 291
Smith, S.F.   208, 218, 219, 225
Smythe, W.E.   278, 290
Smythies, J.R.   331, 335
SNOBOL   196, 231
Sobek, R.   149, 179
Social implications   264, 315–33
Software crisis   326, 327
Sommer, T.   165
Sounds   72, 73, 111, 112, 114, 115, 120,
    229, 231, 233, 234, 250
Sparck Jones, K.   109
Spatial reasoning   138
Spatio-temporal images   125, 126
Spaulding, C.H.   137, 153, 184
Spector, M.   15, 28
Speech acts   101
Speech analysis   115, 118
Speech processing   17, 26, 105
Speech recognition   111, 115–17, 119
Speech synthesis   112, 115, 116, 118, 120
  see also Natural language generation
Speech understanding   112, 113, 115–17,
    119
Sperling, G.   228, 259
Spiegelhalter, D.   192, 199
Spiro, R.J.   290
Spreading activation   249–52, 267, 286–88
Sproul, R.F.   132, 136
SPSS   221
Statistics   276, 277, 281
Steele, J.   42, 47, 105, 110
Stefik, M.   105, 110
Steppers   38
Stevenson, C.N.   142, 183
Stiffness   160, 163
Stone, P.   215, 224
Stonham, T.J.   214
Storage management   37, 43
Stories   94, 97, 99–101, 273, 281, 284
STRIPS   103
Structured programming   23, 327
Suffixes   75–78
Summers, P.D.   184
Surfaces   127, 129–31
Sussman, G.J.   105, 110
Sutherland, I.E.   183
Sutherland, S.   8

Symbolic computation   33, 36, 38, 50–52, 197, 229, 232
Symmetries   22
Syntax
  editor   36, 39
  LISP dialects   62
  memory rules   236
  natural language   75, 79–83, 89, 91, 93, 95, 104, 105
  rule induction   207, 210, 222
  speech recognition   117, 118
Systemic grammar   91
Szpakowicz, S.   17, 28

Takeyasu, K.   141, 162, 179
Tanner, J.E.   152, 165–67, 183
Tarski, P.   71
Taylor, R.H.   154, 155, 163, 184
Teitelman, W.   40, 47
Television   165, 316, 324
Templates   116, 119
Tendons   146–48
Terzopoulos, D.   141, 169, 184
Testing   14, 26, 27, 277, 282
  see also Implementability
Text processing   105
Texture   127, 128, 134, 168
Thatcher, M.   111
Theorem proving   17, 24, 141, 191
Theories   20, 26, 195, 275, 276, 278, 280, 282, 283, 285–87
  see also Models
Thinking   294, 297, 298, 302
Thompson, H.   290
TIDY   221, 222
Tippett, J.P.   136
TLC   286
Tomkins, S.S.   290
Tomography   122, 126
Tools   169, 170, 175, 318, 319, 321
TOPs   286
Torque   144
Torrance, B.   263, 264, 292, 310, 312, 314
Touretzky, D.S.   63
Tracers   38, 59
Trainable classifiers   212
Transition networks   83–86, 88, 89
Transformational grammar   91, 283
Trevelyan, J.P.   139, 161, 162, 184
Tsai, S.J.   149, 151, 182

Tsuji, S.   169, 184
Tulving, E.   228, 259
Turing, A.   7, 292, 296, 297, 314
Turing machine   304, 305
Turing test   270, 294, 296–300, 302, 305, 311
Turner, R.   320, 336
Turner, T.J.   285, 290
Tweney, R.D.   277, 291

UK   5, 306
Ullman, S.   129, 136
Uncertainty   138, 140, 141, 154, 192, 196
Unemployment   316–18
Unimation PUMA   137, 159, 160
USA   5, 7, 316
User interface   61, 62
User modelling   27

Vaiiett, M.   149, 179
VAL   137, 153, 184
van Valin, R.D.   108
Vander Brug, G.J.   137, 179
VED   43–46
Vehicle guidance   122
Verification conditions   71
Vidler, A.R.   178
Villiers, P.   137, 184
Vilnrotter, F.   184
Virtual machine   43, 44
Vision
  AI techniques   113
  algorithms   17, 24
  3-D   122, 123, 126, 129–32, 134, 139
  human compared with computer   122, 129, 132
  machine learning   212, 213
  memory models   230, 231, 233, 251
  neurophysiology   14, 212, 249
  paralle processing   249, 305
  robotics   122, 139, 164, 165, 168, 172
Vocder   114, 116
Voices   117, 119, 120
Von Neumann architecture   27, 247, 249

Wahawisai, J.J.   145
Wargames   209
Warren, D.H.D.   91, 108
Wason, P.   8

Wassel, G.   212, 225
Waterman, D.A.   109, 110, 139
Waters, R.   164, 183
Watkins, A.   169
Watson, L.T.   168, 179
Wave forms   113–15
Weber, S.   312
Weiss, S.   199
Weizenbaum, J.   9, 59, 63, 272, 292, 297, 298, 314, 325, 330, 331, 336
Wesley, M.A.   153, 185
WHIM   117
Whitney, D.E.   140, 143, 161, 162, 185
Wiesel, T.N.   129, 136
Wilensky, T.   63, 281, 286, 292
Wilkes, K.   276, 292
Wilkes, Y.A.   110
Wilkie, R.A.   214
Wilkins, A.J.   287, 292
Wilson, E.O.   331, 335
Winograd, T.   8, 97, 98, 110, 236, 259, 290, 326
Winston, P.   8, 9, 16, 18, 20, 28, 29, 63, 139, 140, 141, 172, 174, 185, 223, 225
WISARD   214
Wishful mnemonics   280
Witkin, A.P.   185
Witten, I.K.   121
Wood, J.   148
Woodham, R.J.   164, 185
Woods, W.A.   83, 91, 105, 110, 120
Word recognition   115, 116, 117, 119, 233, 250, 251–54, 281
Wrenches   173–75
Writing   160, 161

X-ray computer tomography   122, 126

Yazdani, M.   10, 28, 47, 269, 271, 292
Yoshikawa, T.   143, 185
Youcef-Toumi, K.   144, 176
Young, K.K.D.   145, 185
Young, S.J.   119, 121
Yuille, A.   169, 177

Zucker, S.W.   126, 136, 141, 185